OXFORD STUDIES IN DEMO

Series editor: Laurence

••••••••••••••••

RETHINKING ARAB DEMOCRATIZATION:
ELECTIONS WITHOUT DEMOCRACY

OXFORD STUDIES IN DEMOCRATIZATION

Series editor: Laurence Whitehead

● ● ● ● ● ● ● ● ● ● ● ● ● ● ● ● ●

Oxford Studies in Democratization is a series for scholars
and students of comparative politics and related disciplines.
Volumes will concentrate on the comparative study of the
democratization processes that accompanied the decline and
termination of the cold war. The geographical focus of the
series will primarily be Latin America, the Caribbean,
Southern and Eastern Europe, and relevant
experiences in Africa and Asia.

OTHER BOOKS IN THE SERIES

Rethinking Arab Democratization

Elections Without Democracy

....

LARBI SADIKI

UNIVERSITY PRESS

OXFORD

UNIVERSITY PRESS

Great Clarendon Street, Oxford OX2 6DP
United Kingdom

Oxford University Press is a department of the University of Oxford.
It furthers the University's objective of excellence in research, scholarship,
and education by publishing worldwide. Oxford is a registered trade mark of
Oxford University Press in the UK and in certain other countries

© Larbi Sadiki 2009

The moral rights of the author have been asserted

First published in paperback 2011
Reprinted 2012

British Library Cataloguing in Publication Data
Data available

Library of Congress Cataloging in Publication Data
Data available

ISBN 978-0-19-969924-7

Printed in the United Kingdom by
the MPG Books Group Ltd

For Jamel, Kaiss, Adann and Yasmina.

To all of those who sacrificed their lives to bring about the
Arab Revolution in 2011

·················
Foreword to the Paperback edition
·················

There have been many "elections without democracy" in the Arab world over the past half century. Tunisia was no exception, even though in many other respects (living standards, the rights of women, levels of education, and engagement with international knowledge networks, among other factors) it was in the vanguard of "modernity" by regional standards. For the first three decades after independence from French protectorate status (in 1956), it was ruled by "enlightened despot" Habib Bourguiba who was eventually elected "President for Life" by the National Assembly in 1975.

But life presidencies beget succession crises, and so it was in this case. Eventually, in 1987, Bourguiba's Minister of the Interior, Zinelabidine Ben Ali, ousted him in a coup on the grounds of senility. But his successor retained extensive formal powers under the still extant 1959 constitution. He could legally select the Prime Minister, rule by decree when the National Assembly was not in session, and appoint the governors of the 23 provinces. Beyond this, he also exercised meta-constitutional powers as effective proprietor of the ruling party chief of police, and of the last court of appeal. By 2011, he was also the well-established head of a family business conglomerate dominating key sectors of the economy.

At first, President Ben Ali spoke of political liberalization, but after two re-elections – won with more than 99 percent of the votes cast – he orchestrated a constitutional referendum to remove the three-term limit, and raised the maximum age for a presidential candidate to 75. Thus, in 2004, he won a fourth term (this time with only 94 percent of the vote), and in 2009, aged 73, he officially secured his fifth – and final – victory. He claimed just under 90 percent of the vote on an 89 percent turnout. Officially his party also won almost 85 percent of the votes and over three quarters of the seats in the National Assembly.

The trouble with such improbable displays of overwhelming national unity and enthusiasm is that they insult the intelligence of the citizens in question. As we now know, when the exasperated population of Tunisia finally came together to express their true feelings about the Ben Ali kleptocracy it was quite a different form of near unanimity that emerged. Within weeks the Tunisian example had helped trigger an upsurge in popular demands for the removal of other long-term arab presidential incumbents, and their families, and for the installation of elections *with* democracy.

In this volume Tunisian scholar, Larbi Sadiki, traces how Arab elections have previously prolonged autocratic strangleholds over polity – notably Ben Ali in Tunisia, Mubarak in Egypt, and Abdullah al-Salih in Yemen (p. 14). But he also lays the groundwork for an understanding of the sources of contestation that would in quick succession render all these three long-standing autocracies unviable. Indeed, the collapse of Ben Ali's regime after twenty-three years was quickly followed by the fall of Mubarak after twenty-nine years, with the President of Yemen teetering on the brink of ouster after thirty-two years in office. In addition, Colonel Mu'ammar al-Qadhafi and his family have been ousted by a mixture of internal democratic rebellion and externally directed bombardment, terminating forty one years of personalist rule (without elections); and the Baath Party's monopoly in power in Syria (enforced under a state of emergency dating back to 1963) is also being severely challenged.

Obviously each of these political upheavals must be understood in its own context. It is also far too early to assess where this dramatic regional concatenation will end. Even in Tunisia and Egypt, where competitive elections are scheduled later in 2011, the interim power-holders are still the armed forces. The Arab monarchies may also be drawn in, with unpredictable consequences (so far only Bahrain and Oman have been directly affected, but the succession issue looms in Saudi Arabia). The king of Morocco has attempted to pre-empt unrest by formulating a package of liberalising constitutional reforms that were endorsed by an overwhelmingly approved, 98 percent popular vote of approval in July 2011. So the challenges of democratization are by no means confined to the Arab republics. Wider repercussions across the whole of the MENA (Middle East and North Africa) region, affecting Iraq, Iran, and Israel among others, will take time to emerge. But a few weeks in early 2011 were enough to expose any surface veneer of political stability and repressive order in the Arab Middle East as unreal. Popular aspirations for political democracy have proved more widespread, more uncontainable, and more potentially transformative than most observers had hitherto acknowledged.

In view of these events, specialists and democratization scholars alike will need to re-examine the established evidence about how politics has been operating in the contemporary Arab world over the past generation. Longstanding assumptions about a supposed Arab or Middle Eastern regional "exceptionalism", or entrenched resistance to democratizing impulses, have proved as unfounded here as they turned out to be in Latin America (its supposed Catholic anti-democratic culture) in the 1970s. Larbi Sadiki's book has the great merit that, before the current upsurge began, he was already scanning the terrain for clues about where this large region might fit in the broader scheme of global democratic developments in the post-Cold War world.

In particular, he monitored the illusions of Arab electoralism in the decades when incumbents still believed themselves beyond the reach of their voters; he reflected on the "salon" democracy gestating in various privileged elite circles; he probed the scope and (major) limitations of western "democracy promotion" from without; and he recognised the potential of the information technology revolution before that had entered into the mainstream of contemporary political analysis. But perhaps the most important contribution of this volume is its attention to the distorted (or even hidden) demands for democratization that were gestating from below. These had been as dismissed as "bread riots" (as purely economic expressions of exclusion that could therefore be countered by subsidies and clientelist consensus from these oil-rich rulers), but Sadiki grasped their broader political significance.

As demonstrated by the self-immolation of Mohamed Bouazizi, which precipitated the regime change in Tunisia, demands from below could be about self-respect, dignity, and fair treatment (the violation of a socially embedded "moral economy") rather than just craven petitions for material favours. Autocracies incapable of concealing their contempt for their subjects therefore exposed themselves to the abrupt and uncontainable loss of their pretended legitimacy. As Sadiki anticipated, the apparent stability of these autocratic regimes was to some extent the artificial product of a climate of fear that was assiduously cultivated from the top. Once this "fear barrier" was broken by some breakthrough such as Bouazizi's action or the occupation of a central public space, it was the protesters who became emboldened, and the rulers who suddenly appeared as fearful. Of course, this insight will require much further investigation and refinement in the light of developments since the first edition of this book went to press in 2009. But this book refutes the claim that this truth was unknown to scholarship before the event. "Rethinking Arab Democratization" has thus set the agenda for a new generation of comparative political research concerning this vital large region.

Comparative experience from elsewhere indicates that the so-called "Arab awakening" of early 2011 is only an early step in an extended political process with no single guaranteed outcome. The first stage in processes of democratic transition is a time of surprise and hope, but what then follows is a complex and open-ended series of manoeuvres including threats and possible compromises. There are many disputes to be resolved, for example about which democratic rights are to be prioritised, and which actors can be counted as democrats. Questions of formal constitutional design will need to be settled, but also informal power relations have to be renegotiated. This will often include the rebalancing of various international alignments. So beyond strictly political issues, these democratization demands also raise complex socio-economic and security dilemmas. There will be much more to write about the fate of these democratic upsurges in the Arab world. Sadiki's opening contribution is to provide their context, and to demonstrate that they did not erupt unforeseeably from nowhere.

September 2011   Laurence Whitehead
                                                                Nuffield College

....

Preface

....

The Arab Middle East is today awash in *electoralism* and what I call *election fetishism*. This is a book that unpacks the nature of *stalled democratic transitions* in this region against this backdrop. But this is not the only background. 'Democratization' has been on the political agenda in the Arab Middle East for 150 years. As early as the 1860s, Egypt's Khedives and the King-Officers of the Beylicate of Tunis briefly experimented with written constitutions, elections, and parliaments. Democratization is one thread that oddly links the pre-colonial and post-colonial political orders. Indeed, it captures many a moment (Islam–Christendom rivalry, Franco-British colonialism, and now American imperialism) in the long history of the encounter with Western political know-how. Capturing how democratization is done and what it means in the Arab world is a tough assignment. Scholarship on Arab democratization continues to be confronted with problems of ahistoricity, exceptionalism, foundationalism, and essentialism/Orientalism. Writing a book on Arab democratization is not on its own a daunting challenge; Endeavouring to go some way towards questioning and answering this formidable foursome is. Throughout the pages of this book, I have quarreled with these four, attempting to obviate some of their assumptions on questions of democracy and democratization in the Arab region.

In the same vein, I attempt to challenge the ahistorical nature of studies to democratization in the Arab world. I deconstruct the Orientalist binary polarities of concepts (democratic/autocratic, agent/object), especially in relation to the narratives and knowing surrounding US democracy promotion. These narratives have typically accorded higher value to their ideals, knowing and doing than their counterparts within the Arab locale. This kind of hierarchy lends itself to a logic of 'enframing' (to use a word coined by Mitchell) the Arab 'Orient' and a logic of superiority and subjugation (to re-phrase Said). To an extent, democracy promotion and that brand of transitology that espouses its ideal uncritically more or less form a quasi 'grand narrative' convinced in its claims to universality and rationality.

Accordingly, my approach throughout this book has been to engage with concepts and methods found in consolidation-oriented transitology. The aim has been to reconceptualize problems of transition in the Arab region through an anti-foundationalist lens. I have, to this end, meshed into my theoretical tools approaches that cast doubt on democratization as a universal and totalizing paradigm as well as on its utility to explain transition across boundaries of time, space, culture, and history. Plus, what some Euro-American transitologists count as consolidation is so only within the framework of ethnocentric social sciences set up against a non-democratic 'other'. Arab democratization is relevant as a 'problematique' for enquiry but not in the unimaginative and ethnocentric templates many social scientists offer. I have benefited from, and deploy, new interrogations and contests within studies of democratization. These new works contest democratization as a quest for universal principles, unmitigated by specificity and unconditioned by time and space. Along this wavelength, I have written a book that does not equate democratic transition with stable and certain outcomes, much less one that is prone to closure. Inspired by these works, I accord the 'locale' importance—particularity matters in democratic transition. Hence I adopt an approach that treats and conceives of transition as historically situated, flexible, contingent, fragmented, nuanced, non-linear, and variable.

I have throughout this book resisted 'normativizing' the Euro-American model as the standard bearer in the study of Arab democratization. This I have done with utmost humility towards learning from the vast comparative work done on Southern and Latin America, Southern Mediterranean, and Eastern and Central Europe. But my aim has been not to sacrifice the specificity or the region's knowledge repository as to capture with maximum integrity and veracity the peculiarities of stalled democratic transition in Arab states. Particularly onerous and demanding is to navigate between territories of political thought in the Arab world and corresponding areas of Euro-American epistemic enquiry. Given the near silence on Arab political thought, this book fills a gap by presenting new knowledge on the emerging branch of Arab transitology. Thus a kind of cross-cultural dialogue ensues between these matrices of thought, and also within them. However, partly, my intention has been to shift the position of the Arab world of passive and silent object to one of active and visible agent. I have allowed a degree of self-representation by lacing my text with written and spoken materials I have been privileged to add to my reference library following long stretches of research fieldtrips over many years in the Arab world.

I have not taken Arab diversity for granted. Rather, I have sought to explore and indirectly celebrate the tapestry of diverse identities in the Arab world. Through my analysis I articulate, in a comparative fashion, the implications of similarities and dissimilarities for Arab democratic transition. While this book constitutes a *tour de force* on democratization *qua* electoralism or *qua* election fetishism I have endeavoured not to obscure, much less sacrifice, difference. The category 'Arab' is not problematic. But the category 'democratic', 'democratization', or 'democratizer' is. This is what the analysis engages, highlighting trends of similarity in democratization amid the rich Arab plurality of political systems, modernities, traditions, histories, levels of development, and electoral experiments.

This book is part and parcel of a wider and continuous cultural project for investigating democracy and democratization in the Arab setting. I am writing as both an Arabist and a student of Arab democratization with a keen interest in projecting to all kinds of readers the worldviews of the silenced voices from the Arab Middle East. A few enquiries are more stimulating, exciting, and demanding. In writing this book, I have incurred the debt of many mentors, many through their published knowledge, and others directly and through engaging intellectual encounters. I owe a special debt to the American University of Beirut, the University of Aleppo, University of Damascus, Heinrich Böll Stiftung (Beirut), the European University Institute (Florence), Institut Europeu de la Mediterrània (Barcelona), and the Carnegie Endowment for International Peace Middle East Centre (Beirut). They have all encouraged and inspired my own take on Arab democratic transitions. The book would not have come to fruition without the unflagging moral support of friends such as Eid Al-Yahya, Jeremy Salt, David Lee, Dr. Hamdi Hasan, Essam Hanafi, Fatima Sumadi, Dr. Ahmed Mella, Sheikh Muhammad Kawtharani, Ruba Farkh, and Professor James Morris (Boston College). The company of Nayna, Beau, and Kelby Cintra made the writing enjoyable even if challenging. In Beirut I have benefited from much friendship and inspiration from the Carnegie Non-Resident Expert Fellowship through engaging and productive encounters with resident scholars such as Dr. Paul Salem and Marina Ottaway. It gives me great pleasure to acknowledge the support and access I was given by the Arab Unity Studies Centre and its director, Dr. Khair Eddin Haseeb, to their Arabic collection of books and periodicals on Arab democratization. The Nuffield College Graduate School seminar series, convened by Professor Laurence Whitehead, is one of the most rigorous forums anywhere in the world for the discussion of democratization and transitology. I am grateful to the seminar series for having acted as a friendly sounding board as well as a constructive critic when it invited me in 2006 and 2007 to try out some of my ideas on Arab democratization.

Through this forum, I enjoyed learning from some of the leading voices on democratization such as Guillermo O'Donnell, Nancy Bermeo, and Thomas Carothers.

My thanks are also due to Cambridge University Press for permission to reprint 'Popular Uprisings and Arab Democratization', which appeared in a shorter in the *International Journal of Middle East Studies*, 32/1 (February 2000), 71–95. I owe a debt of gratitude to the British Academy who awarded me a research grant in 2003 and some of the research contained in the book is the result of its generous support. I am most grateful to the Leverhulme Trust for funding my 2007 sabbatical without which this book would not have seen the light of day. I thank Nonno Sebastiano and Nonna Cosima Lapi for their encouragement, and Mark Herzog, Mohammad Moussa for their professional assistance with indexing some research for this book, and for their help with the preparation of the bibliography. My thanks go to Sarah Grey for her competent preparation of the transliterated glossary. Lastly, I owe special thanks to Eric Brough for his patience and the wonderful artwork he produced for the book's cover.

I consider it both an honour and a challenge to be given the opportunity to inaugurate with my book a discussion on Arab democratic transition, a discussion which has been missing from the graceful list of the Oxford Studies in Democratization Series. I am most grateful for the independent referees and for the editors, Professor Laurence Whitehead and Dominic Byatt, for their decision to fill this gap in this outstanding series. At OUP I would like to thank Louise Sprake, Elizabeth Suffling, and Maggi Shade for their tireless editorial support and constructive and professional feedback.

I do hope my past and present students of democratization in the Arab world and the Middle East at the University of Exeter find in this book much food for thought.

Contents

List of Tables

....

Abbreviations

....

AHRO	Arab Human Rights Organization
AME	Arab Middle East
APN	National Popular Assembly (Algeria)
APO	Association of Police Officers (Sudan)
ASU	Arab Socialist Union (in Nasser's Egypt)
AUSC	Arab Unity Studies Centre
BMEI	Broader Middle East Initiative
CDHR	Committee for the Defense of Human Rights (Saudi Arabia)
CHRLA	Centre for Human Rights and Legal Aid (Egypt)
EHRO	Egyptian Human Rights Organization
EU	European Union
FAOO	Free Army Officers Organization
FFS	Front of Socialist Forces (Algeria)
FIS	Islamic Salvation Front or Front Islamique du Salut (Algeria)
FLN	National Liberation Front, Algeria (Front de Libération Nationale)
GCC	Gulf Cooperation Council
GDD	Group for Democratic Development (Egypt)
GPC	General People's Congress (Yemen)
GMEI	Greater Middle East Initiative
HCS	High Council of State (Algeria)
IAF	Islamic Action Front, Jordan
ICG	International Crisis Group
IMF	International Monetary Fund
JCP	Justice and Charity Party, Morocco (Al-Adl wa Al-Ihsan)
JDP	Justice and Development Party, Morocco (Al-Adl wa al-Tanmiyah)
LTDH	Ligue Tunisienne de Droits de L'Homme
MDA	Algerian Democratic Movement
MDS	Movement of Socialist Democrats (Tunisia)
MEPI	Middle East Partnership Initiative
NED	National Endowment for Democracy
NDP	National Democratic Party (Egypt)

NGO	Non-Governmental Organization
NIF	National Islamic Front (Sudan)
PPC	Political Parties Committee (Egypt)
RCD	Rally for Culture and Democracy (Berber party, Algeria)
RCD	Democratic Constitutional Rally, Tunisia (ruling party)
RND	National Rally for Democracy (Algeria)
SLP	Socialist Labour Party (Egypt)
SP	Socialist Party (Yemen)
TNA	Transitional National Assembly (Iraq)
TNC	Transnational Corporation
UNFP	National Union of Popular Forces (Morocco)
USAID	United States Agency for International Aid
WMDs	Weapons of Mass Destruction
YRR	Yemeni Reform Rally (known as Iṣlāḥ)

....

Glossary

....

I have adopted a very simplified transliteration system inside the text, with the 'ain [ع] taking the form of an accent: ' (as in Shi'ite), and the hamzah [ء] noted thus: ' (as in Qur'ān).

To satisfy linguistic purists, I have produced the glossary in full transliteration, adopting the Library of Congress system, which uses the following transcription system of the Arabic alphabet:

ء	'
ا	ā
ب	b
ت	t
ث	th
ج	j
ح	ḥ
خ	kh
د	d
ذ	dh
ر	r
ز	z
س	s
ش	sh
ص	ṣ
ض	ḍ
ط	ṭ
ظ	ẓ
ع	'
غ	gh
ف	f
ق	q
ك	k
ل	l
م	m
ن	n
ه	h

و	*w / ū*
ي	*y / ī*
'adālah	justice
ahl	kin/partisans
aḥzāb siyāsiyyah	political parties (singular *ḥizb siyāsī*)
akhawiyyah	brotherhood
akh	brother
al-mujtamaʿ al-ahlī	Primordial society or association
al-mujtamaʿ al-madanī	civil society
al-ṣāniʿ	apprentice
ʿāmmiyyah	uprising or revolt (specific to nineteenth-century Lebanon)
ʿaṣabiyyah	group feeling or solidarity (a term coined by Ibn Khaldun)
aṣnāf	guilds (also translated as *ṭawāʾif*)
aswāq	*sūqs;* markets
azmah	crisis
baltajah	or *baltagah*, Egyptian slang for 'thuggery' (used by security forces against opposition)
barakah	Godly providence
bilāṭ	palace; or royal court
būlītīk	Maghribi slang for the French word *'politique'* (politics), denoting distrust of politicians
daʿawī	missionary
daʿm	subsidization
damaqraṭah	democratization
dawlah	state
dīmuqrāṭiyyat al-khubz	'democracy of bread'
dīwāniyyah	traditional male forums (specific to Kuwait)
dustūr	constitution
fatwā	religious counsel
farr	retreat (Ibn Khaldun uses this term in conjunction with *karr* to describe a medieval Arab warfare technique.)
fallāhīn	peasants; farmers
fitnah	trial; schism
ghulb	superiority (in a military or coercive sense)
ḥadīth	sayings by the Prophet Muhammad
ḥaqq	right
ḥārah	neighbourhood
ḥāʾiṭ	wall

ḥārāt	hoods (sing. *ḥārah*)
ḥijāb	headscarf
ḥiraf	crafts
ḥizbiyyah	partyism
ijtihād	independent reasoning
ikhwān	brethren
imām	prayer leader (also used to refer to Shi'ite religious authority)
imārah	principality (administrative and political unit, pre-nation-state system in Lebanon)
infitāḥ	open-door policy
inqilāb	*coup d'état* (plural *inqilābāt*)
inḥilāl	collapse
intifāḍah	uprising (plural *intifāḍāt*)
iṣlāḥ	reform
istidrāj	recruitment
jāh	authority/power
jamā'ah	group (plural *jamā'āt*)
jihād	holy war (it has non-martial meanings)
karr	literally, attack
khubz	bread
madīnah	city
maghrib	Arab West
majālis	traditional councils (for meeting as well as consulting)
majlis al-sh'ab	People's Assembly
majlis al-shūrā	consultative council (equivalent to parliament in some Arab states)
manābir	political platforms (specifically in Sadat's Egypt before parties were legalized)
mashriq	Arab East
mu'allim	artisan
mubtadi'	unskilled beginner (in crafts)
mudawwināt	blogs
muḥtasib	market superintendent
mukhābarāt	Secret police
muqāṭa'ah	boycott
muṣālaḥah	reconciliation
nahḍah	liberal age of Arab thought; Arab renaissance (also referred to as *'asr al-nahḍah*)
naksah	setback
ni'am	Godly favours or bounty

qāḍī	judge
rij'ī	retrograde
ṣadaqah	voluntary almsgiving
ṣāḥib al-shurṭah	police chief
shadd	promotion ceremony
sharī'ah	Islamic law
shar'īyyah	legitimacy
shaykh al-ḥirfah	the master artisan
shaykh al-sūq	market's grand master
shūrā	Islamic process of consultation
shuyūkh	spiritual instructors (plural of *shaykh*)
tabdhīr	excessive consumerism
taḥawwul dīmuqrāṭī	democratic transition
tajwī'	starvation
taqahqur	reversal or retreat
tarāḥum	mutual compassion
ṭarīqah	Sufi order (plural *turuq*)
ṭawā'if	sects
tekke	Sufi hospice
thaqāfah dīmuqrāṭiyyah	democratic acculturation
thawrāt	revolutions (sing. *thawrah*)
'ulamā'	religious scholars
ummah	Muslim non-territorial global community; community of faith
walā'	loyalty
wālī	Governor
waqf	religious endowment
wilāyah	province (plural *wilāyāt*)
zakāt	compulsory alms tax in Islam
zāwiyah	Sufi teaching mosque (known also as *ribāṭ*)

Introduction

The curious fact is that—a quarter-century into the 'third wave' of democratization and the renaissance it brought in comparative democratic studies—we are still far from consensus on what constitutes 'democracy'. And we still struggle to classify ambiguous regimes . . . [Ambiguous regimes] are all (or mostly) something less than electoral democracies: competitive authoritarian systems, hegemonic-party systems, or hybrid regimes.

Larry Diamond[1]

Democracy . . . is the quintessentially contested concept . . . [T]here have never been so many rulers who claim that their regimes are democratic . . . [I]t is that across most of the globe today, the ultimate claim of a political regime to be legitimate—or at least acceptable—rests on the kind of popular consent that purportedly finds expression in the act of free voting . . . Democracy is ultimately based not on voters, but on *citizens* . . . [A] third set [of countries] wherein elections, even if held, are not reasonably fair and many political freedoms are seriously curtailed. There are democracies pour la *gallerie*, especially the international *gallerie*. They are 'electoral authoritarianisms' that have recently been drawing much attention in the scholarly literature.

Guillermo O'Donnell[2]

How do the countries of the Arab Middle East (AME) 'democratize'? This is the key question that guides the book's analytical trajectory. The enterprise is intellectually exciting and yet daunting. Exciting in the sense that thinking about democratization comprises a wide variety of styles, presuppositions, approaches, and of comparative data. Students of democratic transition have sought to explain the acquisition of democratic government or its breakdown juxtaposing the theoretical and the empirical, the national/local and international/global, the political and the economic, the institutional/structural, and the attitudinal/cultural, and the top-down and bottom-up. This plurality has made thinking about democratization equally challenging and daunting. Diamond and O' Donnell are not stating the obvious when they note above that democracy is an essentially contested concept. They are restating the daedal nature of determining what qualifies as 'democratic' when 'democracy' itself is the subject of continuous disagreement over meaning and substance. If the 'what' (democracy) is contested, the 'how' (democratization) has to be equally contested, Whitehead avers.[3] Democratization may be the 'paradigm' which frames the enquiry into democratic transition or emergence of Diamond's 'hybrid regimes'. However, it is not a 'regulative paradigm'. If it were one, Carothers has some time ago declared its 'death'.[4] The diversity of approaches, styles, and assumptions has dictated against singularity and fixity. Students of democratization display a firm grasp of a golden democratic rule: their methodological plurality has undermined the imposition of a single authoritative approach. Similarly, the contests they engender have denied the rise of a singular democratization narrative. The book has benefited from this diversity in narrating a 'story' of democratization in the AME. The contests over democratization and the various assumptions and considerations underlying them are reflected in its text. One assumption that informs the book is that of the conditioned, indeterminate, and unstable nature of processes of democratic transition. Neither determinacy nor stability typifies processes of democratization in the AME.

Thinking about democratization in the AME departs from the considerations offered by both Diamond and O'Donnell of 'hybrid regimes'. Regimes, as they agree, hold elections but produce little or no democracy. The labels for these regimes are legion: 'authoritarian democracy', 'electoral authoritarianism', 'hegemonic-party systems', and 'competitive authoritarianism'.[5] Diamond explains that this hybrid variety performs below the 'substantive test' or 'threshold' typical of electoral democracies. He puts down the failure to transcend the threshold of electoral democracy to three reasons. Electoral administration may be lacking in autonomy and professionalism; opposition parties may be hampered from freely campaigning and having equal opportunity to defeat the incumbent regime; and the allocation of parliamentary seats to unelected representatives.[6] O' Donnell's test partakes of the two dimensions of inclusiveness and competition of polyarchy with emphasis on what he calls 'decisive elections', elections that place winners in the seat of power with full constitutional protection for alternation and tenure of office.[7] The template of civil and political rights that enable competition, O' Donnell insists, must be present for elections to mean more than a periodic cosmetic exercise intended to impress the IMF or the donor international community.

In thinking about democratization in the AME, I have sought to document and capture the rise of 'electoralism' in the late 1980s in Egypt, and since the mid-1990s the routinization of 'election fetishism'. By any other label 'election fetishism' is 'electoral authoritarianism' or what Brumberg deftly calls 'liberalized autocracy'.[8] Regime tutelage, 'divide-and-rule' tactics, monopoly of material and immaterial resources, and weak civil society in Brumberg's 'liberalized autocracy' correspond with the reservations expressed by Diamond and O' Donnell about the impasse of electoral processes that have voters but produce no citizens, and mediate no alternation of power fairly or freely.

Through *Rethinking Arab Democratization: Elections without Democracy* I am seeking to answer the question of how Arab countries democratize and whether they are democratizing at all. The book pays attention to specificity, highlighting where relevant and possible the peculiarities of democratic transitions in the Arab region. In so doing, it situates the discussion of such transitions firmly within their local contexts, but without losing sight of the global picture. It rejects 'exceptionalism' by showing that the Arab world is not immured from the global trend towards political liberalization. But by identifying new trends in Arab democratic transitions and highlighting their peculiarities, it pinpoints the contingency of some of the prerequisites underlying Western theories of democratic transition when applied to the Arab setting. Arab electoralism has since the 1990s been shadowed by Islamism, the Palestinian uprising, increasing US encroachment, economic malaise, two major wars, including the sacking of Baghdad in 2003, and new forms of organizing dissidence and protesting state hegemony. The book is written with these dynamics in mind. In assessing electoralism, it provides a balance sheet of the state of Arab democratization from 1975 to 2008.

I have throughout favoured an interpretive style in the belief that 'third-wave' theory, as argued by Whitehead, panders more to consolidation whereas in the AME the question is one of 'transition'. The democratization I attempt to narrate adopts the emerging 'revisionism' that views transition as 'open-ended' and 'tentative'.[9] To this end, the book examines Arab electoralism over two periods: 1975–97 and 1998–2008. Chapter 1 problematizes and criticizes scholarly approaches to explaining democratic transitions in the Arab world. It tests categories such as 'third-wave', 'civil society', and 'pacted transition' and critically assesses their relevance to the AME. The book avoids the silence in other works on Arab democratization and critically reviews an emerging brand of 'transitology' in Arabic under the auspices of the Arab Unity Studies Centre (AUSC) in Beirut. This new discourse provides an indigenous perspective on democratization in the AME. Chapters 2 and 3 rethink ways of understanding the catalysts and restraints of democratic transition with focus on state tutelage. Using the Khaldunian rubric of *karr* (attack) and *farr* (retreat), Chapter 3 describes the electoral processes of 1975–97 as being forms of democratic attack and retreat, that is, reform and breakdown. Arab reforms are not unlike the warfare technique described by Ibn Khaldun (the fourteenth-century Arab philosopher of history). I use his terms of *karr* and *farr* to refer to the sea-sawing between phases of progression/reform and retrogression/breakdown. In addition to describing the progressive and retrogressive patterns of electoralism in the AME, the chapter analyzes their inherent contradictions and inconsistency with human rights. Good government cannot obtain, it seems, without prejudicing the political, civil, and religious rights of excluded social and political forces in the key Arab 'democratizers'—Algeria, Egypt, Jordan, Kuwait, Lebanon, Morocco, Tunisia, and Yemen. Chapter 2 presents a comprehensive and systematic evaluation of the initiation of electoralism of the 1980s and provides a background for understanding the routinization of electoralism of the 1990s.

Chapters 2 and 3 are a narration of the 'story' of top-down Arab democratization. Chapter 4 tells the story of democratization from without, focusing on US democracy promotion. To this end, the chapter provides a critical deconstruction of the Greater Middle East Initiative (GMEI), the United States's 'road-map' for democratizing the AME. The investigation looks at the language of the GMEI and the power asymmetry in terms of dictating the 'knowledge' of democracy or the substance of democratization in the AME. Here democratization via contagion (Arab Gulf), intimidation (Palestinian Territories and Lebanon) and invasion (Iraq) are deployed, benefiting from comparative studies on Latin America. The contradictions of US democracy promotion are illustrated through acts that concomitantly promote (Iraq) and undermine (Palestinian Territories/Hamas) democratization.

Chapters 5 and 6 re-narrate the 'story' of Arab democratization by shifting the focus on democratizing catalysts from below. Chapter 5 considers the role of protest, specifically bread riots, and the collapse of the 'bread' pact of post-independence between the rulers and the ruled in the AME—subsidized goods in return for political deference. This is an important dynamic the literature on Arab democratization remains silent on. The notion of a tacit pact between the rulers and the ruled is best encapsulated in the Arabic term 'democracy of bread' (*dīmuqrāṭiyyat al-khubz*). The explanatory power of the quasi-moral economy of 'bread' and the trade-off between providential and electoral politics are analyzed. Pressure from below in the 1980s, in the form of bread riots, led to involuntary relaxation of control from the top in the form of an ambiguous politics of renewal. The clear purpose of this political renewal thus far has been regime survival by other means. Freedom arrives in other societies following the solving of economic problems or solid economic performance, as Lipset claims. The chapter tests and refutes the Lipset hypothesis in the context of the austerity programmes of the late 1980s. Limited forms of political equality have emerged in some Arab countries at the back of economic woes. The final chapter examines the impact of al-Jazeerah satellite TV, the Internet, and blogs and their roles in consolidating democratic struggles and the nascent Arab public opinion.

The analysis seeks to capture the richness of the Arab political tapestry, from Mauritania in the Arab West to Bahrain in the Arab Gulf. I use examples from the entire AME noting both the similarities and dissimilarities, past and present. For practical reasons I had to shrink the history of democratization in the AME to the post-colonial period from the mid-1970s to present. However, I have noted the pre-colonial history of reform from the nineteenth century when the first councils for limited representation were set up. The colonial period had its own parliamentary 'ornaments', which in post-independence military coups were to dissolve and close in the 1950s and 1960s. I have embedded into the text interview materials from leading opinion-formulators from within the AME. I use them to supplement written materials unused before in analyses of Arab democratization. Once again, the 'Occident' returns to the 'Orient' through 'civilizing' ideas that today travel in a borderless world. Thus the use of indigenous voices, where relevant, makes for a two-way flow of information. The book shows that these voices have significant agency in determining the terms of their encounter with democratization. In so doing, they add to the multivocal parley and fierce contest of democratization as I elaborate in the next chapter.

Notes

1. Larry Diamond, 'Elections without Democracy: Thinking about Hybrid Regimes', *Journal of Democracy*, 13/2 (April 2002), 21–2.
2. Guillermo O' Donnell, 'The Perpetual Crises of Democracy', *Journal of Democracy*, 18/1 (January 2007), 6: 8–9.
3. Laurence Whitehead, *Democratization: Theory and Experience* (Oxford: Oxford University Press, 2002), 30.
4. Thomas Carothers, 'The End of the Transition Paradigm', *Journal of Democracy*, 13/1 (2002), 5–21.

5. In addition to the articles by Diamond and O' Donnell, which mention these labels, see the articles by the authors in the section on 'Elections without Democracy', edited by Diamond. An example is by, Steven Levitsky and Lucan A. Way, 'The Rise of Competitive Authoritarianism', *Journal of Democracy*, 13/2 (April 2002), 51–65.
6. Diamond, 'Thinking about Hybrid Regimes', 22.
7. O' Donnell, 'The Perpetual Crises of Democracy', 7.
8. Daniel Brumberg, 'The Trap of Liberalized autocracy', 13/14 (October 2002), 56–68.
9. Whitehead, *Democratization: Theory and Experience*, 27.

....

1

....

Rethinking Democratization
in the Arab Context

If 'democracy' is viewed as a contested and to some extent unstable
concept, anchored through the invocation of practical knowledge
and a deliberative filter or collective deliberation, then democratization can only come about through a lengthy process of social
construction that is bound to be relatively open-ended. However, although the resulting processes of democratization may be
lengthy, erratic, and contested, they should generate quite enough
evidence to confirm their existence.

Laurence Whitehead[1]

It is time to recognize that the transition paradigm has outlived its
usefulness and to look for a better lens ... [T]he almost automatic
assumption of democracy promoters during the peak years of the
third wave that any country moving away from dictatorship was in
'transition to democracy' has often been inaccurate and misleading.
Some of those countries have hardly democratized at all. Many
have taken on a smattering of democratic features but show few
signs of democratizing much further and are certainly not following
any predictable democratization script.

Thomas Carothers[2]

In this chapter, I attempt to rethink democratization in the context of
the AME. Democratization has ceased to be the 'high priest' many still
claim it to be. Scholars from Carothers to Whitehead interrogate the
'transition paradigm' and 'third wave' democratization. Interrogation
is doubly fierce when 'word' (theory) meets 'world' (context, practice).
No matter how normatively appealing democratization theory neither
has neat boundaries nor is uncontested. Moreover, its application to
the Arab setting poses difficulties as shall be argued in this chapter.
However, this is not specific to the AME. Democratization has its

travails, trials, failures, and successes elsewhere—Southern and Latin America and Eastern Europe. What route should democratization take and what processes and outcomes should typify it in the AME? Do the concepts that belong to the nomenclature of Western democratization readily apply to the AME? To address these questions, I follow a twofold analytical agenda. As a prelude to the discussion around these questions, I first situate democratization within the broader scholarly discourse, paying special attention to the contestability of democratization. I principally focus on the 'dialogue' between Samuel P. Huntington and Laurence Whitehead. Whitehead's notion of democratization being essentially contested informs the ontological position of this book. Democratization speaks to time and space and its progression is reflected spatially and temporally. This discussion briefly extends to the nascent scholarly effort from within the AME to understand and adapt the 'democratization paradigm'. I draw on the key writings, which have been totally ignored by students of Arab democratization, providing a critical assessment. In the absence of an indigenous analogue to Euro-American studies of transition it will remain difficult to exclusively view reforms in the AME through a 'Western' lens. What characterizes this emerging 'Arab transitology' is the borrowing of Western theoretical frameworks and concepts that do not always explain Arab peculiarities. This is despite the wide usage of neologisms such as '*damaqraṭah*' or '*taḥawwul dīmuqrāṭī*', respectively, the Arabic terms for 'democratization' and 'democratic transition'. Second, the chapter tests the concepts of 'pacted transition' and 'civil society' in the AME. Their rendition with reference to the AME attests to the difficulty of transposing the 'dogmas' of Eurocentric democratization as well as to the variability of both interpretation and application.

Contesting Democratization

Arab states and societies are caught in the vortex of the challenges brought about by the global travel of democratization to the AME. Vogue Euro-American paradigmatic approaches and explanatory universals come and go. The study of the AME has since the 1960s had its share of the analytical fads invented by political scientists. Only recently, modernization has ceded to democratization. The pressure to democratize is from within and without. The global diffusion of democracy and human rights as new standards and legitimators in domestic politics has impacted on all Arab societies and polities. Crises of economic performance and of de-legitimacy from the inside (e.g. bread riots) have forced many Arab ruling elites to embark on previously unthinkable political reforms.[3] Arab societies are grappling with the challenge of learning political organization in order to carve out a margin of existence in largely corporatist settings. Epistemic communities are equally challenged by the 'travel' of democratization. How students of Arab politics harmonize word and world poses more questions than provides answers. Some of these questions concern the prerequisites of democratic transition. Others revolve around the compatibility of Islam and democracy. In particular, the assignment of scholars to invent or apply theoretical frameworks for analysing progression towards and retrogression from substantive democratic government has not been uncomplicated. There are reservations about whether Western democratic theory is for export.[4] But claims to universality are as reproachable as defensiveness in the name of specificity. In the AME, the merits of relativism must be weighed against the trap of 'exceptionalism'.[5] Privileging indigenous models of democracy or democratization has historically worked to sidetrack genuine political reform. Indeed, democratization as a moral imperative must be defended. Euro-American paradigms for explaining democratic transition may not be applicable outside their original milieu. However, the AME can learn from the limitations, if not the successes, of these paradigms. There is plenty of learning to be had in undoing the polarities between structure and agency, state and society, institution and attitude, and between the domestic and international. To some extent this book attempts to seek some answers to the peculiarity of Arab political liberalizations. It does this by trying to bridge the gap between top-down and bottom-up as well as internal and external dynamics.

Caught unprepared by the early 'democratic' stirrings of the early 1990s and keen to explain transformation along the path of modernity, students of the AME have sought clues in Euro-American scholarship.[6] The theoretical and conceptual lag in the study of Arab politics makes this exercise imperative as well as inevitable.[7] The various analytical approaches (from behaviouralism through rational choice down to Marxism) that vied for proving their scientific credentials and establishing their pre-eminence in political science have all coloured the content and direction of the study of politics in the AME. This explains the focus up to the mid-1990s on elites' political behaviour or institutions such as the military in Arab polities to the detriment of investigation of civil society.[8] Indeed, opportunities in the Arab world are slowly unfolding for greater participation and contestation—the two dimensions of Dahl's polyarchy.[9] Arab political liberalizations have not hitherto led to popularly constituted and accountable government, rule of law, or revitalized intermediary institutions. Nor have they put an end to abuse of office and serious violations of human rights.[10] Nonetheless, democratization is the paradigm through which they are interpreted. By and large, the experiences of Southern and Eastern Europe, Latin and Southern America, regions that find themselves in states of transition far more congenial with transcending the democratic threshold, form the comparative framework for the study of Arab democratic stirrings and initiatives. The state of flux observable in most Arab political liberalizations suggests that Eurocentric paradigms, especially democratization, are not easily applicable to Arab democratic experiments. That is, unless they are supplemented with indigenous forms of explanation and interpretation in which political realities and phenomena are conceived.[11] Hence there is a need for a process of dialectic, as against a synthesis. Indigenous forms of explanation and Euro-American frameworks and knowledge practices from 'East' and 'West' must engage in cross-cultural 'fertilization' or 'cross-cultural dialogue'.[12] However, such dialogue is still a long way away. Western scholarship on democratization in the AME ignores indigenous representations of the problem. Indigenous representations, on the other hand, access and apply Eurocentric knowledge practices—dependency theory or democratization. But there is one problem. This access tends to lack critical engagement. This is evident in the rendition given to democratization in Arab scholarship in which, for example, emphasis on structure outweighs that on agency, a point to be returned to below.

Concepts such as 'civil society' or 'pacted transition' which accompany democratization in its global travel are not always neat or clear in their new geographies. No matter how potent and functional in the milieu in which they are conceived, Euro-American interpretive frameworks cannot be expected to fit comfortably when being transplanted in a new milieu. Moreover, they are not always congenial with the different forms of interpretation upon which they are imposed. There are as many forms of interpreting and explaining a given political phenomenon. The diversity of interpretations corresponds with the world's vast tapestry of cultures and categories of thought. Naturally, this does not preclude the possibilities of either overlap or exchange. Relatively detached Euro-American paradigms may not serve well to explain the dynamics of Arab politics. This is true with regard to the so-called third wave[13] of Arab democratizations and transitions[14] to good government. This problem has been foreshadowed by a number of students of democratization in the AME.[15]

Recent analyses of the complex dynamics of Arab movements towards liberalizing the authoritarian structures of the various police (*mukhābarāt*) states are fragmentary. Until very recently, democracy has been considered to be irrelevant to the Arab context. 'Democracy' and 'Arab' have been paired as an 'oxymoron'. Hudson deprecates this exceptionalism, the by-product, *inter alia*, of the genre of Orientalist literature that excludes the AME from the study of democratization, for instance.[16] An extension of this Orientalist bias is the often assumed incompatibility of Islam and democratic practices. But there are counter-arguments.[17] The prejudicial view against Islam has roots in an adversarial history with Christendom.[18] Knowledge-making and practices in the study of Arab politics are not neutral: They are embedded in the historically biased attitude of Euro-American ideas towards Islam and Arabism.[19] The corollary is that 'the West feels that its stereotypes constitute "knowledge" of the Middle East'.[20] Generalizations about Islam and Islamists and their assumed hostility to democracy aside, 'Islamic and Western democratic values tend to overlap', and include basic concepts of equality, justice, and so on.[21] The post-1945 democratic model, filtered through American pluralism, cannot and should not be precisely reproduced in the AME. This is not to argue either that democracy should be 'occidentalized' as exclusively Western or that the Arab democratic model will be *sui generis*. At least in theory, the common denominator already exists. Islam's concepts of consultation and consensus jostle for recognition as equal to and compatible with democracy's most basic principles of participation and contestation. Islam's principles of equality and justice, claim many Muslim scholars, have analogues in Western democracy.

The call for political science to be critical and more self-consciously interpretive is apposite.[22] As mentioned above, analytical paradigms created with special reference to European and North American contexts will no doubt defy transposition to different settings. The democratization paradigm must be fluid, flexible, and sensitive to linguistic, historical, and cultural factors in the AME. Hence the relevance of a process of dialectic: a component of this paradigm is not inappropriate to understanding political phenomena in the AME. Indeed, democratization ought to be defended and instituted in the AME. However, the danger of homogenizing meanings of democratization is for them to be captured by a single framework (such as 'third wave') to the point that they cannot speak to a different setting. For such meanings are trapped in a single way of understanding the world. A paradigm that speaks with the singularity of 'truth' requires reassessment of its basic precepts. What follows is a look at how 'third wave' democratization is subject to critical reassessment. Special reference is made to the work of Laurence Whitehead who is a key critic of Huntington's brand of 'Third Wave' democratization with its emphasis on consolidation.

Third Wave Transition: A 'Dialogue' Between Huntington and Whitehead

The search for 'third wave'[23] democracies and democratization in the Arab World is an exercise in futility. Scholars seem to pay too much deference to the premises of 'third wave' democratization. Is 'closure' the defining test of democratic transition? Are two consecutive multiparty elections an adequate test for successful democratic transition? The 'dialogue' between two seminal scholars of democratization is invoked here not so much for the purpose of finding answers. Rather, the chief aim is to highlight the indeterminate nature of democratization in countries such as in the AME where transition is still inchoate and fledgling. Both our scholars are driven by the normative appeal of democracy as an ethos and as a system of government. In his *Third Wave*, Samuel Huntington makes the case for democratic consolidation. This he does with an air of certainty. 'Closure' is the end-point in his conceptualization of how countries democratize. Laurence Whitehead, by contrast, is more circumspect. In his book *Democratization: Theory and Experience* Whitehead questions Huntington's brand of democratization. In its global travel, democratization stumbles upon a variety of experiences and contexts, he proposes. The gulf between what theory suggests and experience displays is indeed wide. Thomas Carothers concurs. Thus Whitehead puts forth an understanding of democratization as an essentially contested concept. He argues that if democracy is an essentially contested concept so is democratization. Instead of Huntington's 'closure', Whitehead counter-argues with his own notion of 'open-ended' democratic transition. The random and cyclic realities of Arab transition generally deny rather than affirm Huntington's brand of 'third wave' democratization. They lack the linearity which sits at odds with 'closure'. The realities of Arab transition approximate Whitehead's counter-argument of protracted processes that are subject to the vicissitudes of space and time as well as, in the case of the AME, the whims of autocrats. Arab 'transitions' collide with democratization orthodoxy, owing to the false starts and uncertainty of Arab political reforms.[24] Huntington's democratization is almost too neat and viable to apply to the contemporary Arab world. The state in some parts of the AME is conspired against within (by patrimonial, corporatist, tribal, and coercive practices) and without (by expansionist impulses). What happens in the Arab World is closer therefore to the script written by Whitehead than that offered by Huntington. The Arab realities of transition dictate against linear, determinate, stable, and measurable consolidation. Consolidation is not even an issue when the existing processes of liberalization in the AME are still marred by state illiberal policies and near total control of the content and pace of reform. Huntington's confidence in democratic outcomes and processes is context and time-specific. His confidence is perhaps more suited to empirically verifiable democratic outcomes in Southern Europe or Latin America. Spatially and temporally, the Arab world has no record of liberalization to match Southern or Eastern European successes. Whitehead views transition as a provisional process and this is more fitting in the AME. Huntington's transition is chronologically short (two democratic and consecutive transfers of power). Whitehead is disdainful of short history. For him, the *longue dureé* would readily show the history of democratization to be littered with reverses and breakdowns. Unforeseen happenings do not guarantee smooth and straight-line democratic transition. Even a single generation may not be sufficient for democratic transition.[25] Whitehead's book stresses, for the benefit of transitologists, the elements of contingency, contestation, and open-endedness as intrinsic to democratic transition.[26]

For this reason the structuralist template and top-down trajectory of Huntington's 'third wave' may not be reliable for measuring democratic transition in the Arab world. Few scholars pay attention to the dispositional and bottom-up angles of democratic construction. The phenomenon of bread riots as a catalyst for liberalization in the 1980s is considered in this book (Chapter 5) in order to account for unforeseen happenings as well as bottom-up dynamics. Among students of democratization in the AME Norton's probing of Middle Eastern civil society and Tétreault and Carapico's investigations, respectively, of Kuwaiti and Yemeni civil societies are noteworthy exceptions to the top-down state-centric enquiry into the state of Arab political reforms.[27] Experience of Arab liberalizations seems hitherto to fail 'third wave' theory. Instead of consolidation, those searching for democracy in the Arab world find 'record of failure', 'liberalized autocracy', 'decline of pluralism', 'depoliticization', 'elusive Reformation', and 'silenced majority'.[28] Empirically verifiable democratization by electoral test alone is doubtful. Huntington affirms his expressly institutional bent by upholding the primacy of the electoral test, holding elections to be 'the essence of democracy'.[29] However, 30 years of elections in Egypt confirm rather than deny O'Donnell's critical reflections about illusive consolidation, especially when electoral activities coexist with authoritarianism in so-called new democracies.[30] Elections have not reversed political singularity and excessive executive power in the Arab world. To rephrase Diamond 'elections without democracy' characterize Arab political reforms.[31] Huntington is aware of the limits of 'electoral democracies' and the electoral test. Elections, he notes, in 'non-Western societies' can display the 'parochializing...not cosmopolitanizing' effects of democracy.[32] Huntington is correct in pointing out how elections, instead of broadening inclusion and widening interests, can place in power autocrats, ideological and ethnic bigots, and religious zealots. To an extent, thus unfolds the 'story' of elections in the Arab world. Elections prolong autocrats' stranglehold over polity (e.g. Ben Ali in Tunisia; Mubarak in Egypt; Abdullah al-Salih in Yemen; Al-Bashir in the Sudan). Southern European Generals and Colonels marched back into military barracks as Huntington records in his *Third Wave* (e.g. Greece, Portugal). Their return to the barracks has no analogue in the Arab world. Huntington credits General Antonio de Spinola with the 'expansion of human freedom' with his 1974 coup whose demonstration effect precipitated democratization outside Portugal.[33] Arab military officers do not hand power to civilian governments. They themselves become the civilian authority (e.g. Yemen, Libya, Sudan [1989], Tunisia). Substituting military for civilian clothing does not constitute a transition.

Democratization theory or what Carothers calls the 'transition paradigm' tends to fail the Arab experience with political liberalization.[34] The study of the Arab experiences with liberalization suffers from being too cemented to the democratization template. It follows too closely the institutional and top-down itinerary of 'third wave'-type transitology. At least four assumptions of the 'democratization paradigm' seem to guide much of the enquiry of Arab political reforms. Transition away from authoritarianism is the first assumption. It speaks to Huntington's original idea of 'third wave' democratization being more of a systematic movement towards democracy than towards authoritarian rule. 'De-liberalization' and 'retreats' observed in the AME from the 1990s are in the opposite direction to democracy, however.[35] The second assumption regards the sequential trajectory of democratization made up of a beginning (opening), a middle (a breakthrough), and an end (consolidation). Manifestations of this linear sequencing in democratic progression are empirically difficult to prove anywhere in the AME. The 'determinative importance of elections', the third assumption, is also difficult to substantiate in terms of engendering democratic citizenship in the Arab world. From Qatar, an oil-rich city-state, to Mauritania, one of the most impoverished and tribal Arab states, periodic elections happen with regularity. But little or no democracy results from Arab elections, as shall be argued in the ensuing chapters. The fourth assumption holds that democratization is more or less an outcome enabled top-down by the choice of rulers and elites. This is no exception in the AME. However, elites' choice of elections is tattered by the benefit of hindsight through observation of increasing 'electoralism' across the AME's vast geography. Electoralism does not equate with democratization. The antidote against the fourth assumption is that most probably in most Arab rulers' reasoning autocracy, not democracy, is the best means for maximizing utility (e.g. survival in power). Elites and rulers possess reform processes and manage them in ways that ensure preordained results at the polls. Which parties are proscribed and which political forces are allowed to participate in elections are among the tools used by ruling elites to ensure that they face no threat in the reforms they introduce. Examples are legion—Algeria, Egypt, Sudan, Tunisia, and Yemen.

Whitehead criticizes 'third wave' democratization for being at once 'too permissive' and 'too exacting' to measure up to the diverse tapestry of transitions in the real world.[36] Explaining democratization through a set of fixed and inflexible theoretical propositions, which may be drawn from specific and ideal-typical case studies, leads to imprecision when mapped out on a wider geography of transitions. Thus democratization cannot be oversimplified into an orderly, predictable, and measurable movement between two polarities—autocracy and democracy—mediated by 10 years of elections, constitutional laws, or 'pacted' agreements. 'Pacted transition' in Spain had democratic outcomes that were not replicated in the 1988 Tunisian copy of it, a case to be examined below.[37] The only democratization therefore that can be envisaged in the Arab World is along Whitehead's lines of 'a complex, long-term, dynamic, and open-ended process'.[38] This process, Whitehead adds, involves 'progress' towards 'a more rule-based, more consensual and more participatory type of politics'.[39] Here Whitehead's 'boat' metaphor of 'anchored' and 'floated' democratization and democracy comes to the fore. Whitehead's reference to 'rule-based', 'consensual', and 'participatory' brand of citizenship is informed by fixed meanings of democracy. Like Huntington, his understanding is 'anchored' in Schumpeter's electoral competition as well as in Dahl's polyarchy with its twin dimensions of participation and contestation.[40] Unlike Huntington, however, Whitehead contests both democracy and democratization, placing 'internal tensions'[41] at the core of the ability of democracy and democratization to draw appeal, elicit interest, spur dialogue, court controversy, and sustain allure through adaptability to time and space. The internal tensions mirror the polarity between 'fact' and 'value'. The former elicit clarity and universality; the latter opacity and particularity. 'Fact' corresponds with 'anchorage' in terms of meaning and practice (e.g. institutions). 'Value' has the potential of eliciting at worst a 'clash', to use a word made popular by Huntington, and, at best, a dialogue in the realm of the non-institutional. The notion of 'tensions' allows Whitehead a 'floated' reading of democracy and democratization. According to this reading both democracy and democratization are in a state of flux demanded by time, space, culture, history, and additional non-institutional factors. Thus it is impossible to pin down either democracy or democratization to singularity or fixity in terms of conceptualization or practice. The understanding of democratization as essentially contested is largely missing in Arabic scholarship on transition, which I examine below.

Democratic Transition in the AME

The AME remains a consumer of theories and ideologies. The invention of 'dependency theory' or 'bureaucratic authoritarianism' to examine the reality of development and authoritarianism in Southern and Latin America, for instance, has never been matched by scholarship in the AME. Even if incoherent, 'Islamization' is perhaps the only originally indigenous 'narrative' that has thus far been invented by the opponents of Westernization. Pan-Arabists, be they Nasserists or Ba'thists, display sensitivity to Islam but still superficially dress up Western socialism in an Arab garb. Now that democratization is the latest vogue in the AME there is a near theoretical and conceptual blank as how to 'filter' it into the realities of the AME. It is perhaps a little ambitious or premature to be at this stage talking about an Arab school of democratization. Democratization as a subfield of political science enquiry is still at its infancy in the AME. As yet there are no original theoretical frameworks to distinguish the Arab examination of democratic transition from more established and theoretically rigorous investigations of the subject in Latin America or Southern Europe, for instance. Generally, however, and despite its infancy, the study of transition in the AME tends to reject democratization from without; it leans towards a teleological and institutionalist understanding of democracy and democratization; and it attempts a kind of 'diagnosis' of Arab political decay, favouring an examination of constraints, more so than opportunities, of democratization. What follows is an attempt to illustrate the presence of these features in the Arabic scholarship of transition in the AME.

For nearly 20 years now the most relatively disciplined and continuous scholarly project on democratization in the AME has been led by the Beirut-based Arab Unity Studies Centre (AUSC). This project is well-documented in the centre's series on democratization launched in the second half of the 1980s and in its quarterly journal *The Arab Future (Al-Mustaqbal Al-'Arabī)*. Students of transition continue to ignore this resource in their accounts of democratization in the AME. The AUSC is not ideologically neutral. As a think-tank it is governed by a pan-Arabist ideology. Thus it champions Arab specificity, autonomy, common identity, and destiny. Iraq's invasion of Kuwait in 1990 forced a rethink of the centre's original ideological identity. Nasserism was a dying ideology and the remaining Ba'thist states (Iraq and Syria) were examples of pariah and failed states whose declaratory policy of Arab unity was failing. Today AUSC still professes the ideal of pan-Arab integration. However, this it does in conjunction with a commitment to the ideal of democratization. The discourse of democratization in the AUSC's series on the subject is marked by an inner contrast. Its pan-Arabist leanings inform its opposition to all outside democracy promotion in the AME, especially by the United States. A series of books on Iraq published since the 2003 invasion makes plain the peril of transformation led by foreign powers. Thus the brand of transitology found in the Arab discourse stands against colonialism and cultural imperialism. The impact of the colonial past still haunts Arab scholars and this has been reinforced by the invasion of Iraq in 2003. In fact, no single factor has damaged US democracy promotion in the AME more than the invasion of Iraq. The very tension with the 'colonial' and 'imperialist' Western 'other' that accompanied the Arab search for modernization in the 1960s and 1970s today rages unabated in the pursuit of democratization. The Arab 'psyche' is once again injured, rekindling fear for identity and sovereignty that was once prevalent in the height of the anti-colonial resistance. The AME is engaging with democratization; but that does not mean democratization from without. The reordering of the Arab house must therefore be engineered by Arabs who alone pick and choose what models, modalities, and routes democratic transition should emulate and follow. The view expressed below by Khair Eddin Haseeb, AUSC's director, illustrates the point:

I recognize that the Iraqi regime is, like many Arab countries, undemocratic . . . But how do we treat this [problem]? Is it through US invasion of Iraq or through work from the inside? Firstly, the Americans definitely do not want democracy in Iraq or in other Arab countries. They co-operated with the Iraqi regime in the 1980s during the Iran–Iraq war; so why do they now want to change the regime? There are suspicions around the subject of Americans and democracy in the Arab region. It is not in the interest of the West, especially America, for democracy to exist in the Arab region.[42]

This is a theme common to Arab discussions of democratic transition in the AME. It gets a particularly elaborate treatment in a recent AUSC case study of democratization in Iraq by scholar Abdelwahab Hamid Rashid. Rashid argues that the United States does not genuinely pursue democracy in Iraq. Rather, the United States wants a pliant Iraq as part and parcel of a broader security and 'pax-Americana' agenda in the AME. The hot items on that agenda, he argues, are as follows: to neutralize Iraq in the Arab–Israeli conflict through the facilitation of a peace treaty with Israel; to impose upon Iraq a ban on non-conventional arms that includes also a major reduction in its conventional war-making capacity and technological know-how; and, subsequently, to eliminate all threats to oil supply as well as Israel's security.[43] Neither democracy nor human rights, Rashid adds, are on the radar of the US foreign policy architects, especially the hawkish neoconservatives. The name of the game in Iraq is control over the Arab Gulf oil and rulers. In addition to this, preventing the rise of an economically and politically independent and powerful Iraq that may serve as a bulwark against US hegemony in the region is another key foreign policy objective.[44] These sentiments are echoed in Arab criticisms of the Broader Middle East Initiative (Chapter 4). There may however be an oversimplification in the contention that Euro-American foreign policymakers are not genuine about seeing democracy flourish in the AME. A key voice in the AUSC democratization project, Yousef Shoueiri, advances an argument that repudiates zealous conspiratorial theorizing. He finds a historical precedent for contemporary Western democracy promotion in the French colonial promotion of consultation (*shūrā*) in Tunisia in the nineteenth century. Consultation, he writes, 'was born in Tunisia carrying two contradictory objectives'. The first, he argues, is an internal objective aimed at solidifying independence in the face of rising European expansionism. The second, Shoueiri adds, is a European desire to see the practice of Islamic consultation implemented as a way of furthering economic interests. European powers promoted the election of local merchants to the councils and assemblies. In so doing, European powers' key objective was to have allies whose role was to facilitate the opening of local markets.[45] In the same vein, US democracy promotion cannot be assumed to be totally disingenuous. If spreading American capitalism is one of the aims of bringing the 'American Century' to fruition, then democracy promotion makes both good economic and political sense. Current US democracy promotion resembles the promotion of consultation by the European colons in the past. The promotion of democracy is not a fully altruistic undertaking.

Yet despite the somewhat adversarial position vis-à-vis the West, the notion of democratization AUSC publications on democratic transition operationalize is largely inspired by Western models and understandings of democracy. There is the odd reverence of Islamic consultation. But there is no elaboration of a model of democracy or democratization that draws on this specifically Islamic institution. This is in spite of the fact that the AUSC series on democratization is mindful of Arab specificity. This specificity, argues Abdelhussein Sha'ban, must not be converted into sentiments against all forms of 'otherness'. Cultural autarchy and exceptionalism must be rejected as they would simply emulate Huntington's 'clash of civilizations' or Fukuyama's 'end of history'. Both, he notes, render Western civilization or democracy the end-point for all humanity and sole stand-bearers of development and rationality. Thus he writes that 'specificity means [affinity with] civilizational, cultural, social and religious pluralism; by working in tandem with global and universal thought, specificity [acquires space to celebrate] its distinction'.[46] For him democratization should not mean the pursuit of modernity in a fashion that ignores the Arab and Islamic cultural heritage. That would spell alienation and leads not to modernity. Accordingly, he contends that the Islamic practice of consultation and democracy can share political space.[47] The question of cultural heritage and its role in modernity as a whole has been a recurring theme in the various Arab attempts to engineer 'transition' to independence, then to modernization, Islamization, globalization, and now to democratization. Accommodation of the cultural heritage, argues Thana Fuad Abdullah, is a prerequisite for a balanced and successful democratization that is reconcilable with pan-Arab and Islamic identity.[48] In the same vein, the AUSC discourse of democratization allows ample room for broad coalitions of moral protest politics to defeat authoritarianism in the AME. It tolerates Islamists as legitimate democratic actors. It also displays sensitivity to Islam as pertinent to the social and cultural fabric of Arab societies. The works by Al-Solh, Al-Kawari, Rashid, Ghalyun, and Shoueiri, all prominent contributors to the AUSC democratization series, corroborate this point.[49] Thus far, however, there has not been an articulation of a brand of democracy or democratization that exclusively speaks to the AME's specificity. Perhaps specificity in the AME is best served by making the most of what both 'East' and 'West' have to offer in the realm of good government. In the absence of a coherent and rigorous project of what specificity should spell for democratization in the AME, the discourse by AUSC has, even if by default, one advantage: syncretism.

Nonetheless, teleology is deeply embedded in the discourses of democracy and democratization as though elections, institutions, and constitutions are the sole progenitors of good government. The end point of elections or institutions must be democracy. This oversimplification of democratic discussion in the AME is reflected in the discourse of the AUSC series. The discussion of democratization panders to institutionalism. Its institutional 'check list' echoes understandings registered in third wave-type treatment of the question of transition. Ali Khalifah Al-Kawari, the series editor and one of the key convenors of AUSC democratization workshops, notes that there is no universal definition of democracy and that AUSC's attempt to define democracy is ongoing. Yet he seems to abandon this provisional thinking in favour of an institutionalist and contractual understanding of democratization. He states two key principles as fundamental to democratization, popular will and citizenship. These two, he adds, must be enshrined constitutionally. He goes on to list political and civil liberties, legality, constitutionalism, institution-building, alternation of power, separation of power, and free and fair elections as essential to democratic transition. Al-Kawari stresses that transitional societies in the AME will need a constitutional court to adjudicate when intricate questions arise as how to harmonize religious and natural laws. As an arbiter, such a constitutional court would help minimize the conflicts between otherwise antagonistic ideological trends that could easily erupt in the course of democratization.[50] This institutionalist bent is found in the key works published thus far. An important work entitled 'Mechanisms of Democratic Change in the Arab Homeland' by Thana Fuad Abdullah allocates the greater part of her investigation to institutionalism. Her 'machinery' of democratic transition rests on multipartyism, rule of law, constitutionalism, and free media.[51] However, while Abdullah's analysis panders to a top-down and institutionalist agenda, there is reference to the importance of civil society. More important is the casual reference in all of the AUSC democratization series to 'democratic acculturation' (*thaqāfah dīmuqrāṭiyyah*). Never has this concept, which holds the key to a non-institutionalist examination of democratization in the AME, been addressed systematically. Yet it is a term that recurs in all of the AUSC workshop proceedings and the books published thus far on democratization. A positive development is the in-depth case studies of democratic acculturation in specific Arab countries. The contribution by Kuwaiti scholar Ismail Al-Shatti sheds light on this process in Kuwait. Al-Shatti succeeds in identifying key features specific to Kuwait's process of democratic acculturation of which pragmatism is the most important. Pragmatism, he argues, derives from the harshness and severity of desert-dwelling. Harshness and poverty in the desert have conditioned Kuwaitis to seek pragmatic solutions. Just as their forebears avoided hunger and sought gain in commercial transactions through moderation, modern-day Kuwaitis deploy the same pragmatism to democratize, by rejecting extremism in all aspects of life.[52] Their pragmatism is underpinned by norms of negotiation and compromise. These norms make Kuwaiti politics amenable to the conclusion of win–win agreements. Kuwaitis are additionally coached into overt forms of protest and criticism. This openness in conflict resolution has rendered the resort to covert action or violence minimal in Kuwaiti history.[53] Al-Shatti finds the rise of early awareness of sovereignty and nationalist identification to be deeply entrenched. This factor is owed to permanent perception of threat from larger and expansionist political neighbours—Ottomans, Wahhabis, and Iraqis. Early nationalist sentiment led to the emergence of political elites that spearheaded the task of nation and state-building. In particular, the influx of political ideas of nationalism, sovereignty, and democracy added sophistication to the country's political elite.[54] That elite, Al-Shatti remarks, was instrumental in leading democratic struggles begun in the first half of the twentieth century.[55] Through these struggles the first building blocks for associational life and civil society were put in place.[56] The traditional male forums (*dīwāniyyah*) held to discuss social, political, and cultural matters are a unique institution in Kuwait's associational life.

I refer now to two additional examples of discussion of democratic acculturation. Despite his institutionalist working definition of democracy and democratization, Sha'ban rates democratic acculturation highly in the crafting of democracy. He compares, but only in passing, Arab and Western histories of acquisition of good government. He finds the history of acquisition of good government to be cumulative and continuous in the case of consolidated democracies. By contrast, it is discontinuous in the course of nation and state-building in the AME. Incidentally, this is a rare even if indirect acknowledgement by Sha'ban of the type of interpretist method applied by scholars such as Whitehead for whom democratization is open-ended and contingent. Unlike in consolidated democracies, Arab processes of nation and state-building have characteristically ignored democratic acculturation. May be such an acculturation has not been deemed to cohere with the aims of nationalist monism. Regardless, the point Sha'ban makes is that the AME abruptly terminated the liberal age of Arab thought (*nahḍah*); thus the didactic potential of that period was never fully fulfilled. Here Sha'ban laments negligence of the intellectual and liberal heritage from the nineteenth century. Had the AME absorbed the lessons of Abdulrahman Al-Kawakib's famous treatise 'The Ways of Despotism' in the same way the French did Montesquieu's *Spirit of Laws* or Rousseau's *Social Contract*, they would have founded a democratic acculturation amenable to democratic transition today.[57] Thana Abdullah concurs. She notes that there is an absence of the 'democratic individual', the individual who partakes in discussions of public affairs, exercises voting rights, tolerates difference, and joins associations.[58] She recognizes the role of education for the purpose of democratic acculturation, noting three rival approaches about how to acculturate Arab societies into democracy. The first aims at the creation of a new Arab democratic culture. Such a culture would be geared towards resistance against cultural imperialism from without and promotion of toleration and alternation of power from within. For the advocates of the second approach building such a culture is not possible without determining from the outset which social forces should steer such a project and develop agendas and strategies for democratic transformation. The last approach weds culture and structure: cultural renewal must be combined with material amelioration of people's livelihoods for the greater sake of wider participation.[59] These propositions have Gramscian overtones about the re-production of culture to resist authoritarianism within and hegemony without. However, they also tend to argue for cultural monism as though the 350 million Arabs can all be governed by a single democratic culture or project of democratic acculturation. Until pan-Arab sentiments reconcile themselves to local specificity across the panoply of Arab states and societies, the legitimate ideal of cultural renewal will be simply rehashing the old totalizing social engineering specific to Nasser's Arab socialism and Saddam's Ba'thism. Their failure to recognize difference accounts for the pan-Arabist and Ba'thist utopia to be practically mapped on the diverse AME.

Thus a great deal of the diagnosis with the AUSC discourse of democratization targets the failed postcolonial ideologies. It is a discourse that tends towards soul-searching and, to an extent, self-doubt. It seeks to outline the anatomy of the crisis (*azmah*) of the macro Arab body politic and its constituent political units. The diagnosis is carried out on a 'sick' and decaying Arab body politic. Systemic 'decay' diagnosed in Arab polities is extended to the Marxist, Socialist, Nasserist, and Ba'thist elites and the ideologies that once were at the vanguard of leading the struggles for independence, national development, and Arab unity. Arab transitology is borne out of disillusionment. Unlike the study of Euro-American transition, it is largely steeped in pessimism. The transition from colonialism to nationalism raised expectations without delivering either political or economic development. The transfer in the 1950s and 1960s of power from the Anglophile and Francophile landed aristocracy, bourgeoisie, and ruling houses to postcolonial rural and military elites substituted the monopoly of one class with another and the injustice of the market with that of the state. The occupation of the state by pan-Arabists (Nasserists and Ba'thists) or Marxists (Southern Yemen before 1994) more or less killed the dream of Arab renaissance, development, and democracy. This is one reason why the task of Arab transitology seems to revolve primarily around understanding the 'crisis' of Arab nationalism and statism and only secondarily around formulating theories of how to transcend authoritarian rule. George Tarabishi, a leading Arab philosopher, finds the legacy of what he calls 'revolutionary and putschist culture' of the old ideologies and their political masters to deny the AME the opportunity to democratize in the near future. He argues that these ideologies have built their political careers in the AME as antitheses to democracy. He finds but expediency in these ideologies' current attempt to reappropriate democracy, which they have disowned in practice when political rule was in their hands, either as Ba'thists or Nasserists. Unconvinced of this technique of buying new legitimacy through democracy he writes that:

[Somehow], effortlessly, and at no cost or labour pains at any time, the miracle of a quick transition from the existing reality of backwardness [autocracy] to development [democracy] is [naively expected] to ensue with [the turning of] the magical key of democracy. Creating a 'miracle' has been the shared destiny of democracy, socialism and Arab unity [in the AME]. However, democracy's mythical status [today] as a saviour has an additional function. To grant a pardon and peace of mind to the Arab political movements that bear the larger share of responsibility for the political assassination of democracy. [Not to mention] for [its] physical assassinations in places where these movements became ruling parties.[60]

Thus Tarabishi finds the kernel of the problem in relation to democratization in the AME to reside not in what democratic culture should prevail as much as in the predominant culture in which two generations of Arabs have been schooled into negating rather than affirming democracy. As he puts it this goes to the heart of the epistemology of radical ideologies whose own *raison d'être* can only mean non-being of all alterity. Democracy as a system, he adds, differs from radical ideologies, in reference to the leftists and pan-Arabists in the AME. Democracy renews itself by way of cumulative knowledge and experience. By contrast, revolutionary ideologies reject what comes before them, refusing coexistence with difference.[61] Tarabishi's diagnosis is typical of the self-criticism the Arab left has undertaken following the atrophy of its brand of social and political engineering around the time when the first winds of change began to blow in the former USSR thanks to Gorbachev's perestroika. It was in the height of that political ferment that the AUSC published its first work, entitled *The Crisis of Democracy in the Arab Homeland*.[62] This was to be followed by similar titles, including the more recent work on the 'crisis of opposition' in the AME.[63] A great deal of this discourse is therefore geared towards critical evaluation of Arab autocracy. The self-criticism is structured around workshops in which focus is placed on political parties, opposition, or consolidation of democratic transition in the

AME. The idealism of the 1950s and 1960s began to falter in the 1980s as the ruling political parties, leftist and pan-Arabist, had no tangible record of military, political, or economic success to justify the correctness of their policies or monopoly over political power. For Walid Khaddouri both the leftist and pan-Arabist forces engaged in deceit and false justification of their policies for the sole purpose of prolonging their stay in power. He agrees with Tarabishi that the crisis of autocracy must be squarely placed on the shoulders of the pan-Arabists, accusing them of eradicating rival forces and movements with credible democratic credentials.[64] However, like Tarabishi, he believes deviation happened as pan-Arabists became entrenched in the business of political power and political survival. Prior to their advent to political power pan-Arabists held democratic ideals. Here Khaddouri, among others, raises an important point about how liberal forces in the AME tend to become illiberal as soon as they make the transition from the realm of civil society to political society. Khaddouri notes the rulers' preoccupation with struggles within (against the old bourgeoisie or redistribution of resources and roles to include the have-nots) and without (the Arab–Israeli conflict) do not excuse autocracy.[65] Instead of democratic practice, pan-Arabist rule routinized singularity, violence, deceit, propaganda, intolerance, and lack of pragmatism and self-criticism.[66]

Just as Tarabishi and Khaddouri find no redeeming features in the practice of revolutionary and pan-Arabist political parties as far as democratization goes, Belqaziz's assessment of opposition in the AME bodes not any better for democratic transition. His diagnosis is damning. Arab opposition, he observes, has no political projects. Trial and error and lack of vision are salient within it. Moreover, Arab opposition has not the kind of programmes to give it either strategic depth or tactical agility.[67] Bluntly, Belqaziz states that Arab opposition cannot aid the cause of democratization. For it suffers from dwindling membership, persistent political failure, lack of imagination, non-representation, primordialism in some cases, absence of internal democracy, and increasingly dependence on or collaboration with foreign powers.[68] With such a bleak picture of political singularity by the ruling houses and failed opposition, democratization in the AME stands little chance in the diagnosis of Belqaziz. He understands the attenuating circumstances of opposition in the AME, namely, a state that 'owns the public sphere' and 'customizes' it according to the rulers' whims and predilections.[69] The practice of politics, he notes, displays the emblems of political modernization, such as constitutions, elected parliaments, and multipartyism. But these bespeak the grim reality of exclusionary, oppressive, and de-legitimized regimes.[70] However, opposition is part of the problem and its own record and practice of politics mirror the state in terms of failure and lack of representation. Both are hindrances to democratization. Belqaziz's analysis is perhaps too pessimistic, especially in its treatment of opposition in the AME, ignoring grassroots struggles, which are not locked in the party politics of the dying genre of totalizing parties. Lack of empirical contextualization and sweeping generalizations weaken Belqaziz's assessment. As Mounir Shafiq notes, in response to Belqaziz, exaggerated pessimism detracts from the work done by emerging forces whose struggles for democracy and human rights is yet to be researched. As a corrective to this pessimism Shafiq proposes disaggregating 'Arab opposition' in order to approximate higher standards of objectivity. He adds that Islamists, pan-Arabists, socialists, the Palestinian, and Lebanese resistance movements cannot all be subsumed under the same umbrella of Arab opposition as they have varying degrees of success and failure.[71]

What must be recorded here is that the above understandings given by the aforementioned scholars to democratic transition are not as eloquent as those found in Latin and Southern America, Eastern or Southern Europe. The latter have developed their brands of study of democratic transition from practical and historical struggles that were successful in unhinging totalitarian regimes. This is precisely the missing link in the Arab discourse of democratic transition. There are ongoing struggles. But there are no practical experiences of democratic change that feed into how to theorize democratic transition in the AME. As a result, the discussion of Arab transition remains largely framed by theoretical and conceptual artefacts and parameters not constructed within the AME. One tension therefore that is inherent to the Arab discourse of democratic transition results from the push factors inspired by outside fashions and trends and the pull factors dictated by reverence of the Arabo-Islamic cultural heritage. Two issues are pertinent in this regard. Generally, in terms of methods the AUSC's series on democratization leans towards structure and institutions. The books reviewed tend to utilize a foundationalist, as opposite an interpretist, epistemology. There is an assumption in AUSC narratives of democratization that there is a 'democracy' or 'democratization' that is independent of knowledge. Little attention is given to the actual meanings and dogmas of Euro-American understandings of such concepts. Part of the problem resides in the disillusionment with Arab systems; thus Euro-American models of political engineering feature large as sources of inspiration for the AME. Both 'democracy' and 'democratization' are a function of knowledge. The academic strategies for knowing about Euro-American understandings of democratization tend to be passive foundationalism. By contrast, in the realm of politics there is no such passivity vis-à-vis either the EU or the United States. Both the EU and the United States tend to be subjected to interpretist analysis that resonates with conspiratorial theorizing and traditional realism. As Rashid's analysis illustrates that genre of discourse looks at the Hobbesian nature of the US-led world order post-9/11 and the invasion of Iraq in which the pursuit of self-interest and hegemony happens at the expense of the Arab side. Euro-American meddling in Arab affairs is rejected and treated critically. But concepts such as 'democracy' and 'democratization', which hail from Euro-American practice of government, are accepted almost uncritically. As a result, AUSC discourse is yet to benefit from the interrogation 'democracy' and 'democratization' in the study of democratic transition. The AUSC-sponsored 'Project for the Study of Democracy in Arab Countries', which meets annually at the University of Oxford, draws a committed and interdisciplinary elite of participants whose discourse is still unknown to the bulk of the Arab public. Nonetheless, the scholars, democracy and human rights activists, politicians, and journalists whose combined work is the driving force of the project are bearers of a moral flame at a moment of democratic impasse in the AME. Their enquiry into autocracy remains the only sustained effort to address the important question of how to emulate the democratic transformations initiated in Southern Europe in the mid-1970s. Studies of transition per se are not as yet a well-defined or established discipline in the AME. However, as an intellectual vocation concerned with transition there is a coherent agenda led by democratic activists, scholars, and public intellectuals working under AUSC's umbrella.

The analysis now considers the difficulties of wedding the concepts of 'pacted transition' and 'civil society' to the AME. This section draws on Arab and non-Arab scholarship. The aim is to further illustrate the disjunction between word (theory) and world (experience). Pacted transition is yet to be replicated in the AME with the same vigour, maturity, and substantive effect as in Southern European countries. The understanding given to civil society in Euro-American settings is not analogous to that found in the AME for being drenched in religious and political realities in which the boundaries of state and society, the individual and the communal, and the political and civil are blurred. Civil society as a bulwark against the state has no presence in the Arab *telos*.

Pacted Transition in the Arab Setting

If the demonstration models in the wide body of democratic transition literature[72] have a lesson, then it is that there is no unique or universally normative route to regime change. There is a variety of historical experiences and a variety of explanations of democratic transition. Nowadays there is therefore no consensus among scholars on a single approach for the explanation of democratic transition or of the nature of the questions asked: how do countries democratize? Or how do they 'de-authoritarianize'? A few of the leading approaches for explaining democratic transition tend to abstract from some of the unique realities of the AME, as shown below. Karl correctly criticizes the early fixation on defining 'identical conditions' to explain democracy and democratization, counseling instead 'more modest efforts to derive contextually bounded approach'.[73] Regime changes since the 1970s in Southern Europe, Latin America, and Eastern Europe have not exactly been replicas of Western Europe's path to institutional and accountable order. Gellner criticizes the early insistence of Eurocentric philosophies of history that Europe's transformations and their attendant problems and solutions 'were firmly inscribed on a universal human agenda... [and] provided the norm'.[74] Despite vast comparative scholarship on regime change, there is no univocal prescription of the conditions that lead to the expansion of participation and contestation, and the contraction of authoritarianism. Rustow distinguishes three paradigmatic approaches to the study of transition. The first stresses social and economic variables, the second 'beliefs or psychological attitudes', and the third 'certain features of social and political structures'.[75] The 'structural approach' emphasizes the economic and social variables largely attributed to the empirical work of Lipset in the 1950s.[76] The 'agency approach', or the so-called choice model, places high premium on ruling elites' support, policy choices, and decisions for democratic transition.[77] The most ardent voices of this discourse[78] draw on the historical experiences of 'pact-making', 'pacted democratization', or 'pacted democracy' such as in Brazil and in Spain.[79]

Pacted transitions are not universally relished. Negotiated transitions are susceptible to breakdown owing to their elitist and exclusionary nature which eventually galvanizes anti-systemic activities from excluded parties or forces.[80] There is also the risk of 'excessive voluntarism' inherent in 'contingent choice'[81] if the 'understanding of democracy... is not placed within a framework of structural-historical constraints'.[82] The elitism inherent in and the potential risks of pacted transition—'democracy by undemocratic means'[83]—is recognized even by those who emphasize its merits, especially, as a way of 'liberalizing authoritarianism',[84] thus setting in motion a historical process of democratization with cumulatively multivariate stages. Hence the potential for viable and stable pacted democracy reasonably reduces the possibility of unruly and violent transition. Pacted transition makes for 'gradual' as against 'dramatic' regime change. It holds the possibility of a consensual and legal route to democratic order temporarily or permanently, especially where there is an institutional and structural void. It presents all contending groups with a unique opportunity for getting habituated with moderation, mutuality, interdependence, compromise, and fundamental democratic values. It gives an acceptable exit from power to incumbent authoritarian elites through minimalist, as versus maximalist, regulative mechanisms that initially limit popular participation. That is, a threat to their 'corporate autonomies and vital interests' could lead to reaction authoritarianism—reversal of transition.[85]

The obvious institutional and structural void in most Arab polities makes pacted democracy one of the potentially best transition processes available to Arabs. However, it must be observed that the case that pacted transition yields stable democracy is exaggerated, as the Brazilian experience shows.[86] Its worthiness for the Arab world is twofold. First, the idea of an 'extrication pact'[87] can potentially facilitate a retreat from the business of governing in militarized ruling polities (Sudan, Libya, Mauritania, Yemen, Syria). Here the onus is on these elites to open up channels of communication with various societal interests via 'interlocutors outside the regime'. To this end, O'Donnell and Schmitter envisage a set of agreements and mutual guarantees ensuring commitment to nonviolence, restoration of freedoms, neutrality of the armed forces, power-sharing arrangements, and influential and representative leaders who sell the terms of the pact to their constituencies.[88] Such pacted transition is thought to stand a good chance of survival especially thanks to the 'civilianization'—demilitarization of polity as in Colombia, Venezuela, and Costa Rica—and the 'resurrection of civil society'. The multiplier effect of the revival and expansion of civil society for the consolidation[89] and inauguration of an initially pacted 'limited democracy' cannot be stressed enough.[90]

Second, transitional military or political pacts, while easier to conclude as noted by O'Donnell and Schmitter, would be best if supplemented by 'some sort of socioeconomic pact'.[91] The aims of such a socioeconomic pact are crucial for the stability of a newly inaugurated democracy where the rights of both workers (welfare) and business (property) are assured.[92] One of the most obvious flaws of Lebanon's 1943 National Pact, which did not spare the Lebanese the perils of two civil wars, was its silence on economic power-sharing arrangements. The 1990 Taif Accord duplicates the same flaw. The Arab world's experience in pact-making and pacted transition is slight.[93] The Jordanian 1991 National Charter, the Algerian 1989 constitution, and unified Yemen's 1991 constitution all amount to multipartite pacts.

The transition to be facilitated by the Algerian and Yemeni constitutional pacts has atrophied. In the latter the constitutional pact's democratic provisions for merging the country's former north and south became the very triggers which undermined the two transitions (to a unitary and democratic system) in the mid-1990s. The catalyst was the 1993 free and fair parliamentary elections in which the southern Socialist Party (SP), the major partner of the northern General People's Congress (GPC) in the pact, performed badly.[94] Fearing its eclipse, the SP, especially with the new and promising oil finds in the south, not only grew estranged from the GPC but also pushed for de-unification. This was unacceptable to the north. A devastating limited civil war ensued in 1994. The Algerian pact bore faint resemblance to the Spanish pact in the late 1970s, especially with regard to civilianizing political life by returning the armed forces to the barracks. The armed forces were charged with defending the sovereignty of the country and by implication the constitution.[95] With the benefit of hindsight, it can be argued that the armed forces lacked any real commitment to disengaging from politics. Indeed, at the first opportunity, they invoked their duty to defend state sovereignty by entering the political fray and aborting the electoral process in 1992.

The Tunisian pact is not without problems as shown by Lisa Anderson's insightful reflections.[96] The pact's insistence on many democratic ideals of dissent, tolerance, inclusiveness, and equality are yet to be fulfilled. Electoral malproportionality persists 20 years after its signing. In the municipal elections of May 1995 the ruling party swept the board, winning 4,084 seats as against 6 for the minor opposition parties, although it must be noted that the opposition had contested only 32 out of 257 districts. If the significance of the pact lies, as Anderson observes, with 'the direction in which it points', then that direction is a long way from polyarchy. The 'interdependence' assumed to set in during the phase of negotiating a pact[97] has not prevailed after the concluding of the Tunisian case. As the pact was the initiative of a regime 'firmly in power',[98] the signatories depended on the regime's goodwill and concessionary political 'handouts'. The regime depended on and mobilized the signatories only at the beginning, and mostly for legitimation purposes. Thus the regime and the ruling party's present dominance cannot be claimed not to have been mandated by the pact's signatories. Thus al-Ghannushi, leader of the Islamist Nahḍah Party, observes:

The pact is impressive not for what it does but for what it does not. In fact there are two pacts: the first is the 13-page document signed in 1988; the second is unwritten and implicit, but, nonetheless, the more important. For, it is the latter that defines the rules of the game. The rules of the former are window-dressing. The most important unstated rule is to normalize and perpetuate the denial of political space for movements like ours. How could the pact be taken so seriously, or be considered inclusive when thousands of Tunisians are either disenfranchised, jobless, jailed or live deracinated in foreign countries as political refugees? Does not the pact enshrine the same rights that the Constitution does, and which did not in the past spare Tunisia repression, nepotism, regionalism, economic malaise and political immobilism? If pacts facilitate democracy, I cannot say the same about our country's pact.[99]

The Tunisian pact is thus inconclusive. It is vague vis-à-vis socioeconomic issues,[100] one of the potential sources of regime delegitimacy and instability, as the track record shows with the near collapse of the First Republic (Bourguiba's) in the mid-1980s. Owing to its hindrance of democracy, it hitherto bears more resemblance to the Brazilian experience rather than the Spanish model it seeks to duplicate. Hagopian's summation of the Brazilian pact is that 'perhaps more subtly but no less important, ... [they] permitted traditional civilian elites to perpetuate many political practices of preceding regimes, particularly that of state clientelism, which imprinted an undemocratic character on the state and on political parties and weakened political representation'.[101] The pact's insistence on the de-politicization of Islam notwithstanding its 'evocations of Tunisia's liberal definition of Islam'[102] effectively discouraged the participation of the Nahḍah party in the concluding of the pact.[103] From a comparative standpoint, regime compromises which are features of Latin American and Southern European pacted transitions do not feature in the Tunisian pact. The fact that the ideals of the pact, especially with regard to the safeguarding of freedoms, were shared by the final signatories was not diminished by the pact being superimposed by the new government. With a few exceptions, many of the signatories were regime clients or co-opted organizations. From this perspective the Tunisian pact amounts to skilful statecraft. The lag in institutional development, the fragility of the licensed political parties, and the co-optation by the state of many associations and unions stymie the growth of civil society. This being the case, the capacity of pacted democracy proven elsewhere is yet to provide more serious opportunities for ushering in Arab good government. Lisa Anderson read too much into the signing in 1988 of Tunisia's National Pact, a quasi-constitutional formula for 'manufacturing consensus' and building confidence between the regime and selected non-state actors and forces. In her usual sharpness and modesty, and with the hindsight of an extra decade of close observation of the Bin Ali regime, Anderson revises her earlier position that a 'pacted' transition modelled on the Spanish example was being replicated in Tunisia:

In the 1980s, I wrote an article hailing the Tunisian National Pact of 1988 as an important step on the road to democracy, comparable to the Pact of Moncloa in Spain, on which it was said to have modelled. By the time my article appeared in print in 1991, it was all too obvious that Tunisia was not on its way to a Spanish-style transition and that the National Pact had played a very different role in Tunisia than its counterpart in Spain... In Spain the [Pact] brought together political actors with independent bases of power in the society and economy and institutionalized and symbolized the compromise that had been brokered among them. In Tunisia, by contrast, virtually all the signatories of the pact represented dependencies of the perennial ruling party; far from a compromise or bargain among equals, the pact was an effort to create the appearance of political pluralism in the absence of political actors with autonomous social and economic power.[104]

Two lessons transpire from the above. One is that there is no single universally applicable route to democratization, an argument which is in line with Whitehead's understanding of democratization as one that lends itself to variable permutations according to time and space. What theory suggests and what experience allows are two totally different things. The other lesson is that Eurocentric modalities and concepts defy transposition. Time is of the essence here. The Spanish pacted transition had the benefit of longer time for the process to take root and gather momentum and advocates. The Tunisian pact was executed in haste and was solely managed by the state. Society's role in it was kept to a minimum. Ideally, however, pacted democratic transition has the potential of presenting Arab states and societies with moments of promise. But for these types of transition to prove a powerful solvent of the democratic impasse in the AME, the most pressing challenge for incumbent regimes and oppositions is to moderate their positions; engage in politics of broad coalition building and consensus; even work with and within existing regimes; and fashion sophisticated strategies that will bring governments and oppositions on the same side rather on different sides, and on paths of collusion rather than collision. This is cumulatively bound to set state–society relations on a more constructive course of equality, mutuality, and reciprocity. Arab regimes must realize that authoritarian rule will not be permitted to continue for ever unchecked (e.g. note intervention in the name of human rights). Nor can they continue on ruling without the support or the know-how and advice of emergent plural civil societies. Similarly, Arab oppositions can ill-afford political wilderness; they have to engage authoritarianism more coherently by establishing themselves as shadow governments capable of the tasks of checking and balancing and by rising above tribal, personal, and petty politics. This is a major challenge for both political society and civil society, the latter being another concept whose travel in the AME raises questions about the utility and adaptability of Western political artefacts.

Civil Society Between 'Occident' and 'Orient'

The momentous political changes in Eastern Europe have provided the impetus for renewed debate over the utility of civil society in democratization.[105] This scholarly tendency is noticeable in discussions of Arab democratization.[106] That the question of civil society with all of its 'confusion' and differing theoretical 'resonances' meets with a wide-ranging reaction and attraction should be of no surprise.[107] Embedding this attractiveness is civil society's 'assumed synthesis of private and public "good" and of individual and social desiderata'.[108] Thus viewed, civil society is 'an ethical ideal of the social order' with the potential to either resolve or, failing that, 'harmonize ... the conflicting demands of individual interest and social good'.[109] The attractiveness of civil society is not universal. Feminists view it as another patriarchal conception of power based on male privilege and female exclusion. Pateman discredits the whole Western political tradition of contractual theorizing geared towards the attainment of civility by men and for men (see Chapter 5).[110] Foucault's understanding of society in terms of power relations that subjugate[111] humans has implications for the understanding of the modern civil society. The 'normalization' of subjugation is multifaceted, taking place through a hierarchy of institutions (prisons, hospitals ...).[112] Just as 'popular solidarities' are negated by 'disciplinary power', so are 'any spaces within modernity for the emergence of new forms of solidarity and association'.[113] With the absence of 'public life' the terrain remains vacated for two principal actors: 'private individuals as well as the state'.[114]

The history of European civil society originated in the sacking of Rome.[115] The upshot was the passing of power into multiple arenas of authority, and the 'separation between political and ideological power'.[116] Thus St. Augustine's *The City of God (De Civitate Dei)* distinguishes between two types of *civitas*, understood to mean society: the city of God (the community of believers, supernatural society, the Church) and earthly/secular society (*civitas terrena*).[117] However, despite the distinctions between the realms, values, and roles intrinsic to both the Church and the State, and given the fallibility of human law and humans, complementarity between the two is necessary.[118] Hence natural law (*ius naturale*), 'the basic moral rules', must inform civil law (*ius civile*) of the political society.[119] This is St. Thomas Aquinas' position in 'The Treatise on Law', in his *Summa Theologica*, as interpreted by Charlesworth.[120] This can be argued the key missing link in the chain of Arab government and theology: the absence of an Aquinas. The complex interactions, and balances and counterbalances that engendered European civil society range from the Church's 'underwrit[ing] of mundane political rule' and king-making for fear of secular absolutism, the landed feudal nobility's carving out of small arenas of autonomy from royal power, to the latter's 'practice of calling assemblies of the estates of the realm' in times of war to seek both moral and material endorsement.[121] All of these factors helped, in a limited way, atomize power and society.[122] Other noteworthy historical benchmarks are the Reformation's institution of the principle of religious diversity (tolerance) within Europe which was boosted by the 1555 Treaty of Augsburg. This was enhanced further in the Westphalian agreement in 1648 which, according to Hall, insisted not just on 'tak[ing] religion out of geopolitics altogether' but also on freedom of religion within European states.[123] By the eighteenth century, civil society became imbued with new dynamism as a result also of the revolution in the means of communication, increased literacy, and the rise of 'mass print culture'. Thus, 'horizontal linkages in society free from state control grew enormously'.[124] The conception of the modern civil society can be traced in the political 'struggles for citizenship' especially under the burden of high taxes, in the rise of capitalism, as much as in the ideas of the Scottish moralists,[125] among many others.[126]

The theoretical treatments of the question of civil society revolve around the nature of the relationship—integration and/or separation—between the individual and another, between the particular and the universal, between the private and the public, and between society and state. In one sense the search for civility can be equated with the search for the most reasonable synthesis of interests and values that predispose cohabitants not only to indefinitely coexist outside the state of nature but also to achieve, maintain, and reproduce optimum 'public good' in the realm of social life. The concern with a permanent exit from the state of nature is embedded in the political thought of both Locke and Hobbes. The utility of some form of civil society underpins the former's regard for the preservation of natural rights (life, liberty, and property) and the necessity of the social contract. Civil society, taking the form of political societies, reserves the right to 'resist' the unjust predispositions of a government, especially one 'that violates the terms of the social contract by usurping powers that have not been handed over to it'.[127] The latter's more pessimistic disposition leads him to invent a 'compelling theory of escape from natural reification and into civil society'. Thus the idea of a 'contract or a covenant', argues Tester, represents for Hobbes the mechanism of the '"Common Power" which could guarantee the symmetric reciprocity of individuals and overcome the egoism, reification and scarcity of the state of nature'.[128] But what must be noted is that for Hobbes the contract founds the state.

Hegel draws a clear distinction between the state and civil society. Although the two are confused in the sense that the latter is 'an immature kind of state' where particular interests are yet to be subordinated to the former, that is, the actualized state where the universal comes to rule over the particular.[129] Civil society, hierarchically located above the family and below the state, is an 'association', predicated on private interests (wants/caprice) and needs, of 'self-subsistent individuals in a universality which, because of their self-subsistence, is only abstract'.[130] But the actualization of particularity is a function of universality. The balance between the two is mediated by an all-time social axiom: 'no person is an island'. Hence, 'the particular person is essentially so related to other particular persons that each establishes himself and finds satisfaction by means of the others ... by means of the form of universality'.[131] Here lies the context of Hegel's civil society: the necessity of utter cooperation for the sake of common 'livelihood, happiness, and rights'.[132] Civil society is a means to an end whereby individuals 'determine their knowing, willing, and acting in a universal way and make themselves links in this chain of social connexions'.[133] Thus conceived civil society is paradoxical; it is at once individuals motivated by self-interest, and whose 'particularity is educated up to subjectivity'.[134] Mutuality is activated such as through policing and administering over legal, social, and economic life. Civil society is also a 'moment' in the development of the state, the rational state which is an end in itself.

Distinction between the state/political society, on the one hand, and civil society, on the other, is clear in de Tocqueville's *De La Démocratie En Amérique*. Therein he distinguishes between civil life (*vie civile*) and State (*État*).[135] Within civil life, both civil and political associations feed on one another, forging a self-governing terrain separating them from both the government and the household. De Tocqueville leaves no doubt how such a terrain, where association being 'the mother of action', is vital for citizenship, liberty, and democracy.[136] Thus he appreciates not only the didactic[137] but also the democratic value of political associations, the media by means of which citizens, mistrustful watchdogs,[138] carve out arenas of autonomy, contestation, and participation for the sake of the public good.[139]

For Marx the egoism of the state of nature that causes scarcity is nurtured by capitalists.[140] The liberal civil society is a 'class society' that mirrors capitalist modes of production with their exploitative practices, and reification of bourgeois values and interests.[141] According to this standpoint, the state is 'a mere excrescence' of civil society, a position that Giner criticizes for completely ignoring the relative autonomy of the state, and Keane for reductionism.[142] This is certainly Marx's position in *The German Ideology*, in which he ties the development of civil society to the bourgeoisie, a byproduct of 'production and commerce', and 'which...forms the basis of the state and...the idealistic superstructure'.[143] Marx's civil society, perceived in materialist terms, is 'the true source and theatre of all history'.[144]

Gramsci's conceptualization of civil society, as laid out in *The Modern Prince*, is understood as a new and bold departure from Marxist orthodoxy. Novelty resides in his stress on the struggle for power, and his insistence that workers counter bourgeois and state hegemony with a hegemony of their own.[145] In a capitalist context, Gramsci's theory of hegemony[146] (moral supremacy) rests on the premise that culture/dogmas/myths/belief systems not only take time to germinate but also represent the particularistic values and interests of the bourgeoisie which universalizes them. Hence the importantly strategic role of intellectuals: they reproduce these systems of thought, as well as 'a new approach to the problems of the intellectuals and the state'.[147] The corollary is a subtly structured 'consent' facilitated by 'civil society' not the 'state-as-force'. Thus for Gramsci, the route to the state is through a bottom-up cultural revolution via and within the terrain of civil society as against the Bolshevik top-down, monolithic, and elitist party-led putschist method. Gramsci's formulations of civil society are not without antinomies.[148] In play, as Cohen and Arato argue, is a dualism whereby civil society as a sphere of 'democratic self-government and social solidarity' coexists with the state, or 'political society', the sphere of coercion/domination. But also in play is the gradual *civilizing* of the 'state-as-force' and its appropriation through the state-to-be hegemonic institutions—civil society—in formation.[149] Hence a distinction is found in the 'the antinomy between civil society as a consolidation or normalization of domination and civil society as a genuinely alternative principle to domination'.[150]

Orientalists' search for either Arab or Muslim civil societies, and for selected staple items on which modernity is taken to be predicated, tends towards essentialization. Marxist as well as Weberian readings of Islamic history have been part of this pathology.[151] The underlying themes that cut across both are the absence of a 'bourgeois class', or of an Islamic 'spirit of capitalism'.[152] If the Marxist materialist perspective regards the absence of landed proprietors and power centralization to be the causes, the Weberian culturalist analysis diagnoses the problem in the aversion to selfish accumulation of wealth within Islamic ethics.[153] Islam, being this-worldly but not ascetic, is not comparable with Weber's 'Protestant ethic' (ascetic and this-worldly) paradigm, and accordingly uncongenial with rationalization and modernity.[154] Seen through the Orientalist intellectual 'hegemonic' optic, the Orient is made up of 'strong' states and 'weak' societies.[155] Just as Oriental societies are invariably assumed to be despotic, as Wittfogel argues in *Oriental Despotism*, autonomous countervailing forces—civil society— are consequently concluded to be absent. Speaking of the modern era, Gellner concludes that Muslim societies, while 'suffused with faith . . . manifest at most a feeble yearning for civil society'.[156] In fact, as Turner correctly observes, 'the deficiencies of Islamic society, politics, economics and culture, are, in Orientalism, located in the problem of an absent civil society.'[157] Approached comparatively in hegemonic discourses, the relation between the Orient and Occident, one in which the latter's 'civility' and 'modernity' is contrasted with the former's 'despotism' and 'pre-modernity', is situated along lines of Occidental 'positional superiority'. Said's iconoclastic *Orientalism* deploys the Gramscian-Foucauldian innovative frameworks for the understanding of the interplay between 'power' and 'truth', especially in terms of their being constitutive of hegemony.[158] Turner maintains that Orientalism cannot be exonerated from its share in the construction of images of the 'other' by highlighting the 'uniqueness of the West'. Turner takes the argument a little further. Contextualizing the despotic narrative in Europe and amidst 'uncertainty about enlightened despotism and monarchy', he argues that

The Orientalist discourse on the absence of the civil society in Islam was a reflection of basic political anxieties about the state of political freedom in the West. In this sense, the problem of Orientalism was not the Orient but the Occident. These problems and anxieties were consequently transferred onto the Orient which became, not a representation of the East, but a caricature of the West. Oriental despotism was simply Western monarchy writ large. The crises and contradictions of contemporary Orientalism are, therefore, to be seen as part of a continuing crisis of Western society transferred to a global context.[159]

Regardless, any Orientalist search for Arab and Islamic civil societies associating their absence with despotism is a prime example of positional superiority structured through knowledge-making. Yet, is the absence of Arabo-Islamic civil societies related to despotism alone, or is it a case of an absence 'constituted by discourse rather than history'? The ontology of civil society in Arab social history presents formidable problems whose nature can only be sketched within the limited scope of this enquiry.

Philologically, the term 'civil society' has no Arabic or Islamic equivalent. Hence the difficulty of trying to account for a phenomenon for

which there is only a linguistic blank. This problem has been overlooked by Norton's *Civil Society in the Middle East*.[160] Kawtharani
makes a worthwhile effort towards the mending of this lacuna.[161] He
finds the term 'civil society' (*al-mujtama' al-madanī*) inadequate, posing not just definitional but also conceptual problems. Brother (*Akh*),
brethren (*ikhwān*), brotherhood (*akhawīyyah*), and kin/partisans (*ahl*)
more accurately encapsulate the historical nature of 'Arab and Islamic
cultural, social and political relationships'.[162] *Akhawīyyah* and *ahl*,
Kawtharani points out,

> originate in a political society whose chief feature is membership of Islam,
> and allegiance to the *ummah* ... on the basis of two interconnected ele-
> ments ... faith and language in accordance with the 'hierarchy' of such an alle-
> giance, starting with neighbourhood (*ḥārah*)[163] dwellers in the city (*madīnah*)
> on to artisans, members of Sufi orders (*turuq*) and sects (*ṭawā'if*).[164]

Primordial society or association (*al-mujtama' al-ahlī*—of *ahl-*) is more
fitting with the Arabo-Islamic political, social, and economic conditions
and the historical structures underlying them. He cautions that primordial association is not conceptually even remotely identical with
the term 'civil society'. However, he does not rule out some form of
common ground, especially with regard to the autonomy of society from
the state.[165]

Methodologically, any ahistorical rendering of the present state of
civil society will be incomplete. Thus the institutions, ideas, arrangements, and even 'dreams' that embedded state–society relations in the
past cannot be bypassed for a thorough understanding of the Arabo-
Islamic lifeworld. In this respect the approaches taken by Kawtharani and Mardin are sound, helping to clarify the analytical tools
and define the trajectory for probing the subject of civil society in an
Islamic context.[166] Mardin stresses the 'incongruity' of the Western
and Muslim 'dreams'. Three levels, ranked in order of importance, are
at the centre of the Muslim dream: 'the Muslim would only bow to
the political obligations set by the [Qur'ān] ... [H]e would accept as an
equivalent the [Qur'ānic] verisimilitude of the [Qur'ānic] commenta-
tors ... [B]ecause neither of these systems were able to assert themselves unequivocally, the Muslim dream shifted to the ideal of a social
equilibrium created under the aegis of a just prince.'[167] In so doing,
Mardin sets the scene for comparing the dynamics of Western and
Islamic values which were to shape the structures of their societies.
He distinguishes two characteristics of the Muslim dream or *telos* that
set it apart from the West. One is its dependence on the charismatic
authority of the just prince to distribute justice, and, consequently,
act to rectify the 'unrealized system of justice'. Mardin contrasts this

Islamic feature with Europe's 'rationalization of legal practice and the self-referential aspect of law'.[168] The other is the Muslim dream of a just prince, being against the 'adoption of a concept concerning the gradual perfectibility of man through man's making of his own history' [is] 'linked with primal time, with a yearning for a return of a golden age'.[169] Accordingly, in the Muslim dream justice is read as freedom, if not even accorded precedence over freedom.[170]

Three themes dominate Kawtharani's analysis. In the first he explores the nexus between state (*dawlah*), Islamic law (*sharī'ah*), group feeling or solidarity (*'aṣabiyyah*), and non-Muslim community in the Ottoman Empire (*millet*) system.[171] Here he explains the interplay of Islamic law and kinship in state formation. The first forms the basis of legitimacy of what Ibn Khaldun calls the authority/power (*jāh*) of the state. For, the Islamic law-based role of the Muslim state is missionary (*da'awi*). The second regards the instrument of summoning, again in the words of Ibn Khaldun, support or loyalty (*walā'*) to achieve superiority (*ghulb*) and, in consequence, power. However, the accession to power of a particular group on the basis of group solidarity does not translate into imposing on the community or *ummah* its own interpretation of Islam. The community has recourse in the Islamic law 'and what, in accordance with its texts, can, in particular circumstances, be viewed as a right (*haqq*)'.[172] Islamic history is fraught with endless examples and 'forms of resistance, opposition and disobedience against the despotic state, and against different schools of independent reasoning in Islamic jurisprudence and of exegesis'.[173] This point, as Kawtharani has first shown, has been clearly captured by Gardet:

It is certain that there had always been in Islam many insurgent voices against what was arbitrary, accepting from the legitimate authority only that which related to [Qur'ānic] laws and rules deduced thereof; when it comes to the content of governmental principles, the notion of *haqq*, the right to defend, to protect and to exercise is absolutely primordial.[174]

Thus Kawtharani suggests that the state–community (*dawlah–ummah*) relations were cooperative, not organic, with local and *millet* related intermediary channels.[175] From the Umayyad up to the Osmanli Ottoman State, power was conquered through tribal solidarity-based superiority, making it impossible for the ruling elites to 'integrate the *ummah*' into its own orbit of control. For the community was not only diverse but also subdivided into rites of jurisprudence, *millet* systems, groups (*jamā'āt*), guilds, fraternities, Sufi brotherhoods, and ethnic communities. These subdivisions not only allowed for degrees of autonomy within and between the various structural substrata but also for mediation of their concerns to the highest levels of the political machine via their own leaders and spokespersons, be they spiritual instructors (*shuyūkh,* plural of *shaykh*) or tribal and community leaders.[176]

The thesis of 'strong' states and 'weak' societies in the Orient is somewhat exaggerated as shown by Lapidus and Burke's accounts of anti-systemic protests.[177] Lapidus documents how pro and anti-systemic activism by Sufi orders permeated Muslim societies during the Ottoman period, noting, at the same time, how the Ottomans appreciated the Sufis' important social work in rural areas.[178] Gellner's 'folk Islam'[179] has equally useful political and spiritual functions: '[it] superviz[es] the political process in segmentary groups, e.g. election or selection of chiefs[; it] superviz[es] and sanction[s] their legal process[; it] suppl[ies] the means for the Islamic identification of the tribesmen.'[180] Other Sufis demonstrated more antagonism towards the state. One such example is the roaming dervishes, named Qalandariya, known for their disregard for Islamic law as well as for political authority.[181] Realizing their potential in inciting anti-systemic resistance, the Ottomans opted in the fifteenth and sixteenth centuries to co-opt Sufi hospices (*tekkes*) buying them with 'permanent endowments and gifts for charitable purposes'.[182] When disconnected from the political centre, the religious scholars (*'ulamā'*), although lacking a sacerdotal hierarchy or a Church-like institutional structure, led, although 'diffusely' and 'sporadically', uprisings 'against the unjust ruler' and thus, more or less, 'constituted a counterpoise to the political hegemon'. However, once 'bureaucratized' and, in a sense, 'bought' by the Ottomans, they assumed the role of legitimators of mundane power. Lapidus observes how their cooption in officialdom, from which they accrued material and professional rewards either as educators or administrators of religious endowments (*waqf*), was achieved at a price. It was at the expense of foregoing their roles as representatives of 'the communal and religious interests' of Muslims and as defenders of 'the people from the abuses of political power'.[183]

Gellner's bifurcated Islam with its High/puritanical/transcendental and Low/folk/communal styles of religious understanding and practice lends itself to both denying and affirming an autonomous space between the people and the state.[184] High Islam of the urban and religious literati, being 'unitarian, individualistic, puritanical, nomocratic, scripturalist', has a long history of serving to underwrite political power. Its history of resisting or opposing central authority is short.[185] It has cyclically acted in unison with tribal solidarity, usually motivated by purification ideals, providing the vehicle for what Gellner calls 'dynasty-initiation'.[186] For Gellner these revivalist movements have the makings of an Islamic 'Permanent Reformation'.[187] Being rural and tribal, Low Islam de-emphasizes literacy and rule-observance, thriving instead on magic, ecstasy, and saintly intercession.[188] These factors along with its anti-establishment bent explain the historical drive by establishment and reformist scholars to eradicate Sufi dogma, practices, and leaders, leading to the cutting off of endowments, closing of hospices, and jailing of Sufi leaders in the seventeenth century.[189] The triumph of 'High Islam' over 'Low Islam' does not bode well for the prospects of a dynamic civil society. Gellner notes that 'the direct transition from communal priests to universalize unitarian enthusiasts ... does not favour the emergence of civil society'.[190]

Bromley applies a more socioeconomic approach to account for the mutual interdependence of the 'tributary state' and the learned scholars of Islam.[191] The Sunni clergy, being plugged in the state hierarchy by virtue of their erudition, administrative and juristic expertise, came to reap the material rewards of their dutifulness to the state. Their surplus extraction capacity, Bromley argues, helped them entrench their position and bolster their prestige through their involvement in 'charity, education, justice and informal social and political leadership'.[192] Their social status as a new notability was the function of their expertise via which they came to enter into a political, social, and economic compact with their Turkish patrons. The latter, with 'no experience of sedentary agriculture and imperial administration', but with much military might and skill, could enforce social peace and order. The former, with no physical force to ensure order, but with ample civil and judicial know-how, 'could organize society'.[193] Accordingly, for Bromley, this invalidates the assumption of Islam's 'institutional continuity' because of a 'distinctively "Islamic history" or "Islamic society"'. It is, he notes, 'a contingent feature of the necessary intermediation in tributary forms of rule and appropriation, and hence relates to the use made of Islam by historically specific social forces.'[194] Thus, located outside the circle of tributary surplus appropriation, Sufi Islam was predisposed to be resistant to incorporation by the centre. Its articulation of a more populist style of Islam and its forging of autonomous material ties placed it at odds with 'the urban tributary power'.[195]

Kawtharani's second theme emphasizes the roles of Sufi orders as well as of markets (*aswāq*), hoods (*ḥārāt*), and crafts (*ḥiraf*). Here he attends to the socioeconomic and political dynamics characteristic of the Islamic city (*madīnah*) where interpenetration between ethnic, productive, religious, and political forces was at play. Multilateral and mutual processes of exchange, communication, and cohabitation were visible. These dynamics and processes were facilitated by the architectural layout and demographic setup of the Islamic city, reflected in its ethnically and religiously differentiated hoods, and in its specialized productive quarters, with the mosque being its hub.[196] Gibb and Bowen observe:

In spite of the existence of a sense of unity...the Islamic city was not in any respect an organic unity. The social organization, as it had been built up under political and economic pressure, and reworked and vitalized by religious influences, was one of dislocated, self-contained and almost self-governing groups, subject only to the overriding authority of the temporal and spiritual powers.[197]

According to Kawtharani the Islamic city's dynamism was articulated in the relations between rulers and ruled, marked by an 'equilibrium between government intervention (*sultan*)—represented in the offices of governor (*al-wālī*), judge (*al-qāḍī*), market superintendent (*al-muhtasib*) and police chief (*ṣāḥib al-shurṭah*)—and social needs (civil) that expressed themselves by inventing forms of organization and institutionalization parallel to the state's'.[198] Traders and artisans/craftsmen formed guilds (*aṣnāf*, similar to those found in medieval Europe). The guilds were distinguishable from corporations (*ṭawā'if*, types of guilds—as translated by Gibb and Bowen). They adopt Sufi rankings. These start with the unskilled beginner (*mubtadi'*), the apprentice (*al-ṣāni'*), artisan (*mu'allim*), the master artisan (*shaykh al-ḥirfah*), and at the apex the market's grand master (*shaykh al-sūq*). This professional hierarchy and organization had the twin effects of articulating relations of authority (according to knowledge of the secrets of the trade) between the lower and higher rankings as well as enhancing communication and mediation between the various guilds, on the one hand, and between the guilds and the state, on the other hand.[199] Kawtharani shows that the mediatory function of the guilds between state and society was widely practised. A striking example is the one in sixteenth-century Hama (Syria) where the grand masters and merchants consensually appoint the market's grand master. He is required to be a pious and ethical figure who meets with the approval of all tradesmen. Their choice is subject to final vetting by the chief judge and the ruler. Kawtharani describes the tasks performed by the market's grand master: 'He supervises over all of the various crafts and trades guilds; mediates between them and both the chief judge and the local governor. No changes take place without his knowledge or advice. In his presence and through his secondment the master artisans are elected.'[200] Religiosity permeates all of these activities, especially during the promotion (*shadd*) ceremony. While the promotion ceremony, in a sense, serves as a display of Islamicity tying the productive forces to the wider Islamic community, it also plays a socioeconomic and political function in which the promoted artisan or craftsman vows, in the presence of masters, grand masters, relatives, and officials, to be committed to quality work, to fair trade practices, and to solidarity with fellow tradesmen. These vows were made in an atmosphere of reverence in which the Qur'ān was read, and came to be known as 'constitution' (*al-dustūr*).[201] 'Constitution' signified both a spiritual contract between the promoted craftsman and God, and between himself and his colleagues, on the one hand, and himself and society, on the other.

For Kawtharani the forms of organization, communication, mediation, and regulation that came to underlie the workings of these structural components of Muslim society amounted to autonomous political formations that acted mostly to mediate with the state, and intermittently to protest against it.[202] He quotes Gibb and Bowen as follows:

The Corporation [meaning *ṭā'ifah,* singular of *ṭawā'if*] served many purposes. It offered the means by which the humblest citizen could give expression to his social instincts, and be assured in return of his place in the social order. This was his field of citizenship, and if he was rarely called upon to play any part in outward political life, he was on the other hand, little interfered with by his political governors, who respected in general the independence and the traditional usages of the corporations. The social function of the corporations was enhanced (not in all, but in most, especially of the craft corporations) by their religious affiliation, usually to one of the great religious orders.[203]

The third theme regards religious endowment and social services. The basis for religious endowment can be found in Islamic law. It is created when a benefactor dispenses of money or property for charity. Pious endowments are created either through voluntary almsgiving (*ṣadaqah*) or compulsory alms tax (*zakāt*). Kawtharani stresses the historical importance of religious endowment not only in the building of social welfare institutions and services but also in the effusion of feelings of mutuality and voluntarism, and the diffusion of an Islamic *esprit de corps* that binds both state and society into working together for the good of the Muslim community. For him, these elements

attest to the ability of Arab society, since the conception of the nucleus of the state in Medina and up to the Ottoman period, within an Islamic communal order, to produce institutions for the public good and for social services. These welfare services range from health, education, orphanages, houses for the handicapped, and hospitals, to free meals and shelter for the needy.[204]

The phenomena of Sufi teaching mosques (*zāwiyah* or *ribāṭ*) and their Turkish counterparts (known as *tekiyyah*) grew exponentially as they assumed welfare functions to go in tandem with their educational and spiritual roles in medieval Islam. Kawtharani cites multiple examples of the historical utility of religious endowment. There were instances when it was utilized to assist the state when faced with financial deficits, especially when pious endowments from cultivable land helped repair bridges. The majority of learning centres in the eleventh century were funded through endowments.[205] Historically, the 'root structural components of civil society, either in a condition of autonomy from or of equilibrium with the state', abounded not just as institutions and practices but also as a consciousness, Kawtharani concludes.[206]

A Critical Reflection

Unlike Kawtharani's historical contextualization, the sense that is given to the notion of civil society in its Arab setting is fairly in tandem with the institutions of democratic capitalism,[207] and with the project of democratization.[208] Hence there is a foundationalist content to the definitions of civil society. They all spell out common normative understandings of a 'space' or 'arena' of public autonomy between the individual and the state. They all stress normative functions of 'demand', 'support',[209] and even 'opposition' of the state. Moreover, they all share a degree of normative *raisons d'être* epitomized in mediation, legitimation, reproduction, or 'replacement'[210] of the state. They all take as givens the normative values of tolerance, mutuality, reciprocity, and even solidarity; and normative methods stressing nonviolence, elections, and legality. Variation exists as to what precisely the boundaries are of or the sphere of activities of civil society. Rau's yardstick for determining the sphere of activity of civil life is freedom from 'organizational or financial state control'.[211] According to this position, even if tendentiously, very few Arab organizations and associations are autonomous from the state. Most are government sponsored, and those that operate outside state control are largely circumscribed.

At a time when the so-called Western model[212] is being questioned, the reinvention of Arab civil society ought to be more critical than has been provided for in recent discourses. Many aspects need reflecting. The extent to which the notion of 'society against state' applies to the Arab context is not clear. Total autonomy of either society or state is a myth. Both share many spaces of interaction, transaction, communication, and publics. Even in the Euro-American setting, varying degrees of corporatist practices integrating the state with both the economic and political societies prevail. If Fascist Italy was an extreme case, modern Sweden is a moderate one. Civil society elsewhere can be described as standing largely for the status quo, and only rarely as revolutionary or radical. 'Status quo' civil societies are nurtured via a common 'normative system'[213] according to which state and civil society's 'interaction is characterized by harmony and directed toward common ends'.[214] Conversely, revolutionary civil society exists where that common normative system is absent. In Eastern Europe, especially Poland in the 1980s, the radicalization of society stemmed from the absence of such a system. The same goes for segments of the still constrained Arab civil society, especially the radical Islamist groups (*jamā'āt islāmiyyah*), such as in Egypt. In fact, Arab civil society can be said to be transitional given that it is struggling to throw off the shackles of state control and red tape for the purposes of self-mobilization and self-constitution. Cohen and Arato envisage 'mediating spheres' whereby civil society's influence is exercised.[215] Thus 'antagonism' arises only when 'mediations fail or when the institutions of economic and political society serve to insulate decision-making and decision-makers from the influence of social organizations, initiatives, and forms of public discussion'.[216] A future autonomous associational civil life should not be taken to prescribe a state–society dichotomy in the Arab World. Functions of reciprocal support, dependence, and integration will be necessary, not only if the common 'dream' informing associational behaviour is to assert the relevance of the Islamic heritage but also, as importantly, if the reality of scarce resources is to be managed by both state and society.

Being the outcome of a specific set of European historic circumstances, civil society cannot exist without the supporting liberal ideology with its emphasis on the freedom of the individual. Turner points out the nexus between the idea of civil society and the autonomy of individuals in Western thought whereby the instrumentality of the former engenders protection of the latter. The Orientalist assumption, he argues, is that 'the absence of civil society in Islam entailed the absence of the autonomous individual exercising conscience and rejecting arbitrary interventions by the state'.[217] Historically, the autonomous individual has found expression only as a member of a group or a community that is defined by a web of group solidarities (*'aṣabiyyāt*—religious, ethnic, tribal, regional, and even gender-related). The challenges are sundry. One would be how to modulate the democratic requirements of individual autonomy without compromising the centuries-long primacy of the community's rights in the Arabo-Islamic setting. Another, as articulated by Salamé, 'is the necessity of keeping communities from confining individuals within them'.[218] The inchoate status of Arab civil society would be set to suffer further from adopting the Euro-American notion of individualism. Its emphasis on the individuals' interests is not easy to reconcile with the

Arabo-Islamic practice of stressing needs (*ḥājāt*). The Western notion of interest entails a specific social order, one that is class-based, that is, one in which 'civil society is, by definition, a class society, for it fosters an unequal distribution of goods and rewards'.[219] Another challenge for the visionaries of Arab civil society is to determine the extent to which privatization of public assets is to be allowed. For privatization has implications not only for the question of social justice but it seems, as Gray maintains, for the 'transfer of initiative from government to society'.[220] Ultimately the challenge is to choose between the vibrant associational life of the Euro-American model in which inequality seems to be an inevitable part of the civil society 'package-deal', and a totally different Arabo-Islamic paradigm where social justice necessitates greater integration of state and society, cooperation not competition, and a civil society bounded primarily by common needs and only secondarily by individual interests.

The search for Arab civil society,[221] like the search for democratization, should go beyond the compass of the conventional modern associational formations to include the pristine prototype social institutions and organizations such as brotherhoods and religious endowments, and transnational Arab social movements and non-governmental organizations (NGOs). The traditionally important social and political role of elders (*shuyūkh*), and the traditional male association (*dīwāniyyah* in Kuwait) type institutions are as important. Despite the widely held view of elders and their councils (*majālis*) as loci of patriarchal authority, their role in engendering participation, in mediating disputes, in representing the preferences of their members, and in providing fora and domains outside state control for discussion and self-help remains largely underresearched. Nonetheless, their contribution to primordial society's self-constitution is beyond question.[222] The council itself can be said to have arisen from the historical practice of elders to congregate and consult. The *dīwāniyyah* is both an essential and unique component of civil society that is specific to Kuwait.[223] In a polity where association has mostly been subject to state proscriptive laws, the *dīwāniyyah*, being home-based gatherings, provides the citizenry with an instrument to bypass governmental red tape as well as an alternative stage for activism.[224] Hicks and al-Najjar adduce much evidence of the significance of these forums as vehicles of anti-centralist protests, as *avant-garde* and ad hoc movements, and a point of contact between leading members of both the political and economic societies and aware and concerned citizens—civil society. They point out how the *dīwāniyyah* protests during 1989 and 1990 not only embodied widespread and society-based demands to restore the National Assembly dissolved in 1986 but also forced the reluctant government to respond to those demands by negotiating the rehabilitation of parliamentary life.[225] The utility of the *dīwāniyyah* is registered in the enduring marks of traditional gatherings and forums and in its relevance by 'acting as a counterweight to governmental autonomy'.[226] With Kuwaiti women initiating their own *dīwāniyyāt* (plural of *dīwāniyyah*) this tradition could only flourish.

The transnational Islamist movements, despite multitudinous differences of temporal and spatial conditions, *modus operandi*, and dogmatic opinion, share a hard core of ideals. That core is rooted in a politico-religio-moral worldview having at its centre a zealous commitment to reforming polity, society, and economy, by bringing them closer to the Medinan model of the Prophet and, at the same time, reconciling them with the requirements of Islamic modernism. The strong impact of Islamists on the self-mobilization and self-constitution of Arab civil society, both as discursive formations and social movements, is without question. Within this framework of Islamism-transnationalism a whole web of networks of 'ruly' and 'unruly', overt and covert, intellectual and material exchange, diffusion, communication, and support is deployed to the bolstering of existing national Islamist forces or the creation of new ones, and to the aggregating of positions and responses.

Conclusion

The travel of democracy and democratization to the AME along with their conceptual and institutional artefacts and dogmas attests to the fact that the Arab world is not in a state of 'exile' as far as the quest for good government is concerned. The problem lies elsewhere. Conceptually, the artefacts tend to be too specific to adequately capture the peculiarities of the different geographies to which they are transposed. Third wave democratization, I have argued, is too linear and too certain to apply to the circularity and fluidity of Arab liberalizations. Arab understandings of democratization tend to be largely mired in Euro-American foundationalist ontology and positivist epistemology. More recent interpretist deconstruction of democratization in Euro-American scholarship is yet to filter to Arab readings of democratization. The travel to the AME of democratization or civil society and their attendant dogmas—elections, individualism, or secularism—is not so simple. Uncritical borrowing involves omission of difference. Cooperation, not opposition, seems to underpin associational life, for instance. Communal identity and loyalty are still embedded socially and politically. After 20 March 2003, the date of the US-led invasion, Iraqi nationalism ceded to primordial modes of identification that outlived the authoritarian nationalist state. Democratization, pacted transition, or civil society all stumble upon experiences that Euro-American democratic theory cannot foresee outside its Western preview. This is why an anti-foundationalist ontology that recognizes that Euro-American democratization is a function of time and context-specific knowledge is needed for Arab re-reading of democratic transition. AUSC discourse of democratization has been shown to be impervious to interrogation of democratization theory. It tends to be teleological. There is obsession with outcomes not processes. It favours an institutionalist reading of democratization as though elections and constitutions are the only building blocs of good government. Such a discourse tends to mislocate its object of Arab democratization as it locates it in fragments of knowledge that are neither Arab nor do they speak to Arab peculiarities. Normatively, the quest for an Arab democratization is correct. Epistemologically, however, little is being done to develop a brand of transitology that thinks outside the 'institutionalist' box. The institutionalist bent is evident in attempts to liberalize the AME top-down and from without (the Greater Middle East Initiative). This has rendered democratic transition in the AME cosmetic and stalled, despite modest advances and gains. In the ensuing three chapters I attempt to elaborate this line of argument.

Notes

1. Laurence Whitehead, *Democratization: Theory and Experience* (Oxford: Oxford University Press, 2002), 30.
2. Thomas Carothers, 'The End of the Transition Paradigm', in *Critical Mission: Essays on Democracy Promotion* (Washington, DC: Carnegie Endowment for International Peace, 2004), 168; 176.
3. See the fine study of recent Arab political liberalizations by Michael C. Hudson, Louis Cantori and others, 'The Possibilities for Pluralism', *American-Arab Affairs*, 36 (Spring 1991), 3–26.
4. See Jacques Barzun, 'Is Democratic Theory for Export?' in Joel H. Rosenthal (ed.), *Ethics and International Affairs: A Reader* (Washington, DC: Georgetown University Press, 1995), 39–57.
5. See Steven Heydemann, 'Is the Middle East Different?' *Journal of Democracy*, 7/2 (April 1996), 171–5.
6. One of the earliest pieces on the question of Arab democracy is by Malcom Kerr, 'Arab Radical Notions of Democracy', in *Middle Eastern Affairs* (St. Anthony's Papers) 3 (1963), 9–40.
7. See, for instance, John P. Entelis, 'Civil Society and the Authoritarian Temptation in Algerian Politics: Islamic Democracy vs. the Centralized State', in Augustus R. Norton (ed.), *Civil Society in the Middle East*, vol. II (Leiden: E. J. Brill, 1996), 45. See also, James A. Bill, 'Comparative

Middle East Politics: Still in Search of Theory', in *Political Science and Politics*, XXVII (September 1994), 518–19.

8. See the good work by Fawaz A. Gerges, 'The Study of Middle East International Relations: A Critique', *British Journal of Middle East Studies*, 18/2 (1991), 208–440.

9. Robert A. Dahl, *Polyarchy: Participation and Opposition* (New Haven: Yale University Press, 1971).

10. Evidence for this view is adduced in the two volumes by Augustus R. Norton (ed.), *Civil Society in the Middle East* (Leiden: E. J. Brill, 1995 and 1996).

11. See a similar idea by Carrie Rosefsky Wickham, 'Beyond Democratization: Political Change in the Arab World', in *Political Science and Politics*, XXVII (September 1994), 507–9.

12. Louis J. Cantori, 'The Old Orthodoxy and the New Orthodoxy in the Study of Middle Eastern Politics', *Political Science and Politics*, XXVII (September 1994), 516.

13. The coinage belongs to Samuel P. Huntington; see his work, *The Third Wave: Democratization in the Late Twentieth Century* (Norman and London: University of Oklahoma Press, 1991). For the application of the term in the Arab context, see Mustapha K. El Sayyid, 'The Third Wave of Democratization in the Arab World', in Dan Tschirgi (ed.), *The Arab World Today* (Boulder and London: Lynne Rienner, 1994), 179–89.

14. A standard text for the study of democratic transitions is the voluminous work by Guillermo O'Donnell, Philippe C. Schmitter, and Laurence Whitehead (eds.), *Transitions from Authoritarian Rule: Prospects for Democracy* (Baltimore: Johns Hopkins University Press, 1986).

15. See Wickham, 'Democracy, Islam, and the Study of Middle Eastern Politics', in *Political Science and Politics*, XXVII (September 1994), 507–19.

16. Michael C. Hudson, 'After the Gulf War: Prospects for Democratization in the Middle East', *Middle East Journal*, 45/3 (Summer 1991), 407–27.

17. John L. Esposito and James P. Piscatori, 'Democratization and Islam', *Middle East Journal*, 45/3 (Summer 1991), 427–40.

18. Louis J. Cantori, 'Introduction', *Political Science and Politics*, XXVII (September 1994), 507.

19. Ibid.

20. Ibid.

21. Korany, 'Arab Democratization: A Poor Cousin', p. 512. Compare with the equally insightful piece by Joshua Parens, 'Whose Liberalism? Which Islam? Leonard Binder's "Islamic Liberalism"', *Political Science and Politics* XXVII (September 1994), 514–15.

22. Cantori, 'The Old Orthodoxy and the New Orthodoxy in the Study of Middle Eastern Politics', 516.

23. Samuel P. Huntington, *The Third Wave: Democratization in the Late Twentieth Century* (Norman: University of Oklahoma Press, 1991). Also see, Samuel P. Huntington, 'After Twenty Years: The Future of the Third Wave', *Journal of Democracy*, 8/4 (October 1997), 3–12.

24. Whitehead, *Democratization: Theory and Experience*, 28.

25. Ibid. 2.

26. Ibid., Chapters 1 and 2.

27. Norton (ed.), *Civil Society in the Middle East*; Mary Ann Tétreault, *Stories of Democracy: Politics and Society in Contemporary Kuwait* (New York: Columbia University Press, 2000); Sheila Carapico, *Civil Society in Yemen: The Political Economy of Activism* (Cambridge: Cambridge University Press, 1998).

28. These are all taken from titles of case studies in the fine collection of essays edited by Larry Diamond, Marc F. Plattner, and Daniel Brumberg, *Islam and Democracy in the Middle East* (Baltimore & London: Johns Hopkins, 2003).

29. Huntington, *The Third Wave*, 7; Huntington, 'After Twenty Years', 7.

30. Guillermo O'Donnell, 'Illusions about Consolidation', *Journal of Democracy*, 7/2 (April 1996), 34–51.

31. Larry Diamond, 'Elections without Democracy: Thinking about Hybrid Regimes', *Journal of Democracy*, 13/12 (April 2002).

32. Huntington, 'After Twenty Years', 8.

33. Ibid. 12; 3.

34. Thomas Carothers, 'The End of the Transition Paradigm', *Journal of Democracy*, 13/1 (2002), 5–21.

35. Eberhard Kienle, 'More than a Response to Islamism: The Political Deliberalization of Egypt in the 1990s', *Middle East Journal*, 52/2 (Spring 1998), 219–35.

36. Whitehead, *Democratization*, 26–7.

37. Lisa Anderson, 'Politics in the Middle East: Opportunities and Limits in the Quest for Theory', in Mark Tessler, Jodi Nachtwey, and Anne Banda (eds.), *Area Studies and Social Science: Strategies for Understanding Middle East Politics* (Bloomington and Indianapolis: Indiana University Press, 1999), 4.

38. Whitehead, *Democratization*, 27; 30.

39. Ibid. 27.

40. Whitehead, 21–6. Huntington, *The Third Wave*, 5–14.

41. Whitehead, 27.

42. Khair Eddin Haseeb in 'Mustaqbal Al-Intiqal il Al-Dimuqratiyyah fi Al-Bilad al-Arabiyyah: Munaqashah Ammah' [The Future of Democratic Transition in the Arab Homeland: A General Discussion], in Ali Khalifah Al-Kawari (ed.), *Madakhil al-intiqal ila al-dimuqratiyyah fi al-buldan al-'arabiyyah* [Pathways to Democratic Transition in the Arab Countries] (Beirut: Markaz Dirasat Al-Wihdah Al-Arabiyyah, 2003), 203.

43. Abdelwahab Hamid Rashid, *Al-Tahawwul Al-Dimuqrati fi Al-'Iraq: Al-Mawarith Al-Tarikhiyyah, Al-Ususs Al-Thaqafiyyah, wa Al-Muhaddadat Al-Kharijiyyah* [Democratic Transition in Iraq: The Historical Heritage, the Cultural Foundations, and the External Constraints] (Beirut: Markaz Dirasat Al-Wihdah Al-Arabiyyah, 2006), 273.

44. Ibid. 274.

45. Yousef Shoueiri, 'Al-Shūrā wa Al-Libiraliyyah wa Al-Dimuqratiyyah fi Al-Watan Al-'Arabi: Aliyat Al-Intiqal' [Shūrā, Liberalism and Democracy in the Arab Homeland: The Mechanisms of Transition], in Al-Kawari (ed.), *Madakhil Al-Intiqal*, 26.

46. Abdelhussein Sha'ban, 'Ma'uqat Al-Intiqal ila Al-Dimuratiyyah fi Al-Watan Al-'Arabi' [Obstacles to Transition to Democracy in the Arab Homeland], in Al-Kawari (ed.), *Madakhil Al-Intiqal*, 245.

47. Ibid. 245–6.

48. Thana Fuad Abdullah, *Aliyyat Al-Taghyeer Al-Dimuqrati fi Al-Watan Al-'Arabī* [The Mechanisms of Democratic Transformation in the Arab Homeland] (Beirut: Markaz Dirasat Al-Wihdah Al-Arabiyyah, 2004), 355–84.

49. Raghid Al-Solh and Ali Khalifah Al-Kawari, 'Mashru li Ta'ziz Al-Masa'i Al-Dimuqratiyyah fi Al-Buldan Al-'Arabiyyah' [The Project of Consolidating Democracy Orientations in the Arab Homeland], in *Al-Mustaqbal Al-'Arabī*, 15/161 (July 1992); also by the same authors see an earlier article on the same topic in *Al-Mustaqbal Al-'Arabī*, 14/155 (July 1992). Burhan Ghalyun, 'Al-Dimuqratiyyah al-Mafrudah wa Al-Dimuqratiyyah al-Mukhtarah: Al-Khayarat Al-'Arabiyyah Al-Rahinah fi Al-Intiqal ila Al-Dimuqratiyyah' [Imposed Democracy and Chosen Democracy: Current Arab Options in Transition to Democracy], in Al-Kawari (ed.), *Madakhil Al-Intiqal*, 267. Shoueiri', 'Al-Shūrā wa Al-Libiraliyyah wa Al-Dimuqratiyyah', 25–32.

50. Ali Khalifah Al-Kawari (ed.), *Al-Dimuqratiyyah wa Al-Ahzab fi Al-Buldan al-'Arabiyyah: Al-Mawaqif wa Al-Makhawif al-Mutabadalah* [Democracy and Political Parties in Arab Countries: Reciprocal Positions and Fears] (Beirut: Markaz Dirasat Al-Wihdah Al-Arabiyyah), 13.

51. Abdullah, *Aliyyat Al-Taghyeer Al-Dimuqrati fi Al-Watan Al-'Arabī*, see Chapter 6.

52. Ismail Al-Shatti, 'Al-Kuwait was Tajribat al-Intiqal ila Al-Dimuqratiyyah', in Al-Kawari (ed.), *Madakhil Al-Intiqal*, 140–7.

53. Ibid. 148–150.

54. Ibid. 145–8.

55. Ibid. 150–3.

56. Ibid. 153–5.

57. Sha'ban, 'Ma'uqat Al-Intiqal ila Al-Dimuratiyyah fi Al-Watan Al-'Arabi', 244.

58. Abdullah, *Aliyyat Al-Taghyeer Al-Dimuqrati fi Al-Watan Al-'Arabi*, 336.

59. Ibid. 346–7.

60. George Tarabishi, 'Al-Idyulujiyyah Al-Thawriyyah wa Istihalat al-Dimuqratiyyah' [Revolutionary Ideology and the Impossibility of Democracy], in Al-Kawari (ed.), *Al-Dimuqratiyyah wa Al-Ahzab fi Al-Buldan al-'Arabiyyah*, 72.

61. Ibid. 73.

62. Saad Eddin Ibrahim (ed.), *Azmatu Al-Dimuqratiyyah fi Al-Watan Al-'Arabi* [The Crisis of Democracy in the Arab Homeland] (Beirut: Markaz Dirasat Al-Wihdah Al-Arabiyyah, 1987).

63. Abd Al-Ilah Belqaziz (ed.), *Al-Mu'aradah wa Al-Sultah fi Al-Watan Al-'Arabi: Azmatu Al-Mu'aradah Al-Siyasiyyah Al-'Arabiyyah* [Opposition and Government in the Arab Homeland: The Crisis of Arab Political Opposition] (Beirut: Markaz Dirasat Al-Wihdah Al-Arabiyyah, 1987).

64. Walid Khaddouri, 'Al-Qawmiyyah Al-'Arabiyyah wa Al-Dimuqratiyyah: Muraja'ah Naqdiyyha', in Al-Kawari (ed.), *Al-Dimuqratiyyah wa Al-Ahzab fi Al-Buldan al-'Arabiyyah*, 39.

65. Ibid. 32.

66. Ibid. 40–4.

67. Abd Al-Ilah Belqaziz, 'Azmat Al-Mu'aradhah Al-Siyasiyyah fi al-Watan Al-'Arabi', in Abd Al-Ilah Belqaziz (ed.), *Al-Mu'aradah wa Al-Sultah fi Al-Watan Al-'Arabi,* 31.

68. Ibid. 28–44.

69. Ibid. 20.

70. Ibid. 23.

71. Mounir Sahfiq's on Belqaziz's paper can be found in Ibid. 75–90.

72. For sample works see Alex Inkeles, 'Transitions to Democracy', *Society*, 28 (May/June 1991), 67–72; John Higley and Richard Gunther (eds.), *Elites and Democratic Consolidation in Latin America* (Cambridge: Cambridge University Press, 1992); the four volumes by Guillermo O'Donnell, Philippe Schmitter, and Laurence Whitehead (eds.), *Transitions from Authoritarian Rule* (Baltimore: Johns Hopkins University Press, 1986); Enrique A. Baloyra, *Comparing New Democracies: Transition and Consolidation in Mediterranean Europe and the Southern Cone* (Boulder: Westview Press, 1987); see also the four volumes on region studies of transition by Larry Diamond, Juan J. Linz, and Seymour Martin Lipset (eds.), *Democracy in Developing Countries* (Boulder: Westview Press, 1988–90); Suzanne Jonas and Nancy Stein (eds), *Democracy in Latin America* (New York: Bergin and Garvey Publishers, 1990); James M. Malloy and Mitchell A. Seligson (eds.), *The Politics of Regime Transition in Latin America* (Pittsburgh: University of Pittsburgh Press, 1987); Alfred Stepan, *Rethinking Military Politics: Brazil and the Southern Cone* (Princeton: Princeton University Press, 1988); Leonard Binder et al. (eds.), *Crises and Sequences in Political Development* (Princeton: Princeton University Press, 1971).

73. Terry Lynn Karl, 'Dilemmas of Democratization in Latin America', *Comparative Politics* 23/1 (October 1990), 5.

74. See Ernest Gellner, 'Introduction', in Jean Baechler, John A. Hall, and Michael Mann (eds.), *Europe and the Rise of Capitalism* (New York: Basil Blackwell, 1988), 2.

75. Dankwart A. Rustow, 'Transitions to Democracy: Toward a Dynamic Model', 337–8.

76. Mahmood Monshipouri, *Democratization, Liberalization and Human Rights in the Third World* (Boulder and London: Lynne Rienner, 1995), 6.

77. Ibid.

78. See, for instance, Frances Hagopian, 'Democracy by Undemocratic Means?' Elites, Political Pacts, and Regime Transition in Brazil', *Comparative Political Studies*, 23/2 (July 1990), 147–70; Guillermo O'Donnell and Philippe C. Schmitter, *Transitions from Authoritarian Rule: Tentative Conclusions about Uncertain Democracy* (Baltimore: Johns Hopkins University Press, 1986); Youssef Cohen, 'Democracy from Above: The Political Origins of Military Dictatorship in Brazil', *World Politics*, 40/1 (October 1987), 30–54; Karl, 'Dilemmas of Democratization in Latin America'; also by Karl see, 'Petroleum and Political Pacts: The Transition to democracy in Venezuela', in Guillermo O'Donnell, Schmitter, and Laurence Whitehead (eds.), *Transitions from Authoritarian Rule: Latin America* (Baltimore: Johns Hopkins University Press, 1986), 196–219; John H. Hertz (ed.), *From Dictatorship to Democracy: Coping with the Legacies of Authoritarianism and Totalitarianism* (Westport: Greenwood Press, 1982).
79. O'Donnell and Schmitter define a pact 'as an explicit, but not always publicly explicated or justified, agreement among a select set of actors which seek to define (or, better, to redefine) rules governing the exercise of power on the basis of mutual guarantees for the "vital interests" of those entering into it.' See their 'Tentative Conclusions about Certain Democracies', 37.
80. Cohen, 'Democracy from Above', 47–8.
81. Which he defines as the fact 'that outcomes depend less on objective conditions than subjective rules surrounding strategic choice.' See Karl, 'Dilemmas of Democratization in Latin America', 6.
82. Ibid. 6.
83. O'Donnell and Schmitter, 'Tentative Conclusions about Uncertain Democracies', 38.
84. See Luciano Martins, 'The 'Liberalization' of Authoritarian Rule in Brazil', in O'Donnell, Schmitter, and Whitehead (eds.), *Transitions from Authoritarian Rule: Latin America*, 72–94.
85. For a summary of these points see O'Donnell and Schmitter, 'Tentative Conclusions about Uncertain Democracies', 37–9.
86. See Hagopian, 'Democracy by Undemocratic Means', 165.
87. See O'Donnell and Schmitter, 'Tentative Conclusions about Uncertain Democracies', 40.
88. Ibid.
89. Maravall and Santamaria describe consolidation as follows: 'Consolidation is the process that, eventually, leads to political-material institutionalization. Briefly defined, consolidation includes the process by which the emergent regime eliminates, reduces to a minimum, or incorporates its initial ideological and institutional inconsistencies; establishes its autonomy in the face of preexisting established powers within the country, especially the armed forces; mobilizes civil society into political forms of expression; and develops and maintains a structured and relatively stable party system, capable of guaranteeing popularly accountable government.' See their 'Political Change in Spain', 73.

90. Here emphasis is no longer on concentration of executive power and an arrangement of mutual guarantees...but on distribution of representative positions and on collaboration between political parties in policymaking...The mobilization following initial liberalization is likely to bring political parties to the forefront of the transition and make the convocation of elections an increasingly attractive means for conflict resolution. See Ibid.

91. Ibid. 45–7.

92. Ibid.

93. Anderson's reflections on the Tunisian model stands as one of very few attempts at applying contingent choice theory to Arab democratization. Lisa Anderson, 'Political Pacts, Liberalism, and Democracy: The Tunisian National Pact of 1988', *Government and Opposition*, 26 (Spring 1991), 244–60.

94. The SP won 56 seats, the GPC 123, and the other northern Islamist party, The Yemeni Ikhwān (reform) Rally, 62.

95. For the Spanish case see Maravall and Santamaria, 'Political Change in Spain', 88.

96. Anderson, 'The Tunisian National Pact', esp. 257–60.

97. O'Donnell and Schmitter, 'Tentative Conclusions about Uncertain Democracies', 38.

98. Anderson, 'The Tunisian National Pact', 244.

99. Author's interview with Rashid al-Ghannushi, 15 April 1993, London.

100. See Anderson, 'The Tunisian National Pact', 246, 256.

101. Hagopian, 'Democracy by Undemocratic Means', 149.

102. Anderson, 'The Tunisian National Pact', 255.

103. The current exclusion of *Al-Nahḍah*, while implicit, from the 'pacted transition' echoes that of the communists from Venezuela's 1958 Pact of Punto Fijo, and hence from 'participation in politics.' See Hagopian, 'Democracy by Undemocratic Means', 151.

104. Lisa Anderson, 'Politics in the Middle East: Opportunities and Limits in the Quest for Theory', in Mark Tessler, Jodi Nachtwey, and Anne Banda (eds.), *Area Studies and Social Science: Strategies for Understanding Middle East Politics* (Bloomington and Indianapolis: Indiana University Press, 1999), 4.

105. See Zbigniew Rau (ed.), *The Reemergence of Civil Society in Eastern Europe and the Soviet Union* (Boulder: Westview Press, 1991).

106. There has, since 1992, been a monthly magazine published by the Ibn Khaldun Centre in Cairo, Egypt, entitled *Civil Society*. The Beirut-based Arab Unity studies Centre published an 879-page volume of the papers and the discussions of the symposium it organized in January 1992, on the question of Arab civil society; see Said Binsaid al-Alawi, *Al-Mujtamaʿu al-Madani fi al-Watani Al-ʿArabi wa Dawruhu fi Tahqiqi al-Dimuqratiyyah* [Civil Society in the Arab Homeland: Its Role in Achieving Democracy] (Beirut: Markaz Dirasat al-Wihdah al-Arabiyyah, 1992). See also, Azzedine Layachi, 'Algeria: Reinstating the State or Instating a Civil society?', in I. William Zartman (ed.), *Collapsed*

States: The Disintegration and Restoration of Legitimate Authority (Boulder and London: Lynne Rienner, 1995), pp. 171–89. Useful and insightful also are the two volumes on the subject by Augustus Richard Norton (ed.), *Civil Society in the Middle East* (Leiden: E. J. Brill, 1995). See also, John P. Entelis and Phillip C. Naylor (eds.), *State and Society in Algeria* (Boulder: Westview Press, 1992).

107. See the preface by Adam B. Seligman, *The Idea of Civil society* (New York: The Free Press, 1992), ix–xii.
108. Ibid. x.
109. Ibid.
110. See Carole Pateman, *The Sexual Contract* (Cambridge: Polity Press, 1988), 3, 11.
111. Tester, *Civil Society*, 118–19.
112. See Cohen and Arato, *Civil Society and Political Theory*, p. 289.
113. Ibid. 290.
114. Ibid.
115. John A. Hall, 'In Search of Civil Society', in John A. Hall (ed.), *Civil Society: Theory, History, Comparison* (Cambridge: Polity Press, 1995), 4.
116. Ibid.
117. Charlesworth suggests that St. Augustine's 'final position' is one which concedes to the State its own arenas of autonomy and of jurisdiction (guarantor of peace and order) in which the Church must not meddle. See Max Charlesworth, 'Augustine and Aquinas: Church and State', in David Muschamp (ed.), *Political Thinkers* (Melbourne: Macmillan, 1986), 40–2.
118. Ibid. 44–5.
119. Ibid.
120. Ibid. 44.
121. Hall, 'In Search of Civil Society', pp. 4–5.
122. Autonomous towns, for instance, 'became islands in the feudal sea in which new ideas and practices could develop.' The calling of assemblies not only helped make Europe 'rule-bound' but also, Hall shows, establish many of the legal axioms such as 'no taxation without representation.' See Ibid. 5.
123. Ibid.
124. Ibid. 6.
125. Christopher G. A. Bryant states that 'for Ferguson, Hutcheson, Smith, Millar, Hume and others, civil society refers to a civilized or polished society in contrast to a rude, barbarous or savage society ... civility for the Scots has to do with manners, education, and cultivation which enjoin respect for the sensibilities or others. What the Scottish moralists imply, but never quite say, is that the constitutional state is not synonymous with civil society but rather complements it by guaranteeing civil and property rights and equality before the law.' See his 'Civic Nation, Civil Society, Civil Religion', in Hall (ed.), *Civil Society*, 143.
126. Hall, 'In Search of Civil Society', p. 7.

127. See C. L. Ten, 'Locke on Political Authority, Property, and Toleration', in Muschamp (ed.), *Political Thinkers*, 96. See also, Keith Tester, *Civil Society* (London and New York: Routledge, 1992), 53.

128. Tester, *Civil Society*, 57.

129. See T. M. Knox, 'Translator's Foreword', in *Hegel's Philosophy of Right* (Oxford: Clarendon Press, 1942), pp. x–xi.

130. Hegel in Ibid. 110.

131. Ibid. 122–3. With regard to this particular point refer to Tester who correctly points out how Hegel 'seems to be anticipating the sociological recognition of the division of labour and its implications for social solidarity.' See his *Civil Society*, 22.

132. Hegel in Knox, *Hegel's Philosophy of Right*, 123.

133. Ibid. 124.

134. Ibid. 125.

135. Alexis de Tocqueville, *De La Démocratie En Amérique* (Paris: C.L., 1888), vol. III, ch. VII.

136. Ibid. 199.

137. De Tocqueville compares political associations with 'free schools' in which American citizens come to learn about the art of association; Ibid. See also vol. II, ch. IV.

138. For this point see vol. II; de Tocqueville states how the American citizen 'looks upon the social authority with a mistrustful and anxious eye', p. 32.

139. Ironically, de Tocqueville's native France is an example of a democratic polity where associational life has not traditionally been vibrant or desirable. With the state and the family being 'highly organized', Kornhauser argues, 'there is a relative paucity of intermediate structures to link' them. See William Kornhauser, *The Politics of Mass Society* (London: Routledge and Kegan Paul, 1965), 84.

140. Tester, *Civil Society*, 55.

141. Salvador Giner, 'Civil Society and its Future', in Hall (ed.), *Civil Society*, 308.

142. Ibid. 308, 323. See also John Keane, *Democracy and Civil Society: On the Predicaments of European Socialism, the Prospects for Democracy, and the Problem of Controlling Social and Political Power* (London and New York: Verso, 1988), 31–2; and also by Keane, *Civil Society and the State: New European Perspectives* (London and New York: Verso, 1988).

143. Karl Marx, *The German Ideology* (New York: International Publishers, 1970), 57.

144. Ibid. 57.

145. See introduction in Antonio Gramsci, *The Modern Prince and Other Writings*, trans. by Louis Marks (New York: International Publishers, 1968), 12.

146. For a discussion of the origin of the notion of 'hegemony' in Marxist–Leninist thought, and for a comparison between Gramsci's formulation of hegemony and Lenin's, see Christine Buci-Glucksmann, *Gramsci and the State* (London: Lawrence and Wishart, 1980), pp. 174–85.

147. Ibid. 185.

148. See Jean L. Cohen and Andrew Arato, *Civil Society and Political Theory* (Cambridge, Mass.: The MIT Press, 1992), 142–59.

149. Ibid. 157.

150. Ibid.

151. See the latest and excellent work by Bryan S. Turner, *Orientalism, Postmodernism and Globalism* (London and New York: Routledge, 1994), esp. Ch. 2, 'Orientalism and the Problem of Civil Society in Islam', 20–35. See also an earlier version of this article by the same title in Asaf Hussain, Robert Olson, Jamil Qureshi (eds.), *Orientalism, Islam and Islamists* (Brattleboro: Amana Books, 1984), 23–42.

152. Ibid. 30.

153. Ibid.

154. See Simon Bromley, *Rethinking Middle East Politics* (Cambridge: Polity Press, 1994), 20–2.

155. See Karl A. Wittfogel, *Oriental Despotism: A Comparative Study of Total Power* (New Haven: Yale University Press, 1957), 49, 101–36. For the question of 'strong' states and 'weak' societies see Joel S. Migdal, *Strong States and Weak Societies: State–Society Relations and State Capabilities in the Third World* (Princeton: Princeton University Press, 1988).

156. Ernest Gellner, 'Civil Society in Historical Context', *International Social Science Journal*, 129 (August 1991), 506.

157. Turner, *Orientalism, Postmodernism and Globalism*, 31.

158. Edward W. Said, *Orientalism* (London: Penguin Books, 1991). For a good article giving a thorough account of orientalist treatments of Islam see Asaf Hussain, 'The Ideology Orientalism', in Asaf, Olson, and Qureshi (eds.), *Orientalism, Islam and Islamists*, 5–21.

159. Turner, *Orientalism, Postmodernism and Globalism*, 34–5.

160. Compare with the voluminous Arab work published three years earlier, *Al-Mujtama'u al-Madani fi al-Watani al-'Arabi* [Civil Society in the Arab Homeland], which has been methodologically more rigorous by being more alert to this linguistic lacuna. See the introduction by Said Binsaid al-Alawi, '*Al-Mujtama'u al-Madani: al-Mafhum wa Tadawuluhu fi al-Khitabi Al-'Arabi al-Mu'asir*' [Civil Society: The Concept and its Usage in the Contemporary Arab Discourse], in *Al-Mujtama'u al-Madani fi al-Watani al-'Arabi wa Dawruhu fi Tahqiqi al-Dimuqratiyyah*, 9–29.

161. See Wajih Kawtharani, 'Al-Mujtama'u al-Madani wa al-Dawlah fi al-Tarikh al-'Arabi' [Civil Society and the State in Arab History], in Ibid. 119–31.

162. Ibid. 120.

163. This term is not easily rendered in English. It refers to an inhabited small area in many Islamic cities. The American slang term 'hood', a derivative of neighbourhood, is its closest approximation in English.

164. Kawtharani, 'Al-Mujtama'u al-Madani', 120.

165. Here he deploys Ibn Khaldun. The latter's use of the term *ahlu al-dawlah* (those who control the state) is distinguished from *'ahlu*

al-'aṣabiyyah wa ahlu al-ḥiraf wa-ṣanā'i' al-ṭuruq wa al-firaq' (solidarities of kinship, of professions, of industries, of Sufi orders and of sections). This Kawtharani takes to be evidence of 'a sociopolitical dynamism with institutions for production and exchange, patterns of culture and independent reasoning, and expressions of political and professional activism.' See Ibid.

166. Serif Mardin, 'Civil Society and Islam', in Hall (ed.), *Civil Society*, 278–300.
167. Ibid. 285.
168. Ibid. 286.
169. Ibid.
170. Mardin demonstrates this point through the example of the search for a Turkish word for 'freedom', introduced into the Ottoman Empire in the 19th century: 'a neologism *serbestiyyet* had therefore to be invented: compassion, respect for the individual as an emanation from one of the divine attributes and respect for justice seen as the harmonizing of rival claims were elements of Islamic/Ottoman civilization; 'Freedom' was not.' See Ibid. 286.
171. Kawtharani, 'Al-Mujtama'u al-Madani', 123.
172. Ibid.
173. Ibid.
174. The author acknowledges having first seen this passage in the Arab essay by Kawtharani. In translating it, the author referred to the original French text. See Louis Gardet, *La Cité Musulmane: Vie sociale et politique* [The Islamic City: Social and Political Life] (Paris: Librairie Philosophique J. Vrin, 1954), 37–8.
175. Kawtharani, 'Al-Mujtama'u al-Madani', 123–4.
176. Ibid. 124.
177. See Ira M. Lapidus, *A History of Islamic Society* (Cambridge: Cambridge University Press, 1991), 322–8. See also, Edmund Burke III, 'Understanding Arab Protest Movements', *Arab Studies Quarterly*, 8 (Fall 1986), 333–45.
178. Lapidus writes that 'Sufi Babas mobilized bands of Turkish warriors and led them to holy war, protected travelers, mediated disputes, and otherwise helped to create social order in rural areas.' See Lapidus, *A History of Islamic Societies*, 325.
179. Ernest Gellner, *Muslim Society* (Cambridge: Cambridge University Press, 1981), 5.
180. Ibid. 41.
181. Lapidus, *A History of Islamic Societies*, 325.
182. Ibid. 326.
183. Ibid. 327.
184. See Ernest Gellner, *Postmodernism, Reason and Religion* (London and New York: Routledge, 1992), 9–11. See also Gellner, 'Civil Society in Historical Context', 506.
185. Gellner, 'Civil Society in Historical Context', 506.

186. Examples of these are the *Wahabiyyah* (Saudi Arabia), *Sanussiyyah* (Libya), and the *Mahdiyyah* (Sudan) movements. See Gellner, *Postmodernism, Reason and Religion*, 12–13.
187. Gellner, 'Civil Society in Historical Context', 506.
188. Gellner, *Postmodernism, Reason and Religion*, 11.
189. See Lapidus, *A History of Islamic Societies*, 327.
190. Gellner, 'Civil Society in Historical Context', 510.
191. Bromely, *Rethinking Middle East Politics*, 38.
192. Ibid. 39.
193. Ibid. 39–40.
194. Ibid. 40.
195. Ibid. 41–4.
196. Kawtharani, 'Al-Mujtamaʻu al-Madani', 124.
197. H. A. R. Gibb and Harold Bowen, *Islamic Society and the West: A Study of the Impact of Western Civilization on Muslim Culture in the Near East* (London: Oxford University Press, 1950), Vol. I, Part. II, 277.
198. Kawtharani, 'Al-Mujtamaʻu al-Madani', 125.
199. Ibid.
200. Ibid. 126.
201. Ibid.
202. Ibid. 127.
203. Gibb and Bowen, *Islamic Society and the West*, 277.
204. Kawtharani, 'Al-Mujtamaʻu al-Madani', 127.
205. Ibid. 128.
206. Ibid. 129.
207. See Norton, 'Introduction', in Norton (ed.), *Civil Society in the Middle East*, 1–25; John P. Entelis, 'Introduction: State and Society in Transition', in Entelis and Naylor (eds.), *State and Society in Algeria*, 1–32.
208. See Saad Eddin Ibrahim, 'Civil Society and Prospects of Democratization in the Arab World', in Norton (ed.), *Civil Society in the Middle East*, 29.
209. Zartman's definition reads: 'Civil society is used . . . to designate the social, economic, and political groupings that structure the demographic tissue; it is distinct and independent of the state but potentially under its control, performing demand and support functions in order to influence, legitimize, and/or replace the state.' See I. William Zartman, 'Introduction: Posing the Problem of State Collapse', in Zartman (ed.), *Collapsed States*, 6.
210. Ibid.
211. See Zbigniew Rau, 'Introduction', in Zbigniew Rau (ed.), *The Reemergence of Civil society in Eastern Europe and the Soviet Union* (Boulder: Westview Press, 1991), 5–6.
212. See John Gray, 'Post-Totalitarianism, Civil Society, and the Limits of the Western Model', in Rau (ed.), *The Reemergence of Civil Society*, 145–60.
213. Rau, 'Introduction', 6.
214. Ibid.
215. Cohen and Arato, *Civil Society and Political Theory*, p. x.

216. Ibid, pp. x–xi.
217. Turner, *Orientalism, Postmodernism and Globalism*, 34.
218. Ghassan Salamé, 'Introduction: Where are the Democrats? ', in Ghassan Salamé (ed.), *Democracy Without Democrats? The Renewal of Politics in the Muslim World* (London: I. B. Tauris, 1994), 10.
219. Gellner, 'Civil Society and its Future', 308.
220. Gray, 'Post-Totalitarianism, Civil Society, and Limits of the Western Model', 157.
221. The state of the fledgling civil society throughout the Arab world has been dealt with in great detail elsewhere, especially in Norton's *Civil Society in the Middle East*. The picture it depicts is generally one of increasingly active and crystallizing associations, parties, and organizations which are still inchoate and subject to state tutelage and control.
222. War-torn Somalia is one country where Adam finds 'the role of the 'traditional elders' (both secular and religious)...both visible and positive', considering them as some of the actors contributing to the revival of the country's civil society. See Hussein M. Adam, 'Somalia: A Terrible Beauty Being Born', in Zartman (ed.), *Collapsed States*, p. 80.
223. Augustus Richard Norton, 'Introduction', in Norton (ed.), *Civil Society in the Middle East*, pp. 15–16.
224. Neil Hicks and Ghanim al-Najjar, 'The Utility of Tradition: Civil Society in Kuwait', in Norton (ed.), *Civil Society in the Middle East*, 190.
225. Ibid. 198–9.
226. Ibid. 199.

Mapping out Arab Electoralism, 1998–2008

> Totally or partially elected parliaments now exist in [most] Arab countries ... However, the right to political participation has often been little more than a [constitutional] ritual ... In most cases, elections have resulted in misrepresenting the will of the electorate and in low levels of representation for the opposition. Hence, elections have not played their designated role as a participatory tool for the peaceful alternation of power. These elections have generally reproduced the same ruling elites.
>
> UN Arab Human Development Report 2004[1]

There is an explosion of 'election fetishism' and 'electoralism' in the AME. In this chapter, I firstly attempt to assess the flurry of electoral activities of the 1998–2008-period. This period is momentous for democratization in the AME. Two gains are noteworthy. The first of these is the consolidation of 'electoralism' in the cluster of Arab states which have been holding elections since the 1980s. Electoralism is behind the rise of 'parliamentarization' in the AME. The second gain is that by 2007 three Arab Gulf polities have held elections for the first time in their history and a fourth resumed elections after a hiatus of nearly 30 years. Thus, for the first time in Arab history, the entire oil-rich Arab Gulf joins the process of what I call Arab electoralism. That is, the occurrence of elections with regular frequency but with limited substantive democratic dividends in four areas. Contestation is not deep enough and hardly leads to redistribution of power or renewal of ruling elites. Participation is yet to be widened as to include new recruits from within civil society. The state's monopoly of the use of coercion is not subjected to any legal checks. Lastly, the symbiosis between wealth and political power and between tribal solidarity and/or partisan loyalty and power has grown exponentially, pre-empting elections of any real value to reorder polity according to the electorate's voting preferences. Nonetheless, the initiation or routinization of elections across all of the AME is an exciting dimension to the study of democratization. This development represents, at least partially, a rebuttal to the Orientalist old habit of viewing this region to be at variance with the rest of the world in democratic struggle, if not achievement.[2]

Elections are now everywhere in the AME, but democracy nowhere. Elections are ubiquitous. But democracy is still awaited. The 'metrics' of elections differ from the metrics of good government. The number of elections is not a credible test of good government without renewal of rulers and equal opportunity for the recruitment of political actors from within civil society. Nor are regularity and frequency of elections without matching respect of human rights. What I call 'election fetishism' has set in. Elections seem to guide most scholarly search for democratization in the AME. They are the first evidence that we all turn to for clues about democratization in the region. Not a month or year passes without an election or more throughout the vast Arab geography. For this reason, in the second part of the chapter, I try to critique election fetishism. I argue that elections belie a state of political decay in most of the AME. Elections are being mapped out onto geographies where neither justice nor power is being redistributed equally. The family is returning to centre stage as an important locus of loyalty and a prime player in state-making. Society is patriarchal to the detriment of equal gender relations.[3] Polity is noted for its singularity and civil societies are in state of siege by leviathan-like states.[4] Economy is mismanaged by corruption and inefficiency of state capitalism.[5] There are qualified exceptions, of course. The 'electoralism' of this period conjures up a not so distant history when weak rulers whose sham powerless parliaments failed to embellish or conceal colonial tutelage. Accordingly, I shall begin by returning to the history of Arab reform in search for linkages with present electoralism. In particular, I briefly consider this history in relation to the so-called waves of Arab democratization.

Arab Democratic Waves?

Not all history of democratization is linear. Arab democratization seems to be following a cyclical trajectory. Elections have not thus far halted the return to the point of departure: autocracy by the same ruling elites and unchecked rule by the same royal houses. The AME appears to remain within the bounds of cyclical history with regard to democratization. Despite the explosion of state-led elections, democratization is unfolding as a 'complex, long-term, and open-ended process', as Whitehead critically views democratic transition. Varying degrees of authoritarianism still resist the 'third wave'[6] of liberal-democratic 'universalism'. It may be argued that there are primordial, social, political, and even transcendental factors that present checks to the triumph of liberal-democratic universalism. None of this, however, validates the thesis that Arab democracy is an oxymoron.[7] Nor does it support the notion of 'exceptionalism'[8] with regard to Arab democratization. Al-Sayyid regards the AME to be experiencing its own 'third wave' of democratization. However, based on the state of play in most Arab polities, this so-called third wave cannot, I argue, be presented as a harbinger of constitutional-representative and accountable government. In fact, it is open to question whether the term 'third wave'[9] could be applied to recent political openings throughout the Arab political landscape without overstating their significance. The Arab world seems to be precariously perched on a precipice of democratization. The flurry of electoral politics that has either happened, or is in the offing, is unprecedented. On paper, the scope of the new reforms, be they institutional, legal, constitutional, or electoral, is remarkable. Whether these reforms merit being qualified as a 'third wave' is questionable. They approximate 'ripples' rather than waves in terms of their impact. The terms 'trends' or 'phases' are more precise than 'waves'. I shall use all three terms interchangeably. Nonetheless, al-Sayyid is right. The temptation to interpret them in terms of 'waves' of democratization seems to be irresistible.[10] Drawing closely on Huntington's chronology, al-Sayyid identifies three 'waves' of political liberalization. The first, in Egypt, was heralded in 1866 by Khedive Isma'il. It spanned some 14 years ending with the country's occupation by the British.[11] The second, concentrated in the Arab East (*mashriq*),[12] was mostly coterminous with independence. It covered a 50-year time span beginning in 1922 with the British-sponsored and landed aristocracy-dominated Egyptian parliament, and ending with the escalation of Lebanon's civil war in the mid-1970s. This wave included Egypt (1923–52); Iraq (1936–58); Lebanon (1946–75); Syria (1946–49; 1955–58); and Tunisia (1959–63).[13] Libya, Kuwait, Morocco, and Sudan also had either checkered or short-lived parliamentary experiments. The 'third wave', according to al-Sayyid, among others, had its roots in the crushing defeat of the third Arab–Israeli war. Such a defeat discredited Arab regimes resting on military/revolutionary legitimacy, and plunged them in a political and even ideological crisis.[14] The momentum of this 'wave' came after the October 1973 war with the revitalization and restoration of pluralist politics in Morocco and Egypt, in 1975 and 1976, respectively. This wave gathered further momentum after yet another war, the Second Gulf War of 1991.[15]

Table 2.1   First wave of Arab reform and breakdown

Period	Date	Place	Reform
Age of Arab Liberal Thought	1860	Tunisia	• Muslim World's first Constitution
			• Grand Council appointed
	1868	Egypt	• Arab World's first election
			• Assembly elected by village headmen Breakdown
Colonialism	1881	Tunisia	French protectorate
	1882	Egypt	British occupation

Establishing time boundaries on Arab reformist trends defies precise definition. Assuming that only three such trends are indeed identifiable, their institutional impacts must not be exaggerated. The first, coinciding with the renaissance/liberal age (*asr al-nahḍah*), was more significant due to the intellectual ferment that placed democracy in the Arabo-Islamic mind-set.[16] The 'elections' of assemblies under Khedives Isma'il and Tawfiq in Egypt were important. But they were not the only event to launch that first phase of reform. If the pioneering institutional pinnacles of that ferment are to be considered with historical veracity, the earliest has to be Muhammad Bey's granting of the Arab world's first constitution in 1860 in Tunisia[17] (see Table 2.1). Neither that Tunisian constitution, which was eventually suspended, and the Grand Council that accompanied it, nor the Egyptian Khedives' assemblies served more than a modicum of constitutional-representative government. In Kedourie's words the former represented 'the façade of constitutionalism without its reality', and the latter 'an empty gesture'.[18]

The second phase of political liberalizations, which coincided with the emergence of the Arab nation-state system, was characterized by its elitist nature. Almost everywhere where parliamentary structures existed the notables had the upper hand. It had a sectarian-confessional basis (Lebanon). It followed an unsteady path. It was punctuated by coups as in Iraq or by civil war as in Lebanon. This second phase of reform was followed by a phase of democratic retreat (see Table 2.1). Revolutionary and military praetorian guards and totalitarian ideologies were wrestling the Arab state by force from the remnants of Francophile and Anglophile liberal elites. Only Tunisia, Lebanon, and Morocco were spared the same fate. The third phase, while still in its infancy despite the passing of two decades since its inauguration in Egypt, Kuwait (which al-Sayyid excludes), and

Morocco in the mid-1970s, is the most far-reaching since the Arab intelligentsia cried out for new thinking and democratization in the 1960s. Although it was launched in Egypt, Kuwait, and Morocco almost contemporaneously with the third wave that began in Southern Europe, its greatest momentum occurred with the April 1986 multiparty parliamentary elections in Sudan that placed the opposition in government. This was an unprecedented happening in Arab political history. Only Mauritania has matched this political feat with the democratic election of a president in March 2007. Despite inherent trepidation, this last phase of political reform is the most serious and significant in the post-independence period. This phase embraced the Arab West (*maghrib*), the Arab East, and Kuwait in the Arab Gulf.[19] Given the fact that the notion of 'wave' denotes both quantity and quality, the third phase of Arab liberalizations did not, therefore, begin in earnest until 1986 in Sudan and then later in the years 1989/1990 when Jordan and Algeria's significant elections took place. These dates mark the launching of the most extensive electoral and institutional campaign in the history of Arab post-independence.

The 'waves' of Arab political liberalizations had resonance in 'waves' of intellectual effervescence and vice versa. Democracy was the most common theme of those intellectual 'waves'. In post-independence three such 'waves' can be identified. If democracy was their common theme, war seemed to be their 'defining event'.[20] Writing in 1986, Hilal identified the June 1967 Arab–Israeli war and the June 1982 Israeli invasion of Lebanon as triggers of intellectual discourse on democracy and human rights. 'Lack of participation and absence of democracy' were the answers provided by intellectuals probing the questions as to 'what happened and why' in 1967 when Arab armies were swiftly routed by Israel.[21] As to 'why there hardly was any Arab popular reaction to Israel's invasion of Lebanon' the discourse provided messages of 'systemic oppression... absence of accountability, and... violation of human rights'.[22] That the Second Gulf War of 1991 galvanized Arab intellectuals into soul-searching and drawing lessons[23] from yet another grave error of miscalculation by an Arab despot needs little emphasis. This third 'wave' of intellectual discourse on Arab democracy has spared no Arab country. However, what is noticeable is the disjunctive nature of the intellectual discourse on democracy. Just as disastrous wars (1967, 1982, 1991) spawn intellectual interest in democracy, partially won wars (1973, Iraq–Iran war) seem mostly to generate silence. Should democracy and human rights matter only when Arab pride is injured? Grotesque cases of calculated state brutality against Arab and Kurdish (Hama and Halbaja) citizens drew little or no criticism (Tables 2.2 and 2.3).[24]

Table 2.2 Second wave of Arab reform

Start date	Country	Reform
1922	Egypt	• 1923–36: Pre-independence MP/E (various dissolutions) • 1936–52: Post-independence MP/E
1925	Iraq	• 1925: Pre-independence MP/E (first Iraqi Parliament) • 1930–58: Post-independence MP/E (various coups)
1926	Lebanon	• 1926–44: Pre-independence MP/E (confessional/sectarian system) • 1944–75: Post-independence MP/E (1958 Civil War)
1927	Syria	• 1927–43: Pre-independence MP/E (various dissolutions) • 1944–48: Post-independence MP/E
1952	Libya	• 1952–60: Post-independence MP/E • 1960–69: Post-independence NP/E
1953	Sudan	• 1953–56: Pre-independence MP/E • 1956–58; 1964–69: Post-independence MP/E
1954	Jordan	• 1954–57: Post-independence MP/E
1959	Tunisia	• 1959–63: Post-independence MP/E (a single election)
1963	Kuwait	• 1963–75: Post-independence NP/E (dissolution 1965–71)
1963	Morocco	• 1963–72: Post-independence MP/E (various dissolutions)

Keys: MP/E: Multiparty elections; NP/E: Elections without political parties.

The matrix from which Arab liberalizations have been launched deserves brief examination. While on the whole these liberalizations constitute related evolutions of a common impulse, they do not preclude variation. Hence, Huntington's caveat applies: 'the combination of causes generally responsible for one wave of democratization differs from that responsible for other waves.'[25] The first pre-colonial phase of reform in Tunis and Cairo, which cannot, by any standards, be called

Table 2.3 End of second wave of Arab reform

Date	Place	Cause
1948	Syria	Coup
1952	Egypt	Coup
1957	Jordan	Ban on elections/parties
1958	Iraq	Coup
1958	Sudan	Coup
1969		Coup
1963	Tunisia	Ban on elections/parties
1965	Kuwait	Dissolution of parliament
1969	Libya	Coup
1972	Morocco	Dissolution of parliament
1975	Lebanon	Civil war

a wave, was the by-product of palace (*al-bilāṭ*) contacts with foreign powers. The reforms ensued from a combination of direct or indirect prodding from outside, and from feelings of backwardness or even inferiority vis-à-vis the European master. As eloquently put by Kedourie, these reforms were a showpiece 'designed to show that [their royal authors were] in tune with the spirit of the age'.[26] The second postcolonial phase of reform was not totally devoid of outside inputs. For instance, the parliamentary structures and party politics[27] that flowed from Britain's unilateral granting of nominal independence to Egypt in the 1920s constituted a tripartite arrangement between the palace, the landed aristocracy and the nationalists, and the British colonialists. Elsewhere mostly Francophile and Anglophile nationalist elites oversaw the flagging and 'parliamentarization' of their newly independent political realms. Only the last phase, noted for the intensity and scope of 'electoralism', is home-grown. It largely reflects indigenous inputs, demands, pressures, and expectations. These are in tune with the 'travel' of democratic norms globally. Those factors that have, in varying degrees, precipitated the last phase of electoral initiatives are both internal and external. The following brief explanations of the occurrence and the timing of third wave democratizations by Huntington coincide, more or less, with those proposed below in relation to Arab liberalizations.

The crisis of legitimacy (*azmatu al-sharʿiyyah*) is at the heart of the most recent Arab democratic stirrings. They largely reflect the failure of the existing unresponsive and unaccountable political structures and practices that fostered narrow-based and top-down decision-making processes. There is also a realization of the limited effectiveness of coercion and traditional modes of legitimation to assert state authority. Eighty years of state coercion over the Muslim Brotherhood have failed to weaken the Islamists. Electoralism and attendant 'parliamentarization' are thus additional tools in the inventory of rulers. They give the state a modicum of institutional-building. Whether elections and parliaments serve as mechanisms to aggregate and mediate public interests is another matter. But having them as institutional décor is intended both for internal and external consumption. The third phase of reform is additionally precipitated by the dismal state record in providing strategic and economic security. The vote is one way out of the contractual obligation to provide for the populace. Huntington relates the legitimacy crisis of authoritarianism to the widespread diffusion of democratic norms, to authoritarian regimes' 'consequent dependence' on living up to the standards of this new democratic universalism, and their 'inability to maintain "performance legitimacy" due to economic (and sometimes military) failure'.[28]

Accordingly, the roots of the Arab authoritarianism legitimacy crisis can be found in military setbacks, the culmination of which was the loss of Jerusalem in 1967, and in the atrophy of state-led ill-planned and ill-guided developmental endeavours. The Arab bread uprisings of the 1980s signaled flashpoints in state–society relations, the management of which could not be maintained by draconian measures alone. The bullet had to be substituted with the ballot.[29] Hence the Sudanese, Algerian, Jordanian, Tunisian, and Egyptian liberalizations had to be engineered (see Chapter 5). The 'electoralism' of the 1998–2008-period, being part of the third phase of Arab reform, deserves closer scrutiny.

Electoralism, 1998–2008: Initiation and Routinization

The 1998–2008-period is fecund with electoral activities. The resulting electoralism can be understood in terms of 'routinization' and 'initiation'. Routinization refers to the process of solidification of elections as an irreversible *modus operandi* in the cluster of Arab 'semi-democratizers'. This cluster includes countries where elections have been taking place, in some cases with interruption, since the 1980s. Kuwait is included in this cluster. Initiation is the process whereby elections are introduced into established Arab states or states under occupation (Iraq) or simultaneously under occupation and in formation (Occupied Territories). These elections have thus far spared only Libya. For the first time since the departure of the European colonial powers, which first designed the Arab state system, elections cover the entire Arab landscape.

Initiation

The Arab Gulf, with the exception of Kuwait, having for so long resisted political modernization, has finally joined the process of electoralism in the AME (see Table 2.4). Saudi rulers have, since the creation of the Consultative Council (*majlis al-shūrā*) in 1993, argued that Islamic Law and government were not compatible with elections. In 2005 they held Saudi Arabia's first elections, a momentous event since King Saud united Najd and Hijaz and founded the kingdom in 1932. The Wahhabi puritanical creed, which is hostile to Western democracy, was not adjusted for the purpose of legitimizing the municipal elections. Instead, it was the Saudi rulers who had to adjust to the electoral contagion from within the AME. They pragmatically agreed to the elections in the face of internal demands for reform and external pressure to conform to the global democratic diffusion. Over three rounds (10 February; 3 March; and 21 April) a partial electorate elected half the councillors for 178 civic bodies. That same year in December 7.9 million Saudis bought shares in the initial public offering of 39 million shares of the country's Yanbu National Petrochemicals Company. Indeed, in 2005 the Saudi state simultaneously opened up to democracy and capitalism. The vote was opened up to a partial electorate—30 per cent of the population. The stock market was opened up to all, men and women. The years ahead will tell whether democracy and capitalism will succeed in redistributing power and wealth. Nonetheless, the twinning of democracy and capitalism in the country where the Qur'ān is a quasi constitution and where the inventions of modernity have until recently been considered heretical is proof the Arab Gulf is responding to the winds of change. In December 2006 the UAE entered the electoral age. Select citizens from six Emirates elected over three rounds half (20 deputies) of the country's Advisory Council (Federal National Council). The smallest states whose rulers deposed their own fathers, Bahrain and Qatar, have redesigned their city-states in line with newly created democratic constitutions, respectively in 2001 and 2003.[30] Like Saudi Arabia and the UAE, Qatar had its first taste of voting in the 1999 municipal elections. It was the first country in the Arab Gulf to adopt universal suffrage. Mobilization and enthusiasm were high, explaining the equally high voter turnout (85%). Bahrain resumed elections in 2002 after nearly 30 years of absolute rule. Like Qatar, universal suffrage was used in the elections of Bahrain in 2002 and 2006. Being the tiniest states in the Arab Gulf, they have sought through reform to make up for what they lack in geographical size and population, especially in comparison with Saudi Arabia and Oman, with democratic distinction. For Bahrain, the consolidation of 'electoralism', which was not boycotted in 2006 by the Shi'ite opposition, was additionally designed to firm up the tiny oildom's conversion to a kingdom in 2002 (see Table 2.4).

Kuwait is, relative to the AME, a consolidated electoral democracy and boasts one of the most vibrant parliaments anywhere in the AME. It is a trailblazer in both electoralism and parliamentarization. What is new in Kuwait is the enfranchising of women in 2005 and exercised for the first time in the June 2006 parliamentary elections. Note that elections quickly followed the dissolution of Parliament in early 2008. So the previous practice of keeping parliament closed for years is no longer an option available to the ruling house. The only option remaining is to dissolve an antagonistic parliament. Oman is the other Arab Gulf state where elections have been taking place since the 1990s. A key reform was the adoption of the universal adult suffrage since 2002, which was implemented in the 2003 parliamentary elections. The move

Table 2.4 Democratic trends in Arab Gulf, 1998–2008

Democratic activities	Bahrain	Kuwait	Oman	Qatar	Saudi Arabia	UAE
Municipal elections/voter turnout %	2002: 52.3 2006: 61	2001: 56 2005: (two women appointed)	No	1999: 85 2003: 38 2007: 51	2005: 64 (first ever)	N/A
Parliament elections	2002, first in 27 years 2006	1999 2003 2006 2008	2000 2003 2007	2009 or 2010 (first ever)	No	2006 (first ever)
Political parties Parliament	Illegal 40 elected 40 appointed	Political blocs 50 elected	Illegal	Illegal 30 elected + 15 appointed	Illegal *Shūrā* Council appointed	Illegal 20 elected + 20 appointed
Female candidates	Yes—first and only woman of 17 candidates to enter parliament in 2006: Latifa Al-Qouhud won uncontested seat	Franchise won in 2005; voted for first time in 2006; five female candidates	1997 first two women win seats 2007–21 ran but none won	Yes: one female won in each municipal election	No	Yes
Electorate	General suffrage; no foreigners	'badun' excluded; no foreigners	General suffrage since 2003	General suffrage; no foreigners	No: women, foreigners; military personnel	5,500 males and 1,189 females
Elections Referenda	2001 Constitution; monarchy conversion 2002	Since 1963 No	Since 1990 No	2003 Gulf's first written constitution	Since 2005 No	Since 2006 No
Independence	1971 from UK	1961 from UK	1951 from UK	1971 from UK	1932 state created	1971 from UK

Figures compiled from Arab Gulf newspapers: *Al-Ittihad, Al-Siyassah, Al-Khaleej, Al-Hayat.*

away from partial electorates in the Arab Gulf, which poses problems of both identity and citizenship, is a positive step in the right direction for women, especially. Naturalized citizens, guest workers, and the *'badun'* (stateless Arabs) are yet to be inducted and included into citizenship, much less voting. The initiation through the practice of elections in the Arab Gulf may be explained by outside pressure for reform, namely, the US Greater Middle East Initiative (see Chapter 4). More importantly, however, is the fact that the Arab Gulf has suffered an obvious imbalance between economic and political modernization. Dubai is a global shopping Mecca. Other Gulf capital cities have got thriving dynamic financial and commercial entrepots. In a way the initiation into elections is one way of redressing the imbalance between economic and political modernization. The rentier state's reliance on surplus extraction from oil wealth spared it the pressure to reform in the 1980s when the rest of the lesser-to-do AME was facing social unrest due to state incapacity to maintain subsidies (see Chapter 5). Oil wealth and distributive capacity still shield the rich Arab Gulf from the kind of political opposition found in Egypt or Morocco. But voluntary state-managed 'electoralism' makes good political sense, domestically and internationally. As the entire Arab Gulf enters the electoral age, there is a need to go beyond the conventional scholarly propositions of the 1980s in order to explain political modernization in rentier states at the turn of the millennium.

Transitologists tend to present two polar opposite positions when it comes to assessing prospects for political transformation in the Arab Gulf. They tend to treat this sub-region in either 'exceptionalist' or 'normalist' terms. In agreement with Abd Allah, it must be asserted that neither position is entirely defendable. At the core of the 'exceptionalist' discourse is the failure of the oil affluence to translate into democratic dividends to match the socioeconomic goods distributed by the rulers. The rulers' political durability is therefore a function of their distributive capacity. Societal challenge to their rule is unlikely under the current fiscal arrangements—subsidies and no taxes. The 'normalist' argument does not differentiate between the Arab Gulf and the rest of developing countries which share unemployment, uncontrolled population growth, and lack of democracy. It contends that the Arab Gulf is undergoing a modernization process, with distribution of political power itself slowly shifting from traditional to modern modes of management. Gulf rulers have no control over the vicissitudes of the international economy, in particular the oil market. Slump in oil prices, as in the mid-1980s, can easily affect the ability of rentier states to fund welfarism and with it political stability and change.[31] An opposing view finds change to be already happening in the form of augmented political opposition. The gist of this argument by Francis Gause is that oil wealth does not just buy political acquiescence. It funds literacy and media consumption with politicizing effects. Politicization is manifest in the new norms of socialization that transcends primordialism and family or clan-based associational habits. Work- and school-based activities are drawing individuals into new socialization and solidarity networks, increasingly rendering traditional associations superfluous. The upshot is increased politicization on the basis of ideology, as opposed to kinship.[32] This may be relatively true of Bahrain and Kuwait where political blocs exist. The rest of the Arab Gulf still bans political parties. Gause gives the example of the new media in the Arab Gulf. He recognizes the media's politicizing role, which is being translated into greater participation. Instructive in this respect is the petitions and processions that challenge the existing political order, such as in Saudi Arabia.[33] In this context, it should be recognized that political liberalization will be in some measure the interplay of attitudinal change by the rulers and the ruled with the newly introduced inquisitive, daring, and independent media, such as al-Jazeerah (see Chapter 6). The adoption of new media technologies and the entry into the Arab Gulf of millions of guest workers all have politicizing effects. Satellite dishes facilitate the travel of 'universals', such as human rights and democracy. Elections in the AME and around the globe, Ukraine's 'Orange revolution' and 'Lebanon's Cedar revolution' travel uninvited into the lounge rooms of Gulf citizens. Satellite dishes, computers, cellular phones, and higher literacy catalyze political learning that cannot go without a response from the top. The elections of the Arab Gulf are partly responses to the global winds of change as well as economic modernization. Economic development has just started to feed into political development. Nonetheless, the initiation into electoralism is state-managed and qualifies as election fetishism—elections with limited substance.

Electoral initiation also has taken place in Arab political units under occupation. In both the Occupied Territories and Iraq the elections followed the departure from the political scene of omnipotent figures who would not have agreed to contests to their authority other than by presidential referendums. The elections represented quasi 'civilizing' processes that were meant to emulate the occupiers' own democratic achievements. Israeli leaders' declarations make a linkage between a democratized and an independent Palestinian state in the future. The United States has been more intrusive in its control of Iraqi democratization (see Chapter 4). The elections in the Palestinian Occupied Territories came as the biggest test to the United States's 2003 declaratory policy to democratize the AME. Despite harsh conditions of siege, impoverishment, violence, and occupation the Palestinians voter turnout at 75 per cent was higher (see Table 2.5) than that of neighbouring Egypt where elections and referenda for the same year averaged less than 25 per cent. The traditional power-holders Fatah (45 seats) came second to Hamas (74 seats) but accepted the verdict of the people (at least initially and before subsequent US pressure to boycott Hamas was applied). It was indeed a political feat by Arab standards. The elections, regardless of their results, were an act of defiance of occupation and a statement of despair for statehood. Instead of statehood the Palestinians were collectively punished for voting Hamas into government. The siege and subsequent isolation of Hamas was 'a test that the United States' Greater Middle East Initiative failed', in the words of Dr. Moussa Abou Marzouq, the number two in Hamas.[34] The elections were also a test for other Arab regimes closely watching the political ascendance of Hamas. This was a source of concern for Jordan and Egypt where Hamas had allies in both countries' formidable Muslim Brethren. For the United States, Israel, and Arab regimes the elections were a barometer by which to gauge Islamist performance. Hamas did not field a candidate in the presidential elections, which were the first that had multiple candidates in the Occupied Territories. But it battled Fatah at the municipal elections fought over 12 months and over four rounds in 2004–05. The fact that elections have not even spared the Occupied Territories, territories without legally demarcated and internationally recognized borders, sovereignty, or peace, says a great deal about the routinization of electoralism. The old modes of legitimation are perhaps not as yet dying out in the AME. But elections, despite many flaws and limitations, have become a new mode of legitimation that enthuse both state and society.

Whereas in the rest of the AME elections are controlled and staged by indigenous power-holders, the Iraqi elections of 2005 (see Table 2.5) was largely overseen by the main occupying force, the United States. The elections were intended to induct not only Iraqis but also the rest of the AME into American pluralism. Iraq had a role to play by lending credence to the United States' Greater Middle East Initiative. Democracy replaced WMDs as the main objective of the US-led occupation. Thus the Iraqi constitution drafted with US mentoring and the subsequent elections were to an extent a trial run of democratization in the wider Middle East. Instead Iraq became the example that the AME has sought to avoid, not emulate. The civil war, sectarian divisions, the poor state of services, unsuccessful reconstruction,[35] and the inutility of the elections have all undermined rather than strengthened the case for an outside mentor of democratization. Even those who were initially receptive to the mentor's role assigned to the United States

Table 2.5 Democratization under occupation

Elections	Occupied territories (Palestine)	Iraq
Year	2006	2005
Parliamentary	Second in 10 years	First since 2003 invasion
Main parties	Hamas: 74 seats	Unified Iraqi Alliance: 140 seats
	Fatah: 45 seats	Kurdistan Coalition: 53 seats
	PFLP: 3 seats	Iraqi Accordance Front: 44 seats
	Alternative list: 2 seats	Iraqi Front for National Dialogue:
	Third Way List: 2 seats	11 seats
	Independents: 6 seats	Kurdish Islamic Union: 5 seats
		Risaliyyun: 2 seats
Voter turnout	75%	68.4%
Municipal	2004–05	N/A
	Fatah: 49%	
	Hamas: 46%	
	Independents: 5%	
Presidential	2005	2005
Key candidates	Mahmoud Abbas: 62.52%	Jalal Talabani, elected by
	Mustafa Barghouthi: 19.48%	parliament

had reservations. Hassanayn Tawfiq Ibrahim was of the view that holding elections in an occupied country where tribalism was on the rise, and where neither reconciled political partners nor social peace existed was like putting the cart before the horse:

> Founding a democratic system in Iraq is not an impossible objective. But this is a complex undertaking. It can be realized over both a mid-term and a long-term time frame. This requires working efficiently to provide the internal requisites of democratization ... For, democracy cannot be superimposed from without. External support remains important to back up democratization. But the role of this support is [secondary and] intended to aid [not to manage]. Thus the exit from the Iraqi quagmire could be for the US to declare its commitment to gradual withdrawal after the holding of the elections, opening the way for a greater UN role in reconstruction ... The elections could be delayed for some time to prepare the conditions for internal reconciliation and political accord.[36]

A democratization that is solely built on elections does not stand the chance of much success; especially when a country is under occupation and its many sectarian and warring foes share not many political values or objectives. Ahmad Abdallah al-Jabbar finds elections to be a sad reductionism with no prospect to help either Iraqi democratization or reconciliation. He observes that democratization must be neither top-down nor elitist and based on superficial institutionalism.[37] Richard Falk concurs. He notes that the Bush Administration has in fact reduced democracy to institutional exercises, namely elections, constitutions, and free market economics.[38] In both the Occupied Territories and Iraq 'electoralism' as initiation has been an exercise that was largely tied to 'rites of passage' into sovereignty. Both the Palestinian and the Iraqi people are still awaiting sovereignty. The electoral exercise has served to point to new ways for locating legitimacy and affirm the civic potentialities of the Palestinian and Iraqi peoples. Thus far, however, it has been vitiated by the incapacity of the United States to assume moral courage or leadership in lending substance to elections, namely, that elections help build democracies, resolve conflict, and earn sovereignty.

Routinization

'Electoralism' in the rest of the AME proceeds apace. In 2007 alone, Algeria, Jordan, Morocco, and Syria, held parliamentary elections. This is in addition to Mauritania's presidential elections the same year (see Table 2.6). Elections are indeed being routinized. There can be no return to a political order without some reference to the AME's electorates. Of course, this is not to say that elections will not be postponed. Following the 2001 dissolution of parliament Jordanians had to wait for two years to elect new representatives. Egypt has delayed the municipal elections due in 2006 by two years. Domestically, reversing an electoral process would mean doing away with sometimes the only and most obvious evidence of political liberalization. International standards of governance forbid democratic reversibility and conditionality is much more stringent. States requiring foreign aid are particularly vulnerable. With the routinization of 'electoralism' comes meaningful gains, potentially if not immediately. Two gains are noteworthy. In the 1998–2008 period, presidential elections have not only become regular and on time. More importantly, incumbent rulers have begun subjecting themselves to some competition. Also, the genre of 99 per cent presidential victories is gradually becoming something of the past. The example of Mauritania illustrates this point. The Maghribi state voted in March 2007 a new president, Sid Ould Cheikh Abdallahi. After two rounds, as in the French system, he emerged as the clear winner against his last rival, Ahmed Ould Daddah. Abdallahi won by 53 per cent. By comparison, in December 1997 Mou'awiya Ould Sid Ahmed Taya, the incumbent, won by 90.14 per cent. However, by 2003 winning elections by such a high percentage was inviting disdain and disbelief. That year Taya won by 67.38 per cent; his rival Muhammad Khouna Ould Haidalla got 18.77 per cent of the total vote. Mubarak (Egypt), Ali Abdallah Al-Salih (Yemen), and Bouteflika (Algeria) all registered lower percentages in their last presidential multi-candidate contests (see Table 2.6). Even Bin Ali (Tunisia) had to do with 94.5 per cent.

The biggest gain from the routinization of 'electoralism' is the opportunity of and potential for democratic habituation this process opens up for both political society and civil society, which have obvious weaknesses. The regularity and frequency of elections are useful for people to sharpen their political skills and get used to contestation and participation. In Algeria, Jordan, Morocco, Lebanon, Mauritania, and Yemen varying degrees of political pluralism and forms of opposition are now firmly entrenched in the political system. Morocco and Jordan have no ruling parties and this is the key advantage of political competition in both monarchies. There are centrist political forces which are amenable to doing business with the palace in both countries. In Morocco, in particular, the absence of a ruling party renders the competition, for instance, over municipalities very much an inter-party contest. Jordan remains cautious to opening up this contest for fear of Islamist domination, already noticeable in the professional syndicates. The fact, however, remains, that neither is a constitutional monarchy and ultimately there is a big difference between what political reform *is* and what it *should be*. In both the monarchy is a system above the system; electoralism does not touch it. In Tunisia the regime has taken steps away from single party rule and exclusivity. Following the 1999 and 2004 elections the opposition has held 34 seats in the 182-member lower house of the National Assembly. This represents 15 seats up under a *pro forma* for including the opposition. The increase in the opposition's quota can be read in two ways: a gain for the opposition and a further decrease in the government's domination of parliamentary politics. With 34 seats the opposition holds nearly 20 per cent of the total seats. Mubarak's Egypt is noted for the regularity and frequency of elections. Despite a ban on religious parties, the Muslim Brotherhood is astute in political survival and the conversion of its permanence, and religious, social, and historical capital into parliamentary visibility. This it achieved in the 2005 parliamentary elections, securing 20 per cent of the total vote, 88 seats.

Beyond 'Election Fetishism'

Consider the following. The United Arab Emirates held its first elections ever in 2006. Precisely, 6,689 citizens, less than 1 per cent of the total population, were the only voters on December 16, 18, and

Table 2.6 Electoralism in Arab semi-democratizers, 1998–2008

Region	Country	Parliamentary elections/voter turnout (%)	Presidential elections/winner's % of vote	Municipal elections/voter turnout (%)	Opposition in parliament
Arab Maghrib	Algeria	2002: 46% 2007: 35.6%	1999: 73.7% 2004: 85%	1999: 30% 2002: 50% 2005: 34%	12 parties hold seats in parliament
	Mauritania	2001: 54.4% 2006: 69.5%	2003: 67.4% 2007: 53%	1999: 16% 2001: 55.8% 2006: 73%	Legalized parties and blocs
	Morocco	2002: 52.6% (first under new King) 2007: 34%	Monarchy	2003: 54.2%	6 large parties and minor parties, and Islamist independents
	Libya	No elections	No elections	No elections	No parties
	Tunisia	1999: 92.5% 2004: 86.4%	1999: 99% 2004: 94.5%	2000: 84.5% 2005: 85.4%	RCD and five opposition banned
Arab Mashriq	Egypt	2000: 25% 2005: 24%	1999: plebiscite 2005: 88.6% first multi-candidate	2002: 42.4% 2006: delayed for two years (2008)	Muslim Brotherhood and other five parties
	Jordan	2001: postponed 2003: 57.7% (first under new king) 2007: 54%	Monarchy	1999: 53% 2003: 58% 2007: 51%	Islamist, leftist, pan-Arabist parties—15 parties
	Lebanon	2000: 45% 2005: 46.5%	1998: vote by parliament (Maronite) 2000: 86.5% (sole candidate)	1998: 58% 2004: 63%	18 sects and affiliated parties
	Sudan	2000: 57%	2007: sole candidate	N/A	Traditional parties
	Syria	1998: 82% 2003: 63.4% 2007: 56%	1999: sole candidate 2007: sole candidate	1999: 66% 2003: N/A	Ruling Ba'ath forms bloc with five minor parties (Jabhah)
	Yemen	2003: 75%	1999: 96.2% (sole candidate—first by popular vote) 2006: 77.2%	2001: 48% 2006: 61%	Two main parties and several minor parties

20. That is, 1,689 more than the idealized number of the ideal Greek polity whose 5,000 select male citizens could fit in a stadium in order to practise democracy directly via deliberation. The UAE's select citizenry conjures up the Greek polis except in democracy. Numerically, it is the privileged that the right to citizenship is bestowed upon. Foreigners and slaves are excluded. The wealth-makers of the UAE, mostly Indians working under the most backward labour laws anywhere,[39] are at once the foreigners and the slaves with no citizenship rights of any kind. There is a concession to women in the UAE that was not available to women in the Greek polis. Women make up 18 per cent of the 'Electoral College'. Thus of the 6,689 voters 1,203 were women. This is the most partial electorate ever invented in the Arab Gulf and possibly the entire world since the Greeks. Moreover, our 6,689 citizens, selected by the rulers of the seven Emirates, elected only half of the Federal National Council, an advisory body with no legislative powers!

How should we read the explosion of elections in the AME? This explosion is the most concrete and outward evidence that a reform of sorts is under way in the AME. Historically, since the expansion of the suffrage in North America and Europe elections have been one of the most important emblems of democratic transformation and consolidation. Elections are an added emblem in a long succession of tools and symbols of state-making in the AME. That succession began with the importing of military *techne* of enlightened Europe and was followed by the European advisor, the *colon*, the flag, the anthem, the borrowed 'isms' of post-independence, and now elections—the *techne* of government. But if elections have become unavoidable, so has election fetishism. Election fetishism, it seems, is equally unavoidable for both governments and students of democratic transition. For governments in the AME elections have become additional emblemata of sovereign statehood and badges of 'liberal universalism' and 'enlightened' rule. Holding elections is a global fashion that regimes in the AME feel compelled to copy. Internationally, Arab regimes know only too well that creeping conditionality renders the business of governance partly dependent on outside approval. Like developing countries, states in the AME are therefore compelled under newly operating norms of governance to meet a minimum threshold of legitimacy. For the lesser-to-do Arab states minimalist good governance is obtained by electoralism. This democratic minimalism is sufficient for maintaining their status as IMF and World Bank clients as well as securing sponsorship by political benefactors in Europe and North America. For students of democratic transition electoral data can be one method of verifying the occurrence of democratization. The figures and the numbers that are produced with every election in the AME tempt empiricists. However, elections are still new in a great part of the AME to allow for large scale studies of Arab electoral systems or voting behaviour across countries or sub-regions within the Arab world. At this juncture voting and elections despite increasing regularity are still novice experiences. The kind of quantitative measurement of political attitudes and disposi- tions that would help the making of inferences about how Arab citizens vote is still far from being realized. This is particularly true in the AME where polling is quite new to the region, and where regimes still treat information about voting with utmost sensitivity. Election results are still disclosed to the world by the Interior or Justice Ministry in most Arab states, few of which have independent specialized agencies that oversee elections and sort out results. The figures and numbers of Arab electoralism are not as yet proof of substantive democratizing trends. They are simply indicative of reform stirrings.

For instance, voter turnout is consistently shown as standing above 90 per cent in Tunisian elections. The figure may be correct. But whether that figure correlates with a rise in civic awareness cannot be established by the figure itself. The estimate of voter turnout is pro- duced by a government department in Tunisia. From this perspective, it is part of a carefully orchestrated campaign the regime wishes to communicate to the public at home and abroad. This is not specific to Tunisia. Complex social and political realities may not always be captured by numerical data that accompany election fetishism. It is these realities that I seek to highlight by reflecting on electoralism and election fetishism. This is why the number of elections in the AME and the impressive figures that come with them must not be allowed to detract from social and political contexts. Focus on electoral statistics leads only to partial assessment of electoralism. In Tunisia, public servants and the labour force at large are tied to a corporatist authoritarian structure. The card showing membership of the ruling party, RCD, is mandatory for government employees. Voting is equally mandatory. Patronage clientelism still reigns high in most of the AME. The Tunisian example of use of the economy by the state to entrench dominance of the ruling party is applicable to other AME corporatist polities (e.g. Algeria, Egypt, Morocco, Syria, and Yemen). The economy has become an additional tool to tighten the regime's control over people's lives and political choice. In Tunisia that choice is between Bin Ali and Bin Ali. A simple economic transaction of applying for a small business loan can turn into a test of political loyalty. A Tunisian speaking to *Le Monde* about his support for Bin Ali states: 'I do not support him. I vote for him; that is different. The other day . . . one of my friends went to the bank to apply for a [micro-credit] loan. He was asked for his voting card; and you want us to have [political] choice.'[40] Another adds, 'in this country the "deal" is simple. We leave politics for the president, and he, in exchange, leaves us eat. We have invented a term for this: "khubzism". One eats and keeps quiet.'[41] The state's control of the economy is being used to further entrench political quietism, whereby so-called khubistes have no choice but to pay deference to the existing political order. It is a quasi-tacit contract between state and society whereby economic goods are exchanged for political deference (see Chapter 5). It is a quintessential example of economic reformism (e.g. micro-credits) being put to the service of political particularism.

Voter turnout figures, even when low and do not give regimes much political capital, are contested. Voter turnout in Egypt's 2007 referendum on 34 amendments to the country's 1970 constitution, which was boycotted by the opposition, was put at 27 per cent by the government, 22 per cent higher than independent monitors' estimate.[42] Elections take place. But when voters have the choice they tend to boycott them. This is not necessarily a result of wide apathy as much as it is an expression of contempt at the pre-ordained nature of results according to George Ishak, one of the founders of Egypt's grass-roots movement for democratic change, Kifayah. For Ishak, Egyptians are politically aware and they largely boycott elections rather than 'partake in an exercise that insults their intelligence'.[43] This 'boycott' (*muqāṭaʿah*) attitude applies to most of the AME. With the exception of Tunisia where high voter turnout explains fear from economic reprisal, in many other Arab polities the figures would have been lower if government clients—public servants and other employees—are not mobilized to vote. They more than any other stratum in society have lots at stake if the employer—governments—were to change. The Islamists are the only groups beside ruling parties that can mobilize their rank-and-file to vote. This has been true of largely Sunni states with strong Muslim Brotherhood organizations that use the ballot to maintain presence and influence, mostly in the face of hostile secular-nationalist forces (e.g. Algeria, Egypt, Jordan, and Yemen). Similarly, sectarian divides play a role in elections where identity assertion and preservation requires mobilization of confessional solidarity (e.g. Bahrain, Lebanon, and post-2003 Iraq).

Election Fetishism: Reflecting on 'Initiation'

The election fetishism that has of late crept into the Arab Gulf, bar Kuwait which is an electoral pioneer in the AME, unlocks very little that can at this juncture be taken seriously in terms of deepening

contestation or widening participation. Even in terms of the actual conduct of elections there is much yet to be improved. Electoral processes
involve the transfer of large sums of money from candidates to voters
willing to elect the highest bidder. Other forms of 'pork-barrelling' are
used to woo voters. These include free food and drink and distribution of material gifts. Not many vote according to political preference,
still a rarity given the absence of political parties in most Arab Gulf
polities. The buying of votes is found in the rest of the AME. All Arab
Gulf polities have partial electorates, including in polities which have
adopted the universal suffrage—Bahrain, Oman, and Qatar. Stateless
Arabs are excluded from the political process. So are guest workers.
Naturalized citizens are not part of the voting citizenry. Kuwait, with
long electoral and parliamentary traditions, has in 2005 extended the
franchise to women. Women represent close to 55 per cent of the total
population and yet not a single woman was elected to parliament in the
2006 or 2008 elections. In Bahrain and Qatar two women won uncontested seats since the initiation of electoralism. Only in Oman two
women are the only exception to the general rule of electoral rejection
in the Arab Gulf. The Kuwaiti voting citizenry is defined according to a
discriminatory law that stresses genealogical purity. Voters must have
an ancestry with Kuwaiti residence since 1920 or 30 years of residence
for the naturalized. Ancestry, gender, and colour can all be grounds
for discrimination in most of the Arab Gulf. Clan-less Saudis are still
looked down upon and even when they are accomplished professionally
they face discrimination, by largely being barred from ministerial jobs.
Arab Gulf societies remain quintessentially gendered societies even
with the franchise given to women in five of the Gulf Cooperation
Council (GCC) states. The franchise may not mean much to women
when personal status codes in the region forbid them from choosing
whom to marry. In Oman marriage to a non-Omani or a Gulf citizen
cancels a woman's civil rights, including employment. 'Coloured' Gulf
Arabs suffer a great deal of discrimination. Informally, it is common
knowledge in the Arab Gulf that coloured citizens are not appointed
to ministerial portfolios. No number of elections can right such wrongs
or conceal lacunae in legal reform, and institutional inclusiveness and
equalization. Electoralism may be no more than a farce when social
and political realities do not support full and universal citizenship.

Only in Kuwait and Oman voters elect the full members of parliament. In the remaining Arab Gulf a 50-50 formula gives the ruling
houses unfettered power in appointing their clients to the mostly 'hon-
orary' national assemblies and consultative councils, which mostly lack
formal powers. Elections are thus decorative acts that are yet to shift
the locus of power from the ruling houses to the populace. In Bahrain,

the al-Khalifah Sunni ruling house uses the appointment of half of the members of parliament in order to keep the Shi'ite majority at bay.[44] A form of gerrymandering is used by naturalization of Sunni Arabs to reduce the Shi'ite numerical superiority. Rumours that the non-voting Saudis cross the causeway linking the two kingdoms to vote in Bahrain's elections are not completely baseless.[45] The leading Shi'ite opposition group, the National Accord Association (Jam'iyyat Al-Wifaq al-Watani), boycotted the 2002 elections to protest the set of tools deployed by the regime to rig the vote. It won 17 seats in the 2006 elections. However, the ruling house has invented a number of measures to contain the Association. A fully appointed second house, the Consultative Council, is on par with the first elected house in terms of suggesting and negotiating legislation. This is more or less the Crown's house. Electoralism and 'parliamentarization' are incipient and neither provides enough of a countervailing force to Emiri authority and or the clout of royal families. Royalty may look more enlightened. But it is not about to share, much less surrender, power, or subject itself to rational laws and democratic scrutiny through parliamentary checks and balances. The very legitimacy earned by the founding fathers— From Saud to Zayed—still serves their royal progeny well in largely deferential societies. The Arab Gulf rulers, like fellow Arab rulers, look upon electoralism as being a resource to contain pressure from within and without to reform. It adds to them; but it does not take away from their power. They confer it upon their societies; and they see it more or less as a 'gift'. More importantly, there should be no illusion as to where the locus of power resides—not in the partially elected assemblies and councils. The princely caste in Saudi Arabia is powerful and permeates every level of political life. The princes dominate local government. The newly partially elected civic bodies will not curtail that domination, especially that the elected councillors owe their seats to princely endorsement. Political and financial power conflates within royal hands everywhere in the AME and initiated electoralism is not intended to take away privileges from families and clans who practically own the state and make full use of petroleum income to ensure continuous possession of it. In May 2007 an Arab daily's front page headline begs the question 'where does oil wealth go?' In answering its own question, it writes:

A minority in Arab petroleum states enjoys oil wealth; it provides them with fairy-tale-like life styles. This has pushed the rest of the people [in their societies] to become resentful and envious. With the political impasse in various states and the domination of royal families over power some youth have turned to extremist groups which conduct vengeful random [terrorist] operations against public property under the guise of religion. In reality, these operations are reactions against corruption, class differences, and political monopoly.[46]

Political monopoly means that the big decisions of national security, petroleum sales, and deals, and foreign relations are all closed to public debate. There are elections and parliaments, all of which are welcome measures of democratic inclusiveness. But there is also increased foreign meddling the populace has no means of consulting rulers about. In the Arab Gulf electoralism as initiation has taken place in states like Bahrain and Qatar. The former is home to the US fifth fleet; the latter hosts al-Jazeerah (not unlike a 'base' in the eyes of many Arab regimes resentful of its 'attacks') and also hosting one of the largest US bases in the AME. As Patrick Seale notes,

An obstacle to change is precisely the overlapping of political power with economic benefit. If losing power means losing wealth . . . then few ruling elites will yield power willingly . . . In spite of huge oil revenues the Arabs seem unable to create effective armed services . . . the Arab liberation struggle of the 1940s and 1950s sought to expel foreign military bases from the region. Today, foreign bases have returned to Arab soil in greater numbers than ever before. Welcomed by host governments, these bases have been used for the invasion of Iraq.[47]

Iraq post the 2003 US-led invasion has hardly lived up to the high hopes pinned on it by the Bush Administration to be a conduit of democracy to the rest of the AME. The 2005 elections went ahead despite advice to the contrary by credible democratization experts such as Larry Diamond. Diamond, who served as an Advisor to the Coalition Provisional Authority, feared that holding elections would lead to underrepresentation of the Sunnis whose majority boycotted the elections. He even proposed constitutional amendments in order to re-integrate the Sunnis into the political process. For Diamond reconciliation and dialogue were more urgent than the elections. His fears that in the absence of a compromise agreement and with the Sunnis remaining disenfranchised Iraq could slip further into a spiral of violence that would lead to a civil war.[48] A 'Truth and Reconciliation' process would have perhaps worked in tandem with elections and or even before jumping onto the bandwagon of electoralism. Elections in the absence of shared political values and under the auspices of occupying forces have clearly defeated the original purpose of democratization. The Kurds have since the 2003 invasion consolidated their control over the north. The emerging Kurdish state, which holds its own elections and has its own president and parliament, has taken advantage of the federal arrangements agreed in the new constitution. The Kurdish leadership reciprocate US de facto backing of their state with democratic procedures and military support. The Sunni–Shi'ite divide is more worrying for stability and for democracy promotion. It has intensified in the fourth year of invasion, leading to the carving of Iraq into sectarian zones policed by militias who dispense of their own law. Grotesque human rights violations at the hands of the Shi'ite new political masters and the Sunni insurgents have been widely recorded. Worse still, the 'liberators' whose job was to 'liberate' the Iraqi people and 'induct' them into democracy committed their own abuses at Abu Ghraib. Similarly, the Palestinian elections of 2006, procedures stipulated in the Oslo Accords, have thus far failed to reconcile Islamist Hamas and secularist Fatah. The interfactional fighting, like in the Iraqi case, has raised doubts in the AME about the utility of elections under occupation. That is, democratization not in tandem with reconciliation and prior to statehood in deeply divided polities. In both instances induction in the ballot has not thus far silenced the tendency to resort to the bullet.

Election Fetishism: Reflecting on Routinization

The chief distinction of electoralism as routinization is that it opens up a vista for some checks and balances through the entry of opposition to parliament. Morocco is a prime example of a parliament with serious opposition despite the presence of a 'courtier' parliamentary wing. It still compares favourably with the 'loyal opposition' in neighbouring Tunisia, and the 'NDP-dependent' parliamentarians, bar the Muslim Brotherhood, in Egypt. However, like electoralism as initiation, routinization provides no exit channels from power to the successive elites that have more or less occupied the state since independence. Even Mauritania owes its briefly democratically-elected president to a coup that deposed Taya in 2005, paving the way for a new start, be it one with candidates with large clan backing. Abdallahi, the eventual winner of the second round in March 2007 multi-candidate presidential elections, like Bouteflika in neighbouring Algeria, has the army's endorsement. Indeed, the very forces that propelled Abdallahi into the presidential candidacy and victory are themselves by-products of Taya's 21-year rule. Despite EU satisfaction with the presidential contest, there are fears that the even procedurally flawless and democratically fair elections can reproduce the previous regime's non-democratic order and practices. One observer writes that 'Taya's regime could return to power via democratic practices—meaning not so much the return of individuals from the former regime, but rather its practices, such as poor governance and financial corruption. Such fears are legitimate given the Abdallahi attained power with the support of a pro-Taya coalition.'[49] The constitutional amendments of 2006 limiting presidential tenure to two terms are one gain. They go against amendments undertaken in Tunisia in 2002 and being considered in Algeria to do away with the two-term tenure. Like in Mauritania, in states like Algeria, Egypt, Sudan, Syria, Tunisia, and Yemen the Army seems to be always lurking in the political background. In Algeria (with weaker but continuous Islamist insurgency) and Syria (still technically in a state of war with Israel) army backing is vital for regime stability. In the other four states the incumbent presidents are former generals whose metamorphosis into their new civilian roles has happened over a lengthy period of more than 20 years in power. With 26 years Mubarak is the longest-serving, a 'sphinx' or a 'pharaoh' for many Egyptians.[50]

The 1998–2008-electoralism coincides with the rise of al-Qaidah after 2001 as a serious threat to centralized authority in a number of Arab states. The 9/11 events have thus strengthened the military's hands in Arab politics, including in the Arab Gulf. Electoralism panders to two diametrically opposed agendas at once: a democratic agenda and anti-terror agenda. Elections serve to soften the anti-terror agenda. Holding elections places the regimes in the good books of the EU and the United States, whose declaratory policies stand for democracy promotion. The anti-terror agenda hardens the stance of regimes vis-à-vis pressure for fast or substantive democratization, often with the tacit approval and understanding from Western governments. Democratic activists, secularists, and Islamists, who are all lumped together as extremists in countries like Egypt, Tunisia, and, to an extent, Morocco, have their share of the public space reduced in the name of combating terror.[51] Winning 88 seats in the 2005 parliamentary elections in Egypt can thus be argued to be no more than a meaningless figure once one transcends the superficiality of election fetishism. Of course, not meaningless in the eyes of the Muslim Brotherhood who in some polling booths had to use ladders to gain access through windows in order to vote. It was one measure to bypass police blocking voters and using force (*baltajah*) to sabotage the Islamist electoral campaign. The existing political realities after the holding of elections confer upon the Muslim Brotherhood no legitimacy within the country's ruling elite, including among the NDP's apparatchiks. Nor do those political realities of exclusion immunize the Muslim Brotherhood against systematic repression. Anti-terror laws are deployed to contain formidable opposition. The 2007 controversial constitutional amendments included the change to Article 179 which empowers the president to send terrorists to any court of his choosing, including military courts.[52] Alarmed by the Madrid and Casablanca bombings, largely executed by Moroccan citizens, and by the rise of al-Qaidah, Morocco's parliament passed an anti-terrorism law in May 2003. The legislation's broad definition of terrorism makes the possession of print material and even apologist thought (which is open to interpretation) on terrorism punishable crimes, and gives police wider authorities in policing mosques and prayer leaders (*imams*). The 2004 UN Arab Human Development Report notes the worsening state of human rights in the name of the fight against terrorism.[53] This security and the democratization agendas clash directly.

At issue here, however, is how to construct a democratic political community that opens up space for all the diverse differences. One genre of problems has to do with the exercise of negative rights. This regards the concern over those categories of difference that exercise such democratic rights of free expression, freedom of the press, freedom to join and form parties, and contest power only to preach extremely non-democratic ideas (e.g. racism, sexism, religious intolerance). In other words, fundamental liberties in the 'wrong hands' may be interpreted as having the potential to undermine or cancel the very foundations of democratic community and political or cultural pluralism. Invoking Islamist fanaticism and the supposed opposition to democracy by the Front of Islamic Salvation (FIS), Algerian generals behaved undemocratically when they aborted what at the time looked to be a uniquely promising democratic process in early 1992.[54] However, since coming to power in 1999 President Bouteflika's *modus operandi* has been twofold. He has included two key Islamist parties, Algerian Hamas and Ennahdah, in the political process. This can be interpreted as a means to assassinate the FIS politically. He has intended, and with some success, the presence of moderate Islamists in government and in parliament to draw as well as rehabilitate FIS defectors and supporters still intent on political activism. Also, as part of his Peace Plan (*Mithāq al-muṣālaḥah al-Wataniyyah*), approved in 2005 in a popular referendum, parties to the bloody conflict are excluded from the political process. This is meant to prevent the FIS return to electoral politics. Hamas and Ennahdah have both participated in the parliamentary polls of 1997, 2002, and 2007. Ennahdah is deeply divided and it won only 3 seats in the 2007 parliamentary elections, a loss of 40 seats from 2002. Hamas, by contrast, has become a solid partner of the state and is the third partner in the so-called Presidential Coalition—also made up of the National Liberation Front (FLN) and the National Rally for Democracy (RND). It won 52 seats in the 2007 elections, gaining 14 seats more than the previous poll. Neighbouring Tunisia and Egypt have insisted on an interpretation of democratic community that excludes political Islam from the democratic process.

Article 5 was part of the 2007 constitutional amendments in Egypt. It was specifically intended to exclude the Muslim Brotherhood. This amendment has been criticized as the ruling NDP is known for juggling double standards on the use religion for political ends. The NDP refers to the country's clergy on most questions, recently 'seeking out the opinions of religious scholars on the law for organ transplants, the passage of which the NDP has blocked'.[55] Similarly, the NDP 'inserted a constitutional article in 1980 naming Islamic law as the primary source of legislation in the country'.[56] Tunisia maintains a more stringent ban on all Islamists, not even as independents. In his July 2005 speech marking the 48th anniversary of the republic, Bin Ali renewed his hostility to Al-Nahḍah's return to politics. The Tunisian Islamists, like the Muslim Brotherhood in Egypt, are victims of their own success. In the first poll held under Bin Ali two years after his 1987 coup, the Islamists won 20–25 per cent of the vote in by-elections in Tunis. The Islamists, perhaps like their Algerian counterparts, rushed too soon into political contestation. The ruling secularists were equally guilty of exaggerating the results as a potential danger to their control over Tunisia. The repression of the late 1980s and early 1990s eradicated the movement from Tunisian soil, forcing it into permanent exile within the EU. Jordan and Morocco have monarchies which claim Prophetic lineage, one means of appropriation of Islam for legitimation purposes. Even with their respectively Hashemite and Sherifian credentials, both monarchies have sought to limit the ascendancy of the Islamists. Jordan's Islamists are more institutionalized than most Islamic movements in the AME and adhere to the rule of the institutional game, having since the onset of electoralism formed the largest parliamentary bloc and opposition in Jordan, even after the 1997 boycott. Morocco's Islamists are more diverse and while Justice and Development Party—JDP (Al-Adl wa al-Tanmiyah), the only legalized Islamist party, plays by the rules of the democratic game, others (e.g. Moroccan Islamic Combat Group with links to al-Qaidah) have contested centralized authority by recourse to terrorism. Like the Muslim Brotherhood in both Egypt and Jordan, the JDP limits the number of candidates to elections. Its objective is not to sweep the board and not to threaten the regime and secular parties. It is a tactful device to avoid confrontation with the regime. In the 2003 local elections it contested only 20 per cent of the municipalities. It also sought to field fewer candidates than it could in the 2002 parliamentary elections, winning 42 seats. The 2005 Law of Political Parties bans religious parties, most probably targeted at the popular and outlawed Justice and Charity Party—JCP—(Al-Adl wa Al-Ihsan) and its leader Nadia Yassine, an avowed republican. The electoralism of the 1998–2008 period has not addressed legalization of moderate Islamist parties. Like the Muslim Brotherhood in Egypt, which has had plan ready for a political party since the late 1990s, the JCP and al-Nahdah prefer to work within the system if legalized. Hamzawy is correct in noting that moderate Islamists are formidable forces that must be engaged and accommodated. These forces have come a long way in negatively adopting democracy and rule of law. The inclusion of Islamists (Islamic Action Front—IAF) in Jordan and Yemen (Reform Party) proves his point about the moderating and stabilizing role of Legalized Islamism.[57]

Perhaps nothing illustrates this democratic dilemma more than the contention within Europe in 2001 over the popularly based political eminence of the Right in Austria. But there is no escape from the following reality. In practice, a non-democracy via democratic means (ascribed to Islamists' use of elections to get power only to deny others inclusion) is the same as a democracy by non-democratic means. The first is feared to abort democracy after the electoral process. The second does already practice exclusion of selected differences. In neither case can the end-result be helpful to democratization in spite of routinized electoralism. The dilemma is how to reconcile the imperatives of safeguarding or building democratic community and of toleration of difference. Must the protecting of democracy entail non-democratic safeguards? To answer the question in the positive is to blur the boundaries between democrats and non-democrats. A politics that rests on exclusion is not worthy of the epithet 'democratic'. To answer the question in the negative is to succumb to the risk inherent within democracy: the occasional unreliability of the democratic process. That is when democracy from time to time becomes a means to an end—in the hands of bureaucrats, technocrats, Eurocrats, autocrats, Islamists, or economic interests. In fact the question of who partakes in the democratic game has been a perennial dilemma in Western history. In the mid-nineteenth century, Irene Collins writes, the liberals equated democracy with the tyranny of the group over the individual and of the majority over the minority. Jacobinism during the French revolution hardened the liberals' case against democracy at the time.[58] This 'fear of democracy', as Collins puts it, swung nineteenth-century liberals against revolution and republicanism. The reason was that both had mass backing, as illustrated by the example of France. The liberals' 'fear of democracy' was in fact fear of too much democracy: 'mass intervention in politics'.[59] Democracy was meant to be the exclusive vocation of the few. Even in Greece, the birthplace of democracy, eminent minds, such as Aristotle and Plato, had a low view of mass-based democracy. Thus nineteenth-century European liberals, resorted to coercion (National Guards) and exclusion (limited franchise) to counteract popular democracy. The Italian Moderates of the 1840s and 1850s were no exception.[60] In France, the electoral law of 1831 excluded millions of well-educated bourgeois.[61]

Electoralism is yet to adjust and tolerate difference. This is a political reality that election fetishism cannot erase. Difference in its many forms and shapes—culture, gender, and ethnicity—is inevitable. Democracy has then to be turned into an end in itself. As an end in itself, rather than an interim game, democracy becomes symbiotic with the enshrining of equal opportunity of all differences for participation, contestation, and representation. Thus conceived, democratic community reads as 'one which permits and perhaps also encourages every man and woman individually or with others to choose the course of his or her life, *subject to recognition of the right of others to do likewise*' (emphasis added).[62] Inclusion of difference, epistemologically, socially, culturally, legally, electorally, and institutionally is the *sine qua non* of democracy.

Democratization must then be the process that lends the above understanding of democracy greater clarity and specificity. That is to say, that it becomes the continuously revisable embodiment of the procedural, legal, institutional, and moral standards essential for integrating difference into the democratic process. This understanding is unlikely to unfold through top-down or institutionally mediated means alone. Democratization, as Parry and Moran correctly point out, is problematic at least in terms of explanation. They caution against the explanatory power of democratization without disaggregation. There is no set of universally applicable conditions under which democratic government flourishes. Thus they caution against studies that tend to explain democratic transition with something akin to scientific exactness.[63] This speaks to Whitehead's argument that accounts for contingency, complexity, and open-endedness in the process of transition. But this criticism can be pushed even further by underscoring the point that the conditions under which democracy develops are subject to change. This is one reason why the above definition insists on a *continuously revisable* process. In the context of the AME, revising regime attitude towards religious parties is perhaps in order. Islamists are unlikely to disappear by way of legal writ or coercion. Accepting the status quo, that is to continue with elections that exclude this group, is tantamount to imposing a permanent political handicap on the AME's fledgling democratization processes. To continue to do so, ruling elites would directly and indirectly condemn their societies to the possibilities of non-democratic and even violent challenges to state authority, national unity, and stability. The spectre of this type of violence haunts many an Arab polity. Varying degrees of it found in Algeria, Egypt, Lebanon, Morocco, Sudan, Syria, and Tunisia. This factor contributes to the impasse of democratization, especially in its crude Arab version of authoritarian electoralism: a process that remains largely desiring in sustainability.

Electoral authoritarianism continues to reproduce singular rule. Irregularities at the polls, especially in the 2007 elections, are widespread according to Algeria Electoral Watchdog. Participation is visibly low. Algeria's parliamentary elections demonstrate the downward trend in voter turnout from 69 per cent in 1997 down to 35.6 per cent in 2007. In the span of 10 years the electorate looks disillusioned with its representatives. On top of the war against terror, the other war that Algeria is yet to win is against corruption. But corruption cannot be won when the people's parliamentarians collectively opposed a law in 2006 that requires state officials and high public servants to declare their wealth. The opposition startled Algerians and the 2007 voter turnout is an expression of disaffection by the populace. Close to one million ballots were spoilt or recorded a 'donkey-vote', again in protest at corrupt officialdom that places itself above the law. Yet Algerian electoralism is a good example of how election fetishism can easily deflect from the social and political realities. Thus far about 13 elections have been held since the cancellation of the 1991 vote in which the FIS looked certain to win. Except that the army moved first to cancel the second round of the vote. The country has 24 legalized political parties. The distribution of seats points to power-sharing arrangements. The FLN won 136 seats, down 63 seats; Hamas 52; and the RND 61 seats, up 18 from the 2002 elections. Even the leftist party led by the only female political party leader, Louiza Hannoune, won 26 seats. On the other side of the political spectrum, with 33 seats, the liberal list increased its seats by 5. The Berber Rally for Culture and Democracy (RCD), coming after a five-year boycott, picked up 19 seats. The independents fared well with 33 elected. Beyond the figures there is the political realities of a Presidential Coalition which runs the parliamentary show on behalf of the executive branch and the President who suggests and approves 80 per cent of all laws. Parliament is thus left with little legislative work. As in the rest of the AME, there are kingmakers who lead. Bouteflika, despite illness, he is no different from Mubarak, Bin Ali, Al-Qadhafi, or the monarchs of Jordan and Morocco. The FLN, despite its dismal record of failure, has been resurrected politically after a decade of blood-letting between the state and the Islamists.[64] The party that was sidelined by the Islamists in the elections of the 1990s is back at the helm. Moreover, should Bouteflika decide not to amend the constitution to run for a third term because of his illness, his prime minister and FLN leader, Abdelaziz Belkhadem, and the RND's president, also a former prime minister, Ahmed Ouyahia, will have the backing of the army and the president to replace him.

Contestation in the AME is yet to open up opportunities for non-establishment contest of leadership. In Egypt, Libya, and Yemen the incumbents' sons are being groomed for inheriting rule. Despite electoralism, Arab republics increasingly resemble monarchical systems. There is political absolutism. The family has returned as a key player in Arab politics. An understanding of civil society as 'beyond the boundaries of the family and clan' and 'short of the state' is problematic in an Arab setting. The symbiosis of state and clan/family or state/party is largely fixed. Families and clans rule several Arab states (e.g. the eight Arab monarchies). In the largely 'monarchical' republics power could be handed down in a hereditary fashion to the incumbent leaders' male progeny. Libya's only organizations that resemble NGOs are founded and led by Qadhafi's eldest son, Saif al-Islam, and daughter, Aicha. Civil and political societies are the exclusive bastion of one family. Thus clan/family solidarity continues to intertwine in the making and unmaking of power and the marking out of the political. Ibn Khaldun is correct. Tunisia's fourteenth-century philosopher of history deploys the concept of social solidarity; tribal kinship (*'aṣabiyyah*) to impart his appreciation of the dynamic of social cohesiveness or lack thereof in the processes of state making and unmaking.[65] The social bond that obtains from tribal solidarity engenders state making. The notion of tribal solidarity persists and is entangled in the political process in the modern AME.[66] For Salamé it hinders democracy in the AME.[67] Electoralism has not in any way refigured the contractual arrangements for leadership recruitment. Tribe/clan/family and, to an extent, ruling party, and the solidarity and loyalty each implies for statecraft, are not affected by electoralism. Lebanon, where consociational democracy is yet to function properly, political recruitment draws on family and on confessional loyalties. Leaders are born in the country's historical political families (Maronite, Sunni, and Druze). Only the Shi'ite community, for long the have-nots and underrepresented of Lebanon, has no model of 'political feudalism'. Thus at once the Arab world's socially most pluralist country is also the most feudal politically. The result is a dysfunctionally pilloried system. In this case, Lebanese electoralism serves and maintains the confessional political system, not democratic transformation. This is in spite of the fact that Lebanon ironically owes its pluralism to the confessional system, which has created multiple vibrant and self-regenerating civil and confessional societies.[68] Citizens are cemented to these societies to which they turn for protection, identification, and political socialization. The state, by comparison, is weak. Thus Lebanon's brand of electoralism is also confessional.

Egypt in 2007 is looking more like Egypt just before the 1952 revolution. There is a quasi 'king' heading the state. There is antagonism in state–society relations. Uncertainty has engulfed civil society, which is increasingly besieged by legal and physical draconian political management. The associations of lawyers, judges, and journalists all have ongoing disputes with the state. The constitutional amendments have, for instance, taken election monitoring away from the judges who disclosed publicly systematic widespread rigging in the 2005 elections. Ayman Nour of Al-Ghad Party in Egypt is languishing in prison for alleged fraudulence in the registration of his party. He is thus far the only non-establishment presidential hopeful to receive 10 per cent in Egypt's first multi-candidate contest against Mubarak in 2005. Competitive presidential elections are an exaggeration. A case in point is the October 1999 elections in which Bin Ali won his third and theoretically last five-year presidential term. Unlike in the two previous presidential plebiscites, two handpicked candidates from the opposition, Muhammad Bilhaj Amor (leader of the Popular Unity Party) and Abd al-Rahman Talili (head of Unionist Democratic Union), ran against him. Between them they scored less than 1 per cent of the vote. Non-establishment politicians such as Munsif al-Marzuqi, a human rights activist, and Abd al-Rahman al-Hani, a known lawyer, were both prevented from standing against Bin Ali in 1999. Bin Ali received 94.5 per cent. Al-Ghannushi seized on the moment: 'Had Bin Ali been intelligent, he would have today been a hero in Tunisia. All he had to do was to win no more than 70 per cent of the vote'.[69] The tendency to reduce the margin of winning in presidential elections visible in Algeria, Egypt, Mauritanian, and Yemen has not been recorded in Tunisia. Moreover, in 2002, through a referendum, Bin Ali abolished the cap on two-term presidential mandates, effectively, becoming a president-for-life, just as was his predecessor. Elections in this Maghribi state approximate the presidential referendums of Syria. Elections are non-eventful; and they are about confirming and rewarding Ba'thist loyalty not contestation of power or participation. The only positive aspect is the one-third quota of independent candidates in the 250-member parliament introduced in 1990. The remaining two-thirds go to the Nationalist Progressive Front (Al-Jabhah al-Taqaddumiyyah), led by the Ba'ath Party. Nonetheless, one analyst refers to these contests as being a case of 'elections without politics'.[70]

The gendered nature of polity visible in the Arab Gulf is less acute in that part of the AME where electoralism is undergoing a process of routinization. It is here that the only female political party leaders have emerged (two in Mauritania; two in Tunisia; one in Algeria; one in Morocco). Also, women either through a quota system (Morocco), appointment and elections (Egypt), and elections affirmative action (Tunisia, Syria) enter elected assemblies and councils. Basically, forms of 'male' and 'state' feminisms abound. These are modes of co-optation more than inclusiveness. Partisan women's entry into parliament is instructive. Being in parliament and having the opportunity to perform as an equal to male deputies are two totally different things. A pioneering work with a feminist perspective on democratization in the AME is the empirical comparative analysis of the parliamentary performance of female MPs in Egypt, Syria, and Tunisia. The study confirms the inequality between male and female parliamentarians.[71] Even in what is theoretically a public institutional space, women are allocated a place and a role in parliament. Partisanship prevents women from voicing criticism of regimes, for instance. Also, women are more or less seen to suit certain debates and not others. Subjects of 'high politics' are marked patriarchal territories. Yet, in terms of numbers, the three countries' parliaments would suggest that substantive inclusiveness is happening in these fairly women-friendly societies.

Conclusion

A striking feature of the Arab world today is a burning sense of impatience, bordering on revolt, with the existing state of affairs. The thirst for change is palpable. From one end of the region to the other—and with very few exceptions—the Arabs are unhappy with the way they are governed. In several countries there is a feeling that an explosion is near. When the Egyptians cry *kifaya!* (enough!)—they are expressing a mood of defiance and insubordination, which is to be found, in one form or another, in many different Arab centres of population. Perhaps the main grievance feeding the movement is the repressive nature of most Arab regimes.[72]

Electoralism has not yet put an end to the state of affairs described in the quote above. However, elections now are conducted in the entire Arab world. The explosion of elections may approximate a 'wave' of reform. Regardless, electoralism in the 1998–2008 period seems to be about democratic self-packaging: having the veneer of democracy without having to be democratic. This is akin to Salamé's phrase about the quest for good government in the AME as being a case of 'democracy without democrats'.[73] Electoralism qua elections is not totally worthless, whether in the stages of initiation or routinization. Elections are meant to reproduce democratic government not authoritarian rule.

They are not in the AME. This is what I have attempted to highlight by going beyond the veneer of elections and election fetishism. Electoralism is undermined by the absence of principled commitment to either deeper contestation or wider inclusiveness. There are measures of pluralist politics. However, singularity has not receded. The standard of equal opportunity for organizing and representing difference that renders a particular liberalizing experiment congenial to or at odds with democracy is still absent. Recognition and inclusion of difference, vital for a multilevel democratic community capable of deliberation, aggregation, and representation of public preferences, is the missing link in the chain of Arab electoralism. A redistribution of power mediated by electoralism will continue to elude the AME in the absence of recognition of difference, an associate of pluralism. Electoralism is operationalized in environments where state-holders manage reform and decide its scope and content. It labours under the duress of existing social and political realities none of which support substantive democratic transformation. There is no single form of electoralism in the AME. Electoralism is subject to specificity. This variable specificity presents democratic opportunities and constraints.

The constitutional reforms, reconciliation packages (e.g. Algeria, Morocco), universal suffrage (Arab Gulf), regular and frequent elections, multi-candidate presidential contests, and multi-partyism all have the potential to guide Arab electoralism away from authoritarian rule. The constraints are legion. Occupation, violence and counter violence, extremism and terrorism, regime brutality, discrimination, nepotism, sectarianism, and gendered societies. In particular, regimes in the AME continue to *possess* the democratic process. They appropriate and deploy all state resources to reproduce their power without much serious competition. In fact, it is no exaggeration to say that electoralism, being the creation of regimes, has become another state resource that the ruling elites use for legitimation purposes within and without. Electoralism does not thus far seem to commit the rulers to governing without recourse to coercive or traditional tools (patronage-clientelism, patrimonial, corporatist, personalist, and tribal tendencies), much less co-governing. The upshot is tailor-made 'electoral' brands of authoritarianism that vary in cosmetic as well as in substantive form and content across the vast AME geography. Generally, electoralism has yet to erode the authoritarian structures of the state. In the absence of a de-gendered society and polity, dynamically associational life, law-abiding government, free press and freely organized opposition, the gains will remain limited.

What is certain is that the top-down institutional reform unfolding in the AME disproves third wave assumptions about transition.

Peaceful transfers of power have yet to take place. Elections must happen. But besides taking place they have to be juxtaposed with other essentially qualitative criteria in order to promote smooth and multileveled democratic transition. In the case of the AME, such a transition is likely to be 'open-ended, complex and contingent'. The electoralism I have described is far from linearity. Diamond's notion of hybrid political systems whose ambiguous democratic transition defies classification applies to Arab electoralism, especially in states in a stage of routinization.[74] That is, Arab electoralism manifests polyarchal aspects of limited contestation and inclusiveness but without the supporting freedoms that produce substantive democratic transition. As though, by engineering state-led electoralism, Arab states step into what Brumberg calls the 'trap of liberalized autocracy', a mix of 'guided pluralism', 'controlled elections', and 'selective repression'.[75] They are staple items on the 'menu of manipulation', designed to be instruments of authoritarian control.[76] The electoralism of the 1998–2008 period was preceded by a discontinuous brand of electoral authoritarianism. It represents an important background without which current electoralism can neither be fully appreciated nor evaluated. In the next chapter I turn to unpacking this background, by focusing on the vacillation between reform and breakdown in the electoralism of the 1975–97 period.

Notes

1. United Nations Development Programme, Arab Human Development Report 2004 (New York: UNDP Regional Bureau for Arab States, 2005), 9.
2. For further details on this tendency, see Michael Hudson, 'Democratization and the Problem of Legitimacy in Middle East Politics', MESA Bulletin, 22/2 (December 1988). Also see, Yahya Sadowski, 'The New Orientalism and the Democracy Debate', *Middle East Report*, No. 183 (July–August 1993), 14–21, 40.
3. Mervat F. Hatem, *The Nineteenth Century Discursive Roots of the Continuing Debate on the Social Contract in Today's Egypt* (Florence: European University Institute, Robert Schuman Centre for Advanced Studies, 2002); Denise Kandiyoti, *Women, Islam and the State* (Philadelphia: Temple University, 1991); *Sondra* Hale, 'The Wing of Patriarch: Sudanese Women and Revolutionary Parties', *Middle East Report*, 16/1 (January–February 1988), 27–8.
4. Larbi Sadiki, 'The Search for Citizenship in Bin Ali's Tunisia: Democracy versus Unity', *Political Studies*, 50/3 (August 2002), 497–513.

5. Clement Henry Moore and Robert Springborg, *Globalization and the Politics of Development in the Middle East* (Cambridge: Cambridge University Press, 2001).

6. See Samuel P. Huntington, 'Democracy's Third Wave', *Journal of Democracy*, 2 (Spring 1991).

7. See the fine article by Michael C. Hudson where he rejects this notion, 'After the Gulf War: Prospects for Democratization in the Arab World', *Middle East Journal*, 45 (Summer 1991), 407–26. See also Michael C. Hudson, 'State, Society, and Legitimacy: An Essay on Arab Political Prospects in the 1990s', in Hisham Sharabi (ed.), *The Next Arab Decade* (Boulder: Westview Press, 1988). Also, refer to the observation by Alan Richards that 'many analysts find phrases like "Arab democracy" or "Islamic democracy" oxymoronic'. See his, 'Economic Pressures for Accountable Governance in the Middle East and North Africa', in Augustus R. Norton (ed.), *Civil Society in the Middle East* (Leiden: E. J. Brill, 1995), 55.

8. See, for instance, introduction by Ellis Goldberg, Resat Kasaba and Joel S. Migdal, in Ellis Goldberg et al. (eds.), *Rules and Rights in the Middle East: Democracy, Law and Society* (Seattle: University of Washington Press, 1993), 3–14; for a good insight into Western views of Arab democratization see Jean-Claude Vatin, 'Les partis démocratiques:—perceptions occidentales de la démocratisation dans le monde arabe' [The Democratic Parties: Western Perceptions of Arab Democratization] *Egypte/Monde Arabe*, 4 (1990), 9–24. See also the article by Bernard Lewis, in which Turkey is regarded to be the only Islamic democracy: 'Why Turkey is the Only Muslim Democracy', *Middle East Quarterly*, 1 (March 1994), 41–9.

9. Mustapha K. Al-Sayyid, 'The Third Wave of Democratization in the Arab World', in Dan Tschirgi (ed.), *The Arab World Today* (Boulder: Lynne Rienner, 1994), 179–89.

10. Ibid. 179.

11. Ibid.

12. Hisham B. Sharabi, 'The Crisis of the Intelligentsia in the Middle East', in Richard H. Nolte (ed.), *The Modern Middle East* (New York: Atherton Press, 1963), 147.

13. Al-Sayyid, 'The Third Wave of Democratization in the Arab World', 179–80.

14. Ibid. 180.

15. Ibid.

16. The nexus between democracy and the renaissance era is suggested by Ahmad Sidqi al-Dajjani in *'Tatawuru mafahimu al-dimuqratiyyah fi al-fikri al-arabi al-ḥadīth'* [The Evolution of the Concept of Democracy in the Modern Arab World], in Saad Eddin Ibrahim (ed.), *Azmatu al-dimuqratiyyah fi al-alam al-arabi* (Beirut: Markaz Dirasat al-Wihdah al-Arabiyyah, 1984), 115.

17. Elie Kedourie, *Democracy and Arab Political Culture* (Washington, DC: The Washington Institute for Near East Policy, 1992), 14. Compare with Albert Hourani who cites the year 1860 not 1861; see his, *Arabic Thought in the Liberal Age: 1798–1939* (London: Oxford University Press, 1962), 64–5.

18. Kedourie explains how Muhammad Bey's Grand Council, an unelected body, was by dint of the 1861 constitution, 'empowered to approve the enactment of new, and the amendment of old laws'. Kedourie, *Democracy and Arab Political Culture*, pp. 14–16.

19. For a general survey of the reforms in these three parts of the Arab world see Steven R. Dorr, 'Democratization in the Middle East', in Robert O. Slater, Barry M. Schutz, and Steven R. Dorr (eds.), *Global Transformation and the Third World* (Boulder and London: Lynne Rienner, 1993), 131–57.

20. See how this term is applied to war in general and to the Second Gulf War in particular in the article by Adeed Dawisha, 'The Gulf War: A Defining Event?', in Tschirgi (ed.), *The Arab World Today*, 123–34.

21. Ali al-din Hilal, '*Al-Dimuqratiyyah wa humum al-'insan al-Arabi al-muasir*' [Democracy and the Concerns of the Modern-Day Arab] in Ali al-din Hilal *et al.*, *Al-Dimuqratiyyah wa huququ al-insan fi al-watani al-arabi* [Democracy and Human Rights in the Arab Homeland] (Beirut: Markaz Dirasat al-Wihdah al-Arabiyyah, 1986), 7.

22. Ibid.

23. See Dawisha, 'The Gulf War: A Defining Event?', 132.

24. See the work by the author of *The Republic of Fear* (then writing under the pseudonym Samir al-Khalil) Kanan Makiya, *Cruelty and Silence: War, Tyranny, Uprising and the Arab World* (London: Penguin Books, 1994). Arab scholar George Juqman cites multiple examples of activities and publications showing the extent of the intellectual discourse on Arab democracy. See his '*Al-Dimuqratiyyah fi nihayati al-qarni al-ishrin: nahwa kharitah fikriyyah*' [Democracy at the End of the Twentieth Century: Towards an Intellectual Map], in Ghalyun et al., *Hawla al-khiyaru al-dimuqrati*, esp. 28–33. On the intellectuals' role in the democratization process throughout the Arab world in general, and in Egypt in particular, see the insightful chapter by Salah al-din Hafiz, '*Al-Dimuqratiyyah wa azmatu al-muthaqqafin*' [Democracy and the Crisis of Intellectuals] in his work *Sadmatu al-dimuqratiyyah* [The Shock of Democracy] (Cairo: Sina" Li-Nashr, 1993), 176–90. Compare with Mundhir Anbatawi, '*Dawru al-nukhbatu al-muthaqqafah fi ta'zizi huquqi a'l-insani al-Arabi*' [The Intelligentsia's Role in Strengthening the Rights of the Arab Citizen] in Ali al-din Hilal et al., *Al-Dimuqratiyyah wa huququ al-insan fi al-watani al-Arabi* [Democracy and Human Rights in the Arab Homeland] (Beirut: Markaz Dirasat al-Wihdah al-Arabiyyah, 1986), 277–312.

25. Huntington, *The Third Wave*, 38.

26. Kedourie, *Democracy and Arab Political Culture*, 16.

27. See Marius Deeb, *Party Politics in Egypt: The Wafd and its Rivals 1919–1939* (London: Ithaca Press, 1979).

28. Huntington, 'Democracy's Third Wave', 13.

29. See Larbi Sadiki, 'The Trials of Democracy: Algeria and Egypt', *Current Affairs Bulletin*, 70 (February 1994), 19–25.

30. Michael Herb, 'Emirs and Parliaments in the Gulf', *Journal of Democracy*, 13/4 (October 2002), 41–7.

31. Abd Allah Abd al-Khaliq, *The Arab Gulf States: Old Approaches and New Realities* (Abu Dhabi: Emirates Centre for Strategic Studies and Research, 2000), 5–40.
32. Francis Gregory Gause, *Political Opposition in the Gulf Monarchies* (San Domenico di Fiesole: European University Institute, 2000), 3–17.
33. Larbi Sadiki, 'Saudi Arabia: Re-reading Politics and Religion in the Wake of September 11', in Shahram Akbarzadeh and Abdullah Saeed (eds.), *Islam and Political Legitimacy* (London: RoutledgeCurzon, 2003), 29–49.
34. Author's interview, Damascus, 2006.
35. David L. Phillips, Losing Iraq (London: Basic Books, 2006).
36. Hassanayn Tawfiq Ibrahim, 'Mu 'awwiqat al-taḥawwul al-dīmuqrāṭī fi al-'Iraq ma ba'da Saddam' [Obstacles to Democratization in Iraq post-Saddam] in Hassanayn Taafiq Ibrahim and Abd Al-Jabbar Ahmad Abdallah (eds.), *Al-Tahawwulat al-Dimuqratiyyah fi al-Iraq: Al-Quyud wa al-Furas* [Democratic Transition in Iraq: Constraints and Opportunities] (Dubai: Markaz Al-Khaleej Lil Abhath, 2005), 44–5.
37. Abd Al-Jabbar Ahmad Abdallah, 'Waqi' wa Mustaqbal al-Khayar Al-Dimuqrati wa al-Dusturi fi al-'Iraq' [The Reality and future of the Democratic and Constitutional Option in Iraq] in Ibid. 90.
38. Richard Falk, 'US Foreign Policy and the Future of the Middle East', in Alex Danchev and John MacMillan (eds.), *The Iraq War and Democratic Politics* (London & New York: Routledge, 2005), 32–3.
39. For further details of UAE labour laws, see Human Rights Watch, 'The UAE's Draft Labour Law: Human Rights Watch's Comments and Recommendations', in *Human rights Watch*, No. 1 (March 2007).
40. C. Simon, 'La Tunisie sous Ben Ali: Un bonheur ambigu' (23 October 1999c), *Le Monde*, p. 14.
41. Ibid. 14.
42. Carnegie Endowment for International Peace, 'Egypt: Referendum Turnout Contested', in *Arab Reform Bulletin*, 5/3 (April 2007).
43. Author's interview, 10 July 2005, Cairo, Egypt.
44. For more details on the status of the Shi'ite in the Arab world see the special issue of the *Middle East Report* (Spring 2007).
45. Author's interview with a former Saudi diplomat, 20 December 2006, London.
46. See 'Ayna Tadhhab amwal al-naft al-arabi?' [Where does Arab Oil Wealth Go?] *Al-Arab*, 17 May 2007, 1.
47. Patrick Seale, 'What Hope for Arab Democracy?' in *Open Democracy*, 21 April 2005.
48. Larry Diamond in 'Viewpoints: Iraq Elections', BBC News, http://news.bbc.co.uk/go/pr/fr/-/1/hi/world/middle_east/4187267.stm, 11/12/05.
49. Azza Galal Hashim, 'Mauritania: Beyond the Presidential Election', in *Arab Reform Bulletin*, 5/3 (April 2007).
50. See Tarek Osman, 'Hosni Mubarak: What the Pharaoh is like', *Open Democracy*, 16 January 2006.

51. See Amnesty International, 'Egypt: Abuses in the Name of Security', Report published on 11 April 2007.
52. Nathan J. Brown, Michele Dunne, and Amr Hamzawy, 'Egypt's Controversial Constitutional Amendments', paper published by the Carnegie Endowment for International Peace, 23 March 2007.
53. UNDP, *Arab Human Development Report, 2004* (New York: UNDP & Regional Bureau for Arab States, 2005), 10.
54. L. Addi, *L'Algérie et la démocratie: Pouvoir et crise du politique dans l'algérie contemporaine* (Paris: La Découverte, 1995).
55. Ibrahim Eissa, 'Egypt: Point/Counterpoint to the Constitutional Amendments—Part II', in *Arab Reform Bulletin*, 5/3 (April 2007).
56. Ibid.
57. Amr Hamzawy, 'The Key to Arab Reform: Moderate Islamists', Carnegie Endowment for International Peace, Working Paper 40 (August 2005).
58. I. Collins, *Liberalism in Nineteenth-Century Europe* (London: Routledge & Kegan Paul), 1–26.
59. Ibid. 11.
60. Ibid. 10–11.
61. Ibid. 11.
62. G. Parry and M. Moran, 'Introduction: Problems of Democracy and Democratization', in Parry, G. and M. Moran (eds.), *Democracy and Democratization* (London: Routledge, 1994), 4.
63. Ibid. 10.
64. William B. Quandt, 'Algeria's Uneasy Peace', *Journal of Democracy*, 13/4 (October 2002), 15–23.
65. Abd al-Rahman Ibn Khaldoun, Trans. by Franz Rosenthal, *The Muqaddimah: An Introduction to History* (London: Routledge & Kegan Paul, 1967), pp. lxxviii–lxxxi.
66. Sami Zubaida, Islam, the People and the State: Essays on Political Ideas and Movements in the Middle East (London: Routledge, 1989).
67. Ghassan Salamé, 'Introduction: Where are the Democrats?', in Ghassan Salamé (ed.), *Democracy Without Democrats: The Renewal of Politics in the Muslim World?* London: I. B. Tauris, 1994), pp. 9–11.
68. Oussama Safa, 'Lebanon Springs Forward', Journal of Democracy, 17/1 (January 2006).
69. Author's interview with Rashid al-Ghannushi, 20 November 1999, London.
70. Omayma Abdel Latif, 'Syria: Elections without Politics', *Arab Reform Bulletin*, 5/3 (April 2007).
71. Nifeen Mis'ad (ed.), Al-Ada'Al-Barlamani Lil-Mar'ah Al-Arabiyyah: Dirasat Halat Misr was Suriya wa Tunis [Parliamentary Performance of the Arab Woman: Case Studies of Egypt, Syria and Tunisia] (Beirut: Markaz Dirasat Al-Wahdah Al-Arabiyyah, 2005).
72. Seale, 'What Hope for Arab Democracy?'
73. Ghassan Salamé (ed.), *Democracy without Democrats? Renewal of Politics in the Muslim World* (London: I. B. Taurus, 1994).

74. Larry Diamond, 'Thinking about Hybrid Regimes', *Journal of Democracy*, 13/2 (April 2002), 21–35.
75. Daniel Brumberg, 'The Trap of Liberalized Autocracy', *Journal of Democracy*, 13/4 (October 2002), 55–68.
76. Andreas Schedler, 'The Menu of Manipulation', *Journal of Democracy*, 13/2 (April 2002), 36–50.

Elections Without Democracy: The False Starts, 1975–97

... Democracy is not so much ritual and the mechanisms of parties, elections, and a free press as it is a spirit and a commitment. The question is not whether the people of Egypt are ready for democracy but whether the regime is prepared to let competing forces achieve power democratically.

Mona Makram-Ebeid, 1989[1]

... The setback (*naksah*) in Arab democratization shows that the demise of dictatorial legitimacy does not automatically mean the rise of democratic legitimacy, or that the preconditions for the realization of democratic legitimacy exist. It rather suggests a historical opening to potentially reorder and change the rules of Arab politics.

Burhan Ghalyun, 1994[2]

No understanding of Arab reform is complete without an examination of the democratic stirrings that took place between 1975 and 1997. They are the backdrop against which current reforms must be read, providing referential material for pinpointing continuity and discontinuity. My first task here is to highlight their significance as well as their inherent contradictions (e.g. elections without inclusiveness) and fault-lines (e.g. political vs. economic reform). To this end, I shall evaluate the democratic initiatives of the 1975–97 period both quantitatively and qualitatively. I will briefly consider the matrix within which they were incubated. I note that elections were central to them and 'electoralism' is their quintessence. Principally, I will argue that the process of Arab liberalization is 'one where progress is followed by retrogression, that is, reversal or partial reversal of earlier democratic gains'.[3] Hence Arab democratic development is not linear. It remains subject to the vicissitudes of Arab domestic politics, to the rulers' whims, and, accordingly, to either retrogression or total retraction. The progressive, retrogressive, and retractive patterns characterizing Arab liberalizations are interpreted here by using the Khaldunian notion of attack/hit (*karr*) and withdrawal/run (*farr*).[4] This Khaldunian phrase encapsulates the crux of democratic advances and retreats or reform and breakdown in Arab liberalizations. Democratic advances between 1975 and 1997 are in many instances signposted by phases of top-down reform (*iṣlāḥ*) or open-door policy (*infitāḥ*)—*karr*—followed by phases of reversal or retreat (*taqahqur*)—*farr*. Democratic development in the AME cannot be said to be unilinear.[5]

Elections Without Democracy

The scope of the democratic stirrings of the 1975–97 period throughout much of the AME was quasi-revolutionary. Those stirrings were perhaps indicative of Arab polities' responses to the latest democratic wave or pressure at home. They were not in any case suggestive of a more serious political reconfiguration, further entrenching the stereotype of a region inhospitable to change. Nonetheless, the statistics and figures were impressive. When considered together, the impact of those reforms was evident in the degree to which they deceptively approximate a wave of democratization—defined by Huntington to be:

A group of transitions from nondemocratic to democratic regimes that occur within a specified period of time; [they] significantly outnumber transitions in the opposite direction during that period of time. A wave also usually involves liberalization or partial democratization in political systems that do not become fully democratic.[6]

Despite occurrences of breakdown as in Sudan, Algeria, and intermittently in Kuwait, the 1975–97 period is marked by a core of 'partial democratizers' or 'semi-democratizers' (Algeria, Egypt, Jordan, Kuwait, Lebanon, Mauritania, Morocco, Sudan, Tunisia, and Yemen). Kuwait is an obvious exception to prevalent political norms in the Gulf oil-rich monarchies, which still did not favour liberalization in the 1975–95 period.[7] These 'semi-democratizers' represented the most identifiable Arab component of political reformism. They gave continuity to the onerous and challenging task of promoting greater contestation, participation and accountability in Arab governance. Their incipient transitions towards more democratic forms of government outnumbered those in the opposite direction, namely, the reverses of democratization in the two hitherto most notable Arab experiments—Sudan and Algeria. However, those reforms also met the criterion that

distinguishes 'fully democratic' from those that are only 'partial'—
as a wave, the degree to which they have a maximum, potential,
or actual reach. The reforms of the period in question were concentrated in the populous and lesser-to-do Arab states, as elaborated
below.

Crafting Democracy in the Lesser-to-do AME

The pointers of Arab reform are legion. None, however, is perhaps
more tangible than the torrent of electoral activities. The flurry of
electoral politics was both unprecedented and impressive. Elections
were held in urbanized and semi-industrialized Egypt as well as in
tribal Mauritania and Yemen. Since the mid-1980s more multiparty
elections took place than in the entire preceding history of the AME.
With no precedent in electoral politics, Mauritania held no less than
four elections between 1988 and 1992. In January 1988, local government elections were held in some 32 districts; in January 1990,
local elections took place in 164 rural communes; in January 1992 the
country held the Arab world's first multiparty presidential elections;
and in February 1992 six political parties and some 223 candidates
contested Mauritania's 79-seat National Assembly.[8] Again, elections
for the Assembly took place in 1995 and presidential ones in 1997.
United Yemen was another example of a political unit hardly versed in
pluralist politics that held multiparty elections in April 1993.[9] Despite
the setback because of the 1994 sixty-day war between northerners
and southerners, the democratic process was resumed with the parliamentary elections of April 1997. Between 1986 and 1995 the number of
Arab multiparty states almost trebled. This period had not only seen
a dramatic surge towards competitive politics but had also heralded
the most remarkable results yet in the history of Arab reform.[10] Of
these, Sudan's April 1986 parliamentary elections remain an unprecedented benchmark: the opposition led by the Ummah Party of Sadiq
al-Mahdi won government.[11] Algeria's first multiparty elections were
another instance of unparalleled Arab democratic achievement. The
stunning provincial and municipal elections of June 1990 were a blow
to the country's ruling *Front de libération Nationale* (FLN), and the
first round of the December 1991 multiparty parliamentary elections
put the *Front Islamique du Salut* (FIS) on the verge of victory.[12]
Jordan's elections of November 1993 were the country's first multiparty elections in nearly 40 years.[13] Like those in Yemen they were
inclusive with legalized Islamist candidates contesting and winning
seats, and also with women entering parliament for the first time.[14] No

women entered parliament in the November 1997 elections which were boycotted by the major political parties and the Islamist opposition. The boycott, however, did not sabotage the electoral process. Lebanon's August–September 1992 three-phase National Assembly elections not only effectively signalled the return to centralized politics but also a revival of pluralism, which remains integral to the country's national identity—given its religious diversity.[15] The 1996 parliamentary elections along with the mid-1998 local elections served to consolidate the electoral process and deepen political reform.

Similarly, Tunisia's elections of March 1994 were eventful with opposition parties entering parliament for the first time in the country's history. After descent into autocratic rule for respectively seven and nine years, in Kuwait (October 1992) and Morocco (June 1993), returned to electoral politics. Egypt, viewed by some as the 'trailblazer' of Arab democratization,[16] launched the 'third wave' of Arab political reform in 1975, through the creation of political platforms (*manābir*), following that with the elections of 1976.[17] Although Egypt is hardly a shining model of democracy, it has since then held periodic elections. It remains the only Arab country to maintain electoral politics for more than 30 years.

Distinction ought to be made between 'strong' and 'weak' Arab electoral performers. The emergence of multiparty politics in this group of Arab 'third-wave' 'semi-democratizers' encouraged very tempered optimism. The same could not be said about the cosmetic elections and proclamations of multipartyism in Iraq and Syria. In both countries the military-bureaucratic Ba'thist state did not seem to be vulnerable to the pressures for change sweeping other parts of the Arab world. In April 1990 Iraq held what on the surface appeared to be pluralist elections noted for the participation of minor parties.[18] Syria followed suit a month later.[19] According to one interpretation the resilience of the personalist minority-based power monopoly in Iraq is owed to the domestic 'legalism of repression', and its constraints on mass politics and on civil society, and to international law's complacency towards repression.[20] Not even the sanctions of the 1990s lessened such resilience in Iraq. In Syria, despite 'political decompression' which had, *inter alia*, entailed a 'freer press', the re-emergence of Ba'thist rhetoric on democracy, lesser stress on draconian tactics, greater religious autonomy, and the regime's recruitment of clientele, especially members of the entrepreneurial and business class, from outside the party,[21] the 'Bonapartist'[22] state still exerted an all-pervasive influence impervious to the currents of political reform in the region. Economic reform was more of a priority, creating a faultline between political and economic reform, as shall be explained below.

Economic versus Political Liberalization

In Ba'thist states there evidently existed a process of economic liberalization without parallel political liberalization. Here the lines between 'semi-democratizers' and 'non-democratizers' become fairly blurred. Almost invariably in all cases of Arab liberalization the economic supersedes the political. Jumping on the economic liberalization bandwagon, especially for the more indebted Arab states such as Algeria, Egypt, Morocco, and Tunisia, was not entirely the corollary of sovereign choice. It was to a great extent conditioned by the wider transformative trend of globalizing the market.

This process has been referred to as 'the new neocolonialism'—an intense dependence on the International Monetary Fund, the World Bank, and major Western countries for the design of economic reform packages and the resources needed to implement them. This leverage has been converted into intensive economic policy conditionality: specific economic policy changes in return for borrowed resources. The primary thrust of these reform efforts is to integrate [third world] economies more fully into the world economy...through a more 'liberal' political economy.[23]

As in the case of Sub-Saharan Africa, although perhaps with much less rigour and without specific programmes except for one inchoate project to sell democracy to the Arab world, political conditionality[24]— more democratic rule—is increasingly seen by external actors as an essential concomitant of economic conditionality.[25] This position is equally adopted by Orientalists in their discourse on governance and democracy in the AME. Nowhere does the discourse even allude to the possibility that perhaps the prospects for democratization hinge on ecologically sustainable development that precludes an out-and-out free market economy. It seems that the dossier of whether alternative economic systems—that may potentially reinforce democratic achievements—can be found has been indefinitely shelved off. Richards argues:

... Successful economic liberalization will require increased political participation in some form. I shall make an 'instrumentalist' case for greater citizen political activity...Coping with the challenges of the food, jobs, and investment will require greater integration into the international economy; such economic changes imply enlarging the role of the private sector, widening the scope of the rule of the law, and more generally restructuring the state's relations with its citizens. In short, expanded political participation will be a necessary tool in the struggle to forge a successful 'Arab'...capitalism in the information age.[26]

One serious limitation of this 'instrumentalist' or 'functional' advocacy of democratization through capitalism in the Arab world is its inherent support of the status quo. More capitalism does not necessarily translate into more genuine or more just democracy. At this juncture it appears that capitalism is accorded first order on the agendas of Arab 'semi-democratizers' and 'non-democratizers'. Although it must be noted that the East Asian crisis, which precipitated the fall of the Soharto regime in Indonesia, put a damper on Arab enthusiasm for Asian tigers-type development. Steven Heydemann, for instance, has rightly challenged the conventional wisdom resting on the assumption that the success of, or prospects, for economic liberalization depend on corresponding political liberalization.[27] The first does not always imply the second.[28] The rigour with which Arab 'semi-democratizers', in particular, and 'non-democratizers', in general, have approached economic liberalization far outstrips that of political liberalization. In elaborating this thesis, Heydemann offers a series of explanations the gist of which supports this view. Heydemann's starting point rejects the notion of a linkage between state and society equally negotiating and striking a 'democratic bargain' the upshot of which is political and economic liberalization.[29] According to the 'democratic bargain' thesis authoritarian regimes, finding it highly liable and taxing to engage in economic reforms with usually dire consequences for many social groups, enter into a 'bargaining' process through the recruiting of partners and the enlisting of wider societal support, a process that entails arrangements for political reform. For Heydemann the resulting 'enforced limited pluralism'[30] is a very good first approximation of a 'social pact' as against a 'social contract'.[31] A social pact lends itself to two conditions that are compatible with authoritarian politics: it neither requires 'public justification' nor requires more than a 'select set of actors'.[32] Hence Heydemann observes that, first, given the nature of authoritarian political management there is nothing to inhibit power holders from liberalizing economically and, second, and subsequently, 'there are a few imperatives that compel authoritarian elites to adopt a democratizing strategy if their aim is simply to liberalize their economies.'[33] Accordingly, three dynamics which explicate more plausibly Arab economic liberalizations are

... (1) corporatist liberalization, or economic reform as a process of coalition management among a restricted set of institutional actors; (2) imposed liberalization, or economic reform as a defensive response to pressure from international lending agencies; and (3) selective liberalization, or economic reform as a process of establishing semi private bargains between regime elites and a limited set of private sector investors.[34]

In applying his analysis to Syria's open-door policy begun in the mid-1980s, Heydemann shows that the rulers had not set out to 'legitimate'

106 *Elections Without Democracy*

the state's very limited decentralization of economic command through greater and more genuine participation and competition. Instead, he argues, the rulers, eager to minimize the destabilizing potential of economic reforms, had, via 'selective and corporatist liberalization', increased the autonomy of those recruited private investors without decreasing their own political power. Capital accumulation was thus at the core of the whole exercise, Heydemann contends, with the power holders aiming at boosting their own surplus extractive capacity—the means by which they could reproduce the state.[35] The most noticeable linkage between the political and the economic in the Syrian experiment was not one where economic and political liberalizations mutually reinforced each other. Rather, the regime's overriding imperative was to shield the existing order from the political damage that could result from the new economic reforms.[36]

The clear prioritization of economic over political liberalization was not cause for being sanguine about the future of democratization in Syria. If the crux of economic reform seemed to be no more than a political utility designed to provide the greatest happiness to the smallest number (power holders, political and economic), the same applied in varying degrees to similar Arab undertakings. In fact, just as in the 1960s state-led modernization was inaugurated via coups (*inqilābāt*) and revolutions (*thawrāt*), in the 1980s and 1990s the modest and inchoate top-down reforms (*iṣlāḥāt*) were preceded by programmes of open-door policy (*infitāhat*, pl. of *infitāh*). Hence economic reforms[37] were initiated in Syria, Iraq, Jordan, Tunisia, Egypt, and Algeria, for instance, long before political reforms. President Chadhli Benjedid's 'de-Boumediennization' (his predecessor was President Boumedienne), in Algeria, and al-Sadat's 'de-Nasserization' (after President Nasser), in Egypt, constituted the first tinkering with liberalization, especially economic.[38] Hence they were first attempts at ditching failed brands of Arab socialism.[39] With regard to ditching socialism al-Sadat's open-door policy was a pace-setter in the Arab world.[40] Limited economic disengagement was pursued more seriously with regard to economy than polity in both countries. In both, economic liberalization preceded the pluralizing initiatives. Liberalization in both countries, especially in Algeria, caused limited state shrinkage in economic management. Al-Sadat's programme[41] sought to charter that path. Mubarak's more or less timid open-door policy[42] freed exchange rates in October 1991 and later on liberalized pricing policy on cotton and labour relations. Mubarak proceeded to privatize a number of state-owned enterprises, singling out medium and small-sized industries for sale. Privatization[43] gained momentum with the creation in 1992 of 27 holding companies in charge of 85 per cent of the country's manufacturing assets. Today the agenda of down-sizing public assets is led by the new technocrats recruited by and allied with Gamal Mubarak, Egypt's 'heir apparent'.

The faster pace with which Arab economies were being liberalized at the time should not, however, mask the significance of the attempts at political renewal in the semi-democratizing states. One point must be illuminated. Like economic reforms, Arab political openings were not strictly a matter of choice. The dynamics at their core range from stifling authoritarianism to deterioration of basic social services and popular unrest in response to a changing world order. External patrons and sponsorship of authoritarianism decreased; and international pressure for pluralization and good governance mounted. The route most Arab states had to follow was that of 'electoralism'. I now turn to explain how democratic initiatives of that period routinized a process of 'electoralism'. As I have explained in the previous chapter, electoralism denotes an explosion of cosmetic elections everywhere but no substantive democracy to speak of anywhere in the AME. This superficiality typifies election fetishism.

'Electoralism'

As noted above, electoral politics were the most unmistakably positive signs of Arab reform in the 1975–97 period. Thus certain dates constitute benchmarks along the Arab path of electoral politics. The years 1976, 1981, 1986, 1992, and 1993 were momentous events for reform in, respectively, Egypt, Tunisia, Sudan, Lebanon, and Jordan. The elections held in those years interrupted the prolonged hiatus of 'non-democracy'. The last multiparty elections took place back in 1950 in Egypt;[44] in 1959 in Tunisia;[45] in 1968 in Sudan; in 1956 in Jordan;[46] and in 1972 in Lebanon. Electorally, the years 1977 and 1981 meant a reactivation of parliamentary life in both Morocco and Kuwait. The elections of 1990 and 1991 in Algeria; 1992 in Mauritania; and 1993 in Yemen inaugurated competitive party politics. Whereas these elections had, more or less, signalled the onset of a quasi re-electoralism of, for instance, Egypt, Lebanon, Tunisia, Jordan, and Morocco, elsewhere, as in Algeria, Yemen, and Mauritania, they represented, even if ephemerally, a first swing away from non-party and non-participatory politics. The most significant upshot of the electoral process was not its potentially corrosive effect on the edifice of the Arab monolithic party (or clan) state as much as it was the immediate institutionalization of elections and their regularity. Between October/November 1976 and November/December 1990 Egypt held five elections for the country's main legislature—People's Assembly (*Majlis al-Sha'b*). That was an average of nearly one election every three years. This average does not take into account presidential and local elections, or the four for the Advisory Council (*Majlis al-Shūrā*) between September 1980 and June 1989. The number of presidential elections rose since 1989 (Algeria: 1995 and 1998; Egypt: 1993; Mauritania: 1992 and 1997; Sudan: 1996; and Tunisia: 1989 and 1994).

The gap between elections decreased markedly in both Tunisia and Jordan. In the former the gap was 22 years between the first post-independence multiparty elections of 1959 and those held in 1981; then 8 years between 1981 and 1989; and finally less than 5 years between November 1989 and March 1994. In the latter the interval separating the Monarchy's last multiparty elections of 1956 and the quasi pluralist (non-party) polls of 1989 was 33 years. That interval was dropped to as low as four years with the country's first multiparty elections held in 1993.[47] Shorter intervals between elections are noticeable in Kuwait and Morocco, two countries who respectively resumed the electoral process in 1992 and 1993. Kuwait held elections in 1996 and Morocco in 1997, effectively making their elections periodic rather than sporadic and discontinuous. These elections represented continuous and unprecedented drills in political and electoral habituation for the Arab citizen.

Proliferation of political parties (*ahzāb siyāsiyyah*)[48] and the rise of partyism (*al-hizbiyyah*) had, through the electoral process begun during this period, contributed to the emergence of both de facto and relatively 'de jure parliamentarization' of Arab politics. The fact of oppositional forces being able to organize, mobilize, field candidates, contest elections, and enter parliament was a positive testimony to the gradual rolling back of single-party rule and autocracy in general. The parliaments of Egypt, Jordan, Yemen, Lebanon, Mauritania, and Tunisia (and Algeria had the initial free and fair electoral process proceeded) acquired forms of institutionalized opposition whose performance, strength, resourcefulness, and independence were still weak. The number of legal parties in Egypt increased to 14 in 1997. However, this numerical advantage translated neither into a rise in the number of deputies in parliament nor into a wider space of the public domain. The role of the opposition to check government was, more or less, clear, even if difficult, in some instances (Egypt, Jordan, Morocco) and remained blurred in others with a quasi loyal opposition (Tunisia) or a form of a coalescence of interests (Kuwait and to a lesser degree Yemen). A welcome initiative was the Moroccan monarch's (the late Hassan II) choice of a veteran opposition leader and human rights activist ('Abd al-Rahman al-Yusufi, leader of the Socialist Union of

Popular Forces) to form a new government following the November 1997 legislative (325-seat Lower House) elections.

In Lebanon those new forces which were conceived in the course of the civil war[49] emerged in the post-war period as formidable power claimants and contestants. These new power claimants embodied the Shi'ite community's demands for inclusiveness, while articulating anti-system (Maronite-dominated) stances. Hence 'Amal and Hezbollah benefited from the new power arrangements, not to mention the Christian boycott (together they received 27 seats) that replaced the old parliamentary 6:5 ratio favouring Christians. The new law passed on 16 July 1992 provided for equal share of seats in the Chamber of Deputies between Muslims and Christians by raising the number of the seats from 108 to 128.[50] In Tunisia the so-called National Pact hammered out between the government and the secular opposition in November 1988 took effect in the March 1994 elections with the maiden entry into the National Assembly of four opposition movements.[51]

A significant feature of Arab electoral politics was electoral participation by independents. Examples can be conjured up in the Algerian December 1991 first round elections for the 430-seat National Assembly in which 3 seats were taken by independents. In the April 1993 Yemeni House of Representatives elections independents, with 47 seats, established themselves as the fourth largest political power—following the General People's Congress (121); the YRR (62); and the Yemeni Socialist Party (56). In Tunisia, independents proved their potential political weight on two occasions. In the June 1990 municipal elections, which were boycotted by opposition groups, independents won 34 seats as against 3,716 by the ruling Democratic Constitutional Rally (RCD). Most significant, however, were the April 1989 multiparty legislative elections—Islamist independents received over 20 per cent of the total vote thus displacing the secular Movement of Socialist Democrats (MDS) as the country's main political force after the RCD.[52] In Egypt the inclusion of independents in the electoral process was new.[53] The government's ban on their activities was revoked after the 1984 elections. In the April 1987 People's Assembly elections independents captured seven seats, whereas in the December 1990 elections the independents' intake, although much higher, was blunted by their co-optation by government.[54] By Arab standards, given the relative resistance to change or its incremental nature, those electoral experiments—regardless of their freedom and fairness, or the lack thereof, and of their substantive outcomes—signalled attitudinal change at leadership level. In the future, as electoral institutions were being routinized, the ballot—rather than the bullet, self-endorsement, or hereditary succession—would define the contours of power and of power holders. This remains a challenge that has thus far been risen to only in Mauritania 2007 presidential elections.

No less important are the legal reforms. Wide-ranging new laws as well as constitutional reforms, favouring at least in theory more open government or competitive politics, were introduced. In 1992 the House of Saud, then still reeling under the negative impact of the 1991 Gulf War that compromised Saudi sovereignty and added to the financial troubles already brewing from Royal profligacy,[55] and under growing local pressure for more equitable sharing of oil wealth and political power,[56] codified the principles of governance. This act, the first of its kind since the monarchy's creation as a united political realm in 1932, approximated a written constitution.[57] The principles were made public in King Fahd's March 1992 speech in which he decreed reforms outlining the Basic System of Governance (al-niẓām al-asāsī lil hukm), the Consultative Council System (niẓām majlis al-shūrā); and the System of Local Administration (niẓām al-manāṭiq).[58] After 32 years of broken promises, Saudi Arabia finally in 1994 got its 60-member Consultative Council—a positive step in the direction of broader participation. Another monarchy, Morocco, had more constitutional reforms than any other Arab state (see Table 3.1). The reform approved in a 1996 referendum, created a bi-cameral parliament. Elections for the chamber of councilors/upper house (majlis al-mustashārīn) were held in December 1997.

Lebanon's Document of National Understanding, the pact popularly known as the Ta'if Accord ratified by the Chamber of Deputies in September 1990 subsequent to its signing in 1989 in Ta'if resort, Saudi Arabia, was not without constitutional significance. This is despite well-placed scepticism that it augured well for both de-confessionalism and secular democracy[59] or for reconciliation and sovereignty.[60] Notwithstanding this scepticism, the Accord provided a preliminary utility for the re-operationalization of state institutions, as through total or partial disarming of the sectarian militias, and for the revival of civil society and resumption of electoral politics. The culmination of the latter was the 1992 elections. The Accord, at least in theory, committed Lebanon's 'communitarian alliances'[61] to (1) parliamentary parity between Christians and Muslims; (2) major limitations on the President's executive powers; (3) more authoritative parliament and council of ministers; (4) redistricting electorates 'on the basis of Muhafadah [province], with its larger and communally mixed electorates'; (5) judicial reform presaging the creation of two supreme and constitutional courts; and (6) administrative decentralization.[62]

Table 3.1 Arab 'electoralism', 1975–97

Year	Egypt	Morocco	Sudan	Algeria	Jordan	Mauritania	Tunisia	Lebanon	Yemen	Kuwait
1997	LE	ME			ME				ME	
1996			E					ME		E
1995	ME		LE		LE	ME	LE			
1994							ME*		CW	
1993	PL	OME			ME*				ME*	
1992	PL	CR		C			ME*		PL	E
1991				ME*	CR	CR		Taif Imp.	CR	GW
1990	ME			LF			LE		Merger	TC
1989			C		E		ME	Taif Acc.		
1988				CR	PD	E				
1987	ME						C			
1986	EL		ME*				E			PD
1985							Infitah			
1984		OME		AR						
1983							PL			
1982										
1981	Mubarak									E
1980		CR		Infitah						
1979				Chadli						
1978	NDP				NCC	C				
1977	PL	ME								
1976	E		AI F							PD
1975	manabir		AC					CW		
1974	Infitah	PD 72			PD				2 States	

(cont.)

Table 3.1 *(Continued)*

In Tunisia, the November 1987 'constitutional' coup[63] by ex-General Zinealabidin Bin Ali, was hailed in official propaganda as the precursor of the New Deal (al-'ahd al-jadīd). Indeed the range of initiatives favoured reformation of the decaying order bequeathed by the octogenarian President Bourguiba—one of the leading heroes of Tunisia's independence. Those initiatives not only defused the anticipated and much feared power struggle over Bourguiba's succession,[64] but also signalled commitment towards multipartyism and constitutional change. Bin Ali's maiden speech of November 1987 contained promises that embodied the new regime's democratic orientation, and stressed that Tunisians were 'worthy of democracy'.[65] Constitutionally, a landmark reform was the dismantling of the 'presidential monarchy'[66]—a reference to the presidential life tenure practiced by Bourguiba since 1974. The July 1988 constitutional amendments limited the presidency to two five-year terms. The amendments limited the executive powers of the Prime Minister, and envisaged greater authority for the Assembly.[67] The new 1988 Political Parties Law relatively removed restrictions on the secular opposition.[68] A few of these parties received government subsidies to run their weekly newspapers and sustain their general activities.[69] Additional reforms concerned the areas of freedom of expression with the July 1988 revamped press code 'preventing monopoly and reducing penalties for code infractions'.[70] Others stressed commitment to human rights through the release of political prisoners, the 'issuing of pardons'[71] to former dissenters, the permission of political exiles to return and for Amnesty International to establish a local branch, and the signing of the UN Convention prohibiting torture. On the judicial–legal front the State Security Court along with the Prosecutor-General of the republic were abolished.[72] The Personal Status Code[73] was declared irrevocable. A number of benchmark administrative reforms were introduced in 1993 with a view to enhancing the bureaucracy's responsiveness to the citizenry.

To this end, for instance, a May 1993 law created an ombudsman office (administrative mediator) charged with handling complaints about the public service from citizens. Various government departments established units to handle relations with citizens by facilitating access, minimizing bureaucratic complications, and responding to citizens' complaints of inefficiency, malpractice, and misconduct by public servants. Central to this reform was a review system of administrative performance in which citizens were to sit along technocrats, senior bureaucrats, and professionals and channel their ideas about how to improve the system.

Algeria and Egypt's democratic openings affected a combined population of 85 million people. Their crossing of the democratic threshold in the future would effectively democratize 35 per cent of all Arabs. The implications of that happening would be far-reaching: a spill-over effect or, at least, a demonstration effect in the rest of the Arab world. Their liberalizations were fraught with tensions and contradictions. In Egypt, al-Sadat created 'his' democracy and chose 'his' opposition. Underpinning al-Sadat's pluralization initiatives was 'traditionalization'.[74] Hinnebusch pinpoints the marks of this traditionalization in al-Sadat's patriarchal politic-speak. Thus al-Sadat 'spoke as if the Egyptian political system were his personal property, referring to "my constitution", "my political parties", even "my opposition"'.[75] Emboldened by the gains of the October 1973 Arab–Israeli War, al-Sadat launched a quasi 'New Deal' with his open economy (infitāḥ al-iqtiṣādī).[76] The initial democratization process began as an Arab Socialist Union (ASU) internal affair. Al-Sadat's quest for what Cooper calls 'semi-pluralism' was motivated by three factors: opposition to, disillusionment, and discomfort with the ASU from the major political tendencies; the regime's needs for containing latently fragmentary forces and widening its power base through an alternative organization; and utilizing this very organization to demonstrate its democratic credentials.[77] Acting on Sayyid Marʿai's presidential committee's recommendation, three political platforms, not proper political parties, representing the ASU's left, right, and centre gained the right for expression, organization, and mobilization. This was a kind of change within continuity.[78] The Parties Law of May 1977 (see Table 3.1) marked the re-emergence of political parties in Egypt after a 25-year ban, and the June 1979 elections the return to competitive party politics after an absence of nearly three decades.[79] In 1978, at al-Sadat's behest, the old ruling ASU became the National Democratic Party (NDP). The change was sold as the actual creation of a new party. In the change, the adjective 'socialist' was dropped, and the populist word 'democratic' was substituted.

Under Mubarak[80] democracy proceeds with its 'halting progress'.[81] Although Egypt's press is considered one of the freest and most diverse in the Arab world, freedom of the press continues to be stifled by the state's censors. Media blackouts on certain news items were know to be imposed from time to time.[82] In 1997, the state moved against irregular newspapers (al-jarā'id al-ṣafrā') with the High Council on Journalism canceling the permits of a dozen newspapers, including the well-known al-Dustour.[83] Egypt's civil society registered some growth in strength, especially between 1976 and 1981 with the number of associations jumping up to 10,731 from 7,593.[84] Also, they more or less, gained more autonomy. But a dynamic civil society does not always mean the state is democratic in spite of legal multipartyism and periodic elections. With some 16 legalized parties and periodic elections, contestation has been evidently higher under Mubarak. In the May 1984 elections the Neo-Wafd-Muslim Brotherhood alliance gained 15 per cent of the total vote, winning 59 seats, in the then newly increased 450-seat Assembly. Again in the 1987 April elections the Labour-Liberals-Brotherhood (Amal-Aḥrār-al-Ikhwān) alliance won 60 seats, 37 of which went to Islamists who displaced the Neo-Wafd (35 seats) as the leading opposition group in parliament.

The independence of the judiciary was perhaps the most redeeming factor in Mubarak's Egypt. In fact, had it not been for the judiciary Egypt's multipartyism would not have grown to its current potential. The Neo-Wafd's legalization is owed to the judiciary's making possible its participation in the 1984 elections after overturning the negative response by the government's Political Parties Committee (Lajnat al-Ahzab) (PPC). With the exception of the diminutive Nation Party (Ummah), also licensed in 1984, the PPC ruled out against all legalization requests it vetted. The High Administrative Court (HAC) acted as a counterbalance to the PPC. Through its bench the Greens, Nasserists, Young Egypt (Misr al-Fatat), the Democratic Unionist Party, and the Social Justice Party were legalized in the first half of the 1990s. The full force of the rule of law was also brought to bear upon the outcome of the 1984 and 1987 elections which discriminated against independents. Both were found unconstitutional owing to the amended 1983 electoral law that prevented unaffiliated individuals from standing for election; to the arbitrary re-districting; and the 8 per cent total vote threshold as a prerequisite for entry into the Assembly.[85]

Algeria's short-lived experiment with pluralist politics appealed to the imagination of democratically minded Arabs and aroused fear among non-democratic regimes, especially in Morocco and Tunisia. Like Egypt, economic liberalization was at the core of President Chadhli's reform. Between 1980 and 1991 he practically reversed all the politico-economic pillars that held up Algeria's system and shaped its authoritarian-bureaucratic polity. His open economy de-Boumediennized, partly de-nationalized, de-ideologized, de-centralized, and, in the process, de-legitimized Algeria's ruling elites. Chadhli's open economy[86] began with the encouragement of privatization, private investment in industry and manufacturing, and managerial autonomy, and ended with IMF and World Bank–instigated austerity measures lowering subsidies for 'strategic' consumer staples, lifting price controls and increasing taxes.[87] Reduced hydrocarbon sales accounting for 95 per cent of total exports ($45 billion in 1984 as against $28 billion in 1986), burdensome foreign debt ($23 billion in 1988), and high unemployment (which more than doubled between 1984 [11%] and 1988 [22.5%]) served as detonators of social discontent and political instability, reaching breaking point in the October 1988 social unrest.[88] Chadhli's political reform developed clarity of purpose and direction only after the bloody bread riots. They amounted to launching not only a 'second republic', but also a second revolution in Algeria's post-independence political development.

The 1989 new constitution laid the foundation for a market economy and a multiparty system. It de-ideologized the system with the dropping of references to socialism, and defined state–society relations. With these changes the breaking up of the historical FLN-state alliance was completed. The constitution enshrined those classical civil liberties and provided, with qualification, for the formation of 'associations of political nature'. A follow-up to this provision was the 5 July 1989 law that cleared the way for the formation of political parties and hence for Algeria's first experimentation ever with party politics.[89] This law further marginalized the FLN which in its November 1988 Congress banned the formation of other political parties.

The February 1989 constitution institutionalized multipartyism and, indirectly, the democratic notion of contestation. Open, free, and fair contestation climaxed twice during Algeria's democratic spring between the February 1989 new constitution and the December 1991 first round National Popular Assembly (APN) elections. The 1990 elections, while boycotted by the Front of Socialist Forces (FFS) and the Algerian Democratic Movement (MDA) and attracting only 65 per cent of the eligible voters, were boon to cultivation of a democratic order. They were significant in three ways: they were pluralist; they constituted a break with the familiar Arab government practice of rigging the vote; and although the ruling FLN suffered a decisive loss it accepted the outcome with the Interior Ministry announcing the results without delay. In the words of one analyst, 'with the 12 June 1990 elections, this former paragon of one-party socialism in the Third World has become the most democratic Arab country'.[90] With more than 55 per cent of the votes cast, the FIS won 32 of the 48 provinces (wilāyāt) and 853 of the country's municipalities. The FLN with nearly 32 per cent of the votes won 14 provinces. Again in December 1991, the FIS won a landslide first-round victory in the parliamentary elections. The Islamists won 188 out of the contested 430 seats and were certain to gain a majority in the second round in January 1992.[91] However, democratic retreats sabotaged democratic progression, as I shall elaborate in the following section.

Reform and Breakdown

Democratic retreats inhibited reformation of Arab polities during the 1975–97 period. Moreover, the reforms' underlying institutions, values, concepts, habits, and modes of operation political institutions expressed were not democratic. Prima facie, the electoral practices and legal reforms of that period could be construed as harbingers of a reformation of Arab polities. However, they, more or less, tended to follow a pattern of adapting old institutions and established hierarchies to emerging realities and new demands, but not radically overturning them. The analysis below attempts to make a mesh of the period's reforms by primarily focusing on the patterns of progression and retrogression—*karr* and *farr*. Arab democratization vacillated between phases of political reform and of breakdown. Progression or *Karr* symbolizes reform or liberalization whereas retrogression or *farr* signifies reversal or breakdown—terminology used in the democratization literature.[92] Those factors—military coups, elite rivalries, and disunity, pressure from assertive and relatively autonomous opposition, a fragmented polity with multiple deadlocked power claims, paper institutions, and personalist leadership—that have usually predisposed Arab reform to breakdown will, when appropriate, be briefly touched upon. Generally, two basic types of Arab regimes were identifiable: democratizing and non-democratizing, which can be either monarchical or republican.

In comparative terms, Arab 'democratizers' differ, for instance, from the democratizing Southern European ideal types (Greece, Spain, Portugal) in the patterns of reform and breakdown in terms of liberalization, and in the varying degrees of fragility, duplicity, and susceptibility to either retrogression or to total retraction of reforms. Hence, being still deficient, especially where the trilogy of participation, contestation, and accountability is concerned, Arab liberalizations have an intermediacy that warrants categorizing them in terms of 'semi-democratization'. In so doing, the aim is not to locate those 'semi-democratizers' somewhere mid-way on a democratization continuum so much as to indicate that Arab democratization is still-born and largely stalled, and has yet more ground to cover. Furthermore, 'semi-democratizers' are pioneer (Egypt and Morocco), incipient (Algeria, Jordan, Lebanon, Mauritania, Sudan, Tunisia, and Yemen), and limited (Kuwait). To illustrate the pattern of reform and breakdown characteristic of Arab democratization the following observations are in order.

Elections, an important democratic institution, or the semblance of an electoral process, cannot yet be decoded as signals that the age of Arab democracy has dawned—rather that the search of Arab democracy is under way. Given the history of retrogression and retraction, Arab elections remain examples par excellence of democratic advance and retreat (karr and farr).

In terms of potential and procedure, Arab elections had in a few instances proven themselves to achieve relative parity with those administered in established polyarchies. Elections in Yemen and Jordan in 1993 and in Algeria in 1991 were instructive. Their reversibility was, however, what undermined the Arab voters' confidence in the ballot and in their leaders' democratic rhetoric. By and large, the period's elections were status quo elections. They were dialectical processes that had paradoxically both fostered and undermined democratization. At their core clashed the state-holders' quest for endorsement and a legitimating gloss of liberalism, and society's yearning for a venue for self-articulation and empowerment. As the latter's empowerment could potentially imply the former's disempowerment, progression, and retrogression ensued when elections either did not endorse the existing political order or produced such potentiality.

The Arab electoral experience is replete with phases where democratic advances either temporarily or permanently ceded to retreats. Pre-revolutionary Libya is a case in point. Libya's democratic experiment between the early 1950s and the late 1960s had mostly been overshadowed by the country's stigma as an anti-international-system state given the radical fervour of its maverick leader, al-Qadhafi. Between 1952 and the September 1969 coup Libya had four general elections for the country's federal Chamber of Deputies. Libyan women won the franchise in 1963 and exercised it in the 1964 and 1965 elections. A quasi two-party system was in place in the early 1950s. The Independence Party and the Congress Party of Tripolitania were politically active, contesting the country's first elections in February 1952. With hindsight, and by Arab standards, such an experiment was quite remarkable. Comparatively, it represented more elections than in democratizing post-independence Algeria in 1991. But in common with Algeria, following the December 1991 elections, democratization was aborted via a military coup. Likewise, the rise of the Free Officers in Egypt in 1952 meant the demise of electoral politics. However, whereas the Libyan retreat remains permanent,[93] Egypt's does not; and Algeria has resumed its liberalization. This pattern of progression and retrogression is not unfamiliar to the rule prevalent in the Arab Gulf monarchies. In December 1973, Bahrain held an election in which voters elected 30 members for the tiny Emirate's National Assembly. Parliamentary scrutiny, being anathema to its ruler, led him to issue a decree in 1975 dissolving the Assembly.

Progression and Retrogression in Kuwait and Morocco

Progression and retrogression stigmatized Kuwait and Morocco's electoral experiments in the 1975–97 period. From an electoral perspective Kuwait represented an interesting case study. Like Morocco, Kuwait was distinguished by both its monarchical system of government, and by the presence of degrees of contestation and participation that originated in 1961 following independence from the British.[94] As in Morocco, the presence of contestation and participation in Kuwait, be it in a more limited fashion, posed no challenge to the ruling family or to the monarchical state structure. In fact, in both systems the central patriarchs remained untouchable by democratization which they whimsically dispensed, organized, and regulated,[95] and the 'dominance of the monarchy'[96] remained intact despite pluralization. Contestation was between the rulers' clients, who were co-opted in the Emirate's patronage system which defined all power distribution, assignment allocation, and interest articulation and aggregation. Elections were the means by which the various actors re-endorsed that system by re-accepting their roles and places and those of their co-players in it, and thus were able to reproduce their privileges. Political opposition under such system had its limitations. Status quo elections gave the whole system the marks of civility and tolerance. Limits aside, Kuwait's electoral activities were, and continue today to be, by Arab standards, quite impressive. They were inaugurated in 1963, and were followed by another six: in 1967, 1971, 1975, 1981, 1985, and 1992.

Kuwait's record of seven elections between 1963 and 1992 compared favourably with most Arab polities, including those which were generally seen to be more liberalized. In the time span of 35 years—between the Emirate's independence in 1961 and 1997—Kuwait's seven elections equal an average of one election every 5 years. The years 1976 and 1986 signal the beginnings of phases of retrogression; direct rule ensued. Those years mark downturns in Kuwait's democratization, usually leading to dissolution of the National Assembly. Accordingly, in the period from 1963 to 1992, direct rule was the norm between 1976 and 1981, and again between 1986 and 1992. Of the 29 years between 1963 and 1992, the dates of the first and the last elections, the total length of democratic breakdown was 11 years of direct rule despite seven elections.

During the same period, Morocco fared in terms of electoral achievement better than most Arab countries, especially its immediate Maghribi neighbours. The obvious qualification was that Morocco's electoral activities did not always meet the standards of freedom and fairness—the very reason why the country's major parties often boycotted them.[97] The exception to this was the December 1997 legislative polls. Discounting non-parliamentary elections, this Maghribi country had five multiparty parliamentary elections since independence in 1956—in 1963, 1970, 1977, 1984, and 1993. In the 30-year period between 1963 and 1993 there was an average of one election every 6 years. If the number of municipal and provincial elections was added, then the total would be substantially higher. Despite the obvious similarities between Kuwait and Morocco, greater degrees of contestation and participation existed in the latter than the former. In Morocco, however, elections were not only noted for their presence but also for their absence. What was conspicuous was the number of elections that had not taken place owing to the delay factor. The elections due in May 1967 never took place; the next elections were held in August 1970, three years later. The elections due in August 1974, given the fact that the supposed life of the country's legislature was four years, were postponed until June 1977. The constitutional reforms introduced following the May 1980 referendum extended legislative tenure to six years. Thus the Chamber of representatives elected in June 1977, which was due to go to the polls in 1983, did not have to do so until September 1984. Similarly, the elections scheduled for 1990 never took place because a referendum held in December 1989 approved the King's decision to hold them two years later. Again the elections planned for December 1992 were put back, and finally took place in June 1993. The 1997 elections were the first to have proceeded according to schedule in 20 years of electoral practice in Morocco.

Like Kuwait, Morocco had instances when the legislature was practically dissolved or paralysed. Following the multiparty elections of May 1963, opposition representatives from both the *Istiqlal* (Independence)[98] Party and the National Union of Popular Forces (UNFP) faced persecution when they pressured the government on the issue of corruption. Many of the leaders of the UNFP, which at the time held some 28 seats in the then 144-member legislature, were imprisoned, tortured, and a few were sentenced to death in relation to an alleged coup against the King. The country's new legislature, which was partly elected by direct suffrage in August 1970, was dissolved two years later. The sum of direct rule in Morocco was 10 years—one-third of the period 1963–93. Dissolutions took place in 1965 and 1972 with each lasting five years.

Progression and Retrogression in the Wider AME

Similar cycles of progression and retrogression in democratization were not unfamiliar to other Arab democratizing polities—Sudan, Egypt, and Algeria. The latter's democratic breakdown in January 1992 was irredeemably the worst reversal in Arab democratization, moving from a potentially powerful and positive demonstration effect to be emulated into a powerfully negative demonstration effect to be avoided. In January 1992 the army usurped control, forcing President Chadhli's resignation. The generals cancelled the election results and the second round of voting. They dissolved parliament, and imposed a state of siege. They replaced the presidency with a High Council of State (HCS) in which a military junta was the most influential.[99] Thus, Algeria's democratization was derailed. The die-hards' self-interest was accorded precedence over the voters' choice. A few patrons of the *ancien régime* continued to describe the voters' choice pedantically and chauvinistically as the 'wrong' choice.[100] The view among the coup leaders was that for the FIS democracy was just a means to win office, only to then revert to a theocratic dictatorship.

Al-Sadat's dicing with democracy also experienced a phase of progression and retrogression. During his last months at the helm al-Sadat literally moved from a phase of political reform into a phase of retreat. His earlier initiatives that appeared to dismantle the structure of the Nasserist authoritarian-populist state and to transform single-party rule were blunted by a return to autocratic measures in order to maintain his power of patronage in the face of more vocal opposition and increasing participatory demands. Al-Sadat's democracy was inherently self-serving. 'His' democracy neither stopped rule by decree and draconian practices under continued emergency rule, nor allowed for formidably genuine opposition and an unfettered press. Following the January 1977 bread riots,[101] al-Sadat, while still maintaining his liberalizing zeal, retrogressed to non-liberal practices. For instance, striking, inciting disorder and anti-government protest, and the formation of political organizations outside the three legalized parties all carried punishment by hard labour for life. When the leftist Al-Tajammu'Party sharpened its anti-Sadat criticism—a taboo in al-Sadat's Egypt—and grew increasingly autonomous, the president banned it along with its weekly mouthpiece 'Al-Ahali'. Likewise, the anti-Camp David Agreement stance by some 15 dissenting deputies from the People's Assembly precipitated its dissolution in 1979.[102] With the 1981 crackdown on official and unofficial opposition, in which the Socialist Labour Party (SLP) was not 'spared',[103] the style of al-Sadat's 'presidential monarchy'[104] seemed incongruous with the requirements and processes of sustainable and substantive democratization.[105] The personalized nature of Arab politics made democratic initiatives inherently tentative or retractable, especially when the rules, procedures, and ends of the democratic game clashed with the rulers' interests.

A few observations are in order. The proliferation of elections and the entrenchment of electoral processes in the 1975–97 period were the most obvious gains. Elections, however, remained far from electoral efficiency much less ordered transition between incumbents and challengers. For incumbents elections seemed to be good only if they endorsed the existing political order, or, at worst, produced no danger to their privileged access to various forms of power: patronage, information, and state resources. The Khaldunian warfare technique of *karr* and *farr* applied. Retreat was retrogressive (Egypt, Morocco, and Tunisia) and retractive (Algeria and Sudan). Evidence pointed to increasing institutionalization of multiparty elections; they were more regular throughout the Arab world than they had ever been during the post-independence era. But evidence of their significance was limited. No serious assault on single-party rule was achieved. The old habits of clientelism, manipulation, and control of the electoral process persisted. The legalization of opposition was not matched by willingness to either let it operate unhindered or to accept it as alternative power-holder. Greater contestation and participation did not translate into greater elite accountability[106] or reduced executive power.

It is in this critical space that assessment of Arab elections and electoral processes are framed. Moench, for instance, focusing on the May 1984 Egyptian parliamentary elections, highlights many of the shortcomings and ambiguities of that process ultimately questioning the honesty and the seriousness of the very 'dispensers' of Egypt's democracy: '[Mubarak] was unable to deliver on his promise of an honest election, and may have hoped for a somewhat larger opposition in the *Majlis al-Sha'ab* if he is sincere in favouring a further democratization of Egypt. On the other hand, he has made no effort to repeal the emergency laws.'[107] Under emergency laws genuine democratization was hardly given a fair chance. Unlike democratic governments in Europe and North America, the Egyptian regime did not operate under legal or constitutional restraints because of the continuing state of emergency since 1981. The absence of restraints meant that the criteria of guaranteed and respected civil rights has mostly been absent in spite of an enlarged voting franchise for the citizenry. The programme issued by the country's opposition parties following the Cairo December 1997 two-day 'Conference of Defense of Democracy, Freedoms and Human Rights' urged the government to call off the emergency rule. It referred to the emergency law, under which serious abuses of human rights by the police and the security forces were quite common, as a 'second constitution' that '[had] dispensed with the original one'.[108] The standards of freedom and fairness leave much to be desired. Both incumbents and challengers were transgressors. While the 99.9 per cent election results genre was dwindling, irregularities were not uncommon. Egypt's infamous multiple voters use names of the deceased, and Kuwaiti candidates resort to rumour and bribes.[109] Owen aptly summed them up as 'elections without choices'.[110] The corollary was lingering 'voter apathy and general cynicism'.[111] For instance, according to Moench and Makram-Ebeid, voter apathy in Egypt's elections was reflected in low voter turnout, generally standing at no more than 30 per cent, and usually being higher in rural areas. As Makram-Ebeid notes, in Cairo, the country's *megalopolis* with its population of 17 million among whom reside the most literate and most politicized, 'voter turnout dropped [to] as low a level as 14 per cent' in the 1984 elections.[112] Although Makram-Ebeid attributes this factor to poverty, illiteracy, and diminutive political awareness, she primarily stresses voter lack of confidence in the electoral process and party politics:

During 1953–77, Egyptians were ruled by a single-party system and since then by a multiparty system, but still by one dominant party. The result is a feeling among the populace that the political balance is already calculated, regardless of their voting, in favour of the major party and that all the opposition parties can do is to improve, to some extent, the position of the minority.[113]

Moench speculates on the potential threat to system stability not just from low voter turnout but most importantly from open hostility:

... The great danger to the regime, other than its inability to cope with the immensity of the problems confronting it, lies in the increasing numbers of Egyptians who have moved from indifference in the political process to the view that the political process itself is not legitimate and must be replaced.[114]

Similarly, Bellin, assessing Tunisia's democratization, notes that the country's 'foray into multipartyism has not introduced sufficient competitiveness to force accountability upon regime elites'.[115] She gives three explanations: first, the constraints on the opposition by regime 'harassment and controls', factors that limit the opposition's 'organizational capacities'. Closely linked to the non-viability of unfettered opposition is the absence of checks on the regime. Second, there was a biased winner-take-all electoral system. Third, the absence of 'secure civil liberties', the regime's ban on religious politics, and its tendency to co-opt sections of the opposition have all hindered the emergence of 'mass-based opposition parties'.[116]

Arab democratization was hampered by exclusion despite markedly higher participation and contestation an, in some instances selective and partial recruitment of formerly silenced or invisible social forces into the political process. The centre's intent on minimalist democracy is without a question. Power of patronage, access to state resources, and law-making capacity continue to seriously handicap unfettered inclusion and formidable opposition.

Arab reform in the 1975–97 period was vitiated by exclusionary practices. By and large, the dynamics of exclusion and inclusion in most Arab polities were gender, family, class, ethnic group, religious and political affiliations, networking and connections, and education. One or a combination of these dynamics explicates exclusion in those Arab democratizers identified above. Political reforms were not about ruling inclusively. Women remained largely excluded from the political process. Kuwait, for instance, is identified here as a limited 'semi-democratizer' given the nature of its 'gendered democracy'.[117] Women had to wait until 2006 to vote.

Exclusion in most Arab 'semi-democratizer's' was a function of partial law-making evidenced in electoral laws and lists, and gerrymandering. Hourani and Brand highlight a number of flaws that came to the fore in the prelude to the Jordanian monarchy's November 1993 elections. An example was the replacement of the 'multiple votes per voter by the new one-person, one-vote' law which was intended by the King as a measure to disadvantage the Islamic Action Front, the political arm of the country's Muslim Brotherhood. Hourani pinpoints other pitfalls pertaining to the inefficiency of voter registration and the issuing of voter cards. For instance, in Amman II only 48.2 per cent of eligible voters placed their names on the electoral roll, and 60 per cent in the Zarqa'a district.[118] The arbitrariness of seat allocation in many districts, often disregarding population size, was another problem. Hourani finds this to be incompatible with free and fair elections as it undermined democratic participation and representativeness. Again,

Amman II with half-a-million inhabitants had three seats, six less than there should be given the size of its population. The city of Zarqa'a, the country's second largest, was allocated six seats; with its 650,000 population it should have had twice the number of seats. By contrast to this underrepresentation, al-Karak, with nine seats, is overrepresented— its population size entitled it to no more than four seats.[119] Brand locates the controversial provisions in the July 1992 Parties Law.[120] It stipulated single partisanship for the 'founding members of political parties' and prohibits affiliation with foreign political parties and organizations. Subsumed under these provisions (Articles 19 and 20) was a ban on foreign-based financial sponsorship, and on political tutelage.[121]

In Egypt the 'centrality' of the centre has been a fixture of political life since the Pharaohnic times. Despite freer political debate and limited administrative decentralization, no genuine delegation or devolution had taken place at the regional government level. Party legalization had to be cleared by PPC which has continuously rejected the application for legalization by the Muslim Brotherhood, potentially the most formidable opposition to the ruling NDP, and its formed political arm, Al-Wasat Party. Nor was it any easier for secular parties to obtain legalization. Although the PPC was supposedly semi-governmental, its neutrality was doubted by the Cairo-based Arab Human Rights Organization (AHRO). A majority of the PPC's board was made up of NDP members including the Consultative Council president and the Ministers for the Interior and Justice.

The December 1992 amendments to the Parties Law (no. 401 of 1977) by the parliament were described by AHRO antithetical to democratization. The amendments banned all activities by political parties until their legalization was cleared by the PPC. The amendments also restricted or made illegal contacts with Arab and foreign parties by existing legalized parties. AHRO questioned the manner and the speed with which the parliament ratified the amendments on 16 December 1992. The amendments proposal was drawn by a meeting of government ministers on 13 December. The next day the Constitutional and Legislative Committee was called on to convene to study the proposal impromptu. This committee's inconclusiveness over the proposal prompted its passing to the Political Parties Affairs Committee to draft new laws of the proposed amendments. The amendments were rubber-stamped by parliament. Of its 454 deputies, a mere 90 were present of which only 76 voted in favour of the new laws.[122]

Similarly, the 17 February 1993 law on professional syndicates and unions was cause for concern within Egyptian civil society. The law, brought about to curb what its legislators call 'minority dictatorship', aims to 'widen democratic participation'. The law, entitled 'safeguards of the professional syndicates' and unions' democracy', was widely recognized as a mechanism to frustrate future Islamist gains within professional syndicates and unions. They were the arena where democratic practice flourished from the mid-1980s to the mid-1990s before sabotaged by the regime. The law came after the September 1992 Bar Association elections when Islamists, with less than 10 per cent of the total vote, beat liberals and leftists to gain control of the country's prestigious and powerful Lawyers' Syndicate. The law made future syndicate and union elections conditional on 50 per cent membership voter participation. Failing that, the government would have the discretion to make appointments to the syndicates and unions' executive committees.[123] This law alarmed the Egyptian Human Rights Organization (EHRO). It feared 'life tenure as a mode of selection for union directorates' would result from government intervention.[124] Islamist scholar Fahmi Huwaydi criticized the law as hypocritical. He pointed out how the parliament of the day was voted in by only 10 per cent of Egypt's total electorate, and how voter turnout for local councils ranged between 5 and 6 per cent.[125]

Regime sensitivity to the rise of centres and forums of public debate, where central power was rivaled, was common place. Assault on associational life saw the temporary closing down—for nearly one year—in June 1992 of the Tunisian Human Rights League (LTDH). The league was outlawed for refusing to comply with the new Law on Associations (March 1992). The new Law, which was rubber-stamped by the Constitutional Council, banned politicians from membership of private organizations.[126] Activists from the LTDH, the Arab world's oldest human rights watchdog, found the Law on Associations unacceptable as it contravened the principle of free association.

While secularists maintain exclusionary policies vis-à-vis Islamists on the basis that separation between religion and state is a democratization prerequisite, they continue to either employ Islamic idioms for legitimation or meddle in religious affairs.

The question of secularization in the AME is a complex one for at least two obvious reasons. First, the ruling secularists administer over political realms the constitutions of which declare Islam to be the state's religion. Constitutions of the secular states of the West mostly do not declare an official religion, even if the preambles of some of them stress the importance of Christianity. Second, while contestable, the overwhelming view is that separation between religion and politics is alien to Islam which has no church. The issue of separation in Arab polities does not stop at the nature of the relationship between religion and politics. Those who champion secularization are yet to seriously consider also separation between the judiciary and the executive; separation between the executive and the legislature; separation between the state and the dominant ruling parties where these exist; and, in other instances, separation between the state and the military.

The quest for democracy has eluded even Lebanon, once a dynamic consociational democracy, because of the complexities and interplay of religion and politics. Lebanon continues its search for formulas and guarantees of stability and democracy amidst the labyrinthine state of affairs of competing 'isms' (Arabism, Lebanonism...) and narrow primordial loyalties.[127] In pondering the future of Lebanon as a viable and united political unit Khairallah sees the solution in nothing less than the total dismantling of the confessional system as a basis for organizing inter and intra-communal as well as state–society relations, which, in his final analysis, must end with the adoption of secular democracy.[128] Confessionalism has assumed two mutually reinforcing functions: the first helps articulate sectarian loyalties and identities; the second disarticulates national loyalty and unity. For confessionalism reproduces itself through its own distributive mechanisms of 'political rights and entitlements' each according to his/her religion, and through the exclusiveness invested in the sectarian hierarchies and interests controlling personal status laws and institutions.[129] Confessionalism then dilutes if not negates citizenship altogether. 'It cements the individual to his [/her] sect... The aspirations of the sect become the goals of its members. If achievement of such goals is thwarted, the culprit is not the state, but another sect or group of sects.'[130] Here the story of the state differs from the rest of the Arab world. The state is on the periphery not the centre. It is almost an accident or an artificial creation. Accordingly, Khairallah observes that 'instead of representing the national will, the state is merely a fragile shell for containing the struggle among sects'.[131] Khairallah's search for Lebanese democracy insists on political de-confessionalism, which must begin with the rejection of the Ta'if Accord. The Accord, as Khairallah puts it, does the opposite, by reproducing confessionalism:

The full extent of the Accord's commitment to de-confessionalization boils down to this: It gives the confessional establishment an unguided, nonbinding, open-ended mandate to abolish itself. Moreover, should a serious threat to the system materialize, the accord comes to the rescue in very precise and binding terms; should 'parliament enact an election law which is not based on religious affiliation records', then, 'concurrent with the election of the first parliament on a national rather than confessional basis, a senate will be created wherein all spiritual families will be represented'... Furthermore, in order to guarantee the preservation of confessional culture and prevent separation between religion and state... the Ta'if Accord gives top religious authorities the right to petition the constitutional council in matters of personal status law, freedom of religious belief and practice, and freedom of religious education. Thus [the Accord]...elevates laws that are at the heart of confessional culture to the level of constitutionally protected rights. Indeed, it bestows upon religious authorities privileges that are denied ordinary citizens with respect to any right under the constitution.[132]

The complexity of the separation of religion and state manifested themselves in the impasse of democratization in both Algeria and Egypt in the 1980s and 1990s. In both countries the Islamists were powerful despite systematic repression. In 1995 Egypt began a systematic crackdown on the Muslim Brotherhood. Mubarak's earlier distinction between extreme Islamists committed to the overthrow of the regime and those Islamists committed to achieving their projects legally no longer applied.[133] In Algeria the powerful FIS was disbanded in March 1992. Egypt's Parties Law of 1977 banned the formation of sectarian (religious) parties. The rulers feared not only from the wide following legalized Islamist parties would be able to muster, but also that the formation of religious parties would trigger similar demands from the country's 10 per cent Coptic community. In Algeria, the Parties Law of 2 July 1989 disallowed religious parties. The view was, and is more so today post-9/11, that Islam should not be monopolized for political ends. Perhaps the starkest contradiction, however, is the continued meddling in religion or its use by secularists for political ends—legitimation. This is the secularists' very basis for objection to mixing religion with politics.

Politicization of the mosque seems to be inevitable. While arguing for prayer leaders and religious scholars, to be non-partisan, the regimes in both Algeria and Egypt appointed their own.[134] In Egypt, Islamist hysteria prompted the introduction of stricter control measures of mosques. Among these were plans to bring all of Egypt's more than 100,000 mosques under the control of the Ministry in charge of religious endowments (*al-awqaf*); to make mandatory prior government approval of Friday sermons in state-controlled mosques; and to impose restrictions on the building of private community mosques.[135] Even when rulers prefer Islam to be relegated to a personal religious experience, interference seems to be unavoidable. Algeria had adopted the 'Tunisian formula'[136] of rendering the headscarf (*ḥijāb*) and beards illegal in the public service. President Mubarak is reported to have described veiled women as *'tentes ambulantes'* (mobile or walking tents).[137]

Perhaps one of the most extraordinary instances of meddling in religious issues was when Tunisia's former president controversially applied the Islamic principle of independent reasoning (*ijtihād*) by applying it to Islamic aspects for which clear Qur'ānic injunctions existed—an act of blasphemy in Islam. In 1974 he sought to interpret the Qur'ānic law regarding inheritance so as to achieve equality between the sexes—an effort that was not without plaudits within and without.[138] In equally notorious cases of political interference in religion, Bourguiba clearly implied that fasting during Ramadan was irrelevant for a Muslim developing country. In both instances the boundaries between Islam and politics, which are often argued to exist and to separate state and religion, were deliberately waived by a politician. The staunchly secularist Bourguiba justified his reasoning on the basis of being the ruler of the land, and thus, in Islamic terms, the 'Commander of the Faithful' (*amīr al-mu'minīn*).

The mobilization of Islam for political purposes by Arab leaders is well known. Piscatori documents their usage of Islamic symbols.[139] The late Hassan II of Morocco adopted the title of the 'Commander of the Faithful'. So did Sudan's Ja'far al-Numayri who enshrined it in the constitution (Article 80) in 1984.[140] Like al-Sadat, the pious president (*al-ra'isu al-mu'min*), he expediently used Islam to placate or co-opt political foes.[141] Al-Sadat enlisted the support of al-Azhar in the form of a religious counsel (*fatwā*) to vet his peace bid with Israel.[142] In 1983 al-Numayri initiated a wide-ranging Islamization programme. The mobilization of Islam by secularist power-holders was well appreciated and thus, in the absence of equally potent modes of legitimation, will continue to be employed unsparingly. Auda's insights capture in a sophisticated fashion the nature of the divide within Egypt's state and society (and with application for other Arab polities): a government-led secular-oriented project harbouring its own Islamically defined sympathies is pitted against a state elite-led but mass-based and religiously defined project for reinventing Islamic tradition:

The tension ... supersedes the conflict between elites and masses or government and opposition. It is a protracted conflict between two different conceptions of society and social change. The rift not only prevails horizontally in the fields of politics, economy, religion, and social affairs but also, and more important, it splits the society and the state vertically. In Egypt, we observe a part of the state elite, supported by factions of the masses and political forces espousing Islamic teachings, in confrontation with another section of the state elite, led by the government and advocating a combination of modern and traditional daily life. In short, in Mubarak's Egypt there are two contending regimes: the Islamic and the government-led.[143]

Notions of Western secularization and democratization are based on respect for the rules and procedures of citizenship and on human rights.

Arab processes are not. The attendant corollary is violence and counter-violence.

Images of the dismal state of human rights abounded in the AME in the1975–97 period. The holding of elections did not automatically improve human rights. The key Arab 'semi-democratizers' continued to figure in the damning reports of Amnesty International, the US State Department's annual country reports, and AHRO. It was then fashionable for Arab governments to create their own duplicate human rights watchdogs. This was usually, as in the case of Tunisia, 'to dilute and countervail the influence'[144] of non-government organizations. Arab regimes became sensitive to accusations of human rights violations, and some eventually staged their own investigations into allegations of abuses by police and security apparatuses. In Tunisia, embarrassment over numerous deaths in custody forced the government to set up a special inquiry into torture in police stations and prisons. However, when it was finally tabled little came out of the so-called Driss Report of 1992.[145] But perhaps nothing illustrated lack of respect for human rights more than the impunity with which abuses by men in power was treated. Nowhere was this more apparent than in the Lebanese government. A few of its members, of many confessional backgrounds, were responsible for large-scale civil war crimes against their peoples and against humanity. Yet they were rewarded with high office from which they reaped undeserved benefits, including immunity from prosecution.

Exclusionary politics, among other factors, accounted for the severe crisis of instability in the 1980s and 1990s. At the end of the nineteenth century the Arab world was divided and ruled from without. Algeria, Morocco, Egypt, Sudan, Somalia, Iraq, Lebanon, and Yemen all experienced varying degrees of break-up of social peace in the 1990s. State violence and Islamist counter-violence gripped both Algeria and Egypt. Violence by excluded Islamists against the state took place in other Arab countries such as Bahrain, Kuwait, Tunisia, Sudan, and Libya. This phenomenon is not going to disappear unless it is seriously and democratically attended to through accommodation, as opposed to repression. Those polities (Jordan, Lebanon, Sudan, and Algeria despite the banning of the FIS) where Islamists were licensed as political parties remain limited. Despite greater 'electoralism' and resulting 'parliamentarization' and the presence of some opposition in many Arab national assemblies, de-militarization of the circuits of power was part of the problem in the 1980s and 1990s. Seven (Algeria, Egypt, Jordan, Mauritania, Sudan, Tunisia, and Yemen) of the key third-wave 'semi-democratizers' were ruled by military or ex-military heads of state. By adding Iraq, Libya, and Syria to the list this translates into more than 80 per cent of all Arabs living under military rule in that period. Whether this factor helps explicate the frequency of human rights abuses during that period will not be speculated on here. But suffice it to say that they must bear some relation. However, the state and its authority seemed to be more stable and less challenged in those Arab polities with a monarchical rather than republican system of government. This is the reverse of the early and mid-twentieth century when monarchies were being rolled back under the assault of Arab revolutionary currents.

The underdevelopment of republicanism in Arab republics accounted at the time for the drifting into social polarization, and the rise of a culture of violence and counter-violence in countries like Algeria and Egypt. The atrophy of democratization in Algeria and its retrogressive nature in Egypt led both polities to an impasse where the rationality of participation and free and fair contestation ceded to the irrationality of exclusion and bloody violence.[146] For the rulers, violence was the state's legitimate prerogative to eradicate anti-democratic forces. For the targets—Islamists—state violence went beyond that mandate. Islamists regard state violence as being executed not by democrats but by anti-Islamic and anti-democratic rulers. Stripped of the political means for empowerment, a few Islamist groups feel justified in resorting to violence in the name of some spurious notion of holy war (*jihād*). The suppression of Algeria's Islamists' certain victory in the polls and the subsequent state violence against the FIS created a bad precedent. That precedent has until now strengthened the hands of radical Islamists who regard Arab rulers as never having been serious about democracy and who, therefore, perceive violence as their only option for empowerment. General amnesties are declared from time to time in various Arab countries. The matter of fact is that these amnesties have never been general. They tend to exclude formidable regime opponents, the secular and religious. For instance, in late 1998 and following the formation of an opposition figure-led government, the Moroccan consultative Commission on Human Rights' plan to release political prisoners did not at the time extend to Islamists who were not considered political prisoners.

Conclusion

The 1975–97 period of reform stirrings in the AME was marked by impressive manifestations of electoral activities. Political liberalization was synonymous with 'electoralism'. Electoral apprenticeship is one gain of the 1975–97 period. But that electoralism smacked of election fetishism. Elections were mostly concentrated in the lesser-to-do Arab states. Kuwait was the only exception in the Arab Gulf. What the analysis above demonstrates is that Arab democratization during the period in question was largely institutionalist in nature with elections being central to it. The outcomes of those elections were cosmetic, proving the point about how Arab political reform can only be as open-ended, complex, and contingent. Elections cannot be taken as a credible test of democratization, especially in the absence of transfer of power. They never translated into unhindered organized political dissent; respect for the rule of law and for human rights, autonomous associational life, and high levels of popular participation, contestation, and of accountability and responsiveness. Duplicity existed. The democratic rhetoric of that period did not always fit with the practice. Exclusionary practices did not cede to political inclusion. Refusal to license formidable Islamist forces as in Tunisia and Egypt, while appropriating Islamist language and projects, were two contradictory aspects of a well-calculated and complete regime response to the popularity of the Islamist current. In Tunisia the RCD 'pre-empted politics ... by incorporating opposition programs (and leaders!) into governmental platforms, in effect virtually reducing the political arena to one that pits the dominant party against a still unrecognized Islamic party'.[147]

Michael Hudson's detailed definition of democratization[148] (italicized text below) offers clues as to the state of Arab reforms of that period.

1. *A process through which the exercise of political power by a regime and state becomes less arbitrary, exclusive, and authoritarian:* despite much improvement and openings in the authoritarian political structure especially through frequent elections, autocracy still persisted in varying degrees in the 1975–97 period.
2. *Bargaining, as opposed to command, takes on increasing importance in power relationships:* although there is evidence of bargaining as was the case in Tunisia, Algeria, Yemen, Jordan, and Egypt, the state-holders were very selective as with whom they bargained with and what they included and excluded when bargaining, as their aims seemed invariably to find loyal but unequal partners in a tutelary democracy.
3. *Public political debate, and the expression of criticism and opposing views, becomes increasingly evident:* higher levels of awareness, and freer opposition press in the 1975–97 period fostered more vocalism. Regardless, regime resources (electronic media and coercion) still ensured strong vertical structures of information control and a capacity to silence dissenting views.

4. *Power holders increasingly recognize the costs of governance by coercion and threat as opposed to persuasion and reward:* this was evidenced by regime rhetoric disowning human rights abuses by transgressors and by the establishment of their own human rights watchdogs in the 1990s (Algeria, Egypt, Morocco, Tunisia).

5. *They increasingly realize that policy goals, such as economic growth and even political stability, may be enhanced by allowing, or acquiescing in, greater autonomy for societal elements in politics. Increased participation, they may come to feel, enhances their political legitimacy; and political legitimacy comes to be seen not as an abstract (and perhaps dispensable) value but as an important political commodity or resource:* The electoral activities initiated in many Arab polities achieved only selective and limited inclusiveness. There is little evidence in the 1975–97 period to show that the liberalizing policies represented a genuine commitment to democracy. Rather, to an extent, they were self-serving devices to cling to power. Arab reforms were procedural, minimalist, and gradualist.

The point about Arab reforms being minimalist and gradualist needs little emphasis. The record speaks for itself. Procedural democracy cannot, in the absence of supporting values and institutions, be expected to deliver more than a minimalist democracy. The retraction of Algerian reform and its retrogression in Egypt, two populous states with the political and geostrategic weight to effect change outside their borders, have deprived the Arab world of two potentially democratic showpieces that may not only have served notice to 'non-democratizers' but also induced emulation. The gradualist nature of reform was a function of the milieu in which democratization was being cultivated. There were no clear directions, agendas, timetables, or even democrats. Those self-declared democrats within and without governments, who feared being swept away by more formidable rival forces, counseled caution and gradualism. In 1992, soon after the Algerian débacle, that very message was, for instance, conveyed to President Mubarak by Egypt's intelligentsia. They warned against 'hasty democratization', and he 'reminded them of some of their earlier criticism of his slow pace of democratization'.[149] For Saad Eddin Ibrahim, 'while gradualism is to be commended . . . these expressions of panic revealed the thin veneer of the Egyptian intellectuals' commitment to the cause of democracy. All of a sudden they remembered that the masses . . . are mostly illiterate and easily manipulated'.[150] Thus the bottom line, as Ann Lesch puts it, is that 'the contradictions inherent in the concept of "democracy in doses" may undermine efforts to extend political reform'.[151]

Gradualism has an external dimension, namely, 'the gradual diffusion of democratic currents' from outside.[152] However, gradualism can also be interpreted as hesitation to respond to pressure to democratize in response to pressure from without. An example of this is the United States's Greater Middle East Initiative. In the next chapter, I attempt to critically assess its objectives and survey reaction to it in the AME.

Notes

1. Mona Makram-Ebeid, 'Political Opposition in Egypt: Democratic Myth or Reality?' *Middle East Journal*, 43 (Summer 1989), 436.
2. Burhan Ghalyun, '*Al-Dimuqratiyyatu 'l-arabiyyah: judhuru 'l-"azmah wa-afaqu 'l-numuw*' [Arab Democracy: Roots of the Crisis and Prospects of Development] in Burhan Ghalyun et al., *Hawla 'l-khiyaru 'l-dimuqrati: dirasat naqdiyyah* [On the Democratic Option: A Critique] (Beirut: Markaz Dirasat al-Wihdah al-Arabiyyah, 1994), 113.
3. Larbi Sadiki, 'Progress and Retrogression of Arab Democratization', *Journal of Arabic, Islamic and Middle Eastern Studies* (hereafter *JAIMES*), 1 (1993), 80.
4. *Al-Karr* (attack) and *al-Farr* (withdrawal) are the warfare techniques the fourteenth century *Maghrib* scholar Ibn Khaldun attributes to Arabs and Berbers. They are applied to describe the pattern of Arab democratization not simply for the sake of viewing it as a kind of battle between state and society, but mostly to emphasize its inconsistency, unassured results, and 'hit and run' style. Ibn Khaldun thus observes: 'Fighting with the technique of attack and withdrawal is not...fierce or...secure.' See, Ibn Khaldun, *The Muqaddimah [Prolegomenon]: An Introduction to History*, trans. by Franz Rosenthal (Princeton: Princeton University Press, 1967), vol. 2, 73–89.
5. For a brief critique of unilinearism see, for instance, Dankwart Rustow, *A World of Nations: Problems of Political Modernization* (Washington, DC: The Brookings Institution, 1967), 141–2.
6. Huntington, *The Third Wave*, 15.
7. See John E. Peterson, *The Arab Gulf States: Steps Toward Political Participation* (New York: Praeger, 1988).
8. The tribal nature of Mauritania's nascent democratization was visible in the parliamentary elections of February 1992. For details see *Al-Hayat*, 29 February 1992. See also 'Mauritania: Democracy in Doubt', *Africa Report*, 37 (May/June 1992), 58–60.
9. For further details on the Yemeni elections see Sheila Carapico, 'Elections and Mass Politics in Yemen', *Middle East Report*, 23 (November/ December 1993), 3–6. See also Renaud Detalle, 'The Yemeni Elections Up Close', *Middle East Report*, 23 (November/December 1993), 8–12. In Arabic see Sami Al-Haj, '*Tawazunat siyasiyyah jadidah tafruduha nata'iju al-Intikhabati al-Yamaniyyah*' [New Power Configurations Imposed by

the Yemeni Elections], *Al-Hawadith*, 7 May 1993, 18–19, and Isam Abd al-Hakim, *'Al-dimuqratiyyatu al-yamaniyyah bayna al-najah wa 'al-fashal'* [Yemeni Democracy Between Success and Failure], *Qad5aya Duwaliyyah*, 4 (March/April 1993), 4–5.

10. For a useful account of Arab political reforms see the article by Mustapha K. al-Sayyid, 'Slow Thaw in the Arab World', *World Policy Journal*, 8 (Fall 1991), 711–37.

11. Details of these elections can be found in Peter Woodward, *Sudan 1898–1989: The Unstable State* (Boulder: Lynne Rienner, 1990), 206–15.

12. There were 231 seats contested in the first round. By winning 188, the FIS was only 27 seats short of a majority. The second winner was the Front des Forces Socialistes (FFS) with 25 followed by the FLN with 15 seats. See Abdeslam Maghraoui, 'Problems of Transition to Democracy: Algeria's Short-lived Experiment with Electoral Politics', *Middle East Insight*, 8 (Winter 1992), 20–6. See also Alfred Hermida, 'Democracy Derailed', *Africa Report*, 37/2 (March–April 1992), 13–17.

13. The ban on political parties in 1957 followed the abortive leftist overthrow of the monarchy. For more details on the November 1993 elections see Larbi Sadiki, 'Jordan's Important Elections', *Asia-Pacific Defence Reporter*, 20 (February/March 1994), 32.

14. In the case of Jordan, Tujan al-Faisal, a former TV personality, is the first woman to win a seat in parliament. Al-Faisal was only 1 in 3 women to have contested the elections with more than 550 men.

15. For an account of Lebanon's political system and the question of democracy see Heather Deegan, *The Middle East and Problems of Democracy* (Buckingham: Open University Press, 1993), 103–18. Being both confessional and pluralist the fragmented Lebanese polity approximates Arend Lijphart's consociational system which is 'deliberately' stabilized by 'the leaders of the major subcultures' in spite of 'subcultural cleavages . . . with [their] tendencies toward immobilism and instability'. See his, 'Typologies of Democratic Systems', *Comparative Political Studies* 1 (April 1968), 20. For those essential conditions that make consociational systems functional see Arend Lijphart, 'Consociational Democracy', *World Politics*, XXI (January 1969), 216. On how the Lebanese system maintained functionalism in the past, on how the 'complex balance of power among the several traditional groups', operated, and how 'Lebanese politicians . . . exhibited an unusually high degree of responsibility in the absence of a controlling authority', see Michael C. Hudson, 'Democracy and Social Mobilization in Lebanese Politics', *Comparative Politics*, 1 (January 1969), esp. pp. 247–9.

16. Michael Hudson, 'The Possibilities for Pluralism', *American-Arab Affairs*, 36 (Spring 1991), 3.

17. For further details on this development see Richard U. Moench, 'The May 1984 Elections in Egypt and the question of Egypt's Stability', in Linda L. Layne, *Elections in the Middle East: Implications of Recent Trends* (Boulder: Westview Press, 1987), 47–85.

18. Pierre-Jean Luizard, '*L'improbable démocratie en Iraq: le piège de l'etat-nation*' [The Improbability of Democracy in Iraq: The Nation-State Trap] *Egypt / Monde Arabe*, 4 (1990), 47–85.

19. Volker Perthes, 'Syria's Parliamentary Elections: Remodeling Asad's Political Base', *Middle East Report*, 22 (January/February 1992), 15–18.

20. Chibli Mallat, 'Obstacles to Democratization in Iraq: A Reading of Post-Revolutionary Iraqi History Through the Gulf War', in Goldberg et al. (eds.), *Rules and Rights in the Middle East*, 224–47.

21. Raymond A. Hinnebusch, 'State, Civil Society, and Political Change in Syria', in Norton (ed.), *Civil Society in the Middle East*, 232–3.

22. Ibid. 219.

23. Thomas R. Callaghy, 'Vision and Politics in the Transformation of the Global Political Economy: Lessons from the Second and Third Worlds', in Robert O. Slater, Barry M. Schutz and Steven R. Dorr, *Global Transformation and the Third World* (Boulder: Lynne Rienner, 1993), 212.

24. Ibid. 213.

25. Ibid.

26. Richards, 'Economic Pressures for Accountable Governance in the Middle East and North Africa', p. 56.

27. Steven Heydemann, 'Taxation Without Representation: Authoritarianism and Economic Liberalization in Syria', in Goldberg et al. (eds.), *Rules and Rights in the Middle East*, 69–101.

28. Another analyst projects a comparable view with Heydemann's observation that 'neither are economic liberalization and democratization simply two sides of one coin'. See Volker Perthes, 'The Private Sector, Economic Liberalization, and the Prospects of Democratization: The Case of Syria and some other Arab Countries', in Ghassan Salamé (ed.), *Democracy Without Democrats? The Renewal of Politics in the Muslim World* (London: I.B. Tauris, 1994), 243–4.

29. Heydemann, 'Taxation Without Representation', pp. 74–80.

30. Ibid. 78.

31. Ibid. 80.

32. Ibid.

33. Ibid.

34. Ibid.

35. Ibid. 81–2.

36. Ibid. 82.

37. According to Perthes two phases have marked the path of economic liberalizations in such countries as Egypt, Jordan, Iraq, Syria, and Tunisia. The first phase, begun in the 1970s and resulting in severe economic crises, was followed by a second phase of 'tangible drive towards a second, or deeper, *infitāḥ* at some point during the second half of the 1980s'. See Perthes, 'The Private Sector, Economic Liberalization, and the Prospects of Democratization', p. 246.

38. See the Algerian example which stressed economic restructuring and delayed political reform in, John P. Entelis, 'Algeria Under Chadli:

Liberalization without Democratization Or, Perestroika, Yes; Glasnost, No!', *Middle East Insight*, 6 (Fall 1988), 47–64. For an insightful account of the roots of al-Sadat's *infitāḥ*, see Esmail Hosseinzadeh, 'How Egyptian State Capitalism Reverted to Market Capitalism', *Arab Studies Quarterly* 10 (Summer 1988), 299–317.

39. Compare the work by Anwar Abdel Malek, *Egypt: Military Society* (New York: Vintage Books, 1968) with the functionalist approaches taken in the writings by Morroe Berger, *The Arab World Today* (New York: Doubleday, 1962), and by Shahrough Akhavi, *Egypt: Neo-Patrimonial Elite*, in Frank Tachau (ed.), *Political Elites and Political development in the Middle East* (New York: John Wiley, 1975), 69–113.

40. Another pioneering economic liberalizer is Tunisia. Perthes observes that 'Tunisia and Egypt officially buried their socialist orientations in the early 1970s'. See Perthes, 'The Private Sector, Economic Liberalization, and the Prospects of Democratization', p. 244. Eva Bellin also observes that 'Tunisia was among the first Arab countries to break with "Arab Socialism" and embark on a "quasi liberal" strategy of development (at least in the sense of consciously promoting the development of private sector commerce and industry)'. See her article, 'Civil Society in Formation: Tunisia', in Norton (ed.) *Civil Society in the Middle East*, 124.

41. Yahya M. Sadowski, *Political Vegetables? Businessman and Bureaucrat in the Development of Egyptian Agriculture* (Washington, DC: The Brookings Institution, 1985), 104–5. For a good account of the 'origin and development' of the *infitāḥ*, see also Paul Rivlin, *The Dynamics of Economic Policy Making in Egypt* (New York: Praeger, 1985), esp. pp. 39–56. See also Nazih N. Ayubi, *The State and Public Policies in Egypt Since Sadat* (Reading: Ithaca Press, 1991), esp. pp. 3–85.

42. Mubarak maintained al-Sadat's *infitāḥ*. He, however, set out initially to slow its pace as well as to 'purify' it by cracking down on corruption with the trial of many *nouveaux riches* including the late al-Sadat's brother, and by curtailing the import of luxury goods. In his maiden speech to the People's Assembly on 14 October 1981, Mubarak identified consumption as his 'principal quarrel with the infitah'. For more details, see John G. Merriam, 'Egypt Under Mubarak', *Current History*, 82 (January 1983), 24–7; 36–7.

43. Privatization is central to the wave of Arab economic liberalizations. Examples of articles that can be consulted on this matter include Fred H. Lawson, *'Liberalisation économique en Syrie et en Iraq'* [Economic liberalization in Syria and Iraq] *Maghreb-Machrek*, 128 (April–June 1990), 27–52; Fred H. Lawson, 'Political Economic Trends in Bathi Syria: A Reinterpretation', *Orient*, 29 (1988), 579–94; Volker Perthes, 'The Syrian Private Industrial and Commercial Sectors and the State', *International Journal of Middle Eastern Studies*, 24/2 (1992), 207–30; on the creation of Syria's stock exchange see Benjamin C. Wedman, 'Let's be Capitalists', *The Middle East*, 214 (August 1992), 28–9; Ilya Harik, 'Privatisation et développement en Tunisie' [Privatization and

Development in Tunisia] *Maghreb-Machrek*, 128 (April–June 1990), 5–26; Abdelsatar Grissa, 'The Tunisian State Enterprises and Privatization Policy', in I. William Zartman (ed.), *Tunisia: The Political Economy of Reform* (Boulder and London: Lynne Rienner, 1991), 109–27; on Tunisia see also, 'Tunisia Makes its Pitch', *The Middle East*, 215 (September 1992), 7; Lynette Rummel, 'Privatization and Democratization in Algeria', in Entelis and Naylor (eds.), *State and Society in Algeria*, 53–71; Alfred Hermida, 'Algeria: Hands-on Management', *The Middle East*, 206 (December 1991), 35; Mushtak Parker, 'Morocco: Headlong towards a Liberal Economy', *The Middle East*, 220 (February 1993), 25; Jon Marks, 'Morocco: "Reform Shakes up a Sleepy System"', *Middle East Economic Digest*, 37 (26 February 1993), 16; Josh Martin, 'Privatization Becomes Urgent', *The Middle East*, 220 (February 1993), 33–4; see also, Egypt special report, 'Shock to the System', *The Middle East*, 213 (July 1992), 39; another special report by David Butter, 'Egypt: Shaking off the Creeping Malaise', *Middle East Economic Digest*, 37 (4 June 1993), 9–18.

44. The 1950 elections were dominated by the Wafdists who won 225 seats. Those parties which partook in those elections besides the Wafd included the Sa'adists, the Liberals, the Socialists, and the Nationalists. The Wafd boycotted the previous elections held in 1945.

45. Tunisia's first post-independence elections were multiparty. The country's Communist Party had two candidates standing against the ruling *Parti Socialiste Destourien* which won all the contested seats.

46. The following year King Hussein banned all political parties. A useful reference on political parties in the Hashemite Kingdom up to 1967 is by Amnon Cohen, *Political Parties in the West Bank under the Jordanian Regime, 1949–1967* (Ithaca and London: Cornell University Press, 1982).

47. For an insightful analysis of Jordan's first multiparty elections of 1993 in 37 years see the excellent article by Hani al-Hurani, *'Intikhabatu 1993 al-'urduniyyah: qira'ah fi khalfiyyatiha, zurufiha wa nata'ijuha'* [Jordan's 1993 Elections: A Reading of its Background, its Circumstances and its Results], *Qira"at Siyasiyyah*, 4 (Spring 1994), 7–25.

48. See some of the figures on Arab political parties given by Saad Eddin Ibrahim, 'Civil Society and Prospects of Democratization in the Arab World', in Norton (ed.), *Civil Society in the Middle East*, 41.

49. For a good account of the spectrum of parliamentary and extraparliamentary forces that are active in Lebanon's politics, including those that emerged during the civil war, see, Ralph E. Crow, 'Electoral Issues: Lebanon', in Jacob M. Landau, Ergun Özbudun, and Frand Tachau (eds.), *Electoral Politics in the Middle East: Issues, Voters and Elites* (London: Croom Helm, 1980), 39–68. See also, in the same book, the fine essay on Lebanon's political elites and their political attitudes by Samir G. Khalaf, 'Parliamentary Elites: Lebanon', 243–71.

50. For a thorough analysis of the Lebanese 1992 elections see Augustus R. Norton and Jillian Schwedler, 'Swiss Soldiers, Taif Clocks, and Early

Elections: Towards a Happy Ending', in Deirdre Collings (ed.), *Peace for Lebanon? From War to Reconstruction* (Boulder and London: Lynne Rienner, 1994), 45–65.

51. Ten seats for the Movement of Social Democrats (MDS); 4 for the Renewal Movement; 3 for the Unionist Democratic Union (UDU); and 2 for the Popular Unity Movement (PUP). The abbreviations correspond with the French names of these parties: *Mouvement des Démocrates socialistes*; *Union Démocratique Unioniste*; and *Parti de L'unité Populaire*.

52. Hermassi, 'The Islamicist Movement and November 7', 200.

53. For a brief account of independents in Egypt's electoral process see Mark N. Cooper, *The Transformation of Egypt* (London: Croom Helm, 1982), 206.

54. Al-Sayyid, 'Slow Thaw in the Arab World', p. 720.

55. According to one analyst the Saudi economy, which had a $140 billion surplus in 1982, has presently a $60 billion deficit, adding that the monarchy's foreign debt shall total $100. See Said K. Aburish, *The Rise, Corruption and Coming Fall of the House of Saud* (London: Bloomsbury, 1994), 303.

56. Ibid. 4.

57. The term constitution is absent in Saudi political discourse. Nowhere does the term appear in King Fahd's March 1992 speech. Instead the word '*nizām*' (system) is used. The reason, as observed by one Arab analyst, is that the use of the term constitution with its secular connotation goes against the monarchy's adoption of the "*Quran* and the Prophet's *Sunna* as 'the supreme source of legislation'. See Saad Eddin Ibrahim, 'On Democracy in Saudi Arabia', *Civil Society*, 3 (March 1992), 2.

58. Details can be found in Ibid. 2–4.

59. See the excellent contribution by Daoud L. Khairallah, 'Secular Democracy: A Viable Alternative to the Confessional System', in Collings (ed.), *Peace For Lebanon? From War to Reconstruction*, 259–72.

60. See the insightful inputs by Joseph Maila, 'The Taif Accord: An Evaluation', in Collings (ed.), *Peace For Lebanon? From War to Reconstruction*, 31–44.

61. Maila, 'The Taif Accord: An Evaluation', 32.

62. For more details on all six points see Ibid. 35.

63. See L. B. Ware, 'Bin Ali's Constitutional Coup in Tunisia', *Middle East Journal* 42 (Autumn 1988), 587–601. The coup has been dubbed constitutional in accordance with its provisions (Article 57) that in case of incapacity power is transferred to the Prime Minister. As I. William Zartman explains, 'The accession to power of Bin Ali occurred on the night of November 6–7, 1987, when he assembled seven doctors and received from the procurator-general their statement of Bourguiba's "absolute incapacity".' See his, 'The Conduct of Political Reform: The Path Toward Democracy', in Zartman (ed.), *Tunisia: The Political Economy of Reform*, 13. The coup is also informally known as the 'medical coup'.

64. For a brief account on the question of power struggle and Bourquiba's endeavours to eliminate autonomous and rival centres of power see Clement Henry Moore, '*La Tunisie après Vingt Ans de Crise de Succession*' [Tunisia After Twenty Years of Succession Crisis] *Maghreb-Machrek* 120 (April–June 1988), esp. 6–7.

65. For full details of the speech see, '*La déclaration de Bin Ali à la radio*' [Bin Ali's Radio Proclamation] *Jeune Afrique*, 18 November 1987, 42.

66. Ware, 'Bin Ali's Constitutional Coup in Tunisia', 597.

67. Rémy Leveau, '*La Tunisie du Président Bin Ali: equilibre interne et envi-ronnemt Arabe*' [President Bin Ali's Tunisia: Internal Equilibrium and Arab Focus]*Maghreb-Machrek* 124 (April–June 1989), 7.

68. In addition to the three established opposition parties—the MDS legal-ized in 1983; the Tunisian communist Party which has been renamed the Renewal party licensed in 1981; and the PUP authorized in 1983—three more parties have gained official recognition since the passing of the 1988 law: the Progressive Socialist Party (RSP); the Social Party for Progress (PSP); and the Unionist Democratic Party (UDU). The abbreviated forms correspond to the Parties' names in French, hence *Rassemblement Social-iste Progressive; Parti Social pour le Progrès; and Union Démocratique Unioniste.*

69. Moore, '*La Tunisie après Vingt Ans de Crise de Succession*', 13.

70. Susan Waltz, 'Clientelism and Reform in Bin Ali's Tunisia', in Zartman (ed.), *Tunisia: The Political Economy of Reform*, 36.

71. Mark Tessler, 'Tunisia's New Beginning', *Current History*, 89 (April 1990), 171.

72. Ibid.

73. Zartman, 'The Conduct of Political Reform: The Path Toward Democracy', p. 21.

74. Raymond A. Hinnebusch, *Egyptian Politics Under Sadat: The Post-Populist Development of an Authoritarian-Modernizing State* (Cam-bridge: Cambridge University Press, 1985), 84.

75. Ibid.

76. See details of the 'October Working Paper', by George Carpozi Jr., *A Man of Peace: Anwar Sadat* (New York: Manor Books, 1979), 63–72.

77. See Cooper, *The Transformation of Egypt*, 199.

78. Veteran Free Officer, Khalid Muhi al-din emerged as leader of the left-ist tendency, *al-Tajammu 'l-Watani 'l-Taqaddumi 'l-wahdawi* (National Progressive Unionist Coalition). Another, Mustafa Kamal Murad, became leader of the rightist tendency, *al-Ahrar* (Liberals). The main centrist platform, *Hizb Misr* (Egypt Party) was headed by the then Prime Min-ister, Mamduh Salim. The latter's victory in al-Sadat's first elections of November 1976 was decisive, winning 280 seats in the *Majlis al-Shaab* (People's Assembly). Independents won 48, *al-ahrar* 12, and *al-Tajammu* only 2. For a summary of these developments consult Moench, 'The May 1984 Elections in Egypt and the Question of Egypt's Stability', pp. 60–3. See also the Ahram Centre's report on Arab pluralism, in *al-Taqrir*

al-Arabi 'l-Istratiji 1989 [The Arab Strategic Report 1989] (Cairo: Markiz al-Dirasat al-Siyasiyyah wa 'l-Istratijiyyah bi 'l-Ahram, 1990), esp. 290–1.

79. Roger Owen, *State, Power and Politics in the Making of the Modern Middle East* (London: Routledge, 1992), 273–7; see also, Mona Makram-Ebeid, 'Political Opposition in Egypt: Democratic Myth or Reality', 423–36.

80. For a good account of Egypt's politics under Mubarak see, Robert Springborg, *Mubarak's Egypt: Fragmentation of the Political Order* (Boulder and London: Westview Press, 1989). See also, Ayubi, *The State and Public Policies in Egypt Since Sadat*, 221–51.

81. Derek Hopwood, *Egypt: Politics and Society 1945–90* (London: Harper Collins Academic, 1991), 186.

82. See, for instance, 'Violence in Algeria and a Media Blackout in Egypt', in *Civil Society*, VI (October 1997), 5–11.

83. See 'Mubarak Reprimands the Press', in *Civil Society*, VII (March 1998), 9–11.

84. Mustapha Kamal al-Sayyid, 'A Civil Society in Egypt', in Norton (ed.), *Civil Society in the Middle East*, 273.

85. For a summary of these points see Moench, 'The May 1984 Elections in Egypt and the Question of Egypt's Stability', 56–7.

86. For accounts of phases of his political liberalization see John P. Entelis, 'Introduction: State and Society in Transition', in Entelis and Naylor (eds.), *State and Society in Algeria*, 17–20.

87. See Scott B. MacDonald, 'The Midde East's New Economic Wave', *Middle East Insight*, 6 (November/December 1989), 47. See also Mansour, *The Arab World: Nation, State and Democracy*, 104–13.

88. Many marginals, who were hit hardest not only by high prices but also by water rationing, took refuge in Bab el-Oued or al-Qobba where Islamists reticulated charity and welfare support systems. For FIS charity work see, 'Taking Up Space in Tlemcen: The Islamist Occupation of Urban Algeria', *Middle East Report*, 22 (November/December 1992), 11–15.

89. This multiplier effect of Algeria's democratization has been described as a *'printemps démocratique'* [spring of democracy]; see Jean Daniel, *'Alger: Le ciel et la rue'* [Algiers: The Sky and the Street], *Le Nouvel Observateur*, 15–21 April 1990, 38–40.

90. Ibid. 31.

91. There were 231 seats contested in the first round. By winning 188, the FIS were only 27 seats short of a majority. The second winner was the FFS with 25, followed by the FLN with 15 seats. See Abdeslam Maghraoui, 'Problems of Transition to Democracy: Algeria's Short-lived Experiment with Electoral Politics', *Middle East Insight*, 8 (Winter 1992), 20–6; see also Alfred Hermida, 'Democracy Derailed', *Africa Report*, 37/2 (March—April 1992), 13–17.

92. See, for instance, Huntington's *Third Wave*; see also, Juan J. Linz and Alfred Stepan (eds.), *The Breakdown of Democratic Regimes: Latin*

America (Baltimore and London: Johns Hopkins University Press, 1978). See also how Saad Eddin Ibrahim applies the tools of advances and reversals to the Arab setting in his, 'Civil Society and Prospects of Democratization in the Arab World', esp. 48–51.

93. Lisa Anderson, 'Liberalism in Northern Africa', *Current History*, 89 (April 1990), 145–8; 174–5; see also, in the same edition, Mary-Jane Deeb, 'New Thinking in Libya': 149–152.

94. Consult the informative and fine article by Kamal Osman Salih, 'Kuwait's Parliamentary Elections: 1963–1985: An Appraisal', *Journal of South Asian and Middle Eastern Studies*, XVI (Winter 1992), 17–40.

95. For a good account of the Moroccan monarch's centrality see John Waterbury, *The Commander of the Faithful: The Moroccan Political Elite—A Study in Segmented Politics* (London: Weidenfeld and Nicolson, 1970), esp. chapter seven, 145–165. See also, '*La démocratie, c'est moi*' [Democracy is Me] *Jeune Afrique*, 2–9 September 1992, 4–7.

96. For more details on the monarchical dominance in Morocco see Mark A. Tessler, 'Institutional Pluralism and Monarchical Dominance', in I. William Zartman et al., *Political Elites in Arab North Africa: Morocco, Algeria, Tunisia, Libya and Egypt* (New York and London: Longman, 1982), 35–91.

97. See the fine article on the Moroccan elections by Mustapha Sehimi, '*Les élections législatives au Maroc*', *Maghreb/Machrek*, 107 (1985), 23–39.

98. See how this party, Morocco's oldest and a leading force in the struggle for independence, was a source of paranoia to the monarchy immediately after independence. In a way, as Waterbury indicates, Morocco's multiparty system was aimed to curtail the *Istiqlal's* power; Waterbury, *The Commander of the Faithful*, p. 145.

99. Marc Yared, '*A la tête de l'Algérie: deux généraux et deux civils*' [At the Head of Algeria, Two Generals and Two Civilians], *Jeune Afrique*, 16–23 January 1992, 5–7; in the same issue see also, Hamza Kaidi '*Comment L'armée fait de la politique malgré elle*' [How the Army makes Politics in Spite of Itself], 7–8; Béchir Ben Yahmed, '*Chadli était la malchance de l'Algérie*' [Chadli was Algeria's Bad Luck], 9; Albert Bourgi, '*Ce regime n'etait plus qu'une coquille vide*' [This Regime was no more than an empty Shell], 10–11. See also André Pautard, '*Algérie: le plan des généraux*' [Algeria: the Generals' Plan], *L'Express* 2115 (24 January 1992), 10–11; Francis Ghiles, 'Algerian Poll in Doubt as President Quits Office', *Financial Times*, 13 January 1992, 1 and 5, see also editorial, 'A Step Back in Algeria', p. 10.; Youssef M. Ibrahim, 'Interim leaders in Algeria Stop Elections for Seats in Parliament', *New York Times*, 13 January 1992, 1, A10; also by Ibrahim, 'Algerians, Angry with the Past, Divided over their Future', *New York Times*, 19 January 1992, Section 4, 3; for the Articles of the Emergency Decree, see, *Middle East Economic Digest*, 36 (21 February 1992), 9; Lahouari Addi, 'Algeria's Democracy Between the Islamists and the Elite', *Middle East Report*, 22 (March/April 1992), 36–8.

100. See the speech by the then Algerian Premier Abdessalam to the Martyrs' Sons Organization Conference in June 1993: '... I shall not consider the three million Algerians who voted for the FIS as enemies. They are compatriots who, for several reasons, did not make the right choice...' Earlier he says: 'We have a duty towards them... [to] convince them that they are wrong and that they are duty-bound to reconsider their ideas and choice... we should try to restore them to the right path... so that they may return to the ranks of the national movement.' In 'Algeria: PM Says There Will Be No Dialogue with Destructive Forces', Reuter Australian Briefing, *Reuters News Textline*, 22 June 1993.

101. Cooper gives a thorough summary of the riots and their dynamics linking them to the failure of Sadat's *infitāḥ*. These riots, which were likened to the 'burning of Cairo' in 1952 when Faruq was overthrown, were quashed with the help of the army. There were '80 deaths' and 560 people were wounded. See Chapter 13, 'The January Riots', in Cooper's *The Transformation of Egypt*, 235–45.

102. Moench, 'The May 1984 Elections in Egypt and the question of Egypt's Stability', p. 62.

103. Hinnebusch, *Egyptian Politics Under Sadat*, 170.

104. Ibid. 78.

105. Gehad Auda, 'Egypt's Uneasy Party Politics', *The Journal of Democracy*, 2 (Spring 1992), 70–8.

106. For a similar idea see Hinnebusch, *Egyptian Politics Under Sadat*, 173.

107. Moench, 'The May 1984 Elections in Egypt and the Question of Egypt's Stability', 72.

108. See 'Egyptian Opposition Parties Issue Program', *Civil Society*, VII (February 1998), 11.

109. Salih, 'Kuwait's Parliamentary Elections: 1963–1985: An Appraisal', 30–1.

110. Roger Owen, 'The Practice of Electoral Democracy in the Arab East and North Africa: Some Lessons from Nearly a Century's Experience', in Goldberg et al., *Rules and Rights in the Middle East*, 38.

111. Ibid.

112. Makram-Ebeid, 'Political Opposition in Egypt', 432.

113. Ibid.

114. Moench, 'The May 1984 Elections in Egypt', 75.

115. Eva Bellin, 'Civil Society in Formation: Tunisia', in Norton (ed.) *Civil Society in the Middle East*, 134.

116. For a summary of these points see Ibid. 134–5.

117. The title of a book. See Anne Phillips, *Gendered Democracy* (Cambridge: Polity Press, 1990).

118. Hani Al-Hurani, '*Intikhabatu 1993 al-'Urduniyyah*', *Qira'at Siyasiyyah*, 4 (Spring 1994), 15.

119. Ibid. 14–15.

120. Brand, '... The Quest for Civil Society in Jordan', 162–3.

121. Ibid. 162.

122. See, '*Al-ta'dilat ala qanuni al-ahzabi al-siyāsiyyah, Khutwah fi al-ittijah al-mu'akis*' [Political Parties Law Amendments: a step in the wrong direction], *AHRO Background Briefing* no's. 60–1 (February–March 1993), 2–3.

123. Scott Mattoon, 'Islam by Profession', *The Middle East*, 218 (December 1992), 16–18; Mattoon, 'A Sense of Foreboding', *The Middle East*, 219 (January 1993), 36–7.

124. See 'Onslaught on Union Freedoms and the Right to Organize', *EHRO Press Release*, Cairo, 21 February 1993.

125. Fahmi Huwaydi, *Al-Islamu wa al-dimuqratiyyah* [Islam and Democracy] (Cairo: Markiz al-Ahram, 1993).

126. For further details see *Le Monde*, 16 June 1992. See also Bellin, 'Civil Society in Formation: Tunisia', 138–9.

127. See the fine work by Kamal Salibi, *A House of Many Notions* (London: I. B. Taurus, 1988).

128. Khairallah, 'Secular Democracy: A Viable Alternative to the Confessional System', 259.

129. Ibid. 260.

130. Ibid.

131. Ibid.

132. Ibid. 263.

133. For details of this earlier distinction see Robert Bianchi, 'Islam and Democracy in Egypt', *Current History*, 88 (February 1989), 93.

134. See the Algerian case in, '*La guerre des imams*' [The War of Imams], *Jeune Afrique*, 17–23 July 1991, 21.

135. Mattoon, 'A Sense of Foreboding', 36.

136. *Manshur* 108 (law 108) was a very controversial law making it illegal for women to wear the *hijab* in public. It was introduced during Burqiba's last years and has been kept by the new regime.

137. '*Moubarak, un rais pas comme les autres*' [Mubarak, a president not like the others], *Jeune Afrique*, 9–16 March 1988, 65.

138. For further details see the response of the Saudi Grand Mufti, Abd al-Aziz Ibn Baz, *Hukmu 'l-Islam* [The Ruling of Islam] (Medina: The Islamic University Publications, 1980).

139. James P. Piscatori, *Islam in a World of Nation-States* (Cambridge: Cambridge University Press, 1986), 32–3.

140. For further details on this point see Saad Eddin Ibrahim, 'The Future of Human Rights in the Arab world', in Hisham Sharabi (ed.), *The Next Arab Decade* (Boulder: Westview Press, 1988), 41.

141. Piscatori, *Islam in a World of Nation States*, 32.

142. Ibid.

143. Gehad Auda, 'The Islamic Movement and Resource Mobilization in Egypt: A Political Culture Perspective', in Larry Diamond (ed.), *Political Culture and Democracy in Developing Countries* (Boulder and London: Lynne Rienner, 1993), 379.

144. Bellin, 'Civil Society in Formation: Tunisia', 140.

145. Accounts of the report can be found in *Jeune Afrique*, 12 August 1992.
146. See Larbi Sadiki, 'Islamists Fight the Secular State', *The Canberra Times*, 13 August 1993, 9.
147. Hermassi, 'Socio-economic Change and Political Implications: the Maghreb', 239.
148. Michael C. Hudson. 'Democratization and the Problem of Legitimacy in Middle East Politics', *Middle East Studies Association Bulletin*, 22 (December 1988), 157–71. Hudson's definition is produced in five italicized points used as criteria by which to assess the state of Arab democratization.
149. Saad Eddin Ibrahim, 'The Betrayal of Democracy by Egypt's Intellectuals', *Civil Society*, 2 (February 1992), 1.
150. Ibid.
151. Ann M. Lesch, 'Democracy in Doses: Mubarak Launches his Second Term as President', *Arab Studies Quarterly*, 11 (Fall 1989), 105.
152. See introduction by Mark Tessler and David Garnham in Mark Tessler and David Garnham (eds.), *Democracy, War and Peace in the Middle East* (Bloomington and Indianapolis: Indiana University Press, 1995), p. x.

4

The Greater Middle East Initiative: A US Democracy Promotion 'Road Map'?

Our commitment to democracy is also tested in the Middle East, which is my focus today, and must be a focus of American policy for decades to come. In many nations of the Middle East—countries of great strategic importance—democracy has not yet taken root. And the questions arise: Are the peoples of the Middle East somehow beyond the reach of liberty? Are millions of men and women and children condemned by history or culture to live in despotism?... Governments across the Middle East and North Africa are beginning to see the need for change... As changes come to the Middle Eastern region, those with power should ask themselves: Will they be remembered for resisting reform, or for leading it?...

Sixty years of Western nations excusing and accommodating the lack of freedom in the Middle East did nothing to make us safe— because in the long run, stability cannot be purchased at the expense of liberty. As long as the Middle East remains a place where freedom does not flourish, it will remain a place of stagnation, resentment, and violence ready for export. And with the spread of weapons that can bring catastrophic harm to our country and to our friends, it would be reckless to accept the status quo.

Therefore, the United States has adopted a new policy, a forward strategy of freedom in the Middle East. This strategy requires the same persistence and energy and idealism we have shown before. And it will yield the same results. As in Europe, as in Asia, as in every region of the world, the advance of freedom leads to peace.

'Forward Strategy of Freedom' speech,
President George W. Bush[1]

In this chapter, I attempt to critically assess US democracy promotion in the AME, focusing on the period following September 11 and the invasion of Iraq in 2003. Declaratory policy, as in the above excerpt from President George W. Bush's 2003 speech, suggests that democracy is America's current *cause célèbre* in the AME. Such a cause has been *célèbre*; but the question regards another 'c'—that of credibility. How credible is such a cause in intending to open up opportunities for democratizing institutions and policies in the AME? To what extent does President Bush's stated goals present the AME with a serious opportunity for institutionalizing democracy? Similarly, what factors constrain the American drive to spread democracy to the Middle East? In seeking to answer these questions I shall follow a twofold analytical trajectory. First, I shall attempt to deconstruct the Greater Middle East Initiative (GMEI), the central plank in President Bush's 'forward strategy of freedom'. My deconstruction highlights the binary knowledge-making and power relations that underpin the GMEI's neo-Orientalist assumptions about the AME. Second, I follow up this discussion by investigating aspects of 'imposition' via 'intimidation' and 'invasion', categories of analysis deployed by Laurence Whitehead in his enquiry into the international context's impact on democratization in Latin America. To this end, I draw on interviews with select key Arab politicians and opinion formulators, thus sampling existing narratives on the US democratization 'road map' in the AME. I shall preface the analysis by considering the international dimensions of democracy promotion. I touch on the difficulty of wedding theory to practice, and account for the democratizing effects of 'contagion' in the AME.

Democratization via 'Contagion' in the AME

The fourth wave of democratization has not incorporated the AME in its geo-political precincts. Thus recurs the problem of disjuncture of theory and experience. Learning gathered in one region may have only limited utility in another. It is the age-old dilemma of reconciling the universal and the particularistic. The fourth wave may have had a global reach starting in Southern Europe and then spreading to Southern and Latin America, Eastern Europe, South East Asia, and parts of Africa.[2] Its globality, however, does not equate with universality. Its explanations of democratic transition from an international perspective may not be universally applicable across boundaries of time, space, culture, history, and levels of economic and political development. Limitations on the generalizable value of democratic transition theory inspired by case studies from other regions should not condemn the AME to Orientalist 'exile'. That is, a region banished from history— 'out of step with history'. To enter and make history is assumed to have a single route: through liberal democracy (Francis Fukuyama's discredited thesis) as experienced from without the AME.

Nonetheless, democratic transition theory has an inquisitive or investigative value. It helps guide the researchers' line of enquiry about democratization in the AME. It equips researchers with a compass for navigating a very vast and difficult terrain. That is, by asking the right questions for investigating, in this case, the international dimensions of democracy promotion; specifically, the extent to which democratization (i.e. elective politics) in the AME has been responsive to 'contagion' or 'control' calls for evaluation. Whitehead, noting the 'contingency, subjectivity, ambiguity, and reversibility' in many transitions, utilizes these categories to re-read historical experiences with democratization.[3] His approach gives due attention to the international context of democratization and how it feeds into domestic processes, actors or events. Thus he, along with Schmitter, among others, question and debunk the conventional wisdom of early transitology that democratization is engineered autochthonously. For the purpose of deconstructing the GMEI, I refer to Whitehead's category of 'control' and 'imposition', which he applies to his special case study of Caribbean experiences with democratization. What is noteworthy here is the healthy 'revisionism' offered by both Whitehead and Schmitter, who, with Guillermo O'Donnell, pioneered the democratization 'paradigm' through the classic three volumes on democratization, *Transitions from Authoritarian Rule*. A common finding by both scholars is that the age of purely autochthonous democratization has ended. The old assumption that 'democratization is a domestic affair *par excellence*' no longer holds true.[4] Schmitter interrogates his previous work, critically and eloquently noting a shift of emphasis on the role of international dynamics away from internal agency.

One of the most confident assertions in the O'Donnell-Schmitter concluding volume to the *Transitions from Authoritarian Rule* project was that 'domestic factors play a dominant role in the transition. Not only does this fly in the face of substantial (if hardly concordant) literature that stresses the dependence, interpenetration, and even integration increasingly embedded in the contemporary world system, but it also seems to clash with some obvious facts surrounding the more recent transitions that have occurred in Eastern Europe.'[5]

There is still a gulf separating Eastern and Southern Europe and Southern and Latin America from the AME. As noted above, the generalizable value may only be of limited utility given the specificity not only of the varied polities within the AME but also of those countries and regions from which a great deal of comparative work has already been accumulated about democratic transition. At the time of the first wave (1840s) many of the existing states in the AME did not exist (e.g. most of the Arab Gulf states). Others were part of the Ottoman Empire, provinces with varying degrees of autonomy from the centre in Istanbul. Algeria was at the time already a French colony, the first but not the last to fall under European expansionism. When the second wave picked up momentum after the First World War the bulk of the AME was without any form of sovereignty altogether. It was reeling under the twin tutelage of a decaying Ottoman rule and a new and more ferocious, sophisticated, and mechanized form of Western colonialism. Still some Arab states at the time did not see the light of day (e.g. most Arab Gulf states, Jordan, Lebanon). By the time of the third wave in the post–Second World War only a handful of nominally independent Arab nation-states emerged. Others were being carved out of the vast geography occupied at the time by the French and British, territory that either belonged or bordered on the dissolved Ottoman Empire since the mid-1920s. The Arab realms of the time did not share the smoother transition to nation-statehood and democracy of the states invented from another defunct supranational realm, the Austro-Hungarian Empire. It would take until the early 1970s for the last colonial powers to leave the Arab world to its own devices, bar of course the still disputed Moroccan–Spanish cities of Ceuta and Mellila, the Israeli-occupied Golan Heights, the West Bank and Gaza, and the Shab'ah farms in southern Lebanon.

Thus only in the course of the fourth wave, begun in 1974, was the AME assuming full control of its own affairs, be it through a modern history punctuated by wars separated by short interludes of peace. This historical background must not be overlooked. It illustrates the difficulty of relating what goes on in other transitions to the AME. Not only the AME's encounter with the nation-state is fairly recent, but also its grasp of democratization is not as firm as in other regions. Latin America's grip over democratization predates the Arab nation-state system. Whitehead writes about the milieu that favoured the rise of democracies in 'Uruguay before the First World War; in Argentina in the 1920s; in Chile from the 1930s, in Costa Rica after 1948;[6] in Colombia and Venezuela since 1958; and more generally in the 1970s and 1980s'. Paradoxically, the exogenous forces (e.g. British, French, Italian, and Spanish) that propelled the Arab nation-state into existence cared little for democratic government in the AME. The French and the British seem to have accorded democratic government more priority in non-Arab colonies (e.g. respectively in Martinique and in Bermuda according to Whitehead).[7] The former metropolitan powers did not dwell much on democratizing the AME despite the aristocratic parliaments and elections that emerged under colonial rule (e.g. in Egypt, Lebanon, Syria, and Tunisia). Those parliaments were more about legitimizing colonialism than creating genuine legitimacy and consultative processes for ending occupation. The former *colons* saw their role as inducting the natives into how to rule and administer not self-govern. This induction was motivated by an ethnocentric civilizing mission that was not purely altruistic. The 'white man's burden' to spread civilized political order aimed more at facilitating mercantilism than democracy.

Preoccupation today by the United States and the EU with democratization in the AME is relatively new when compared with other regions. The United States, for instance, has since the nineteenth century actively promoted democracy, be it unevenly at times and through non-democratic means throughout the twentieth century, in Central and Latin America and the Caribbean. Such a commitment, not always motivated by principled ideals but by realpolitik and by pursuit of national interests, necessitated extreme measures such as intimidation (e.g. Nicaragua) and invasion (Panama, Haiti).[8] President Reagan's National Endowment for Democracy (NED) accorded priority for democracy promotion during the 1980s to Europe and Asia with little or no attention to the AME.[9] The indigenous inheritors of the post-colonial state fare not any better than the ex-colons in this regard. No sooner had the elites that were at the vanguard of the nationalist resistance against colonialism 'colonized' the newly founded states than they set out to erase all of the vestiges of foreign rule. They dismantled the emergent independent states' democratic façade, namely, political parties and parliaments. They made no effort to revamp, reform, or found on these institutions more representative and accountable government. The absence of an indigenous contagion effect, a democratic model, from within the AME has contributed to the routinization of autocracy in the AME. I turn now to this aspect of 'contagion' in order to illuminate the nexus between autochthonous agency and the exogenous impact on political reform in the AME. I have divided this discussion into contagion from within and from without the AME.

Contagion from Without the AME

Discussion of democratic transition by Whitehead and his co-authors illustrates the difficulty of drawing clear-cut boundaries between autochthonous and exogenous democratizing effects. Nor does neutral contagion preclude overlap with control, as Whitehead affirms.

Similarly, Schmitter argues the case for conditionality without over-looking its imperfection as a democratizing mechanism. He notes that even under conditionality some element of domestic voluntarism is required to set the scene for democratization. The extent to which the tone for cautious endorsement of democratic rule by Arab status quo ruling groups has been set by exogenous factors cannot be established conclusively. Foreign meddling in Arab affairs largely served to inhibit rather than foster democracy. The value of Huntington's 'snowballing' and 'demonstration effects' of pioneering third-wave transitions[10] is not fully evident in Arab democratic stirrings. This is not to be taken as a proposition that the Arab body politic is immune to worldwide trends. The reverberations of the emergence of democracy in 1989 as still one of the most important issues in world politics, and the impact of the revolutionary grass-roots-based transformations ensued by the fall of Stalinist regimes in Eastern Europe, were felt polit-ically and intellectually throughout the Arab world. Arab regimes were no doubt dismayed by the 'power of the powerless' that brought about the downfall of dictators. For instance, in a joint European Community–Arab League meeting in Paris in December in 1989, the news of the downfall of Romania's Nicolae Ceausescu elicited no more than an icy reaction from the Arabs: 'While the European ministers clapped and cheered, the Arab delegates sat in stony silence. Some of them, no doubt, were uneasily aware of the similarities between their own countries and the unlamented dictators.'[11] While the impact of such monumental events should not be underrated, it equally should not be overstated. For Arab regimes showed resilience in the face of the Iranian Islamic Revolution of 1979, one of the prodigious events of the twentieth century and one which presents them with greater cultural and geographic propinquity. These very regimes have also weathered the implications, even if further afield, of the 1986 Philippine Revolution whose deposed dictator Marcos held consider-able resemblance to many Arab rulers. Most important, however, were the 1985 people's power upheaval in Sudan (precipitating the coup which ended al-Numayri's 16-year dictatorship), and the multiparty elections the following year in which opposition won government for the first time ever in the AME. The failure of this Arab precedent to be replicated elsewhere in the Arab world raises legitimate ques-tions as to the value of European or South American demonstration effects. Furthermore, both the Algerian and Jordanian reforms of the late 1980s preceded the Eastern European 'democratic revolution'. Nonetheless, cascading changes elsewhere have often inspired limited political adjustments in the AME. Gorbachev's perestroika is a case in point.

The so-called Gorbachev phenomenon with its twin declaratory policies of *perestroika*[12] (restructuring) and *glasnost* (openness) relatively and indirectly sets the tempo of political liberalization in the Arab world. Like elsewhere, Gorbachev's *perestroika* and *glasnost* became a kind of a beacon for political reform in the Arab world. Their main lesson was reform or perish . . . hence the notion of Arab *perestroika*.[13]

A good example of the former Soviet Union's reforms' limited trend-setting effect at the level of leadership was al-Qadhafi's embracing of perestroika—one that was minimalist and superficial.[14] His own brand of perestroika prompted him to deprecate and disown many of his past policies and ideological positions presented in his *Green Book*, to attack the popular committees—the putative instruments of self-government—accusing them of 'murder and terrorism',[15] and to reconsider economic liberalization: 'Suddenly, he has become a champion of human rights, political freedoms and the black market . . . [and] even saw fit to offer advice to Mikhail Gorbachev on how the Soviet Union should conduct its own perestroika.'[16] In spite of this, Gorbachev's perestroika cannot be said to have had great effect in the Arab world. Whatever substantive significance they might have had has acted more in negative than in positive terms. The former Soviet Union's reorientation from totalitarianism to a form of rule more congenial with pluralism and human rights, and its reprioritization of its foreign relations towards the West at the expense of its satellites and clients (owing primarily to its economic development which was stunted by a costly arms race with the United States) meant less willingness to sponsor its protégé dictatorial regimes in the AME. The unavailability of that sponsorship put, for instance, the Marxist regime in the People's Democratic Republic of Yemen (formerly South Yemen) in a very shaky position for which it sought a solution through unification with northern Yemen in May 1990.[17] Emboldened by territorial gains against Iran, Iraq sought to reinvent its *raison d'être* by invading Kuwait in 1991. It can be argued that Gorbachev's perestroika was a factor in the weakening of Arab pariah or failed regimes which, to a limited extent, owed their political legitimacy within the international community to the former Soviet Union's patronage in the 1970s and 1980s. Marxist Yemen is no more. The edifice that was Saddam Hussein's Iraq no longer exists. Libya has given up its adventurism (at the cost of hefty compensation payments to the Lockerbie victims' families, and the handing over of its rudimentary nuclear programme to the United States), and has since 2003 sought to rebuild its foreign relations and with it its image of a 'rogue state'. It has switched sides from Moscow to Washington and is currently working to secure an association agreement with the EU. In spite of its partial isolation the Syrian regime, also a former Soviet client, lacks not the pragmatism needed to seek closer ties with the EU and the United States. However, finding in the AME identical analogues to the plethora of case studies of successful democratic transitions either directly engineered by external agency or fostered by international power politics is a tough assignment. Marxist Yemen is a qualified exception. There was no 'Berlin wall' separating North and South Yemen, and South Yemen never was militarily, industrially, ideologically, or politically the satellite East Germany, for example, was to Moscow. Literally, South Yemen was a peripheral satellite, one that was governed like a 'personalist' regime (to paraphrase Max Weber) notwithstanding the ruling elite's communist ideology. Loss of Soviet tutelage and material sponsorship weakened the state but never cancelled out the ruling elite's chance of political survival. Through unification with the North the elite intended to reinvent itself in the same fashion former communists in Romania, for instance, embraced democratic politics in the post–Ceausescu era. Nonetheless, the infectiousness of the Gorbachev factor and the post-Soviet international order in terms of political reform in the AME is limited. This is so at least when compared with other international factors. In this respect, the elective politics that followed the 1991 Gulf War and, more specially, after the September 11 terrorist attacks on the United States in 2001, and the invasion of Iraq in 2003 stand out, a discussion I shall return to when considering contagion from within the AME.

States in the AME have not been immured from international contexts that, as Whitehead and Schmitter argue, can serve to promote, but sometimes demote, democratization. Decolonization represents a historical moment, yet a missed opportunity, for liberalizing politics in the newly founded Arab states. Soon after independence elections, political parties, and parliaments existed only ephemerally. Libya and Syria are by current standards the furthest from democratization. Yet both had in the mid- to late 1950s democratic institutions. Had these institutions survived both countries would have provided a democratizing contagion effect within the AME. In fact, the 1958 Constitution is the shared platform for the secular and Islamist opposition in Syria. Like decolonization, the Cold War served more of a constraint than a catalyst for democratization within the AME. The Cold War not only divided the global polity into camps but also served to sideline democratization as a moral standard in the behaviour of nation-states. Whitehead observes that 13 of the 61 states described in 1990 by Freedom House to be 'free' used the Cold War to justify their undemocratic systems.[18] To an extent, this was true of a number of Arab states (e.g. Egypt under Nasser, Algeria, Syria, Iraq, Libya, Southern Yemen) which were clients of Moscow in the heyday of the Cold War. Alliance with Washington or with Paris entailed no pressure to democratize either. Jean Kirkpatrick's cliché phrase about 'good dictators', in reference to authoritarian regimes allied to the United States, applied widely in the bipolar world of the 1970s and 1980s. Her tautological phrase 'bad dictators' was reserved for the former Soviet Union client regimes, including a few Arab states.[19] The Cold War context played a restrictive role with regard to democratization. By contrast, it can be argued that the post–Cold War context has relatively had a positive effect on democratization. This positive aspect of the international context's impact on democratization is not as apparent in the AME as in Eastern Europe, for instance. Theory, it must be stressed again, gleaned from comparative studies of democratic transition does not readily apply to the AME. Democratization scored a major victory expanding the global reach of the fourth wave following the collapse of the former Soviet Union in the late 1980s and early 1990s.[20] No single Arab state featured in that fourth wave, even though Schmitter considers the Algerian and Tunisian reforms of the late 1980s to be the qualified exceptions.[21]

Contagion from Within the AME

The discussion now turns to the investigation of this aspect of democratization by looking at contagion from within the AME. The problem here is that there is no shining 'democratic models' in the AME. There have of course been exemplary competitive and fair elections (e.g. Palestinian elections of 2006; the first round of Algerian parliamentary elections of 1991). What matters most here is not so much the presence of a 'model' Arab democracy to inspire emulation or facilitate diffusion of democratic norms of behaviour. The backdrop against which contagion from within has unraveled in the AME is, in the absence of a single Arab democratic 'model', as important. Pertinent to this background are three destabilizing events: the 1991 Gulf War, September 11, and the invasion of Iraq in 2003. The 1991 Gulf War and its aftermath produced more democratic hype than democratic practice. Everywhere in the AME polity and society seemed enmeshed in the democratic discourse. The whole Arab body politic was gripped by a sense of foreboding. This was triggered by the realization, within and without the AME, of the calamitous state of political play under continuous autocracy. Saddam Hussein's miscalculation would have been restrained had there been democratic checks and balances in

Iraq. Elsewhere in the AME the war displayed the wide gulf between the rulers and the ruled. The mass popular demonstrations against the war and Arab participation in it against a fellow Arab country, Iraq, showed wide public disaffection with Arab rulers. From Morocco on the Atlantic to Yemen on the Straits of Hormuz hostile Arab public opinion to the 1991 war confirmed the suspicion that what the rulers willed and what the ruled expected were at loggerheads. The demonstrations were not in vein. Eventually, they forced adjustments on the part of the regimes of the Arab coalition whose armed forces fought alongside the United States. They discontinued direct support for the US-led forces soon after the liberation of Kuwait.

In terms of democratic practice, the 1990s saw a flurry of electoral activities, which were reactionary—mostly knee-jerk responses to domestic problems in the lesser-to-do Arab states. Elections picked up momentum in the AME, as already discussed in Chapters 2 and 3. But only Kuwait and, eventually Oman, in the Arab Gulf held elections in the late 1990s. In 1999 Qatar experimented for the first time in its modern history with civic council elections. The events of September 11 and the invasion of Iraq were by far the most catalytic events in terms of setting into motion infectious electoral effects. Countries that were at the time of the 1991 Gulf War totally devoid of electoralism have in a few years after September 11 and the invasion of Iraq entered or re-entered the age of elective politics. Bahrain and Qatar, respectively one and two years after September 11, drafted and adopted by popular referenda new constitutions. In 2002 Bahrain resumed elections after an interruption of electoral and parliamentary life for nearly 30 years. Kuwait, Oman, and Qatar consolidated their electoralism by adhering to the practice of periodic elections. Saudi Arabia and UAE waited, respectively, two and three years after the invasion of Iraq (which itself held its first democratic elections in 2005) to hold their first elections since their founding as nation-states. The elective momentum, even if cosmetic in one or two instances, forbade democratic inaction in the region. If all else was equal and neither event took place, Kuwait would be the natural choice for an elective Arab Gulf model. But that model during the period in question was missing. Rather, than being triggered by a norm or trend-setter, the contagion derived from a sense of urgency by the political atmospherics following two devastating and costly wars in the region, and the world's most spectacular terrorist attack on the only superpower. Caught in the vortex of these violent events, the entire Arab Gulf body politic came under closer scrutiny as an oddity of modernity and tradition, benevolent rule and political absolutism, hydrocarbon and commercial dynamism, religious and political inertia in contrast to effervescence in the arts and the media, and of interconnectedness resulting from globalization contrasted by cultural insulation.

The Gulf region was in the midst of an identity crisis and adjustments had to be made urgently given the overpowering realities on the ground. These realities included the heavy militarization and increase in US bases in the Arab Gulf with some loss of sovereignty. The rise of US power had to be adjusted with absorption of the 'bitter pill' of a modicum of democratic affinity with the United States. It is a minimum and immaterial conditionality tacitly written in the new Pax-Americana in the Arab Gulf: no protection without a form of representation. US protection and sacrifice of its citizens' lives in the Arab Gulf must be met with corresponding fine-tuning in the arena of political values. After all, the United States invaded Iraq with a democracy promotion agenda, though this was not the initial policy objective. It would be overtly a case of juggling international double standards to promote democracy in Iraq and overlook autocracy in the Arab Gulf. From Bush Senior to Bush Junior, US administrations fought wars to, unwittingly and concomitantly, corrode dictatorship in Iraq and protect non-representative and non-accountable rule in the neigbouring Arab Gulf states. In this case the rise of US power demanded, and, subsequently, resulted in electoral activity in all of the Arab Gulf states. Somehow the rise of electoralism in the Arab Gulf is tantamount to a minimalist act of disassociation with Saddam Hussein's dictatorship. For, American and world public opinion finds little to distinguish Saddam Hussein's rule from that of his neighbours. Both lack in legitimacy, accountability, and representation. This poses a moral dilemma for US administrations conducting unpopular or illegal war, which applies to the invasion of Iraq. To an extent, the timing of the introduction of elective politics in Qatar (first parliamentary elections in 2009 or 2010), Saudi Arabia, and the UAE, and their resumption with regularity in Kuwait and Bahrain has been determined by the United States. The coincidence with the GMEI must be recorded here, a point to be taken up below. Even if the Arab Gulf electoralism is not principled (as the rulers' power is not up for grabs), it partly accommodates the US agenda to democratize the Middle East. There is no deviation here from the election fetishism taking hold in the rest of the AME. This electoralism has equally been demanded by self-preservation by ruling houses whose only legitimacy is based on performance legitimacy, a function of distribution of welfare goods. The proliferation of US bases, the rise in the armament bill, the partial loss of sovereignty, the incapacity to protect resources and territory all have demanded political adjustments, limited measures of participation and inclusiveness. What is contagious here is the psychology of survival through the ballot, the only form of distribution not attempted in the Arab Gulf except in Kuwait. But these elections are not designed to challenge the status quo. The vote is thus added to the other 'goods' distributed by the state: health, education, welfare handouts, employment, and consumer bargaining power. It is almost a case of the vote being another symbol of affluence; it upgrades citizenship to a higher level of satisfaction that buys off more durability in power for the royal houses. Those citizens who can drive the best cars and other luxury items that money can buy can now also vote. Even the vote has been commodified, and is exchanged for pecuniary rewards in most Arab Gulf states, a practice found also in Egypt, Jordan, Lebanon, Syria, and Yemen.

The other non-conventional conditionality factored tacitly into the power equation in Arab Gulf–US relations is the fact, especially where Saudi Arabia is concerned, that the perpetrators of September 11 were largely Saudi and Gulf citizens and punitive measures have been taken against only a handful of Saudi financiers. The September 11 event is like an axe to grind when need be to extract concessions from the Saudi rulers whose civic councils elections of 2005 can be surmised as a minimalist response to US pressure to reform. Exogenous machination determined the timing for Arab Gulf elections. However, the pace and substance of elective politics have been entirely determined by autochthonous agency. Here manifestation is strongest of 'contagion' effects in the AME and elsewhere. Contagion processes in the case of Eastern Europe have flowed from 'non-coercive and neutral transmission mechanisms'[22] cumulatively leading to genuine and substantive openings, geared towards augmented participation and contestation, and supported by dynamic civil societies. Contagion processes in the AME seem to involve a degree of veiled coercion in a moment of political uncertainty and insecurity, not confidence about democratizing polity substantively, forcing the rulers into defensive reforms managed by the centre. The veiled coercion stems from the fact that the prevalent political systems of the Arab Gulf, particularly, and the AME more generally, have become suspects in an atmosphere of hubris, following September 11. Osama Bin Laden became a damning symbol of the Arab lag in democratization and human rights. Saddam Hussein's regime became shorthand for Arab misrule, an indictment of all political systems in the AME. Basically, there was urgency to reform. The sacking of Baghdad became a powerful reminder to all Arab rulers of the fate that could befall non-reformers. The Bulgarians, Checks, Poles, East Germans, Hungarians, and the Romanians enacted their reforms in the 1989–90 period of Soviet decline with confidence to steer a more autonomous and democratic political destiny. The electoralism in the states of the Arab Gulf, at the turn of the new millennium, and in the rest of the AME since the 1990s, coincides with US ascendancy in the political and military affairs of the AME at a cost of varying degrees of sovereignty in many an Arab state. It is thus debatable whether the contagion hypothesis, as deployed by Whitehead, is sufficient in precipitating Arab electoralism without working in tandem with additional forms of control, including imposition and invasion (e.g. Iraq).

Contagion as a trend-setting process is not unknown to the AME. The most evident contagion effect in the 1950s and 1960s was that of Nasser's military revolution of 1952 and attendant pan-Arab ideology. The spill-over effect of that revolution took the AME away from, rather than towards, democratization. A quasi domino effect unfolded as coups in Algeria (1965), Iraq (1958), Syria (1954), Sudan (1958), Libya (1969), and North Yemen (1954) propelled the military into power. Similarly, the Ba'thist coup in Iraq in February 1963 proved infectious in neighbouring Syria whose own Ba'thists staged a coup a month later. Negatively, the prevalence of patrimonial and autocratic rule in the AME has historically served to shield Arab regimes from pressure. Even a single democratic model in the AME would have made it difficult for Arab regimes to resist the tide of democratization for so long. Kuwait, the Arab country most versed in parliamentary politics and electoralism, has never been taken seriously as a democratic model for a number of reasons. It is a 'clan-state'; for the so-called Arab republics clan-politics is looked down upon as retrograde (*rij'ī*) and belonging to the era of Bey and Khedive-based rule. The irony is that at the turn of the millennium at least three Arab republics (Egypt, Libya, Yemen) could see hereditary transfers of power from father to son. In a fourth, Syria, hereditary rule is already in place. Another factor is the small size of Kuwait, a country with a demography dominated by expatriates. Current politics in the AME bespeaks the myth that the democratizing model should come from large Arab states (e.g. Egypt).

However, to assign contagion a democratizing effect may be far-fetched. The explanation for this is simple given the meaning 'contagion' denotes in democratic transition. Whitehead understands it be the 'neutral transmission mechanisms that might induce countries bordering on democracies to replicate the political institutions of their neighbours'.[23] To apply the contagion hypothesis to the AME, I follow Whitehead's 'parsimonious procedure'. 'The procedure is first to establish a binary classification of countries according to some simple and schematic objective tests, and then to observe the geographical distribution of the countries classified as democratic, and how it changes over time.'[24] This exercise, as Whitehead explains, uncovers clusters and sequences, leaving no room for 'random association', as well as substantiates 'contagion through proximity'. Two problems arise when applying this procedure to the AME. First, there are no democracies in the AME. But instead of democracies there have been democratic stirrings, mostly manifest in the initiation and routinization of electoralism. For the purpose of this exercise these may be called 'electoral polities'. Second, the time span is too short, especially in the case of the Arab Gulf, to uncover meaningful sequences or trends of electoral consolidation. Nonetheless, two distinctive clusters are noticeable of old and new 'electoral polities'. Egypt (1984); Sudan (1986); Jordan (1989); Tunisia (1989); Algeria (1991); Mauritania (1992); Kuwait (1992); Lebanon (1992); Yemen (1993); and Morocco (1997)—all within 13 years—constitute the first sequence. This first sequence builds on electoral processes initiated in Sadat's Egypt in 1976, Morocco in 1977, and Kuwait and Tunisia in 1981. These coincide with the Carter years and the messages transmitted neutrally around the world re-opened the questions of human rights and democratic government. Sadat was effecting the most dramatic changes in Egypt's internal and external politics since the death of Nasser. He curtailed military and economic reliance on the former Soviet Union, kept the Kremlin's influence at a minimum, and began to switch alliance from Moscow to Washington. Economically, the message was attuned to Washington's value system and the *infitāḥ* policy was introduced in 1974, followed in 1976 by political openness, and eventually a peace treaty with Israel mediated by President Carter. This was a revolution that did away with Nasser's Arab socialism and, to a lesser extent, state-centered pan-Arabism. Political parties were once again legalized and the scene was set for multiparty politics. Algeria (1980) and Tunisia (1985), and eventually Morocco, set to emulate Egyptian openness through their own brands of market-oriented reforms or *infitāḥ*. These economic open-door policies and the political reforms resulting from them coincided with the beginning of an upward trend of US influence against a downward trend of decline in that of the former Soviet Union in the AME. Whether Egypt is the sole inspiration is a moot point. The elections of the early 1990s in Jordan and Algeria provided a demonstration effect in terms of rigour (freedom and fairness) to elicit responses in countries where elections suffered from either absence (e.g. Tunisia, Yemen) or discontinuity (e.g. Kuwait, Lebanon, Morocco). The initial neutral transmission mechanisms were first state-to-state—United States to Egypt and from there on to the rest of the AME. In the second stage the messages of openness were transmitted, may be not so neutrally, by the institutions of the Bretton Woods system, namely, the IMF. Egypt, Morocco, and Tunisia all experienced riots during that period resulting directly from IMF austerity programmes and messages of structural adjustments programmes from the World Bank. The message of openness was thus not decoded as receptively in the rest of the AME. The rentier states could through petrodollar largesse maintain subsidies, and, countries, such as Libya and Iraq, regarded the message to threaten national sovereignty. In the poorer Arab states there was not much room for maneuvering except by unavoidably relaxing economic and political '*dirigisme*', a discussion to be taken up in the ensuing chapter.

To an extent, the second sequence gives plausibility to the hypothesis of contagion through proximity. What is noteworthy here is the due recognition that must be accorded, even if in small measure, to the Kuwaiti role as a trend-setter in the Arab Gulf region. Kuwait has held elections since the early 1960s and has had a written constitution for as long. Its own election process was re-launched in 1992, one year after liberation and consolidated in 1999 despite the duress of reconstruction in the aftermath of a devastating war, which drained resources and popular and elite morale (especially under an ailing ruler and an equally ailing Crown Prince a the time). Given its geographical and political membership of the GCC, Kuwait belongs to the second cluster. Kuwait (1999)-Oman (2000)-Bahrain (2002)-Saudi Arabia (2005)-UAE (2006)-Qatar (2007)—all within eight years constitutes the second sequence. The transmission mechanisms of the message of unavoidable democratization are not confined to state-to-state channels. NGOs, including Amnesty International, AHRO, Middle East Watch, political parties, and various Arab human rights watchdogs have all absorbed the message and propagated it to the Arab publics. In the Arab Gulf the vociferous dissident movements in exile and at home, such as the Committee for the Defense of Human Rights (CDHR, Saudi Arabia), the women's movement in Kuwait, and the Shi'ite opposition in Bahrain, have all been proactive since the 1991 Gulf War. In particular, the petitions by the Islamist dissidents from within Saudi Arabia have been one form of pressing the royal house for just and non-corrupt rule in accordance with the Islamic principles of *shūrā*. Dissidents such Salman Al-Awdah and Safar Al-Hawali have stood out in these ongoing campaigns for reform. Some pressure came from inside the royal house itself, moderating the historical hostility of the rulers to democracy— or at least elections.[25] The media also have played a leading role in entrenching the message of reform. Media deregulation and the rise of satellite television, ironically funded by Gulf royalty, have pushed the democracy and human rights agenda furthest into the domain of public discussion. Al-Jazeerah, as I show in the final chapter, has been a beacon of change, helping consolidate Arab public opinion and provide a channel for voicing dissidence. However, as noted above, the short time-span necessitates future monitoring of these incipient electoral processes in the Arab Gulf. This monitoring is essential to see when Saudi Arabia upgrades civil elections to parliamentary elections, and when the UAE holds elections using universal suffrage. Proximity has plausibly proved infectious. Even if imperfect the electoralism in the first cluster has had spill-over effects. But as mentioned earlier the message transmitted by the United States, that reform has become inevitable in the post-September 11 and in the post-Saddam era, carried within it enough of a veiled threat to galvanize Arab Gulf rulers into defensive democratization must not be dismissed lightly. This is one reason why Whitehead notes the overlap between contagion and control/imposition.[26] I now turn to deconstruction of the GMEI, an analysis which will touch upon issues of control and imposition.

Enter the Greater Middle East Initiative

The United States in the AME and Democracy Promotion

No deconstruction of the GMEI would be complete without an equal understanding of the United States, the only superpower. This deconstruction is vital given the scepticism and reductionism that shroud the US role as a self-appointed 'prophet' of democracy. Whilst such scepticism and reductionism are commonplace in the AME, they are not specific to it. Sceptics question the United States' selflessness and high morality in its globally missionary democracy promotion, following the Cold War and more specifically, in relation to the AME, after September 11 and the invasion of Iraq. Others reduce the United States' democracy promotion to an example of an activity geared towards empire-building. Both ignore the fact that in the pursuit of this agenda the United States commits more funds than any other global actor, states and NGOs alike.[27] Moreover, the US moral commitment to democracy promotion cannot be belittled or simply dismissed as 'democratic imperialism'. The commitment is neither new nor disingenuous. It has grown exponentially in tandem with the United States' new status as the sole superpower. Hence the United States' ambition to reshape global culture by diffusing democratic norms is not misplaced.[28] Nor is such an ambition an historical aberration. The Greeks, the Romans, like the Babylonians and the Pharaohs before them, aspired to spreading their material and immaterial genius beyond their borders. So did the Christians and the Muslims. The scepticism and reductionism are the more accentuated in the case of the United States for its warring in the name of democracy. Eric Hobsbawm, the distinguished British historian, sums up the widespread scepticism revolving around the notion of a new US hegemony and imperialism. He notes that US militarism since 2001, under false pretenses of containing growing barbarity, resulted not only in illegal wars such as in Iraq, but also, and more importantly, has made the case for permanent interventionism and a world imperial hegemon, the United States. He calls this 'the imperialism of human rights', which had its origins in Bosnia.[29] The United States resolutely and selflessly intervened, Hobsbawm adds, to end the bloodshed with supposedly no apparent motive of self-interest. He rejects interventionism as barbarism even if couched in the moral or just cause of standing up to barbarity, real, or imagined. Wars are barbaric and therefore there is no 'good' and 'bad' barbarism.

It is fundamentally flawed by the fact that great powers in the pursuit of their international policies may do things that suit the champions of human rights, and be aware of the publicity value of doing so, but this is quite incidental to their purposes, which, if they think it necessary, are today pursued with the ruthless barbarism that is the heritage of the twentieth century.[30]

Hobsbawm's point is succinct and eloquent. Nonetheless, in making one relevant point he misses another, which is equally important. Specifically, the United States is one superpower but one with multiple identities. Unless the US global role, in general, and democracy promotion, in particular, are thus viewed the multifaceted and multilayered 'persona' of America is sacrificed. Simply pandering to the rhetoric of realism, in which states are held to be unified actors driven by the perennial search for security, will not allow better understanding of the state in a pluralized world. There is more to America than the oversimplified cliché phrase of empire building.

A more holistic picture of the US can be depicted through a constructivist, rather than a purely realist, lens.[31] To reduce the US to merely a new hegemon is a gross oversimplification of a superpower with multiple 'identities' as a global player in the AME. To demystify 'America' one has to search for the multiple 'Americas' within the overarching signifier that is the 'United States'. Realism tends to be rather static, cementing the understanding of nation-states to a fixed conceptual apparatus that over-does notions of balance of power, security, and self-interest. The constructivist approach opens up possibilities for rereading the US role in the AME away from the reductionism of neorealism and neoliberalism. Generally, constructivists reject to view the structure of the international system as either materialist (the former's emphasis on material forces) or institutional (the latter's stress on institutions).[32] Within this paradigmatic scheme, in the society of states international politics is socially constructed and so are the actors. Constructivists pay particular attention to the following areas. First, constructivists privilege norms and ideas, departing from an ontology that gives primacy to the causal significance of ideas. That is, they affirm the constitutive role of normative and ideational structures. Human agency is grounded in systems of knowledge that assign meaning to material capabilities. According to Wendt 'material resources only acquire meaning for human action through the structure of shared knowledge in which they are embedded'.[33] That shared Knowledge is thus the cognitive 'toolkit' with which individuals (i.e. states as members of the international society) cognize their material world, access it, make sense of it, map it out, navigate it, and act in relation to it. Thus the shared knowledge and the meaning systems it enables form the actors' template of social identities. Accordingly, the constructivists' second ontological standpoint holds that interests and actions are mostly constituted by these social identities. They shape interests and actions. Wendt elaborates this point: 'state identities and interests are in important part constructed by social structures, rather than given exogenously to the system by human nature or domestic politics.'[34] In other words, there are no interests 'out there' outside of the social context within which states associate with other states through variable situations that call for specific actions. In relation to this point Wendt writes that states 'do not have a "portfolio" of interests that they carry around independent of social context; instead they define interests in the process of defining situations'.[35] When situations are new, states construct meanings and by implication their interests, either via 'analogy or de novo', he adds.[36]

For our purpose, what is of relevance to the task at hand is the symbiosis or the constitutive mutuality between identity and interest and identity and action in the construction of American foreign policy in the AME. The discourse and practice that flow from America's identity and the cognitive regime of systems of knowledge and the meanings or interpretations underpinning it inform the US foreign policy. Just as Wendt declares 'anarchy to be what states make of it', Steve Smith pronounces that 'foreign policy is what states make of it'.[37] Conduct can be situated within a context of ideational or normative structures. Even if one proceeds from the assumption that America's 'regime of truth', as Smith refers to the normative and ideational structures,[38] is fixed across time and space, democracy is a recurring theme not only in terms of self-identification but also in self-other process of identification. Such a process, especially when carried out with the conviction that one's 'regime of truth' is 'self-evident' and 'universal',[39] inevitably leads to the cutting up of the world into smaller 'worlds' of democrats and autocrats, and of friends and foes. Within this context, conduct via foreign policy becomes a device for devising policies for dealing with allies and adversaries or rivals, ranging from consolidating or creating new alliances to placating, co-opting, winning to one's side, or containing adversaries. The linguistic and semantic world of foreign policy and its agents illustrates the 'wording' and 'worlding' that animates international politics, ranging from the language of international cooperation to that of war. Two issues matter for our purpose. The first is the knowledge practice that underpins America's identity as a democracy. The second is the multiple and both overlapping and yet contradictory operative 'personalities' (almost a case of quasi schizophrenia) that come into sharp focus in the course of US conduct in the AME. The constitutive role of social interaction within the society of states allows for multiplicity of 'personalities', and subsequently, of interests and actions. US–Arab interactions in relation to democratization reveal a number of tensions. The United States promotes democracy in Iraq, for instance, but seems to oppose it when elections benefit Islamists (e.g. Hamas, Muslim Brotherhood). I shall return to this when I consider Arab opinion-formulators' response to the GMEI.

The GMEI: 'Road-mapping' Democracy in the AME

The gist of the exercise in this section is to deconstruct the GMEI. I shall attempt to do this through a combination of discourse analysis of the key GMEI text leaked to the London-based Arabic daily *Al-Hayat* on 13 February 2004 and through cross-reference with its successor, the Broader Middle East Initiative (BMEI), adopted in June 2004 by the G-8 Sea Island Summit, Georgia. The United States initiated both projects. The BMEI transpired from the initial discussion in April 2004 by the G-8 'sherpas' and subsequent talks by the G-8 and five Muslim leaders of a draft paper principally aiming to give President Bush's 'forward strategy of freedom' an institutional and policy framework.[40] Road-mapping democratization in the AME is filtered initially through an American moment and post the Sea Island Summit through a more internationalized and multilateral moment. The first is noted by its intrusive, coercive, and unidirectional character, the second by a spirit of cooperation, voluntarism, and sensitivity to specificity (see Table 4.1).

A few observations are in order. Democracy will not be one of President George Bush's legacies in the AME. Nonetheless, some credit is due to him. He lent moral support to the wide and vigorous Arab

Table 4.1 GMEI and BMEI: A comparison

Grater M-East initiative	← Programme →	Broader M-East initiative
United States	**Origin/ownership**	US + G-7
Arab world primarily + Muslim world	**Target**	AME, Afghanistan, Iran, Israel, Pakistan, Turkey
Top-down/unidirectional	**Flow of ideas**	Top-down + bottom-up
Unilateral	**Partnership**	Multilateral
Democracy and good governance Knowledge society Economic opportunities	**Pillars**	Forum for the Future Democracy Assistance Group Foundation for Democracy Literacy Corps G-8 Microfinance Pilot Project
Region-wide	**Approach**	Country-by-country
Intrusive/coercive	**Style**	Consultative
Obligatory	**Participation**	Voluntary
Short time span	**Transition**	Process/long-term
Imposition + invasion (Iraq) + funded programmes targeting civil society in AME	**Execution**	State-to-state consultation State-to-society consultation Funds Induction + training
MEPI Arab Human Development Report 2002 Arab Human Development Report 2003	**Foundation**	US-led MEPI Barcelona Process Japan–Arab Dialogue Initiative Arab League Tunis Summit Declaration Alexandria Declaration Sana'a Declaration
September 11 + Iraq invasion + war on terror	**Context**	September 11 + Iraq invasion + war on terror + EU response to GMEI + Arab criticism of GMEI

debate on the question of reform. This debate shall persist after the Bush Administration. Bush's America is the first to propose a plan of action for tackling the Arab democratic deficit, a deficit linked in the 2002 and 2003 UN Arab Human Development Reports to deficits in knowledge and women's empowerment, and even the Arab–Israeli conflict in the 2003 report. The United States' main competitor is the EU. It has been engaging the Southern Mediterranean Arab states through the 1995 Barcelona Process. I shall not look at this process, which is the subject of wide academic discussion.[41] Suffice it to say that the Barcelona Process is neither rigorous nor solely focused on democracy promotion. President Bush's first administration must be credited with the boldest and most ambitious plan to democratize the AME. The plan, still continuing through his second term, is a quasi 'road map' for democracy promotion. President Bush will also go down in history as the only US President to summon the courage to engage in self-criticism about American and Western aiding of autocracy and, by implication, inaction on democracy promotion in the AME for 60 years. Lisa Anderson concisely explains the United States's conduct during those 60 years. The United States has generally colluded with Arab misrule based on 'fixed elections' and 'human rights fakery', thus providing 'a fig leaf' for both patron and clients 'to continue in the game'.[42] Indeed, this is at the core of the US credibility gap in the AME. Madeleine Albright recognizes this problem in her 'Task Force Report' entitled *In Support of Arab Democracy: Why and How*.[43] Marina Ottaway concurs. She notes, in light of Arab publics' suspicion and mistrust of US past record, that the United States has no option but to keep up the pressure for reform in order to close that credibility gap. Closing that gap requires an organic connection between rhetoric and practice in order for the United States to 'build credibility as a pro-democracy actor'.[44] It is a case of a 'pro-democracy actor', without credibility in the AME, vying for a credible role in the realm of democracy promotion.

Plenty of ink has already been spilled over the GMEI. The key criticisms have been rehearsed in a number of fine articles. Ottaway and Carothers view the failure to address the Israeli–Palestinian problem to be the key lacuna in the GMEI's 'working paper'.[45] Reform would be incomplete, they argue without addressing the conflict. After all, it is the conflict that has in no small measure contributed to militarized polities and negligence by scholars and rulers of democratization for over 50 years. Ottaway and Carothers find a 'fundamental flaw' in the GMEI's 'abstract logic over political reality'. What Ottaway and Carothers stress most is that the GMEI is not sufficiently 'pathbreaking' to qualify as a new 'paradigm' for US dealing with the AME. Interest, they point out, still guides the construction of US foreign policy, still favourable to friendly engagement with autocracies in the region.[46] Ottaway and Carothers correctly point out that missing in the GMEI are specific measures that Arab states must take: lifting restrictions on political parties; empowering judiciaries and parliaments; raising levels of political inclusiveness; and subjecting non-elected rulers and their institutions to elective politics. Sifting through the differences in opinion between the GMEI's 'working paper' and its much watered-down BMEI, Tamara Coffman-Wittes is correct in noting Arab preference for 'modernization' (the European input to the new draft, BMEI, with its socio-economic focus) over 'democratization' (the US proposal, with its political focus [see Table 4.1]).[47] For, 'modernization' renders transformation open-ended without pinning down

Arab regimes to specific 'tests' for tackling democratic deficits be they in the area of greater toleration and inclusiveness of civil society or media freedoms.

A return to the 'modernization' paradigm is a return to the quasi authoritarian–bureaucratic developmental models whose records for failure, politically, economically, socially, and militarily, are not in need of substantiation across the AME. Her main concern is that a return to the socio-economic approach is a return to gradualism, which reflects her sympathy with the United States' preference for a shorter time frame (see Table 4.1). Coffman-Wittes notes that a purely socio-economic focus does not suit the current historical juncture of 'anti-Western terrorism' being a 'primary threat'. Assuming terrorism to be in the 'post–Madrid world', as she put it, to be solely 'anti-Western' is imprecise. Iraq had minimum terrorism prior to the US-led invasion and has since 2003 been turned into a 'haven' for all kinds of extremists, including al-Qaidah. Terrorism in Iraq has claimed more Arab and Muslim lives than the entire death toll from September 11. This aside, exclusively political or economic approach may not be enough for tackling either reform or terrorism. The problem of designing democratization plans that panders to the 'war on terror' will re-prioritize security over political equality, and order or stability over democracy. This is a reason why Madeleine Albright expresses concerns about the concessions given to friendly autocracies in the AME in the context of combating terrorism and fighting an un-winnable war in Iraq. Elections alone and representation will not assuage extremists; it will co-opt many terrorists or would be terrorists into the political process. However, it will not stop hardcore extremists whose values and motivations cannot be addressed via democratization, which groups like al-Qaidah reject outright. May be some form of a juridical approach (truth and reconciliation, amnesty along with rehabilitation programmes) or dialogue should be added to the inventory of how to engage terrorists.

Nonetheless, Coffman-Wittes is correct in noting how the reformed BMEI partly panders to Arab autocrats. She writes that the BMEI 'menu will allow Arab governments to focus their "partnership" on issues more palatable to them and reject or ignore those that are unpalatable'.[48] Indeed, the voluntary approach to reform is both positive and negative (see Table 4.1). It is positive in that it gives freedom to Arab states to engage reform by choosing from the five baskets or pillars those activities and programmes that suit their own specific needs. It is negative in that it gives them the option of not participating. The BMEI text (the 'G-8 Plan of Support for Reform' that was agreed in the Sea Island Summit) denotes voluntarism not compulsion. It contains phrases such as 'willing partners', 'willing countries', 'interested countries', and 'partners'. The introduction to the text reads as follows: 'The initiatives herein offer a broad range of opportunities from which governments, business, and civil society in the region can draw support as they choose.' Ottaway and Carothers, Madeleine Albright, among others, have proposed alternatives for 'road-mapping' Arab democratization. Carrie Wickham's critique raises concerns about the GMEI being no more than a 'public relations' exercise with no substantive commitment to democratization. What is at stake is the United States improving its image more than improving governance in the AME.[49] This critique reflects many Islamists' stance on the GMEI, a project they find to be insensitive to local culture and to indigenous forms of good government. In short, what Whickham calls 'coercive democratization' is rejected by Islamists who see it as being motivated by US hegemonic impulses rather than genuine concern for good government, especially that the United States maintains very good relations with non-democratic regimes.

My own critique revolves around aspects of knowledge-making and practice. These aspects resonate with Orientalist assumptions about the AME. My deconstruction brings into sharp focus the construction of power relations of domination and subjugation through textual reading of the initiatives—the GMEI and BMEI. The usage of terms like 'greater' or 'broader' Middle East is a classic example of the persistent Orientalist understanding of the AME. The monolithic label 'Middle East', already vague, is now rendered even more imprecise as its boundaries are stretched further afield to include in addition to the AME Afghanistan, Iran, Israel, Pakistan, and Turkey. The term that still begs the question 'Middle of where East of what' now calls for definition as to 'greater' or 'broader' in what sense. Even though the use of 'broader' is considered a European refinement to its precursor—'greater'—it is intriguing as to why Arab rulers or peoples would find it less imprecise or more acceptable. Generally, there is a tendency by Arabs to view with suspicion attempts to 'lump' them together with non-Arabs. Such schemes, many argue, derail the search for an Arab community of interests. The GMEI is a successor to a plethora of schemes super-imposed top-down and from without. Like its precursor, the Middle East Partnership Initiative (MEPI), the GMEI points to the persistent road-mapping the United States began under Bush Senior (e.g. New World Order) following the liberation of Kuwait in 1991. Subsequent to the Madrid Conference, there were calls for a 'New Middle East' (Shimon Perez being among its original inventors) by George W. Bush in 2003 and Condoleezza Rice in July 2006 (in the midst of the 33-day war between Hizbullah and Israel).

The terms GMEI or BMEI illustrate non-nuanced rendering of a region that continues to baffle policymakers who slot the 'world out there' into generalized categories or large 'boxes'. Their preference for totalizing labels over detailed 'mapping' lends itself to devising policies of the type 'one size fits all'. Even a perfunctory reading of the more recent UN Human Development Reports reveals differences not only within the AME, but also between it and the other non-Arab states. Development indices, such as the gender development index or literacy, show that the diversity and levels of development defy situating these countries in a single 'box'. It follows then that the generalizing category of either 'GMEI' or 'BMEI' equally defies 'one size fits all'-type policies. Some of these countries are far more advanced on elective politics (e.g. Israel, Turkey); some have endured or still do face the threat of social upheaval or civil war (e.g. Afghanistan, Iraq, Lebanon, Pakistan); a few are under occupation (e.g. Iraq and the 'Palestinian Territories'); a few are in a state of no peace no war (e.g. Israel, Syria, Pakistan); one is an occupying state (Israel); several are heterogeneous (e.g. Afghanistan, Algeria, Bahrain, Iran, Iraq, Israel, Jordan, Lebanon, Morocco, Pakistan, Saudi Arabia, Syria, Turkey); several are oil-rich quasi 'clan-states' (e.g. Arab Gulf states); and others are 'monarchical republics' (e.g. Syria, Libya, Yemen).

The GMEI's 'working paper' published by *Al-Hayat* newspaper in London represents a discourse of power. The ownership of its text is American. The rationale given for the GMEI is American. So are the Strategies. The text maps out power relations in which the Arab side is subordinate—silent. The text deftly invokes the UN Arab Human Development Reports as if to record Arab prior agreement of the GMEI. It is a text that smacks with unilateralism. Through the text the only superpower is attempting to order the AME in its own image: the three pillars of democracy, knowledge society, and capitalism reflect not only American values but also criteria of success as noted by President Bush in his NED speech of 2003. Those criteria view successful countries as passing the following tests:

Successful societies limit the power of the state and the power of the military— so the governments respond to the will of the people, and not the will of an elite. Successful societies protect freedom with the consistent and impartial rule of law, instead of selecting applying—selectively applying the law to punish political opponenents. Successful societies allow room for healthy civic institutions—for political parties and labour unions and independent newspapers and broadcast media. Successful societies privatize their economies, and secure the right of property. They prohibit and punish official corruption, and invest in the health and education of their people. They recognize the rights of women. And instead of directing hatred and resentment against others, successful societies appeal to the hopes of their own people.[50]

Note that a feature of the power relations of domination and the discourse of power is blaming global problems on the AME. Such a discourse of power pinpoints the root cause of 'extremism, terrorism, international crime and illegal migration', as noted in the GMEI's working paper, on political and economic disenfranchizement in the AME. US unilateralism is the assumption that the problems of the AME (e.g disenfranchisement, extremism, terrorism) threaten the 'West'. The perception of threat justifies meddling, which takes many forms in the AME. These problems are affirmed to 'pose a threat to the stability of the region, and to the common interests of the G-8 members'. The silence is impressive: 'common interests of the G-8 members?' One can only wager that oil and security are two of these interests. Democracy promotion in the AME is not one of those 'common interests'. Rather, it is a new *modus operandi* for securing those common interests. The text is patronizing in more than one way. There is no responsibility attibuted to the G-8 members, largely a club of imperial powers at one stage or another of their ancient and contemporary history. For instance, President Bush's criticism in his NED speech of Western governments' collusion with misrule in the AME has not been repeated in the GMEI's working paper. It absolves the G-8 of all wrong-doing even though at least two G-8 members are occupying powers in Iraq and permanent Security Council members (France, UK, and Russia) have done little to use their power to find a solution to the Arab–Israeli conflict. The silence is glaring, not so much the silence on the conflict as an additional pillar as most critics point out. The silence is on Western powers' responsiblities. Security Council members share some blame; so does Israel as do Arab states.

The binary knowledge-making typical of Orientalism is manifest in the GMEI's 'working paper'. This Orientalist content of the GMEI and the BMEI is both 'dramatic' and dangerous. The divisions into neat categories are reminiscent of the nineteenth-century pre-colonial ordering of the world according to Western criteria of 'civility'. Stability, democracy, capitalism, women's empowerment, and moderation are the new norms. The polarities, both explicit and implicit, are between democracy and autocracy, stability and disorder, and moderation and extremism. The 'GMEI' and the 'BMEI' are not simply totalizing worlds. Rather, they are worlds that contain within them sub-categories and sub-worlds. Within those 'willing countries' there are boundaries between those 'willing' and 'unwilling'—the 'moderate' and the 'extremist', etc. The 'working paper' and the text agreed by the G-8 following the Sea Island Summit draw additional lines between knowledge producers and knowledge-makers. Despite reference to the region as being 'once the cradle of scientific discovery and learning' in the BMEI text, both initiatives assign the G-8 club the exclusive role of knowledge makers and transmitters.

This is one aspect of the GMEI and the BMEI that critics have invariably ignored. There is a one-way flow of information, knowledge, know-how, and values. The BMEI adopts the GMEI's initial three pillars addressing the three deficits—democracy, knowledge, and economy—and expands on them (see Table 4.1), by toning down the American stress on the political and through emphasis of 'dialogue' and 'partnership'. However, there is no equality in either. The G-8 side is clearly the knowledge-maker with exclusive ownership over the content of the initiatives. The BMEI text literally opens up candidacy for 'apprenticeship' into good government and governance. The mentoring is top-down. The learning is unidirectional. What the BMEI practically sets up is a form of 'classroom' for 'coaching' the AME into measuring up to globalization. In this 'classroom' Jordan is the most proactive 'pupil', practically partaking in all activities and benefiting from most funds. Whilst Jordan clamours for the 'carrots' of training and funding at the levels of state and society, the Arab Gulf states have the financial largesse and a margin of comfort that make these very 'carrots' not sufficiently tempting. There are discretionary 'carrots' (e.g. the United States concluding a deal with Morocco days before its September 2007 parliamentary elections to reward democratizing steps taken by King Mohamed VI with US\$ 697.5 million of grants under the Millennium Challenge Corporation).[51] There are no 'sticks' in the initiative, as Ottaway and Carothers point out. But this is not entirely correct. The 'sticks' are implicit in the risk of missing on the 'train' of 'modernization', stability, moderation, and reform, and pecuniary rewards for countries that choose not to partake in the BMEI's activities. The oil-rich Arab Gulf states need not the initiatives and beyond the assistance available in limited programmes, especially in relation to WTO membership, they can choose to keep their participation to a minimum. The lesser-to-do states cannot do so, despite the non-binding nature of the BMEI. The 'mentoring' is assigned to Canada (e.g. voter registration and electoral transparency in Afghanistan), the EU (e.g. Palestinian elections and electoral commission), France (e.g. elections in Yemen), UK (e.g. parliamentary capacity in Bahrain), UNIFEM and Canada (e.g. development of women's rights in Algeria, Jordan, Lebanon, Morocco, 'Palestinian Territories', and Tunisia), Germany (e.g. gender equality in Jordan, Morocco, and Yemen), Italy (e.g. 'education for all' in Afghanistan and Libya), Japan (e.g. women's empowerment in Egypt, Jordan and the 'Palestinian Territories'), United States (e.g. funding regional women's campaign schools in the AME). There are additional mentoring roles for the G-8 countries in media training, public administration, strengthening civil society, improving education systems, and local development.

There are two missing links in this chain of learning and mentoring. First, because the GMEI and BMEI are built on assumptions of G-8 leadership in knowledge-making and diffusion, little or no effort has been made to explore 'local' knowledge in the AME and opportunities of intra-Arab learning. The AME is constructed, and this is reminiscent of colonial power relations, through denial of equal moral agency and knowing. Not all of the 'goods' that could be deployed for democracy promotion are in the sole possession of the G-8 states, the mentors. Individual states in the AME have deficits in democracy and knowledge. However, as a whole the AME has forms of knowledge, be it dispersed across the vast Arab canvass, with the potential to help democratization. I cite the following examples that are worthy of diffusion and emulation for the sake of locally engineered 'democratic learning':

- Algeria and Saudi Arabia's programmes of national reconciliation (*muṣālaḥah*) for reducing terrorism and rehabilitating terrorists into society;
- Morocco's 'Truth and Reconciliation'-type committee (a mode of transitional justice) for addressing past human rights violations committed under the late King Hassan II;
- Tunisia's Personal Status Code for women's empowerment;
- Jordan's inclusion of Islamists into the political process;
- Morocco's multi-partyism;
- Egypt's assertive judiciary and professional syndicates;
- Qatar's media freedom and professionalism, especially the model set up by al-Jazeerah;
- Dubai's financial and commercial development;
- Kuwait's parliamentary capacity;
- Lebanon's plural civil society;
- Micro-credits and national solidarity funds in Egypt, Jordan, and Tunisia;
- Religious freedom in Lebanon, the 'Palestinian Territories', and Syria; and
- Largely free and fair elections such as in Algeria (1991), Mauritania (2007), and the 'Palestinian Territories' (2006).

Second, neither the GMEI nor the BMEI provide a facility for a two-way flow of learning. The deficits in democracy or knowledge or the problems of stability and terrorism demand the United States and its G-8 partners to assume some humility towards learning. They have placed the blame of these problems squarely on the AME—and the Muslim world. Accordingly, having absolved themselves of all responsibility for 'global' problems, they have put themselves above learning from the AME, including finding about 'local' forms of knowledge relevant to the tough assignment of reform. From the outset there was no attempt at synergy. Like the GMEI, the BMEI is framed with singularity in the area of knowledge. More can be done by the G-8 countries to invest in the learning of Arabic, about Islam and specificity on a country-to-country basis. Only through greater understanding and a firmer grip of the AME's problems can genuine 'dialogue' and 'partnership' take place. Both dialogue and partnership require reciprocity and equality. Neither is evident in the GMEI and the BMEI. The aim of pushing reform correct as it might be will not be served by one-sided, singular, and unidirectional know-how, underlying Orientalist thinking abut an area of vital importance to the rest of the world.

Binary knowledge-making is further reflected in what I consider to be the most dangerous aspect of the GMEI and BMEI. That is, the focus on the various schemes for training and educating AME civil societies by the G-8. Tapping into the global repository of know-how is indeed vital and unstoppable. However, hijacking civil societies from their own states is a daring attempt to partake, if not rival states in the AME, in the tasks of nation and state-building by the G-8. This leaves the central state in the AME with little control over its constituents. An undertaking of this large scale is typical of colonial refiguring of the colonized—acculturation and linguistic and technical training. This is one reason why Arab civil societies have grown sceptical of various American training schemes and workshops hosted in the United States for youth, journalists, women, etc. Jordanian journalist, Fatima Al-Sumadi, who participated in one of these training schemes, uses the terms co-option and recruitment (*istidrāj*). She views *istidrāj* as systematic attempt to socialize pockets from within Arab civil societies into American pluralism. The aim, she adds, is to assign the trainees into becoming 'trainers' and diffusers of US values in their own societies.[52] She notes that the US Department's 'International Visitor Leadership Programme' has two agendas. Its overt agenda is about engaging the select few who are admitted into it through sessions on cultural understanding and exchange, women's empowerment and inclusiveness, rule of law and democracy, and civic education. Its hidden agenda aims at entrenching US values—liberal rationality and the secular outlook—and promoting the building of bridges with Israelis. Al-Sumadi gives the example of the 'Muslim Women in America' workshop, a programme she took part in. It turned out to be a platform for meeting Jewish and Israeli women (which she refused to participate in, causing her difficulties with the organizers and the US government). She observes that whilst the deliberations were conducted in an atmosphere of candour and free expression, the hidden agenda weighed heavily in favour of aims that served US foreign policy objectives. Three objectives stand out: defeating Islamist ideology and extremist forces, which includes changing and reforming educational syllabi and 'de-Islamizing them; promoting human and minority rights and democracy by sponsoring and funding activists in these areas; and inducting participants in American values in order to improve the standing and image of the United States in the Arab world. Al-Sumadi deems the systematic recruitment for the 'International Visitor Leadership Programme' to verge on imposition in the pursuit of reform in the AME. For, it amounts to co-optation of Arab 'publics' into the US strategy of democracy promotion from without.[53]

It exclusively applies to the United States. It has a direct platform in Iraq from which it can by-pass the central state to produce its much vaunted 'democratic model', a model that is naively hypothesized to lead the way in the AME. This is, at least, in theory. But by-passing Arab states in training their civil societies with the view to strengthening citizenship is somewhat unrealistic not to mention 'patronizing'. Again, this displays the failure to value 'local' knowledge as a vital resource and medium for 'local' solutions.

Iraq is now outside the purview of the AME. The GMEI and the BMEI are not concerned with Iraq. The former makes only one mention in passing to Iraq. Its mention is made in the context of legitimizing the proposed GMEI and G-8 leadership in it as well as establishing the bona fides: 'The Euro-Mediterranean Partnership, the U.S. Middle East Partnership Initiative, and the multilateral construction efforts in Afghanistan and Iraq demonstrate the G-8's commitment to reform in the region.' The latter's detailed mentoring programmes under the five pillars include every Arab country with the exception of Iraq. What is obviously conspicuous is that the GMEI and the BMEI do more than legitimizing the G-8. More importantly, they legitimize the US sole guardianship and tutelage over Iraq's nation and state-building. If the AME is clustered in a single 'classroom' to be drilled into the *sine qua non* brand of learning vital for the globalized world, Iraq is slotted in a different 'classroom' for 'private' and exclusive tuition by the United States. The 'Greater' or 'Broader' Middle East has lost Iraq. Thus the G-8-led workshop, primarily under the auspices of the

United States, is a two-track workshop in reforming the AME. One track combines all of the Arab states in addition to a few non-Arab states. The other is reserved for Iraq under the sole mentoring of the United States. Naturally, the United States is more concerned with Iraq than its G-8 partners. It is the one that will stand before the 'court' of history to answer for its successes and failures. Plus, the moral impulse is greatest for the United States, which led an illegal war, and wants to prove its actions and choices correct. This explains the US obsession with 'victory' in Iraq. Increasingly, as the possibility of a military victory is wearing thin, President George W. Bush has since 2007 humbly redefined 'victory':

Victory will not look like the ones our fathers and grandfathers achieved. There will be no surrender ceremony on the deck of a battleship. But victory in Iraq will bring something new in the Arab world—a functioning democracy that polices its territory, upholds the rule of law, respects fundamental human liberties, and answers to its people. A democratic Iraq will not be perfect. But it will be a country that fights terrorists instead of harbouring them— and it will help bring a future of peace and security for our children and our grandchildren.[54]

However, neither democracy nor security look like a certainty at the moment. 'Democracy via undemocratic means'—intimidation and or invasion—does not work. However, the rhetorical unity of purpose and direction in the Bush Administration's discourse of democracy promotion is an impressive factor. It is noted for its boldness, system- atic approach, evincing wide interest, and raising high expectations. President Bush, Colin Powell, and Condolezza Rice,[55] all exemplify the unity of rhetoric on democracy promotion. President George W. Bush's NED speech resonates with democratic teleology. Eight months earlier President Bush sacked Baghdad. His November 2003 speech marked more than the 20th anniversary of a Reaganite institution for democracy promotion, NED. It signaled a new departure point for a more aggressive foreign policy on behalf of democracy promotion. Fifty years earlier America was deposing nascent democracies in the Middle East. The speech's sub-text may be a defence of the US-led illegal inva- sion of a sovereign Arab nation-state couched in the language of high moralism. As if invading a country on the moral grounds of democracy- promotion and breaking with 60-year statecraft of 'waltzing' with Arab dictators make for a 'just war'.

As State Secretary, Powell was at the forefront of building the rhetorical and diplomatic momentum for democracy promotion in the AME. His 2002 MEPI seeks to hit a few 'birds' with the 'stone' of democratization: support for women's empowerment, free trade, and for a vociferous citizenry.[56] William J. Burns, Assistant Secretary for the Bureau of Near Eastern Affairs, defines MEPI's key objective to be 'change'. To this end $365 million, to be channeled into a variety of educational and civic projects and schemes through USAID, were initially earmarked for the task for the Fiscal Years 2002, 2003, and 2004.[57] As National Security Advisor, Dr. Rice speaks of the 'march of freedom in the Muslim world'.[58] The 'march', however, has also been military. Therefore no amount of correct rhetoric about 'road-mapping' democratization can erase the invasion of Iraq. It is an important background against which evaluation of the GMEI must be considered. The *telos* might be democracy in the AME. But the rhetoric discloses more than one item on the democracy promotion agenda: security and the fight against terror. This is what vitiates the moral substance of the GMEI. It is not a comprehensive road-map for democratization *qua* democratization. The spectre of the 'war against terror' haunts and guides democracy promotion under the GMEI. The rhetoric is dia-glossic: combating terrorism via democracy promotion, or a democracy promotion with one of its key objectives combating terrorism as stated in the excerpt form Bush's 2007 'the New Way Forward in Iraq'. Pres-ident Bush has since 2003 up to present reaffirmed the linkage with consistency: 'As long as the Middle East remains a place where freedom does not flourish, it will remain a place of stagnation, resentment, and violence ready for export.'[59] In 2007, the rhetoric is consistent. Refer-ring to Iraq, President Bush urges Arab states to rally to the cause of stable, united, and democratic government in Iraq. For, 'defeat in Iraq would create a new sanctuary for extremists.'[60] Linking terrorism to democratization and *vice versa* has tainted the GMEI. Democracy promotion by conventional means (e.g. diplomacy, aid conditionality, information) cedes to democracy promotion by non-conventional and non-democratic means (e.g. invasion, intimidation). This is conspicu-ous when the invasion of Iraq is factored into the wider picture of the September 11 tragedy. This leads me in the brief discussion below to canvass 'intimidation' and 'invasion' in US democracy promotion. I do this through an examination of political rhetoric, with special reference to Condoleezza Rice, and of US engineering of democracy in the AME.

US Democracy Promotion: Intimidation and Invasion

As State Secretary, Dr. Rice maps out the 'march of freedom' on the Arab political geography using a rhetoric that is rather imperious. In Egypt, she states in her famous American University in Cairo Address (20 June 2005), the regime 'must put its faith in its own people'. She defends pro-democracy activists' rights to protection from violence. She adds 'the day must come when the rule of law replaces emergency decrees—and when the independent judiciary replaces arbitrary justice'. Calling on the Mubarak regime to come good on its own rhetoric— note the use of '*must*'—Dr. Rice says:

The Egyptian government must fulfill the promise it has made to its people— and the entire world—by giving its citizens the freedom to choose. Egypt's elections, including the Parliamentary elections, must meet objective standards that define every free election. Opposition groups must be free to assemble, and participate, and speak to the media. Voting should occur without violence or intimidation. And international election monitors and observers must have unrestricted access to do their jobs.[61]

The rhetoric has a 'coercive' tone to it. Dr. Rice opened up her speech lauding the 'greatness' and 'leadership of Egypt epitomized by the 'reform-minded' Muhammad Ali Dynasty, the Wafd Party's liberal politics, and Sadat's visionary peace-making statecraft. Yet in a series of sentences instructing the Egyptian regime what it 'must' do to pass the litmus test of democracy, she effectively demolishes her own image of 'greatness', 'leadership', and 'vision' she ascribes to Egypt. Indeed, the question arises as whether the tone used suits the role she assigns for 'Egyptians' whom she says 'can lead and define' the 'future' of their democracy. Dr. Rice's style must have, at least partly, contributed to suspicion and fear among the AME's patrimonial rulers (e.g. Saudi Arabia, Egypt, and Tunisia—the countries which boycotted the launching of the Broader Middle East Initiative in the Sea Island G-8 Summit). Mubarak or King Abdullah would have read the United States's approach to democratization as coercive and intrusive. The United States is aware of this and Dr. Rice is somewhat defensive in lashing out at 'those who say democracy is being imposed'. 'Democracy is never imposed' she adds. 'It is tyranny that is imposed.' She is impervious to the context: the US invasion of Iraq. Indeed, Dr. Rice is correct, as she notes in her Cairo address, that in the 'Middle East, the fear of free choices can no longer justify the denial of liberty'.[62] She errs, however, in misjudging public opinion in the AME. The invasion of Iraq, in majority opinion, even under the guise of democratization, does not constitute 'free choice'. Dr. Rice has praise for Jordan's education reforms and decentralization of power. She displays respect for the Iraqi renewed search for their 'round city', 'a city in which no citizen would be closer to the centre of justice than any other'. She notes the milestones ahead in holding elections and writing a democratic constitution in Iraq. In Palestine and after the presidential elections, she expresses enthusiasm for the vision of building a democratic state beside that of Israel, saying nothing about on what or how much land or why the United States is not doing much on that account. Whilst noting the fight against terror by both the Palestinian and Iraq people's, she offers only deafening silence on freedom from Israeli and American occupation. In Lebanon, however, she correctly offers support to freedom from 'foreign masters'. She voices unequivocal support for democracy in Syria and for its dissidents. She welcomes the civic polls in Saudi Arabia and the enfranchisement of women in Kuwait in 2005. The speech's style varies according to the subject. Dr. Rice attacks Iran's political arrangements, considering them non-democratic. Yet in addressing Saudi Arabia and Egypt the tone is coercive but nonetheless cautious. Hence she pours praise on Egypt (by reference to its 'greatness') only to take it away by imperiously telling the rulers what must be done to upgrade the regime to a democratic government. Yet what is puzzling in all of this is what Dr. Rice fails to mention in reference to Iran relative to its Arab neighbours. Despite being partly a closed and exclusionary polity, Iran has more political competition than Saudi Arabia and Egypt. Iran has since 1979 changed its political ruling cast nearly as many times as the United States. This is an area where the 'operative personalities' come into play: In assuming the roles of 'friend' (to Egypt and Saudi Arabia) and 'foe' (to Iran) America tends to exercise economy with regard to 'truth'. Thus the rhetoric varies according to the degree of proximity from an autocracy. Proximity translates into 'soft' and 'mild' criticism or silence. The obverse is true. This selectivity weakens US credibility. Despite a coercive tone vis-à-vis Egypt, for instance, Dr. Rice has not described Mubarak's regime as authoritarian. The same applies to Saudi Arabia. This is akin to the United States turning a blind eye to fraudulent elections (e.g. Nicaragua and Panama), when these seemed to serve foreign policy objectives or political actors sympathetic to them in Latin America the area with the United States's longest record of democracy promotion.[63]

In the post-September 11 world and the 2003 invasion of Iraq the AME has come under intense and critical external agency projected through a new regime of regulation and 'control' in affecting change from without. The 2006 elections in Gaza and the West Bank and the 2005 Iraqi elections must be understood against this backdrop of increased 'imposition', two non-neutral modes of democracy promotion. The Palestinian elections have as a frame of reference the Oslo Accords of 1993 (Declaration of Principles). Under Article III there are three provisions: (1) Palestinian self-government by way of a 'council' (parliament) via internationally supervised 'direct, free and general elections'; (2) agreement on 'the exact mode and conditions of the elections in accordance with the protocol' (Annex I of the Accords); and (3) the elections being 'a significant interim preparatory step toward the realization of the legitimate rights of the Palestinian people and their just requirements'.[64] The democratic game, which is historically bound up with a territorial political unit, is organized by the Oslo Accords prior to Palestinian territoriality. What is unprecedented in this case is the fact that democratization is 'de-territorialized'—territorial sovereignty being de-linked from democracy. This regime of 'control' from without can be explained in two ways. The first is owed to outside intervention, namely, by the United States. Whitehead confirms similar intervention in one-third of the transitions that were complete in 1990. Being the sponsor of the Oslo Accords, the United States ensured a 'democratic content' is built into the agreement as a measure of 'consolidating its dominance'. Whitehead's reference is to the post-1945 world and victories in Europe and Japan.[65] To an extent, this is akin to the post-1990 world—the United States emerging as the sole superpower, owing to the dissolution of the USSR, and democratic transformation in Eastern Europe. Marking the Accords with democratic provisions adds not only to the prestige of the historical moment of the signing of the Arafat-Rabin agreement but also signposts the entry into a new era under the victorious superpower, the United States as a leader in and promoter of democratic values. The second regards a moment of quasi-decolonization, at least in theory. The colonial power, in this case Israel, seeks to secure democratization and security as preconditions for decolonization. Whitehead has discovered identical harmonization to apply in former British colonies. Locking an independent Palestine into the Western sphere of influence requires security (for Israel), free market economic policies, and democratic government.[66] The Oslo Accords under US sponsorship were designed for a statehood process that begins with elections but within a tightly guided framework from without—serving both the United States and Israel.

Democratization via Intimidation: Lebanon & the Occupied Territories

In the years 2006 and 2007 are particularly significant for the emergence of 'intimidation' as a weapon of democracy promotion in the US foreign policymaking. Lebanon and the 'Palestinian Territories' are unique in illustrating intimidation. In both cases, the prime method of intimidation relies heavily on a politics of 'polarization', taking advantage of pre-existing sectarian (Lebanon) and ideological ('Palestinian Territories') cleavages. The United States has visibly allied itself with the so-called 14 February Forces, the anti-Syrian Sunni and Christian bloc. In so doing, it has not only assumed a hostile posture to the Michel Aoun-Hizbullah coalition (also known as the 'March 8 Bloc') but also made itself party to a complex political stalemate that has frozen the country's fragile institutions. Hizbullah leaders, according to author's interviews, view United States meddling to sabotage rather than help democracy. For instance, Hizbullah's leader of the party's Parliamentary wing in the country's National Assembly, Mohammad Ra'ad, notes that the United States's hostility to Syria and Iran, on one hand, and alliance with Israel, on the other, have been reflected in its biased embroilment in the Lebanese crisis. He adds that the United States's declaratory policy suggests support for safeguarding Lebanon's democracy. In practice, he notes, by taking sides in an internal disagreement concerning national priorities, including resistance against Israeli occupation, the United States has undermined its own policy of democracy promotion. He says

the US unconditionally backs the 'March 14 Bloc' as it sees it as its arm to implement its foreign policy agenda of making the Arab world free of legitimate resistance against continued Israeli occupation. The US has fully sponsored the bloc as its political survival is crucial for implementation of UN Resolution 1559, aiming at disarming Hizbullah, which is engaged in a legitimate fight for territorial liberation from Israeli occupation.[67]

Hizbullah's Deputy Secretary Shaykh Na'im Qasim, sees the bias in the fact that the United States has rewarded the 'March 14 Bloc' by ignoring their obdurance in ignoring the constitution. He states that

our constitution stipulates a two-third quorum in parliament to elect a president. We are trying before November 24 to reach any compromise, which would include our own concession to drop our demand for a government of national unity as a trade-off for a consensual president. The United States is not interested in our constitution. It is interested in its own agenda of getting rid of our weapons after the failure of Israel to eliminate us in an illegal and brutal bombing campaign sustained with explicit US approval and US weapons. Our constitution says nothing about a half-plus-one vote, which the pro-US March 14 Bloc is threatening to carry out if we do not join the vote for a pro-US and pro-Israel president.[68]

Hence he interprets the US political backing of the March 14 Bloc, including its willingness to flout the constitution, to undermine constitutionality in Lebanon. Thus Ra'ad criticizes the US method of 'divide and rule' in its meddling in the Lebanese crisis, noting how it defeats democratization. He states that helping one party at the expense of another undermines democratization. It polarizes polity and civil society and feed tension into the political process. Democracy promotion requires neutrality in order for the ideals of equality and consensus-building to triumph. We have played the democratic game in Lebanon fairly and with full respect of our laws and specificity, which outside neither understand nor respect. The US cannot fault us on our democratic record as we have worked with all Lebanese sects since the first post–civil war elections of 1992 up to the last ones in 2005.[69]

Democratization, he notes, is aimed at securing the political survival of a force that espouses 'economic liberalism' with 'pro-Americanism'. For him the US intimidation aimed primarily at his party took so many forms from hostile diplomacy in the UN to war by proxy. He remarks that the United States is interested in promoting a particular brand of democracy that leaves the AME governed by a single pro-American political current.

Indeed, the deepening divide between Fatah and Hamas in the Palestinian territories and the ostracism of the latter partly validates the view above of how US democracy promotion risks producing singularity not plurality. The same tactic of polarization noted in Lebanon has been deployed in the 'Palestinian Territories' with dramatic consequences not only for democracy promotion but also for the coherence and unity of the Palestinian political community pursuing the twin goals of self-determination and democracy. Between the elections of February 2006 and the US-sponsored Middle East conference held in Annapolis in November 2007, America relied on the tactic of polarization and intimidation in its management of the twin aims of brokering peace and promoting democracy. The United States has sided itself with Fatah and Mahmoud Abbas against Hamas despite the latter's having a democratic mandate to govern since the 2006 elections. The twin assignment of brokering peace and promoting democracy proved to be a dangerous mix. The United States has pursued a diplomatic mission of advancing peace by securing recognition of Israel and renunciation of violence in disregard for promoting democracy. For, Hamas' refusal to both demands—despite offers of a ceasefire and openness to a partial deal on the basis of Israeli withdrawal from all territories occupied in 1967—the United States has sought with the approval of its weak Quartet partners and most world governments to isolate Hamas. Moreover, and to the detriment of Palestinian–Palestinian relations, the United States's tactic of polarization led to a rift punctuated by armed fighting between Hamas and Fatah. The economic embargo and the siege now imposed on Gaza since its Hamas takeover in June 2007 have done irreparable damage to democracy promotion at least in the eyes of the Hamas leadership. Khaled Mish'al, Hamas's leader, echoes views expressed by Muhammad Ra'ad by saying that the United States accepts democracy only when it suits its interests. He observes that

Hamas and the Palestinian people are collectively punished for voting, for choosing Hamas, and for doing their part to building democracy for a future Palestinian state. But this democracy has upset America and Israel because it seems that at the current historical juncture what is required by US foreign policy is clients not free citizens ... No amount of intimidation shall nullify the democratic legitimacy obtained in free elections by our people. It is not Hamas that has failed the democratic test. Rather, it is America who has failed to live up to its own agenda of democracy promotion, which was announced to the entire world a few years ago.[70]

A hallmark of the United States's policy, especially when relying on polarization, is the tendency to proceed with intimidation without first recourse to a policy of incentives. Intimidation would perhaps be justified when preceded by confidence-building measures and bridging of differences in order to win over forces seemingly disinclined to make overtures towards the United States. Whitehead contrasts the approach of the United States such as vis-à-vis Cuba with that of the EU, which prefers incentives over sanctions in the pursuit of political reform.[71] In fact, the US campaign of intimidation against the Hamas government led by Ismail Haniyyah is comparable to the harassment of the Sandinistas in the 1980s by the Reagan Administration.[72] That campaign, which led to the weakening of the Sandinistas, employed a range of measures similar to those used against Hamas: 'covert operations, economic sanctions, and political warfare—"intimidation" for short.'[73] Hamas' representative in Lebanon, Usamah Hamdan, notes that from day one of after the 2006 parliamentary victory the international and regional pressure signaled that democracy is not wanted in the AME despite the rhetoric by the United States and others. He elaborates:

The campaign of intimidation began with placing pressure on Mahmoud Abbas not to accept our invitation to Fatah and other Palestinian factions to join us in a national unity government. At least one non-Hamas politician we offered a ministerial portfolio to was threatened with bans to enter the US or meet US politicians if he accepted to be in a Hamas-led cabinet. Much later on, Fatah was again manipulated into refusing to deal with Ismail Haniyyah with Abbas practically maintaining a boycott of ministerial meetings presided by the Hamas Premier. Then when Fatah and Abbas came round to the idea of a national unity government the conditions were to dismiss Mahmoud Zahhar, the Foreign Minister, and Said Sayyam, the Interior Minister. They went but no progress was realized as there was never any intention to work with us and Fatah was itself victim of US and Israeli pressure. After the failed attempt on the life of Haniyyah Mohammad Dahlan's forces began a military campaign against Hamas in Gaza. All of this was possible through US arms, funding and training of special forces allied with Fatah, with other help coming from US client regimes in the region...But worst of all is the collective punishment of Gaza, which has been turned into a huge concentration camp. Inside it are close to two million Palestinians who are embargoed...and are made to go with little food and medicine, and no money...not to mention frequent cut-offs of power by Israel to increase pressure on Gazans aimed at instigating a rebellion against Hamas.[74]

Like in the case of the Sandinistas, the aforementioned intimidation tactics have no doubt weakened Hamas, limiting its room for maneuvering in a largely hostile international atmosphere. But Hamas survival is owed to one factor that the Sandinistas lacked: commitment to a political cause in the name of religion. Not even the robust Marxist ideology of the Sandinistas could have saved Daniel Ortega and his government from the onslaught of the aggressive Reaganites. Indeed, the intimidation campaign, especially after the takeover of Gaza has shaken Hamas, leading it to commit many mistakes through draconian acts against rival Palestinian factions, especially Fatah's members. What is saving Haniyyah is the devout Gazan population. The state of siege and embargo made Gazans more steadfast in rallying behind Hamas and refusing to be broken by US and Israeli pressure. The irony is that the very democratic process that has subjected Hamas to intimidation and isolation, has thus far in Gaza combined with religious faith to spare Haniyyah the fate of Ortega. In his critical assessment of democratization via intimidation in Latin America Whitehead observes that it has two adversary effects. The first concerns the 'home democracy', in this instance the United States, damaging 'the qualities of trust, co-operation, and lawfulness'.[75] This is caused, Whitehead adds, by deception of Congress and of public opinion, and by diversion of funds, for instance. The most vocal and trenchant of US democracy promotion and uneven-handedness in relation to the various Arab–Israeli disputations are Americans such Jimmy Carter and former Attorney General Ramsey Clark.[76] The inputs of the Baker-Hamilton and Albright all point to the divided state of public opinion not only democracy promotion but also the damage caused to the standing of the United States in Arab public opinion. The second adversary effect of democratization via intimidation concerns the target country; it breeds 'cynicism and opportunism'.[77] Between the time of its declaration in 2004 and 2007, the cause of US democracy promotion has lost credibility. The views expressed by Hamas and Hizbullah leaders may not be expected to do justice to the United States, considered right or wrong the key ally and sponsor of Israel. Two views from 'establishment' opinion-formulators show congruence in terms of cynicism vis-à-vis the US 'road map' for democratizing the AME. Both are former Prime Ministers. Tahar Al-Masri of Jordan, Premier (1991) notes that neither the United States is ready for a democratic AME, and nor the AME is ready for democracy. For him the GMEI, whilst signals long time overdue attention to the question of good government by the United States, it lacks the credibility as it protects all of the constitutive elements of authoritarianism from repressive states to hegemonic clans and classes. Thus for him, the GMEI

is contradictory because it has no intention of withdrawing support to the very apparatuses of power that produce authoritarianism in the first place. The United States is a key ally to autocrats in the region and it wishes not see them swept away from power. That would imperil its interests. Plus, the US plan for Arab democratization lacks sensitivity to Arab specificity. Democracy without an independent Palestine is unachievable.[78]

Salim Al-Hoss, Prime Minister of Lebanon in the years 1976–80, 1987–90, and 1998–2000, concurs. He notes that America cannot be equally serious about democracy promotion and about maintaining friendships with Arab autocrats. He adds:

I invite the US to reflect on its actions throughout the Arab world and find one single act it has done to promote democracy. Democracy promotion needs more than a declaration [GMEI] ... It needs principled US Administrations ... Since Bush Senior the Arab world has been made weaker, more divided, more autocratic, and increasingly more in the hands of the rich few not the moral publics who struggle for dignity, equality and liberation from dependence and occupation ... Plus, America has nothing to teach the Arab world in democracy when it ignores world public opinion and invades a sovereign Arab state [Iraq] in the name of democracy promotion. That is not democratic.[79]

It can be expected that Iraq, like the Palestinian cause, feed into Arab cynicism about US democracy promotion. I now turn to the invasion of Iraq to briefly assess US democracy promotion since the 2003 invasion. To this end, I shall refer to the book by Ambassador Paul Bremer III in which he documents his work with Iraqi leaders to build a democratic state.[80]

Democracy Promotion via Invasion: Iraq

Investigating democracy promotion through invasion in Iraq can be attempted only tentatively. For, the task lacks the historical long span that marks the pursuit of democracy promotion by the United States in Latin America.[81] The Iraqi example is dramatic since it ensued with a violent process lacking in legality. Thus it epitomizes an unprecedented undertaking in the AME whereby democracy promotion is pursued through invasion and occupation. This sets Iraq apart from the rest of the AME. By invading Iraq, the United States has acquired a capacity for exercising direct control over the content and substance of political reform. Such a capacity for direct control over authoritarianism is what the United States has lacked in the AME. To an extent the GMEI and the BMEI are instruments for empowering the United States to have some control over Arab democratization. Iraq will be the only polity where the United States stands to be judged on its democracy promotion more so than in other AME states. Iraq joins a long list of countries where the United States pursued democracy promotion 'by force of arms'.[82] The list includes Germany and Japan post-1945 and Haiti and Panama in the 1990s.[83] The difference between Iraq and these states is the varying degrees of institutionalization these countries have enjoyed prior to United States direct intervention and control over democratization. Exercising direct control defeats the very purpose of free choice that Dr. Rice takes to be central to democratic government. Imposing democracy via invasion and occupation is a contradiction in terms. An illegal means (invasion) is deployed for a putatively legal end (democratization). This process is a form of 'democracy . . . by undemocratic means', for which the United States has a historical track record according to evidence marshaled by Whitehead from the Caribbean.[84] Whitehead points out that in line with their traditional commitment to democracy promotion and the resulting successes in many parts of the world, US foreign policy makers see no contradiction in the notion of 'democracy by imposition'.[85] He notes how this commitment makes America unique among hegemonic powers past and present. America's 'self-proclaimed commitment to the promotion of democracy [is] an integral element of its foreign policy, and its long-standing confidence that "all good things" (US influence and security, economic freedom and prosperity, political liberty, and representative government) tend naturally to go together'.[86] The invasion of Iraq is at least partly rooted in the belief that it is morally justifiable since it would lead to 'good things' and in the confidence that America's past democratizing successes would be once again confirmed in the AME.

Two years are not sufficient to canvass the depth and width of the United States' effort to road-map democratization in occupied Iraq. Thus the extent to which the means or method, that is, invasion, justifies the end, democratization, is difficult to confirm or deny objectively. However, political fluidity, the spectre of uncertainty, lack of consensus and unity, and weak legitimacy do not thus far substantiate the thesis of 'good things' in the current US-led democratization in Iraq. What can be sketched are the travails of such a process, noting its pros and cons. The process, as Paul Bremer III, Iraq's Presidential envoy (May 2003–June 2004) calls it, is a 'road map to democracy' in Iraq.[87] On the positive side, the year 2005 marked a turning point in Iraqi history in two ways. First, on three elections that year Iraqis cast their votes: 30 January, to elect a Transitional National Assembly (TNA), 18 Governorates' Councils, and Kurdistan Regional Government; 15 October, a referendum to ratify a draft constitution; and 15 December, to elect a permanent 275-member Assembly of Deputies. Second, the same fever of electoral fetishism gripping the rest of the AME infected Iraq, producing key gains. The January 30 vote was the first in the country's contemporary history to be considered relatively free and fair. There is a departure point not only from pre-ordained elections such as that of 2002 in which the late Saddam Hussein won the residential plebiscite by 100 per cent. The new constitution has reserved a 25 per cent parliamentary quota for women, giving the country's Council of Deputies more female representation than the US Congress. In fact, a source of pride for Paul Bremer III is the fact that women won 31 per cent of the national vote, twice as many women in the American Congress.[88] The country has a modern constitution even if its long-term fate is not assured when the Americans leave Iraq. More importantly, generally, most ordinary Iraqis seem to be pleased by the overthrow of Saddam and his henchmen even if they lived more comfortably under his rule than the prevailing conditions of unemployment and poverty. This is confirmed, for instance, by findings obtained in focus group sessions with ordinary Iraqis by the US National Democratic Institute for International Affairs.[89]

The process of democratization via invasion in Iraq has been far from straightforward or smooth. Bremer's 'road map to democracy' had to be revised and supplemented by at least one 'new road map'.[90] As he notes in an unusually transparent style that building democracy is 'a messy process'.[91] One fortuitous factor seems to have contributed to the hurried nature with which the process of democratization has been executed in Iraq. Somehow Bremer's own private life had crept into the shaping of history in the course of managing the process of democratization. Bremer was a committed family man and was eager to go back home without delay. He agreed with President Bush to limit his assignment as a reluctant colonial administrator in Iraq to mid-2004. Thus he gave himself a tight schedule during which he had to lay the infrastructure for the transfer of a degree of self-government to the Iraqis.[92] The rushing of the process has had detrimental effects on Sunni representation and the overall process of consultation over the drafting of the constitution and subsequently its ratification by referendum in 2005. Bremer is well aware of this fact as he affirms himself in relation to the rushing of the constitutional convention through a fast pace favoured by the United States and not by its key Iraqi allies among the Shi'ites and Kurds.[93] This is one key criticism of the US-led democratization in Iraq that recurs in several studies. The deadline of 15 August 2004 for completing the drafting of the constitution is widely regarded as arbitrary. As a result the proviso in Article 61 (F) for making use of a six-month extension was ignored by the United States despite willingness to do so by members of the political and civil societies in order to give more time for public discussion and consultation.[94] The United States was eager to display procedural rigour and deliver results to ease off pressure from world opinion opposed to the war. A report by the International Crisis Group (ICG) entitled 'Iraq: Don't Rush the Constitution', favoured extension as a beneficial mechanism. It would have permitted longer time for educating the public about the constitution and accommodating the excluded Sunnis as well as civil society at large.[95] ICG notes that rushing the drafting of the constitution did not bode well for the legitimacy of the democratization process. For, a Sunni majority chose to boycott the January 2005 elections. Thus the make-up of the TNA—140 Shi'ites from the United Iraqi Alliance and 75 seats for the Kurdistan Coalition List against only 17 seats for the Sunnis—required a longer time frame for the purpose of recruiting the Sunnis into the political process. Note the TNA elections were instrumental for choosing the committee tasked with the drafting of the constitution. ICG points out the fact that only 2 of the 55 members of that committee were Sunnis.[96] Obviously, Sunni participation is vital for the durability and legitimacy of the democratization process. But somehow this factor did not seem to matter to the United States. Although Bremer provides evidence of efforts made to include them be it still within the ambitious and inflexible schedule he devised for his 'road map to democracy'. As an insider, Noah Feldman, who served as a Senior Advisor for constitutional law to the Coalition Provisional Authority, was equally critical of the arbitrariness of the date for the completion of the draft constitution at the expense of more pressing issues like Sunnis' rights for inclusiveness.[97]

Iraq's permanent constitution lacks legitimacy and the 'no' vote is a measure of the protest against a process Sunnis actively boycotted and others by design or due to time inflexibility excluded them from. A 'no' vote by two-thirds of the registered voters in 3 out of the 18 governorates was required for the new constitution to be rejected. In Salah Al-Din and Anbar Sunni Provinces, homes to the most sustained and ferocious resistance to the US-led occupation, the no vote was highest, respectively 81 and 97 per cent. Sunnis Claim that fraudulence explains the 55 per cent vote in Neenawa, which was expected to reject the new constitution. Overall, the new constitution received 79 per cent of the public vote and that firmed it up as the 'magna carta' for the 'new Iraq'[98] the Bush Administration set out to create. The obsession with quick results and procedure on the part of the United States in its administration of democratization ignored vital dimensions. Some of these have to do with new approaches to constitution-making. Specifically, in his Congressional testimony on Iraq, one expert stressed the need for longer time to 'engage in meaningful civic education'.[99] The rush to deliver the 'good things' hypothesized to come with US democracy promotion goes against the grist of democratization as 'open-ended' and requiring civic education. Linz and Stepan insist on democracy being 'routinized and deeply internalized' socially, institutionally, and attitudinally.[100] Hyper-electoral fetishism, three elections in one year in a country under occupation and divided along ethnic and sectarian lines, may in the long run prove inimical to substantive democratization. Here comparison must be made of the 2005 elections in Lebanon and those of January 2005 in Iraq. Both were the first in both countries' histories to take place after the departure of Ba'thists as occupiers in Lebanon and autocrats in Iraq. The United States, which was behind Resolution 1559 that led to evacuation of Syrian troops in 2005, maintained its rhetoric of safeguarding 'democracy in Lebanon'. On that basis the United States welcomed credible elections in occupation-free Lebanon; yet in Iraq it hurried the electoral process in spite of occupation, division and bloody violence.

As noted before, the constitution-making process lacked wide public consultation and what Bremer reveals in his book is that his Shi'ite and Kurdish interlocutors were using the process of rebuilding a 'new Iraq' as representatives of narrow sectarian interests not impartial leaders working for the public good. What transpires from the book is a parochial elite blinded by primordial loyalties to the slightest notion of shared values. Bremer deftly caricatures the profiles of the Kurdish and Shi'ite leaders he dealt with directly or had to deal with as a guarantor of law and order as the administrator of Iraq. His profiling gives an insight into the moods and minds of the men chosen by the United States in its bid to democratize occupied Iraq. Bremer's 'memoirs' show that in seeking to democratize Iraq, the United States had to work with the human resources available from within the clique that supported occupation. The United States did this with the full knowledge that the profiles leave much to be desired in terms of political virtue and commitment to public service that is not tainted by ethnic, sectarian, or ecclesiastical interests. Sometimes,

Bremer appeared as a loner fighting for his 'new Iraq', whilst Kurds and Shi'ites were scrambling for maximizing sectarian sovereignty, territorial geography, and autonomy. On the question of de-Bathification, Bremer appeared more reasonable than the occupied country's political elite which had no notion of national reconciliation as can be gathered from some of the clumsy decisions. Like Kurdish and other Shi'ite leaders, Chalabi executed a de-Bathification policy that rendered thousands of teachers unemployed.[101] This unnecessary vengeful act could only serve to widen the rift between society and the new political elite. Bremer envisaged a limited de-Bathification that targeted Saddam's henchmen and inner power circle. For the United States Kurdish and Shi'ite partners the only calculus of power seemed to be separatist potentialities. Masoud Barzani (President of Kurdistan) and Jalal Talabani (President of Iraq post-2005), the Kurdish leaders, worked with Bremer in the context of the consultation over the constitution and designing other governing arrangements to advance a Kurdish agenda. They insisted on Kurdish autonomy, federalism, retention of the Peshmerga, and had other territorial concerns, especially regarding Kirkuk, strongly represented.[102] Arabization of Kirkuk was Barzani's *cause celèbre* and the analogue of 'Jerusalem' for Kurdistan in his rhetoric.[103] They were not alone in their parochialism exaggerated by decades of suffering under oppression by Saddam. Abdul Aziz Hakim's Supreme Council for the Islamic Revolution in Iraq sought 'preferential treatment' from Bremer by having a deputy in the Governing Council[104] as well as securing Shi'ite command for the new army.[105]

Others like Sharif Ali whom Bremer calls the 'Pretender to the Throne' was driven into the process by opportunism. He impressed Bremer more with his 'Englishness', Savile Row suit, Rolex, and private jet than with his political skill,[106] having tried and failed to make political capital for himself on the back of the Sunni insurgency. His pretences to be able to conclude a truce with the insurgents proved empty.[107] Both Bremer and the insurgents of Fallujah put a swift end to his monarchical illusions in Iraq. Another opportunist recruited for the purpose of democratization via invasion is Ahmad Chalabi. Again, Bremer could see through the characters whose support was vital for running occupied Iraq. When Chalabi opposed elections early in the stage of re-organizing the war-torn country, Bremer's psychoanalytic mind was quick. Chalabi 'was apparently aware of his very low support in the Iraqi population. So while he wanted a sovereign government soon, he probably believed he could wield more influence if it were selected by a simple expansion of the Governing Council instead of by elections'.[108] Bremer was also aware of allegations of business impropriety in Chalabi's past.[109] Bremer found Adnan Pachachi, a veteran Iraqi politician and a partner in the Governing Council to be sensible but self-conceited. In 2003, Bremer made him adopt the idea of interim constitution as his own. Thus Bremer deftly facilitated placing it as an item on the agenda of the often garrulous and indecisive Governing Council.[110] The US democratization via invasion used the instrument of co-opting and recruiting broadly from within the Iraqi exiled elite whose members were vital for legitimizing occupation. The United States did that despite full knowledge that many were motivated by self-interest or by the interests of ethnicity, sect, and tribe. In a way, the US democratization process is the only bind that brought these fissiparous sub-political cultures together.

In the footsteps of Lord Kitchener and others who ruled the colonized East, Bremer's Orientalism comes to the fore in moments of frustration. Whilst managing the democratization process on behalf of the Bush Administration, Bremer at times tends to essentialize Iraqis into a violent lot. He rejected requests to hold the electoral process back because of violence, making the sweeping generalization that Iraq 'is a violent society, like Columbia'.[111] Moreover, despite frequent and wide consultation with the cabal of leaders recruited by the occupying power to rebuild the country the United States guided the process of democratization very tightly. The big decisions were all made in Washington and when in Baghdad ownership of knowledge was Bremer's alone. The resonance with French monarchical absolutism ('I am the system' genre) is strongest when the UN was approached to release monies for the so-called national crop. Addressing, in Baghdad, recalcitrant UN bureaucrats who refused to release the funds, protesting they belonged to the Iraqi government, Bremer retorted: 'I am the Iraqi government for now'.[112] Indeed, Bremer wielded power with skill, professionalism but also firmness to get 'the job done' as assigned by President Bush. Thus the process of democratization via invasion was both top-down (Bremer) and from without (the Bush Administration). The power asymmetry in favour of the United States ironically worked to deliver results. It was difficult for the Iraqis sometimes to agree on sitting arrangements or sharing the same room during meetings. Bremer assumed the role as sole arbitrator when decision-making eluded him. This he did by lecturing and blackmailing. Early in the process, meetings were unruly and unproductive. Bremer had to give mini lessons in democracy: 'Democracy is truly great, I said. But democracy is majority rule, with the protection of minority rights. It is not indecisive rule by consensus, which can lead to paralysis.'[113] When the Governing Council was not forthcoming on agreeing a plan of action for selection of delegates to the caucuses for the Constitutional Convention, with the Shi'ites and to a lesser extent the Kurds dithering and competing for domination, Bremer threatened to go public and blame the lack of progress in the transfer of sovereignty on the Iraqi leadership.[114] That eventually got him results.

The irony was that the electoral process was never a first choice for Bremer or the Bush Administration team, including Condi Rice, then National Security Advisor. It was Grand Ayatollah Sistani and his *fatwā* that elections be adopted for legitimizing the drafting of the constitution and its founding fathers whom he insisted should be Iraqis. Whilst the Administration and Bremer were genuinely guided by an early transfer of power, the modality of doing so was never clear from the outset. Donald Rumsfeld and Colin Powell were concerned with security.[115] Dick Cheney feared early elections would benefit extremists and Islamists, which is the view held by the secularists in the Iraqi leadership.[116] Dr. Rice shared with Bremer the general feeling within her team against elections at that juncture; instead they favoured 'an appointed government with no constitution'.[117] Bremer adds that Dr. Rice's own position was for the protection of minority rights and a constitutional structure.[118] Democratization via invasion in Iraq, as can be gleaned from Bremer's book, competed with an additional powerful interest: what he calls 'garrison mentality', in reference to the security priorities. Even here the military was not united.[119] Some generals did not link progress along the path of democratization to satisfactory resolution of the security situation. Excessive force, especially in the Sunni triangle, and the Abu Ghraib violations, proved once more the hazards of democratization via invasion. The case of usurping rights through invasion only to grant them later through democratization is yet to be convincingly made in Iraq.

Conclusion

Empirically, if the GMEI is a plan, Iraq displays the flaws of implementing it. Similarly, the experience in the Palestinian territories displays the gulf between the GMEI rhetoric and reality. In Iraq, as an occupying power the United States has had an opportunity to 'teach' or 'demonstrate' to the AME how democratization is engineered. The result, only several years into the process, is that the United States is yet to transcend the same election fetishism found elsewhere in the AME. This is an interesting culmination of the most illegal, costly, divisive, rushed, ill-thought, one-sided, tragic, and violent democracy promotion effort in history. But there is one difference.

Iraq's future hangs in the balance. It may not outlive the constitutional, pluralistic, and legal machinery of democratic government—all of which positives—the United States has helped put in place. The United States is partly to blame for the fragile, contingent, and stalled nature of Iraqi democratization. Democratization via invasion and from without is not a quick solution for ending the reign of Arab authoritarianism. Conceiving of itself as possessing a unique inventory of democratic knowledge, experience, and history, the United States approached democracy promotion in Iraq with little or no humility and uncritical missionary zeal. But such a formidable inventory was never tested genuinely in the AME. Iraq is not Haiti. Other clues for stalled or failed US democracy promotion are found within Iraq where the collapse of an 'over-stated' authoritarian nationalism has given rise to atomized loyalties and identities each taking sanctuary in exaggerated forms of primordialism. The 'fight' is in and over Iraq, but not for Iraq. Rather, it is for competing loyalties in the name of God for some and in the name of tribe and *ethnie* for others. Iraq is one example that shall be returned to by students of democratization in the AME to assess whether Iraq as a trial-run of the Bush Administration's GMEI can produce a redeeming case study. Palestine compounds the democratization trial-run. Like in Iraq, the unfolding of democratization in a nation without either territory or sovereignty does test not only the GMEI but also the seriousness of the United States' declaratory policy in support of democratization. In the Occupied Territories, the twin quest for statehood and good government still evades the two 'road-maps' for peace and democratization. When the United States appears to sabotage or ignore the verdict of the voters (e.g. 2006 elections), the loser is not Hamas. Rather, it is the United States and the GMEI. Democratization is not 'one size fits all'. But the rules of democracy are meant to be the same everywhere: majority rule as Bremer keeps reminding the feuding Iraqis. Here Egypt's most known contemporary author Mohammed Hasanayn Heikal's reflections on the American Empire invite Arab sympathy. He writes that the 'American empire's use of force, along with its concentration or monopoly...has discarded [recourse to or the need for] all higher moral and humanist additions.'[120] He likens its immorality to that of its now defunct former Soviet rival. The former Soviets promised paradise; in practice, they drove people to hell by a thick baton. He states that 'the same is true of US President [George W.] Bush whose general rhetoric is replete with expressions to "ennoble" Arab peoples with the gift of democracy—but by launching scud missiles on any of them as he chooses'.[121] On the other side of Heikal one finds Iraqi writer Kanan Makiya, a champion of both human rights in the AME and of US occupation of Iraq for the purpose of spreading democracy to the Arab world. Despairing at the prospect of a Saddam defeat and of Arab armies helping topple his regime in the 1991 war, Makiya, naively, did the unthinkable 'I called upon the Allied coalition to finish the war by taking out the tyrant and opening up the possibility of democratic change in the Middle East.'[122] Democratization by imposition, whether via intimidation or invasion, has not repeated its success in Latin America. This brand of democracy promotion in the AME validates Whitehead's finding in relation to Latin America that it 'express[es] a radical inequality between the power and rights of the country acting and the country acted upon'.[123] If Makiya represents one extreme, Heikal represents another. Nasser's former Minister tells only one story about the United States. As a master of sensationalism he is caught in a realist and Cold War imagining of world politics. In the context of democracy promotion, the United States cannot be reduced into a single 'identity'. A constructivist reading would reveal contradicting identities—'friend' and 'foe' of democracy. The United States both actively promotes and demotes democracy. Its pressure on the side of democracy has led to diffusion of electoral practices in the Arab Gulf, including Saudi Arabia. Yet the same pressure against democratic outcomes (Hamas and Muslim Brotherhood in Egypt) has undermined its own democracy promotion and the GMEI.

Democracy promotion top-down and from without, as argued in the foregoing chapters, seems thus far to lead to election fetishism. The story of the rise of election fetishism in the AME can be renarrated by looking at bottom-up democratic struggles, thematic foci I shall specify and carefully assess in the last two chapters.

Notes

1. George W. Bush, 'Remarks by the President at the 20th Anniversary of the National Endowment for Democracy', United States Chamber of Commerce, 6 November 2003, Washington, DC.
2. Philippe C. Schmitter, 'The Influence of the International Context upon the Choice of National Institutions and Policies in Neo-Democracies', in Laurence Whitehead (ed.), *The International Dimensions of Democratization: Europe and the Americas* (Oxford: Oxford University Press, 1996), 37.
3. Laurence Whitehead, 'Three International Dimensions of Democratization', in Whitehead (ed.), *The International Dimensions of Democratization: Europe and the Americas*, 4.
4. Schmitter, 'The Influence of the International Context', 27.
5. Ibid.

6. Laurence Whitehead, 'The Imposition of Democracy: The Caribbean', in Whitehead (ed.), *The International Dimensions of Democratization: Europe and the Americas*, 60.

7. Ibid. 67.

8. Whitehead, 'The Imposition of Democracy', 71–83.

9. See testimony by former NED President, Carl Gershman, in 'The National Endowment for Democracy in 1990: Hearing before the Subcommittee on International Operation of the Committee on Foreign Affairs', US House of Representatives, 28 September 1989, 31.

10. Huntington, 'Democracy's Third Wave', 13.

11. See 'The Arabs Dicing with Democracy', *The Economist*, 3 February 1990, 34.

12. Mikhail Gorbachev observes that 'perestroika is an urgent necessity arising from the profound processes of development in our socialist society. This society is ripe for change...any delay in beginning perestroika...would have been fraught with serious social, economic and political crises'. See his *Perestroika* (New York: Harper and Row Publishers, 1987), 17.

13. It unleashed new forces; it inspired Arabs with a new sense of confidence and reformist zeal; it introduced new meaning to the conception of human rights, freedom and good government; it spawned a critical revision of the existing orders and introspection among the intelligentsia of their place in the system and their role as society's voices and interpreters of the major contemporaneous political, social, and economic questions; and it spawned the expectation that a new beginning was looming. One observer notes:

    Thousands of articles, hundreds of announcements and tens of conferences at all levels have shown the Arab interest in perestroika...As a desideratum, Arab perestroika is the endeavour to reunite the two Yemens, to end the civil war in Sudan, to convene a meeting...to solve the Lebanese tragedy [and] to create a high level Study Group on a single Arab trading bloc...An Arab perestroika is also, and in particular, the release of all Arab political prisoners, clearing the way for multi-party and free elections in all Arab countries. See Basim Al-Jasr, '*Al-Birustruyika al-arabiyyah al-manshudah*', [The Desired Arab Perestroika], *Al-Hawadith*, 23 March 1990, 24. See also the article on *Perestroika* by the same author in the same issue, 20.

14. Dirk Vandewalle, 'Qadhafi's "Perestroika": Economic and Political Liberalization in Libya', *Middle East Journal*, 45 (Spring 1991), 216–31.

15. Adeed Dawisha, 'The Colonel Does it His Way', *The Middle East*, 168 (October 1988), 17.

16. Ibid.

17. For further details on this point see Larbi Sadiki, 'Why Yemen Matters', *Asia Pacific Defence Reporter*, 21 (October/November 1994), 18, 27. See

also, Larbi Sadiki, 'Why Yemen is at War', *Current Affairs Bulletin*, 71 (October/November 1994), 41–3.

18. Whitehead, 'Three International Dimensions of Democratization', 3.
19. Noam Chomsky, Towards a New Cold War (London: Sinclair Browne Ltd., 1982), 6.
20. Whitehead, 'Three International Dimensions of Democratization', 4.
21. Schmitter, 'The Influence of the International Context, 37.
22. Whitehead, 'Three International Dimensions of Democratization', 6.
23. Ibid.
24. Ibid. 5.
25. This hostility was expressed by the late King Fahd to democracy on the grounds of its incompatibility with Islam. See, John L. Esposito and John O. Voll, *Islam and Democracy* (New York and Oxford: Oxford University Press, 1996), 193.
26. Whitehead, 'Three International Dimensions of Democratization', 4.
27. For evidence of this refer to the chapter by A. Van Rooy and M. Robinson in A. Van Rooy (ed.), *Civil Society and the Aid Industry* (London: Earthscan Publications, 1998).
28. See S. Halper and J. Clarke, *America Alone* (Cambridge: Cambridge University Press, 2004), 80.
29. Eric Hobsbawm, Globalization, Democracy and Terrorism (London: Little, Brown, 2007), 6–7.
30. Ibid. 7.
31. For a good piece on constructivism and its lineage from critical theory see, Mark Hoffman, 'Restructuring, Reconstruction, Reinscription, Rearticulation: Four Voices in Critical Internal Theory', *Millennium*, 20 (1991), 169–85.
32. For more on the crisis of International Relations after the collapse of the Soviet Union and the end of the Cold war, see John Ruggie, *Constructing the World Polity: Essays on International Institutionalization* (London: Routledge, 1998). Compare with Robert O Keohane, 'International Relations: Old and New', in R. E. Goodin and H. Klingemann (eds.), *A New Handbook of Political Science* (Oxford: Oxford University Press, 1996).
33. Alexander Wendt, 'Constructing International Politics', *International Security*, 20 (Summer 1995), 73.
34. Alexander Wendt, 'Collective Identity Formation and the International State', *American Political Science Review*, 88 (1994), 385 [384–96].
35. Alexander Wendt, 'Anarchy is what States Make of it: The Social Construction of Power Politics', *International Organization*, 46 (Spring 1992), 398.
36. Ibid.
37. Steve Smith, 'Foreign Policy is What States Make of it: Social Construction and International Relations Theory', V. Kubalkova (ed.), *Foreign Policy in a Constructed World* (London: M. E. Sharpe, 2001), 38.

38. Steve Smith, 'The United States and the Discipline of International Relations: "Hegemonic Country, Hegemonic Discipline"', *International Studies Review*, 28/2 (2002), 83.
39. Ibid.
40. Tamara Cofman Wittes, 'The New US Proposal for a Greater Middle East Initiative', Saban Centre for Middle East Policy, Memo No. 2, 10 May 2004.
41. Volker Perthes, 'America's Greater Middle East and Europe: Key Issues for Dialogue', *Middle East Policy*, 11/3 (2004), 85–97. See also, Eberhard Kienle, 'Destabilization through Partnership? Euro-Mediterranean Relations after the Barcelona Declaration', Mediterranean Politics, 3/2 (1998), 1–20; Richard Youngs, 'Europe's Uncertain Pursuit of Middle East Reform', Carnegie Endowment for International Peace, Working Paper No. 45, June 2004.
42. Lisa Anderson, 'Arab Democracy: Dismal Prospects', *World Policy Journal,* XVIII/3 (Fall 2001), 59.
43. Madeleine Albright, *In Support of Arab Democracy: Why and How*, 'Task Force Report', Paper No. 54 (New York: Council on Foreign Relations, 2005), 11.
44. Marina Ottaway, 'Promoting Democracy in the Middle East: The Problem of U.S. Credibility', Carnegie Endowment for International Peace, Working Paper, No. 35 (March 2003), 6.
45. Marina Ottaway and Thomas Carothers, 'The Greater Middle East Initiative: Off to a False Start', Carnegie Endowment for International Peace, Policy Brief no. 29 (March 2004).
46. Ibid. 1–2.
47. Tamara Coffman-Wittes, 'The New U.S. Proposal for a Greater Middle East Initiative: An Evaluation', Saban Centre for Middle East Policy, Memo No. 2, 10 May 2004.
48. Ibid.
49. Carrie Wickham, 'The Problem with Coercive Democratization: The Islamist Response to the US Democracy Reform Initiative', *Muslim World Journal of Human Rights*, 1/1 (2004).
50. George W. Bush, 'Remarks by the President at the 20th Anniversary of the National Endowment for Democracy', United States Chamber of Commerce, 6 November 2003, Washington, DC.
51. The Millennium Challenge Corporation rewards performance in three areas: just rule, investing in people, and promoting economic freedom.
52. Author's interview with Fatima Al-Sumadi, 18 March 2006, Amman, Jordan.
53. Ibid.
54. George W. Bush, 'The New Way Forward in Iraq', President's Address to the Nation, 10 January 2007.
55. Condoleezza Rice, 'Transforming the Middle East', *The Washington Post*, 17 August 2003.

56. See, 'Powell is 'Marketing' the Mid-East Initiative' [in Arabic], in http://www.aljazeera.net?NR?exeres/044E2452-D1E6–4575–9054–4D62E52601E6.htm, 25/09/04.

57. William J. Burns, 'Priorities in the Middle East and North Africa', Testimony before the Senate foreign Relations Committee, Washington D. C., 26 March 2003. See also his previous testimony, 'Political and Economic Goals of a New Generation in the Middle East', Testimony before the Senate foreign Relations Committee, Washington D. C., 19 March 2003.

58. Condoleezza Rice, interview in *Financial Times*, 23 September 2002.

59. George W. Bush, 'Remarks by the President at the 20th Anniversary of the National Endowment for Democracy'.

60. George W. Bush, 'The New Way Forward in Iraq', President's Address to the Nation, 10 January 2007.

61. Condoleezza Rice, 'Remarks from Dr Rice Cairo Speech at AUC', 20 June 2005, http://arabist.net/archives/2005/06/20/condoleezza-rices-remarks-and-excerpts-from-her-htm, 29/06/05.

62. Ibid.

63. Whitehead, 'The Imposition of Democracy: The Caribbean', 80.

64. See 'Text: 1993 Declaration of Principles', Middle East Media Research Institute, http://www.memri.org/docs/oslo1.html, 12/11/01.

65. Whitehead, 'Three International Dimensions', 9.

66. Ibid. 12–13.

67. Author's Interview with MP Muhammad Ra'ad, 20 September 2006, Beirut, Lebanon.

68. Author's interview with Shaykh Na'im Qasim, 12 September 2007, Beirut, Lebanon.

69. Author's Interview with MP Muhammad Ra'ad.

70. Author's interview with Khaled Mish'al, 3 January 2007, Damascus, Syria.

71. Whitehead, 'The Imposition of Democracy', 87.

72. Ibid. 80.

73. Ibid.

74. Author's interview with Usamah Hamdan, 12 September 2007, Beirut, Lebanon.

75. Whitehead, 'The Imposition of Democracy', 81.

76. Jimmy Carter, *Palestine: Peace not Apartheid* (New York: Simon & Schuster, 2006); Ramsey Clark, *The Fire this Time: US War Crimes in the Gulf* (New York: International Action Centre, 2005).

77. Whitehead, 'The Imposition of Democracy', 81.

78. Author's interview with Tahar Al-Masri, 19 March 2006, Amman, Jordan.

79. Author's interview with Salim Al-Hoss, 23 June 2005, Beirut, Lebanon.

80. L. Paul Bremer III and Malcolm McConnell, *My Year in Iraq: The Struggle to Build a Future of Hope* (New York: Simon & Schuster, 2006).

81. Whitehead, 'The Imposition of Democracy', 60.

82. Ibid.

83. Ibid. 59, 61, 76.

84. Ibid. 59.
85. Ibid.
86. Ibid.
87. Bremer III and McConnell, *My Year in Iraq*, 210–43.
88. Ibid. 397.
89. Thomas O. Melia and Brian M. Katulis, *Iraqis Discuss their Future: Post-War Perspectives from the Iraqi Street* (Washington, DC & Baghdad: National Democratic Institute for International Affairs, 28 July 2003), 5.
90. Bremer III and McConnell, *My Year in Iraq*, 229.
91. Ibid. 305.
92. Ibid. 228.
93. Ibid. 210.
94. Jonathan Morrow, 'Iraq's Constitutional Process II: An Opportunity Lost'. Special Report No. 155, United States Institute of Peace, December 2005.
95. ISG, 'Iraq: Don't Rush the Constitution'. Middle East Report No. 42, International Crisis Group, 8 June 2005.
96. Ibid.
97. Noah Feldman, 'Agreeing to Disagree in Iraq', *The New York Times*, 30 August 2005.
98. Bremer III and McConnell, *My Year in Iraq*, 213.
99. 'Constitution-Making Process: Lessons for Iraq', testimony by Neil Kritz before a joint hearing of the Senate Committee on the Judiciary, Subcommittee on the Constitution, Civil rights, and Property Rights; and the Senate Committee on Foreign Relations, Subcommittee on Near Eastern and South Asian Affairs. United States Institute of Peace, 25 June 2003.
100. Juan Linz and Alfred Stepan, Problems of Democratic Transition and Consolidation: Southern Europe, South America, and Post-Communist Europe (Baltimore: Johns Hopkins University Press, 1996), 5.
101. Bremer III and McConnell, *My Year in Iraq*, 297.
102. Ibid. 59–9; 214; 230; 275; and 286.
103. Ibid. 271.
104. Ibid. 96.
105. Ibid. 59.
106. Ibid. 87.
107. Ibid. 277.
108. Ibid. 217.
109. Ibid. 46.
110. Ibid. 214.
111. Ibid. 225.
112. Ibid. 35–6.
113. Ibid. 213.
114. Ibid. 231; 233.
115. Ibid. respectively 217, and 218 and 226.
116. Ibid. 218.
117. Ibid.
118. Ibid. 226.

119. Ibid. 221.
120. Mohammed Hasanayn Heikal, *Al-Imbraturiyyah al-Amarikiyyah wa al-Igharah ala Al-Iraq* [The American Empire and the Conquest of Iraq] (Cairo: Dar Al-Shurooq, 2003), 101.
121. Ibid. 107.
122. Kanan Makiya, 'Arab Demons, Arab Dreams, 1967–2003', in George Packer (ed.), The Fight is for Democracy: Winning the War of Ideas in America and the World (New York: Perennial & HarperCollins, 2003), 155.
123. Whitehead, 'The Imposition of Democracy', 88.

5

Catalysts from Below: Democratic Transition and 'Bread Riots'

The Euphoria in the wake of the October War and the promise of the economic Open Door policy died suddenly amid the Food Riots on 18 and 19 January 1977, one of the worst Egyptian upheavals in recent memory. The working masses, from Alexandria to Aswan, spontaneously arose in reaction to the sudden decision of the government to increase the prices of some essential commodities as part of the austerity...measures ordered...under pressure from the International Monetary Fund. (...) On these two days, the masses took to the streets, and every object that reminded them of the authorities and the profiteers of the *infitāḥ* were attacked. The police stations, the transportation system, and the casinos along the Pyramid Road in Cairo were objects of their fury. The government retaliated by calling in the security forces and the army. In the ensuing clashes, some 73 people were killed. (...) In the face of overwhelming popular opposition, the government was forced to rescind its decision to cut food subsidies. Although Sadat dismissed the whole affair as an 'uprising of thieves', the events...were sufficiently traumatic to call for a complete reevaluation of the country's foreign and domestic policies.

Hamied Ansari[1]

In this chapter I propose that there are restrictions on the effectiveness of applying Western paradigms to explain the significance of bread riots (as well as '*Khubz*-istes' and '*ḥiṭ*-istes') in Arab democratization. I argue that domestic political conflict presents opportunities for positive change with long-term effects despite the 'inherent plausibility' of its harmfulness. This line of enquiry challenges the Lipset hypothesis about the organic link between economic prosperity and democracy. I test this position using examples of Arab bread riots in the context of the rise of Arab electoralism of the late 1980s and 1990s. The rise of electoralism (e.g. Sudan, Algeria, and Jordan) has its roots in pressure from below. Elsewhere (as in Tunisia and Egypt), similar pressure helped consolidate or, at least, place political reform on the agenda of de-legitimized ruling elites. By following this trajectory my intention is twofold. I re-narrate the story of the rise of Arab electoralism, thus re-reading the role of society in it. The previous chapters analyze electoralism and election fetishism focusing on statist agency. Here, I consider the role of domestic political violence in the rise of Arab political activities. This angle has been completely overlooked in relation to political reform in the AME. The bias has generally favoured order and stability as harbingers of democracy. Study of liberalization presents awesome challenges with regard to defining the role of what is often considered to be an amorphous force or 'apolitical clay' identified here as the *khubz*-istes and the *ḥitistes*. *Khubz*-istes and *ḥit*-istes are economically and politically disenfranchized strata of Arab societies. The ideas embodied in these two terms are useful interpretive tools which can provide a new perspective on this specifically bottom-up process of liberalization in the AME.[2] The riots have implications for the political, especially when they are linked to notions of distributive justice and moral economy. For this purpose, I explore the normative side of anomie and the role of Islamists in it.

'*Khubz*-istes' and '*ḥit-istes*' are hybrid terms; Arabic nouns joined to French adjectival endings. The derivation of the two nouns alone points to the post-colonial phenomena they have been coined to describe. Each deals with a kind of political quietism, a quietism which is, however, fragile in certain circumstances. The *khubz-iste* is the quietist in times of material plenty, but ruptured in his quietism at the moment his daily bread (*khubz*) is imperiled. The *ḥitiste* is a more sinister quietist; a despondent and unemployed victim of economic restructuring, who will leave off leaning on his *ḥā'iṭ* (wall) the instant sufficient political unrest occurs for him to be able to revolt with anonymity. The etymologies may be clarified with care, but the usage and history of each word, as with all dialectical neologisms, is obscure. The word '*khubz-iste*' was widely used in the mid-1970s in the Maghrib, specifically Tunisia. In fact, the former Tunisian president, Habib Bourguiba, referred to it a number of times in his well-known demagogic and prolix speeches of the 1970s. The term '*ḥitiste*', however, is a more recent coinage, a by-product of the events of the 1980s in the Arab Maghrib, especially Algeria.

Islamists, Bread Riots, and the Arab Social Compact

Food protest is not specific to Arab history as the seminal article by E. P. Thompson on this phenomenon in eighteenth century England demonstrates.[3] Thompson makes a number of interesting suggestions that have relevance not only for the premodern but also for the contemporary Arab world. He opposes the claim that food protests in eighteenth century England are mob or riot activities; that they are just 'rebellions of the belly', or responses to economic hardship.[4] For Thompson, claims like these are historically bound;[5] the common people were not seen as historical agents before the French Revolution.[6] He argues that such food protests can be explained as expressions of outrage or as the results of violation of community consensus. According to his 'moral economy of the poor',[7] the lower strata had the right to livelihood and economic justice[8] partly legitimated by paternalist support of the authorities.[9] They were not to be undermined or compromised by dealing, milling, or marketing activities which could cause high rises in the price of bread. These food protests, then, were not compulsive but were self-activating. In fact they were 'highly complex form[s] of direct popular action, disciplined and with clear objectives'.[10]

Burke applies Thompson's thesis of a 'moral economy' to the Arab world between 1750 and 1950, identifying three phases of Arab protest: 1750–1839; 1840–80; and 1880–1925.[11] The pattern, organization, style, and ideology of protest differed from one phase to another. In the third phase, for instance, the symbolic language of Islam was replaced with that of secular nationalism.[12] Here Burke cites the example of the Druze and Syrian rebels of 1925.[13] Similarly, the strategy of resistance shifted to more sophisticated tactics to counter more formidable adversaries. In the 1880s Egyptian peasants (*fallāḥīn*) resorted to 'rent strike' and 'land invasion' to counter high Mamluk taxes; and Moroccan peasants and 'Abd al-Karim anti-French resistance in the 1921–25 uprising imitated European warfare tactics.[14] Burke sees the changes in the ideology and strategy of Arab social movements as indicative of the changes engulfing the Arab world (as in social structures), partly owing to the influx of European colonizers.[15] Burke's analysis conceives of Arab protest movements, although historically discontinuous, as an arena of social assertion and dynamism. Thus his analysis lends significance to anti-Orientalist and historical approaches to the questions of state–society relations and governance in the premodern era.

Fieldwork data collected by the author from Sudanese Islamists, who under the leadership of Hasan al-Turabi were organized under the banner of the National Islamic Front (NIF) between 1985 and 1989, and from Jordanian Islamists from the Islamic Action Front (IAF) suggest two important points. One is that the notion of moral economy has a strong basis in predominantly Islamic societies. The other is that food protest was a leading factor in influencing government policy towards democratic reform in Sudan in 1986 and Jordan in 1989.

Conceptions of economic activity by Islamists from the NIF and the IAF are closely bound up with Islam. Their ethical precepts are therefore grounded in revelation which defines the regulatory code of the believers' covenant with God—the permitted and the forbidden, duties and entitlements. The code is also clear about the ends of that covenant: a balance between the herenow and the hereafter. In fact, Qur'ānic language gives many references to this world and the hereafter, often stressing that the former is transitory, and that the latter is 'better and more lasting' [Q: 87:17]. But what is certain is that actions in this life have consequences for the next. Accordingly, although the morality of economic activity in Islam is clearly vertical, it has a strong horizontal dimension. It is one where theology and pragmatism intertwine. Theology or divine authority, as al-Turabi puts it, makes 'Islamic' economic activity morally superior to that found in the West, for example, liberal or state capitalism.[16] Jordanian Islamists concur.[17]

NIF and IAF Interviewees refer to many verses that ground the ethics of economic activity in divine authority. There are clear Qur'ānic injunctions against excessive consumerism (*tabdhīr*), usury, and theft. A few verses urge Muslims to honour contracts and agreements. Others speak directly to the kind of unfair dealing, milling, or marketing activities that could lead to exploitation of the have-nots as in Thompson's moral economy of the poor. One injunction commands Muslims to 'keep up the balance with equity' and not to 'fall short in measure' [Q: 55:9]. In fact, there is a whole chapter in the Qur'ān on the *mutaffif*, he who cheats by giving short measure or short weight. More specifically, the Qur'ān exhorts the devouts to practise *infaq fi sabil Allah*, that is, to spend in God's way (e.g. [Q: 57: 7; 10]). Underlying the notion of spending in God's way is the idea that all providence come from God. Hence the verse 'Allah is the best of Providers' [Q: 62:11]. These Godly bounties or favours (*ni'am*) must be managed in accordance with God's sanctions, by balancing the earthly with the heavenly as well as the individual with the communal. Like all precious possessions, wealth is a trial (*fitnah*) in this life [Q: 64:15]. 'Abd-Allatif 'Arabiyyat, the former IAF leader, makes the point that a Muslim's wealth is governed by communal obligations that stress the right (*haqq*) of the needy/the poor (*al-miskīn*), the orphan (*al-yatīm*) and wayfarer (*ibn al-sabīl*).[18] Thus the Qur'ān not only obligates Muslims to pay the poor-rate (*zakāt*) but also resonates with exhortations to the believers to engage in other voluntary donations (known as *sadaqāt*). It promises those who answer the commandments of 'offering Allah a goodly gift' [Q: 73:20] and 'striving in Allah's way with [their] wealth' [Q: 61:11] eternal bliss in paradise. Conversely, those who fail the trial of wealth—'those who love wealth with exceeding love' [Q: 89:20]—their accounting (*ḥisāb*) on Judgment Day will be severe.

Like al-Turabi, Ishaq Ahmad al-Farhan, IAF leader between 1992 and 1997, believes that moral conduct in economic activity or any other sphere of mundane life is essential for worship and religious practice (*'ibādāt*).[19] This is the pragmatic and practical side of a morally based economic activity in Islam. The end of economic activity is to ensure that Muslims are provided with an environment that facilitates, not complicates, the practice of Islam, maximizing submission to God and not to pecuniary distractions (in the case of the rich) or to concerns with survival (in the case of the poor). One interviewee mentions the saying (*ḥadīth*) by the Prophet, 'Poverty verges on unbelief' (*kāda al-faqru an yakūna kufran*) in support of the idea that material need compromises ethical propriety.[20] Ethical behaviour in economy, and for that matter polity, is necessary for being Muslim. There is a normative dimension to this. The Qur'ān guides the believers to the rules and ways that ought to make Muslims happy in this life and the next. The upshot of this strong basis for a moral economic system in Islam, as most interviewees confirm, is the primacy of social justice (*al-'adalāh al-ijtimā'iyyah*) within the Islamic framework.[21] Social justice in Islam consists in the running of mundane affairs according to Godly sanctioned ethics for advancing public utility, that is, the good of the *ummah*. Formulations of social justice in Islam may vary in practice and scope according to context, but what makes its conception paradigmatically distinct and common to all Muslim societies is its community-based redistributive system. Through this system, the offsetting of material inequalities and injustices is equally binding on all members and groups constitutive of the Islamic community. Inequalities are attended to through voluntary donations and obligatory taxes for the poor. Injustices are managed by way of observing Godly laws governing fair trading as well as through more formal means, legal, and administrative. The gist of social justice in Islam places an obligation on the not so poor and the well-off to undertake a measure of self-sacrifice in order to improve the conditions of the needy. For inequalities to become just and Islamically acceptable, a portion of the benefits of material bounty bestowed upon the rich Muslims by God must be passed on to the needy. The general welfare of the *ummah* is contingent upon mutual compassion (*tarāhum*). This is one reason why social welfare has always been a top priority for Islamic movements like the NIF and the IAF.[22]

The IAF has since its inception in the early 1990s elaborated a detailed policy on social welfare and staple foods. The sub-section on alimentary policy (*al-siyāsatu al-tamwīniyyah*), in the party's 1993 electoral program booklet, shows food security (*al-amn al-ghidhā'ī*) to be high on the Islamists' agenda in Jordan.[23] The sub-section is prefaced by an affirmation of a philosophical viewpoint that holds that food security is fundamentally essential for the citizenry's psychological and material well-being. The linkage between spiritual and material well-being is a theme that recurs in Islamist discourses from Sayyid Qutb to Rashid al-Ghannushi. The seven points subsumed under the sub-section on alimentary policy are logically sequenced, interacting with the Islamists' broader stress on Islamic interdependence, Islamic economic conduct, state welfarism, economic protectionism, and centrally controlled pricing. Arabo-Islamic interdependence for the purpose of securing food self-sufficiency, in point one,[24] highlights a concern within the IAF that reliance on imported foodstuffs leaves the region and its poorer people at the mercy of fluctuating international prices and dependence on the West. Neither price hikes of foodstuffs nor food insufficiency bode well for food security, argues al-Farhan, one of the IAF's top leaders.[25] The Islamists of Jordan share a fundamental belief with fellow Islamists everywhere that failure to pool Arab resources together for the purpose of realizing alimentary self-sufficiency will prolong dependence on the external world. The idea of Arabo-Islamic interdependence to secure food self-sufficiency, points al-Turabi, has been a difficult web to weave with the longstanding plan to turn Sudan into a bread basket for the region remaining low on the priority of states and individual investors alike.[26] The Islamists in Jordan fear nothing more than dependence on their Westward neighbour, Israel. They argue that unemployment, lack of state protection for the local production of wheat, and price increases would benefit the Jewish state through the import of cheap Jordanian labour, and the export of agricultural produce.[27] Moreover, the Islamists look eastward and draw comparisons from the sanctions on Iraq. The crux of their comparisons is that the government policy not to protect the local production of wheat amounts to starvation (*tajwī'*) of the Jordanian people in the same way the United States did with Iraq via the sanctions.[28] Islam's own brand of 'moral economy' through the prohibition of price overstating for the sake of consumer protection is encapsulated in the second point of the sub-section on alimentary policy. Points four and five speak to issues of state interventionism and protectionism. The former calls for continued commitment to a policy of subsidization (*da'm*) of basic food commodities.[29] Again, for al-Farhan, that is not a huge price to be paid by the state for the greater sake of social justice and well-being of all citizens, especially the needy.[30] The latter point about protectionism stresses state support for farmers, especially in times of drought and poor harvests.[31] Thus 'Arabiyyat is puzzled by the contradictory behaviour of the United States, the world's largest free trading nation, which practises protectionism through subsidization of its own farmers. Yet it, along with the IMF, presses poorer countries to abandon policies aimed to protect their own farmers.[32] For the IAF, a measure of state welfarism and economic interventionism makes good economic sense if it goes a long way in securing people's livelihoods. Hence point six encourages the creation of consumer cooperatives for the provision of subsidized commodities; and point seven opposes decentralization of pricing regimes, insisting on the necessity of strong state control over them.[33]

To state that bread can be a matter of life and death, physically as well as politically, in the AME is no exaggeration. It is a powerful signifier in Islamist and non-Islamist discourses.[34] In the Egyptian as well as Maghribi vernacular, bread is sometimes referred to as living/livelihood (*'īsh*). Hence any policy tinkering that results in price increases is regarded by Islamists as a direct assault on the citizenry's living and livelihood. The lifting of subsidies on bread and fodder in August 1996 by the Kabariti government, which had an ambitious agenda of sweeping economic reforms outlined by the IMF, was a case in point. In the prelude to the lifting of subsidies, the IAF's spokesperson, Hamzah Mansur, warned Kabariti not to cross what he called the bread 'red line':

We have warned the government since its first day [in office] from touching the citizenry's food and clearly affirmed in a discussion [in parliament] that [daily] bread is a red line that must not be approached. When we felt that the government is going ahead with its policy, we...warned against the hike in the bread prices.[35]

For Mansur and his fellow Islamists, daily bread, which evokes strong passions within the country's Muslim Brotherhood and the IAF, is treated as a 'red line'. It is a matter of principles committing the movement and its political arm to issues of social justice in line with Islamic teachings and traditions of mutual compassion in Jordan's predominantly Muslim society. He rejects as cynical suggestions the claims[36] that the Islamists' vociferousness on bread and butter issues is aimed at recruiting adherents and boosting the IAF's popularity.[37] Indeed the Islamists, who until 2007 remained the largest opposition bloc within the parliament, led in the 1990s the most intensive and sustained discussion of the hike in the bread prices in the history of the country. From mid-July to mid-August 1996 the Islamist deputies and independent members joined forces, turning what began in early July as short question time sessions in which they quizzed the government on its intended elimination of food subsidies into an extraordinary session. Only in the aftermath of the August 1996 bread riots in the south of the country and after royal intervention was the extraordinary session, in which Kabariti and his government were virtually put on trial, terminated. When the increases were finally introduced in August, the Islamists called on Kabariti to resign; when he failed to do so, most of the Islamist deputies threatened to step down.[38] Not even the offer by the government to compensate every Jordanian with a monthly allowance of JD 1.82 placated the Islamists.

As far as the IAF is concerned, redressing Jordan's economic imbalances must not burden the disadvantaged majority of Jordanians,[39] who, according to Mansur, are weighted down by no less than eighty types of hidden taxes and a general sales tax.[40] The Islamists' argue that the brunt of balancing the books must be borne by the rich such as by taxing luxury goods, instead of staples, and by cutting off the fringe benefits of high officials.[41] Also, they urge tighter audits of the finances of government agencies and departments to guard against embezzlement and raiding of the public purse.[42] That is not much to ask from a group of people whose zeal for Islamic justice and commitment to the ideal Muslim society propel them to volunteer their skilled labour free of charge in hundreds of social welfare projects. 'Moonlighting' for these Islamists is to raise funds for charity, the building of clinics and schools, and for the improvement of life in the Palestinian refugee camps. The Islamists feel very strongly about daily bread because they touch base with ordinary Jordanians in the course of their social activism, coming in contact not only with their material modesty but also with their generosity. Modesty has never stood in the way of generosity. For, Jordanians, observes former IAF deputy Bassam La'mush, contribute generously to the building of universities and mosques—they give more than they take.[43] Thus it is not difficult for the Islamists to stand up for maximum social protection and safeguarding of daily bread. This they do not only in redemption of their people's sharing quality but also in prevention of the kind of social 'diseases', such as crime and prostitution, that have the potential to erode public morality and social cohesion in Jordan, as noted by former parliamentarian, Ibrahim Zayd al-Kilani.[44]

All interviewees from the NIF and the IAF ascribe moral bankruptcy to the blueprints of economic management that deepen and widen inequalities in their countries. These blueprints hurt low- and middle-income earners as austerity programs did in Sudan in 1985 and in Jordan in 1988. Islamists question the wisdom of implementing strategies instigated by IMF officials with no real experience of the abject poverty and the daily struggles for survival faced by millions in the Arab world. In the words of a leading Jordanian Islamist: 'IMF officials hardly leave their comfortable offices. When they visit countries in our region they stay in five-star hotels. May be they should venture into our slums and refugee camps to learn how their strategies for basic services cutbacks cause hunger and despair.'[45] Another from the NIF places the blame squarely on insensitive and dependent secular-nationalist development strategies: 'to a point, the IMF is to blame for the widespread misery caused by its [austerity] programs. But I question the local official who is supposed to be close to the people and mindful of their welfare why he implements them.'[46] IAF spokesperson, Mansur, describes the implementation of austerity measures in Jordan as a policy of starvation (*siyāsat tajwīʿ*). For him, the government was ill-advised to embark on major cutbacks without putting in place compensation schemes for those most at risk.[47]

Criticisms of these austerity measures are not leveled on just purely moral grounds. A veteran Islamist unionist with Jordan's Engineers Syndicate, Tariq Al-Tall, point outs that the IMF's policies devised in New York are not always well suited for social conditions in the AME. He considers its blueprints of monetarist stabilization programs for Arab debtor countries to verge on blackmail. For, without their implementation, these poor countries face being penalized with disapproval of debt service relief and loss of badly needed foreign aid. There has been a long-term price, he argues, for pursuing these short-term benefits: erosion of economic and political sovereignty. Also, from his perspective as a unionist, he charges that IMF instructions in the area of macroeconomic policy are inimical to the interests of workers and the freedom of unionism. Very often austerity programs counsel keeping a lid on wages and labour discipline, a euphemism for getting tough with unions' freedoms and workers' rights. IMF's recipe of greater role for the local private sector can be disastrous if self-interest becomes the overriding dynamic of economic activity. Al-Tall notes that Islam does not oppose the rise of a dynamic domestic private sector; rather it opposes the concentration of advantages within very few hands. It is the concentration of wealth that led Mansur to declare that the country's middle class has been decimated, noting that there are two classes, one living in opulence, the other in subsistence.[48] His fellow Islamist, La'mush, uses the term sharks (*ḥitān*), which is widely used in Jordan and other neighbouring Arab countries, to refer to the wealthy who keep on getting richer at the expense of the poor.[49] Ideally, the Islamic way stands for the distribution of benefits for the sake of the less fortunate in the community of believers. A major contradiction Al-Tall finds with some of the IMF's proposals for growth and economic management in the AME regards the encouragement of export-oriented agriculture at the expense of agrarian production geared to realizing food self-sufficiency. He correctly points out that a large portion of Arab foreign debt is incurred from paying the rising food-imports bill.[50]

Islamists from al-Turabi to al-Farhan consider the state's providential role towards its poor citizens both a civil and religious duty.[51] Failure to fulfill this duty renders state–society relations vexatious, actually and potentially. For them the incidents of food protest exemplify how such vexatious relations lead to clashes between central governments and the people. Jordan's longest serving parliamentarian and a leading IAF member, Yusuf al-'Azm, argues that just as central government's policy impinges on people's capacity to sustain themselves, so do the actions of the populace affect the ruler when they rise up against exorbitant prices on essential alimentary items. Bread riots, as he puts it, are meant to 'prick the rulers' conscience' and 'send them messages' that something is amiss in their rule.[52] The Caliphs, especially 'Umar, points out al-Sanusi of the NIF, made it their job to enquire about the welfare of their peoples, ensuring that all were reasonably fed and clad. Their example, he adds, is worth following because they had the wisdom to realize that living below poverty disturbs religiosity, civility and stability.[53] Accordingly, Abu Faris, a theologian from the IAF, argues that anything that impinges on the believers' dignity (*karāmah*) and upsets the moral and social fabric of society, as do price increases on food items, must be opposed.[54] So it is this opposition to deteriorating living conditions and the widespread backlash against them that led to political reforms in Sudan and in Jordan. Interviewees from the IAF and the NIF directly link the democratic breakthroughs in their respective countries to the domestic unrest resulting from the social costs of the austerity measures. 'Arabiyyat, who also served as speaker of parliament for two consecutive terms in the early 1990s, clearly sees that link:

The sense of unease and uncertainty caused by reductions in government expenditures in social services and food subsidies is behind the bread riots of 1989. Reductions directly affect the poor. But they do affect society as a whole because they widen the gap between the rich and the poor, deepen inequities and create divisions. These divisions upset social peace for everyone. The riots themselves were bound to happen; they erupted when the suffering became unbearable and anger with government policy unstoppable ... The people took a stand like that by our people in Palestine and, as a result, they won democratic reforms.[55]

Not only 'Arabiyyat makes a link in his statement between bread riots and democratic openings but also between the riots in Jordan and the Palestinian uprising. NIF Islamists take the bread riots of

1985 in Sudan to have been decisive (*ḥāsimah*) with regard to the democratic politics they instigated between 1986 and 1989. Al-Turabi himself notes that the Sudanese have a long history of challenging central authorities and winning concessions and political or economic reforms from them. He considers that tradition to be typical of the true believers' duty to translate into action the divine commandment of prohibiting the reprehensible (*al-nahy 'an al-munkar*). Al-Turabi affirms that the democratic phase ensued directly from the people's determination to impose their will through peaceful protest.[56] Su'ad al-Fatih observes that the bread riots in Sudan demonstrated to the rest of the Arab people that popular protest can deliver victory against dictatorial forces no matter how well-equipped they are.[57] This is perhaps one reason why al-Turabi observes that the riots in Sudan tested and disproved the 'myth that autocrats like al-Numayri were invincible'.[58] Hafiz al-Shaykh al-Zaki, a prominent legal expert and a prominent figure in the NIF, refers to the riots as the call of justice (*nida al-'adālah*), noting that 'in the end justice always triumphs and the overthrow of al-Numayri ... an example of how the people decided to defeat injustice and succeeded'.[59]

Burke lists a number of points that can be seen to favour democratic norms, corroborating the Islamist linkage between food protests and political reforms in Sudan and Jordan. His analysis supports the presence of Islamic principles internal to the notion of moral economy. He challenges the conventional Orientalist bias premised on the notion of Oriental despotism, rejecting theories of the Islamic state being an all powerful edifice that is the exclusive domain of manipulative and corrupt rulers and bureaucrats whose 'politics is a game'.[60] These Orientalist views, Burke argues, diminish the significance of revolts in Arab societies. His analysis gives evidence of frequent popular protests between 1750 and 1925, which represented a historical praxis of societal resistance. This historical praxis of resistance indicates that the premodern Islamic state was neither the chief agent of change nor irresponsive to the demands of the variety of social movements (millenarian, revivalist or economic). Burke observes that for nearly two hundred years covering the period 1750–1925, society did not pay total deference to the state. On the contrary, there was a two-way flow of societal demands and state responsiveness. Society formed delegations to represent and communicate its demands directly to the rulers. Mediation between state and society was not always direct. Protesters, for instance, dispatched letters of grievance to the rulers. In either case, rulers responded to these demands and grievances by society to buy peace. This they did, among other things, by disinculpating themselves and blaming their ministers.[61] Burke calls attention to a very important point of this two-way flow of protest and responsiveness: the fact that these delegations and other forms of mediation between rulers and ruled suggest that 'Middle Eastern societies were governed in accordance with tacit moral understanding...about how much was too much'.[62] Intrinsic to this moral understanding was the Islamic notion of social justice. Burke views Muslims, both as individuals and communities, to be endowed with a mission to struggle for justice, stipulated in the Qur'ānic instruction to enjoin the good and forbid evil.[63] The enactment of justice is invested in the authority of a just prince. The office of the market superintendent or *muḥtasib* is delegated this task in practice. Being charged with ensuring fair dealing in the marketplace in such matters as prices, weights and measures, and with prevention of hoarding, the superintendent and the duties he performed were in effect a public trust, which for Burke has special significance in the context of the premodern Islamic state's commitment to social justice:

...there was indeed an Islamic analogue to the West European Christian notion of moral economy, and . . . it centered upon the application of the *sharī'ah* [Islamic Law] by a vigilant Muslim ruler. In particular, according to the *sharī'ah*, the government was obligated to enforce a series of measures of direct economic relevance to the inhabitants. These included the prohibition of usury and the insistence that only Quranically sanctioned taxes be imposed, that only Quranically approved coinage be permitted to circulate officially . . . In addition, there was the further general understanding that it was the duty of governments to ensure the supply of grain to the market at reasonable prices. Taken together these obligations amounted to an Islamic social compact which provided the moral basis of society.[64]

The Islamic social compact Burke describes here represents the doctrinal and customary frame from which the historical praxis of resistance derived its legitimacy. Protest movements in Muslim societies amounted to cries by society to enact the Islamic *telos* of justice and defend age-old liberties, particularly the right of the quarter, the tribe, and other social groups to subsistence.[65] Such protests provided rulers with the opportunity to bolster their own legitimacy by looking into society's demands and by reasserting the Islamic principles of good government on the basis of justice. The praxis of resistance, especially in the form of bread protests, continues to be embedded in Arab societies. These protests represent the discontinuous practice of democracy by society and serve as forms of pressure from below which often succeed in bringing about change from above.

The Collapse of 'Democracy of Bread'

The notion of a tacit pact between ruler and ruled is best encapsulated by the Arabic term 'democracy of bread' (*dīmuqrāṭiyyat al-khubz*). Thus Professor Ahmad Shalabi of Cairo University describes 'Abd al-Nasser's politics.[66] Tunisian Islamist leader, Rashid al-Ghannushi, observes that 'democracy of bread' refers to a value (*qīmah*) that fosters a moral quality in the political process. This value, he argues, must be binding on politicians of all colours. At the core of this value is the obligation to deploy all resources to secure a good living standard for all citizens. For him 'hardship creates neither good citizens nor good Muslims. Godly instructions for mutual compassion do not only concern individual acts but also encompass the realm of governance'.[67] Al-Ghannushi thus views humane governance holistically. In it material and spiritual qualities intertwine: the vote and the bread are not interchangeable; they are essential 'goods' for fulfilling political, economic, social, and religious obligations. Akin to the democracy of bread is the notion of the 'democratic bargain'.[68] Essentially, its chief premise is that post-independence Arab rulers have been paid political deference by their peoples in return for the provision of publicly subsidized services—education, health care, and a state commitment to secure employment. Political deference has been traded off for bread. 'Bread' is used here in a generic sense to refer to free education, health care, and other services. In a sense the arrangements represented by the concept democracy of bread are similar to Burke's idea of a social compact as they represent the moral basis of polity and society. As an explanatory tool, the concept democracy of bread is significant in that it stresses the socioeconomic basis of Arab political power: Arab authoritarianism has not reproduced itself by relying solely on brute force, but also on 'elements of negotiation and accommodation'.[69]

The catalytic role of the failure or collapse (*inḥilāl*) of democracy of bread can be seen in the most recent Arab democratic stirrings. The politics cultivated by democracy of bread is largely deferential and non-participatory, conditional on the state's providential capacity. One consequence of this politics is what the Algerian intellectual Malik Bin Nabi calls *būlītīk* (a bastardization of the French term '*politique*').[70] This popular and pejorative Maghribi term refers to politics as an undesirable game of power, subterfuge and counter-subterfuge; as talk but no action; it conveys a general feeling of distrust which leads to the avoidance of politics.[71] If Arab peoples tend to disown their regimes, *būlītīk* aptly explains why. The support networks provided by the tribe or the family have generally helped Arabs maintain distance from authority. Before the emergence of the nation-state system, the

Arab individual's main desire was livelihood without interference from nature or from authority (tax collection). The undisturbed and apolitical world of the Arab individual is captured in the popular Maghribi saying: 'food we eat, until death we meet' (*na'kulu al-qut wa nistanna al-mut*). The ultimate provider was not the state; it was God and His providence (*barakah*).

In the post-state period, the residue of that folk culture can be noticed in another popular Maghribi term: *khubz*-iste. The term *khubz*-iste describes an attitude of distrust toward the political system coupled with deferential political behaviour. The difference now is that the state is in the picture. A departure has occurred from the world of non-conceptual icons to one of conceptual symbols; from one where providence is imparted directly by God to one where providence is associated with the state; and from one where politics had little relevance to one where politics has more relevance. In both, however, politics has relevance only where the balance of physical existence was impinged upon by authority. If Arab individuals are *khubz*-istes, so are Arab states. The latter create an expectation in the former to seek what it can provide. The *khubz*-iste individual is quietist; the *khubz*-iste state is providential.

Since the *khubz*-iste is quietist only in so far as the state is providential, economic downturns have eroded the providential platform of Arab polities. Subsequently, under societal pressure, the tacit contract between ruler and ruled has become tenuous, leading to involuntary relaxation of control from the top in the form of ambiguous politics of renewal—limited participation and contestation—the clear purpose of which has thus far been regime survival. Economic malaise is at the root of both societal pressure and political changes. Nowhere has that societal pressure been more evident than in the phenomenon of bread uprisings (intifādāt al-khubz). Recent Arab history is littered with numerous examples of such uprisings: Egypt, January 1977; Morocco, January 1984; Tunisia, January 1984; Sudan, March 1985; Algeria, October 1988; Jordan, April 1989 and in 1997; Lebanon, in July 1997 and in February 1998.

Bread riots can be explained in terms of cause and effect. In all these countries bread uprisings were triggered by soaring food prices, housing shortages, high unemployment, and, in Algeria, even rationing of water supplies. In Morocco, Sudan, and Tunisia the trends since the mid-1970s up to the mid-1980s had been of rising prices and declining living standards for a significant percentage of the population.[72] For instance, Morocco's cost-of-food index more than tripled between 1973 and 1983,[73] and in the mid-1980s it was estimated that over 40 per cent of its population was living below the poverty level.[74] During the same period, about 25 per cent of Tunisia's total labour force was either unemployed or underemployed, and a high percentage of 'households in the southern interior live[d] at or below the level of basic subsistence'.[75] Like them, the Sudan experienced increasing trends of pauperization, owing either to government economic mismanagement or to poor harvests.[76] In Jordan, soaring food prices followed IMF-approved economic austerity measures, a situation that was aggravated by mounting foreign debt and a plummeting dinar.[77]

The examples of Algeria and Egypt are equally instructive. In neither country was the professed brand of Arab socialism godless or about class struggle.[78] Both, however, were authoritarian and economically inefficient. Egypt's military setbacks against Israel further delegitimized Nasser's Arab socialism. The ditching of socialism in Egypt in the late 1970s and, more so, in Algeria in the 1980s was conceived in a milieu of economic malaise: soaring foreign debt,[79] high unemployment, housing crises and heightened social polarization between rich and poor. The state welfarist inducements, which in the 1960s and early 1970s served to depoliticize the masses, were in the 1980s stretched too thin because of larger populations. Egypt's high military expenditures and Algeria's dwindling revenues from oil rents (which decreased from 45 to 28 billion dollars between 1984 and 1986 by more than one third) were intolerable burdens on both countries' economies.[80] For the educated jobless in both countries, where unemployment still ranges between 20 and 30 per cent of the active workforce, disillusionment with the regimes was vented in the bread riots of 1977 in Egypt and 1988 in Algeria.

In the impoverished Arab states, unemployment will always remain a potential detonator of social discontent and political instability. Like *khubz*-istes, *ḥiṭ*-istes are ubiquitous. The pressure of population growth further compounds economic hardship. The annual population growth rate, fluctuating between 2 and 4 per cent, is very high given these states' modest resources. This not only means further pressure on housing, water, food, employment, education, and health care but also presents the still more daunting prospect of a doubling of the total population by the year 2025.

The contraction of job markets is further squeezing these countries' economies. In almost all of them, only 23–31 per cent of the total population is fully employed. This has heightened despair among the youth, considering that in 1989 sixty per cent of all Arabs were less than 19 years of age.[81] The prospects of improvement are poor for the alienated and disillusioned Arab youth. The doors of immigration have been closed. To put brakes on future immigration, the former European Community (EC) devised a package of aid to 12 non-member

Mediterranean states, seven of which are Arab—Algeria, Egypt, Jordan, Lebanon, Morocco, Syria, and Tunisia. The aid package, known as the Revised Mediterranean Policy, was a combination of $500 million in grants and more than $4 billion in loans. It was prompted by fear that economic malaise and surging Islamism could spark an exodus from these countries to Europe: 'Today the phrase "boat people" refers to refugees from Vietnam', said one [EC] official. 'In the future it may refer to illegal immigration across the Mediterranean'.[82]

Unequal and selective development that benefits a certain social group or favors a certain region has created a great deal of polarization between the poor and the *nouveaux riches*. Algiers, for example, illustrates the chasm between the haves and the have-nots with its middle class suburbs and the abject poverty of the overcrowded and unsanitary slums in the Qasbah area.[83] Al-Sadat's economic policy of *infitāḥ* has not been beneficial to the poor. Concomitant with the 'prosperity' of the Free Trade Zones was the misery and marginalization of millions of Egyptians—some actually living in cemeteries—outside of the formal economy. Mostly geared to liberalize the economy, encourage foreign investment and privatize public assets, the modest windfall of the *infitāḥ* policy was confined to the Egyptian bourgeoisie, the clientele of the al-Sadat regime, creating a kind of economic apartheid.[84] While this policy freed Egypt from dependence on the Soviets, it failed to free it from dependence on the United States and international capital:

This meant the incorporation of the Egyptian bourgeoisie into new relations with imperialism, and its transformation into a comprador class dependent on foreign capital ... Egypt became a part of the world economy, fulfilling its role as emergent neo-colony of transnational capital dominated by the United States.[85]

The *khubz*-istes' disaffection with inexorably deteriorating economic and living conditions can be singled out as the main factor that created a socially and politically explosive atmosphere—the stage of breaking point. It is against the backdrop of economic malaise that *khubz*-istes and dissident forces take to the streets *en masse*. In these protests the people's taste for participatory politics is nurtured, and their dissidence is unleashed by directly challenging political authority. The rebellious street binds together political dissidents, marginals, the unemployed, and the disillusioned youth. They acquire a spontaneous solidarity and, in their common consciousness of being actual or potential victims of the regime, they direct their anger at high status and regime symbols. The Algerian riots of 1988 are instructive:

From the cities of the coast to oases of the Sahara, Algerians went on [the] rampage and destroyed whatever, in their eyes, represented the regime: city halls, police stations, courts...They also vented their rage on the political headquarters of the country's only legal party, the FLN...Inevitably, stores were ransacked and cars burned, turning the main commercial streets of Algiers into scenes of devastation.[86]

These riots provided a catalyst for the reforms that followed in 1988. The point must be made that bread uprisings represent an economic and political phenomenon.[87] The protests following the waiving of state subsidies[88] for strategic commodities (sugar, tea, kerosene, flour, bread) and price hikes can mislead if strictly interpreted as 'rebellions of the belly'. In all cases these uprisings amounted to protests against social inequality, corruption, nepotism, authoritarianism, and regime incompetence.[89] Egyptian protesters also targeted the government.[90] Cooper stresses the significance of the fact that the January 1977 riots in Egypt followed the November 1976 parliamentary elections and primarily targeted the People's Assembly:[91]

[t]he rioters [did] not look on [the People's Assembly] as an object of attack; rather, it seem[ed] that they want[ed] to use it as a forum in which to be heard. (...) These elections in particular aroused and politicized large numbers of people and, with the capricious raising of prices, the demonstrators felt that the elections and the Assembly had failed them.[92]

If by targeting the Assembly Egyptian rioters disowned the abuse of due process and non-responsive institutions that, in waiving food subsidies, failed to prevent a decision that was impervious and inimical to their interests, the Algerian rioters expressed similar disavowal of their regime.[93] According to Roberts, that disavowal was translated into open contempt for president al-Chadhli: 'as the rioters put it, "we don't want butter or pepper, we want a leader we can respect" (*ma bghina la zibda wa la filfal, lakin bghina za'im fhal*).'[94]

The reference to bread riots, especially those of Algeria and Jordan, as 'uprisings' (*intifādāt*, plural of *intifādah*), recalling the Palestinian *intifādah*, is deliberate. The magnitude of public participation, especially among the youth; the intensity of the outbursts; their semi-peaceful nature (with stone-throwing being the main means of engagement) and their spontaneity lend credibility to the proposition of the infectiousness of the Palestinian *intifādah*. That is, Arab uprisings, especially in Algeria and Jordan, are modeled on the Palestinian uprising. The *intifādah* is an outburst against a 'foreign' occupier. The Jordanian and Algerian riots were outbursts against local authorities which represented some degree of 'foreignness' in the eyes of the rioters: their dependence on foreign aid and expertise; their imported ineffective 'isms' and ideologies employed for nation-building; their economies which have been plugged into the international economy; and their limited autonomy, with many regimes being seen as puppets. Like the *intifāḍah*, the Jordanian and Algerian riots amounted to a cry for justice, equality of opportunity, and emancipation from poverty and despair:

> ...those who sympathize with the rioters often call the October Revolt the *intifāḍah* (uprising)... There can be no doubt that the school children battling in the streets of Algeria took their cue from the Palestinian teenagers of the West Bank and Gaza. Witnessing almost daily television scenes of that uprising, Algerian youngsters set out to enact their own *intifāḍah*. One young demonstrator was quoted as saying, 'they aren't afraid, so why should I be?'[95]

This serves as a confirmation of the view expressed by West Bank activist Jonathan Kuttab in 1988 that Arab regimes harboured fears of an *intifāḍah* spillover into their own streets.[96] The *intifāḍah* assumed a spiritual importance in the eyes of millions of Arabs, epitomizing hope that people power resistance may one day enable disaffected Arabs to achieve their objectives of justice, equality, and emancipation. Like the youth of the *intifāḍah*, the new generation of Arabs stages uprisings in defiance of the status quo. Unlike their parents and grandparents, Arab youth have known only the post-independence order, an order where the gap between their rising expectations and the ability of their regimes to meet them increasingly widens. They have little reason to feel grateful or beholden to their regimes. No amount of rhetoric about a glorious past or a brighter future, couched in the language of nationalism, pan-Arabism or development, is good enough. It means little to the *ḥit*-istes in many an Arab café or street, the hungry Sudanese or the cemetery-dwelling Egyptian.

Accordingly, if bread riots seem to have aroused the Arab people's appetite for open defiance of the status quo in the 1980s, what then are their consequences?

- Economic malaise and the limitation or un-affordability of state welfarism produced twin, opposing effects: politicization of both *khubz*-istes and *ḥit*-istes on the one hand, and erosion of regime legitimacy in many impoverished Arab states.
- Bread uprisings can be interpreted as kinds of indirect elections in countries where no pluralist politics have existed since independence. Uprisings amounted to votes of no confidence against the incumbent regimes. The rioters rebelled to express widespread feelings among the masses of ingratitude toward regimes that still based their legitimacy on past achievements of little relevance

to the people's present struggle for bread. Despite their economic roots, these uprisings have definite political content and motivation. According to Cooper, Egypt's 1977 riots had 'signs of organization [with] identical anti-regime literature appear[ing] simultaneously across the . . . country . . . [of] systematic attempts to cut internal communications . . . [of] coordinated attacks on neighbouring police stations . . . [of] selectivity of targets, concentrating on state property.'[97] Seddon draws similar conclusions about evidence of political organization in the uprisings of Morocco, Sudan, and Tunisia in 1984 and 1985.[98]

- the 'democracy of bread' gave way to political democracy (*al-dīmuqrāṭiyyah al-siyāsiyyah*). 'Bread', the powerful idiom of the past, ceded to the idiom of the present: the vote. In immediate post-independence the vote was denied to the Arab masses in return for bread. In the 1980s the regimes failed to deliver bread. When the masses took to the streets demanding bread they were given the vote.

The democratic openings that resulted from popular uprisings in the 1980s in Algeria and Jordan are instructive. The pressure from below—the uprisings of the Jordanian and Algerian streets—has been a prime factor in forcing both countries' regimes to democratize. The price was paid in human lives: 12 Jordanians in the April 1989 riots, and up to 500 Algerians in the October 1988 riots.[99] From this perspective, democratization has not come easily to Jordan or Algeria. It was fought for. The protest for bread turned into a protest for rights. In Jordan, the 1989 sacking of Rifa'i and the promise of early elections calmed the situation,[100] and in Algeria, only the promise of democracy provided a temporary relief for the FLN.[101] The rulers in Algiers and Amman came to the realization that repression has its limitations, and the still vivid memory of the overthrow of al-Numayri in the 1985 Sudanese bread riots was a reminder of them. As Gene Sharp observes, 'the brutalities of repression against non-violent resisters trigger a process of "political jiujitsu", which increases the resistance, sows problems in the opponents' own camp, and mobilizes third parties in favour of the non-violent resisters.'[102]

Like in Algeria and Sudan before it, Jordan's 1996 bread crisis became a focal point around which the opposition, unions, and students ordered their discourse and orchestrated their actions, by highlighting the government's depleted store of legality and legitimacy. The bread crisis was discoursed in conjunction with the crisis of freedoms, democracy, and lack of consultation; and the protests against the elimination of subsidies became demonstrations for greater freedoms.

Hamzah Mansur observes how the crisis strengthened the resolve of many parliamentarians, especially the Islamists, that they wanted a democratic quality that went beyond the procedural minimum, that is, periodic elections. For, he notes, the Kabariti government was alerted to the consequences of cuts to subsidies and yet it went ahead with their implementation. Had the government heeded that advice of most parliamentarians, he adds, events would not have reached a boiling point between state and society in mid-August, leading to bloody clashes and fatalities in the south.[103] But the opposition was heard by the street. Like, the Egyptian rioters, demonstrators in Jordan marched to the National Assembly to lend support to the deputies' opposition to the increases and vent their protest against the hikes directly to the government. Islamist IAF MP, Muhammad 'Uwidah, deplored how the peaceful protest turned the grounds of the National Assembly into a military barrack.[104] The Islamists' call for Kabariti to resign was echoed in graffiti in at least one city.[105] On every occasion and in every forum where the bread crisis was discoursed it was twinned with the deficiency in freedoms and in the country's incipient democratization. When the Islamist opposition requested an audience with the late King Hussein, they identified the cuts to subsidies and unlawful detention of dissidents as the two topics of discussion with the monarch.[106] For instance, the detention of political dissidents and protestors against the hikes before and after the August riots was highlighted by the Islamist opposition as another blot on the record of the Kabariti government. Bassam La'mush reproached the government for the imprisonment of protestors, whose only crime was to abuse the government verbally, while it pusillanimously ignored the country's sharks who raided the public purse for personal gain.[107] This shook the confidence of the government, forcing Kabariti and a few of his ministers to hold meetings with the opposition to explain the fate of detainees and go public every time a group of protesters or dissidents were released.[108] In a move calculated to control the damage from the negative publicity over the cuts to subsidies and the heavy-handedness used in the riots, the government orchestrated the release over a couple of weeks in order to attract maximum favourable media coverage.

Throughout the bread crisis, the Islamists maximized their political capital by banking on the Kabariti government's folly in ignoring hostile public opinion to cuts in subsidies and overwhelming opposition against them in the National Assembly. The Islamists proved themselves to be adept at politics through three mutually reinforcing strategies. Within parliament, they led the opposition against the subsidies, showing themselves to be bound by legality and proceduralism and capable of the democratic game. Outside parliament, they helped inform and mobilize the street against the government's food policy, astutely legitimizing themselves as spokespersons on behalf of the have-nots. Moreover, with the government's escalation of repression and muzzling of free speech, they succeeded in entrenching themselves as representatives of all victims of authoritarianism. All along, their discourse was couched in the language of Islam along with the language of democracy. Hence when 'Arabiyyat, one of the IAF's leading public figures, had to engage secularists in open debates about the bread crisis, he identified dialogue along the lines of democracy and *shūrā* as the proper framework for resolving problems.[109] In its standoff with the Kabariti government, at no stage did the Islamist opposition attack the monarchy. Just it did define for the government the issue of bread subsidies as a red line not to be crossed, it defined for itself the royal house and the monarchy as a red line not to approach. The Islamists were keen not to drive a wedge between themselves and the monarch whose own support among the various clans was rock solid. By attacking the monarchy they would be committing political suicide—leaving them open to repression and confrontation with the state as well as losing popularity among the people. In fact, the Islamists resorted to the palace to act as an arbitrator in their disputation over economic matters with the Kabariti government. Furthermore, as an act of faith in the monarch and the monarchy, Islamists reaffirmed their allegiance to the late King in the aftermath of the bloody clashes between the people and the state in the south. The then IAF deputy, Ahmad al-Kasasibah, from al-Karak, delivered a speech welcoming the late King to the region, confirming loyalty to God, King, and country, and committing his constituency to renewed support of the Hashemites.[110]

The catalytic role of the collapse of the democracy of bread and bread riots in a few Arab democratic openings can be noticed in the overthrow of al-Numayri's authoritarian regime in 1985. This event was like a historical reenactment of the October 1964 downfall of another Sudanese autocrat, General 'Abbud. Not a single authoritarian regime in the contemporary Arab world has fallen victim to people's power except in the Sudan, where this has occurred twice. Nowhere else, with the exception of Algeria and Jordan in the late 1980s, did clear-cut democratic experiments ensue from 'people's power': the first from 1964 to 1969, the second from 1986 to 1989. These outcomes refute Bienen and Gersovitz's thesis that subsidy cuts-based anomie has only short-term implications for political stability.[111] More importantly, long-term political repercussions of Arab bread uprisings challenge both the near silence of the literature on democratic transition

regarding the role of anomie, and the functionalist faith in modernization and social change embedded in some Western epistemological
circles. Evidence from the Arab world supports the idea that democratic transition (electoralism) can be the result of social disorder
triggered by bread riots. Raising food prices, like raising or imposing
taxes, can trigger rebellion and civil disobedience against authoritarian regimes.[112] If civil disobedience led to the cancellation of food price
increases (Tunisia, Morocco,[113] and Egypt[114]), followed by incremental
but continuous, though token, pluralization in Sudan, Algeria, and
Jordan, it produced some clear examples of political liberalization.

The Sudanese people's uprising in March–April 1985 represents
the example *par excellence* of an economic-based but politically motivated protest. It was a politically purposeful anti-centralist protest
by civil and non-civil collectivities, some of which were both aware
of and dissatisfied with their peripheral positions. Many forces from
the country's civil society (associations representing women, doctors,
lawyers, engineers, trade unions, and students) as well as non-civil
forces (Association of Police Officers [APO], Free Army Officers Organization [FAOO]) joined in a political movement espousing radical
change, that is, nothing short of bringing down al-Numayri's regime.
For some of these forces, participation in the protest was not just part
of a larger mobilizational effort against a de-legitimized authority but
also part of a strategy of aspiring power claimants with their own
political agendas.

Throughout the *intifāḍah* the confluence between the economic and
the political was clear-cut. Leaflets, such as those distributed by hos-
pital doctors, referred to al-Numayri's government as 'a regime of
hunger'.[115] The same leaflets nevertheless articulated radical political messages and defined clear political stances with the people and
against the regime, for good government and against authoritarian
rule. Hence the APO not only expressed that its members would 'dis-
obey any orders to use force against the people of Sudan' but also
adopted the slogan 'no to [al-]Numa[y]ri and no to dictatorship'.[116]
Similarly, the FAOO's message was that 'the Sudan Armed Forces side
with the popular revolt against hunger, ignorance, and misrule, and
for social justice and equality'.[117]

The Peculiarities of Arab 'Democratic' Transitions

Obviously, the progression to democracy in the AME does not necessarily reflect the Western experience.[118] The Western model of linear change through feudalism and then the bourgeoisie has had no

exemplar in the Arab world. The Arab search for democracy seems to traverse the 'authoritarian road': the survival of personalist regimes and the experience of reversals in 1958 and 1975 strongly illustrate the persistent challenge of Arab democratization. Although the scholarly discourse on political transformation presupposes the presence of prerequisites or preconditions for transition to democracy, it remains indeterminate. Rustow cautions against confusing correlation with causation injects an insightful input into the discourse, especially with reference to socioeconomic variables, noting that the transition processes and dynamics are not uniform.[119] In the following discussion, the socioeconomic correlate of democracy will be examined with special emphasis on the collapse of the bread pact between rulers and the ruled in the Arab world.

The focus here is on the Lipset hypothesis, widely accepted association of high economic performance with corresponding high levels of democracy. In his words:

> ... the more well-to-do a nation, the greater the chances that it will sustain democracy. From Aristotle down to the present, [people] have argued that only in a wealthy society in which relatively few citizens lived in real poverty could a situation exist in which the mass of the population could intelligently participate in politics ... [120]

Lipset establishes a linkage between wealth and democracy but does not link economic fairness (equal distribution of wealth) and political fairness, that is, democracy ('one person, one vote'). Thus for Lipset, an increment in general wealth would mean political participation without necessarily eliminating socioeconomic inequalities.[121] Dahl, however, while of the view that a fairly high GNP per capita 'threshold' can be conducive to higher levels of contestation and participation, cautions that higher GNP levels per capita beyond a minimum threshold do not necessarily 'affect [polyarchy] in any significant way'.[122] Furthermore, Dahl gives the example of American democracy in the nineteenth century which had neither an industrial base nor a high GNP per capita.[123] Huntington's findings point to an 'economic transition zone' that can correspond to a 'political transition zone' where movement from non-democracy to democracy occurs.[124] This transition, however, is not irreversible. Lipset's correlation applies to the Arab setting only in one sense:[125] it explains the unsustainability of 'competitive' (Lebanon) and 'semi-competitive'[126] (Egypt, Morocco, Tunisia, Jordan) politics in the not so 'well-to-do' Arab countries.

In the 1980s and beyond, the view in many parts of the Arab world, rightly or wrongly, is that democracy is amenable to high economic development, not vice versa. Pioneering Arab 'democratizers' are the

Table 5.1　Discrepancies between GNP and competitiveness

Country	GNP per capita (US$)	Number of elections 1977–1997
UAE	19,600	0
Qatar	15,670	0
Kuwait	15,500	3
Saudi Arabia	7,700	0
Bahrain	6,630	0
Libya	6,200	0
Oman	5,650	0
Iraq	5,500	1
Algeria	2,300	3
Tunisia	2,000	4
Jordan	1,600	3
Lebanon	1,600	2
Syria	1,200	3
Morocco	1,100	4
Egypt	800	6
Mauritania	600	2
Sudan	550	2
Djibouti	300	1
Somalia	200	0

'relatively populous, poor, and politicized'.[127] The 'well-to-do' Arab rentiers states are, with the qualified exception of Kuwait, the furthest from democratization qua electoralism (see Table 5.1). Higher income per capita does not automatically translate into greater competitiveness or contestation (electoral activities). Of the 33 legislative elections that have been held in the AME since 1977 and up to 1997, only 4 took place in oil-rich countries where per capita income ranges between US$ 5,500 and US$ 20,000. Egypt and Morocco whose combined per capita income is less than US$ 3,000 account for the highest number of elections in the AME, respectively held six and four parliamentary elections. Internal and external factors explain why the poorer Arab countries are election-active than the rich ones. Internally, the ruling elites can ill-afford to control their societies by way of coercion alone. This device is a kind of a redistribution of political power, even if cosmetic or minimalist, to placate the populace in the poor and populous Arab states. The analogue for this in the oil-rich is to redistribute financial largess—economic power—to delay participation. Externally, the poorer Arab states are more vulnerable and sensitive to the winds of change in the global arena. Electoral politics is necessary to meet minimum standards of governance and qualify for the financial services of the donor community. These services are not as yet needed by the oil-rich states.

How can these last two deviations be explained? The anomaly in the Arab hydrocarbon states[128] owes in part to the artificiality of oil wealth—one of a number of various possible factors. The huge returns from external oil rent have contributed primarily to aggrandizement of the state and its political oligarchic patrons—the rentier class.[129] This aggrandizement applies to both oil producers and non-producers. The former directly accrued billions of petrodollars from external oil rent. The latter, only peripheral oil-producers, profited from the Arab oil boom which facilitated greater Arab economic integration and interdependence. This latter group has become partly rentier economies. They rent labour, skills, and expertise to the scarcely populated Arab oil-producing states and thereby earn billions of dollars in remittances. Transfers of millions of Arab petrodollars either in the form of aid or investment are another factor in the equation. Petrodollars have endowed the Arab state with an independent resource to cement and reproduce itself. A prime function of this resource has been the ability to buy political patronage, legitimacy, and time. Hence the oil paradox: the strength and relative domestic autonomy of the Arab state stems from dependence on external oil revenue.[130] Petrodollars have also enabled power holders to assert their authority by expanding state involvement in all socioeconomic spheres. Most socioeconomic functions are state-led. This interventionism has largely inhibited the rise of autonomous societal power centres. The large size of the state bureaucracy has turned much of the working population into de facto state clients whose livelihoods depend on the public purse. According to one estimate of the late 1970s, state bureaucrats formed 30 per cent of Egypt's labour force and 60 per cent of Jordan's.[131] In fact, according to Springborg, the *infitāḥ* has not stemmed the growth of Egypt's state bureaucracy. It quadrupled between 1970 and 1986, reaching 4.8 million—10 per cent of all Egyptians were state employees.[132]

Dividends from oil-rich to oil-poor have helped consolidate the states of the latter, creating political interdependence.[133] External extraction of oil surpluses has bestowed upon the oil-rich both internal and regional distributive powers. These powers have in turn given them regulative functions calibrated according to interest—exclusion of foes and inclusion (pork-barreling) of allies. The recipient Arab states distribute and regulate using the same formula. What Farsoun calls a 'wide economic base' operates both internally and externally:

Regime stability derived domestically in part from this wide economic base, which has been a direct consequence of the expansion of state functions. This would have been impossible without the capital surpluses for the oil-producers and capital transfers for the oil-poor states.[134]

Extraction and distribution of petrodollars have given regimes regulative leverage resulting from the acquisition of a 'wide economic base' through all-encompassing patronage. As Farsoun correctly notes, this has enabled the state to 'pre-empt and deflect opposition'.[135] Political monopoly and the reproduction of the authoritarian state are not only functions of passive exclusion (preemption and deflection) but are also active undertakings. Hence, the police (*mukhābarāt*) state, with its military and police apparatuses, has been made possible by the oil boom. It continues to be able to reproduce itself and to perfect its coercive capacity.[136] For Farsoun the Arab state is the 'syncretic state-in-three'.[137] It is the 'historic state' thriving on political patronage through limited distribution of power (status, prestige) and economic opportunities. Also, it is the 'modern state' with its corporatist character combining interdependent and yet autonomous and semi-autonomous interests and power clusters—bureaucracies (civil, military and police), bourgeoisie (including ruling elites), and technocrats (including information holders and dependent theocrats). It is self-serving, nurturing legitimacy through welfarism and symbolic functions[138] (to enhance a sense of community, of safety, of patriotism), and nurturing clientelism by creating the opportunities and environment for 'capital accumulation by the elite'.[139] Lastly, it is the *police* state that ensures the survival of the regime and its allied interests.

Huntington relates the failure of oil-rich states to democratize to state enrichment from petrodollars which discards its need for tax revenue. It seems that these states are comfortable with the status quo, that is, non-competitive polities in which there is neither representation nor taxation.[140] In contrast, he notes, industrial economies are amenable to a 'much more diverse, complex and interrelated economy, which becomes increasingly difficult for authoritarian regimes to control'.[141] Tax-paying citizens in consolidated democracies subject their governors to the rigor of accountability and checks and balances. The point is that oil wealth has contributed to the viability of authoritarianism, not of democracy. If one is to accept the association between high economic development and democracy, arguments can be made for more equitable distribution of oil wealth in such a way that it brings Arabs near those 'thresholds' or 'zones of transition' that would make Arab democracy viable. For such transfers to happen, democracy is needed first.[142] The anomaly with regard to democratizing Arab states resides in the fact that medium to low economic development, which is generally taken to be a constraint on democratization, has in fact been a catalyst. While this might be an exaggeration, the fact remains that openings initiated by a few authoritarian Arab states have been the result of economic downturns, not high performance.[143]

Conclusion

In the short term, even if limited and controlled, political change in the AME is more likely to continue to ensue from the phenomenon of bread riots than from a voluntary refashioning of the existing fixed and singular power relations. This is increasingly becoming the case in a world where nation-states in North and South are learning, with varying degrees of success, how to come to grips with globalization and the revitalized neo-liberal agenda that sustains it. Perhaps no element of globalization and the neo-liberal agenda are likely to lead to the conditions that trigger bread riots more than the weakening of nationally and autonomously economic decision-making in the pursuit of objectives of equity, social justice, and protection of the have-nots. Losing sight of these objectives, especially as the AME is experiencing a second wave of open-door policies in parallel with international trends to seek integration in the global economy, can be detrimental for equal distribution, socioeconomic security and, by implication, social peace. Both the design and implementation of economic policy that takes account of these objectives require not only commitment to issues of social justice and equity but also effective state institutions to implement them. The AME must seek to learn and gain from the potential benefits of the global without losing sight of the local.

In a globalizing world where economic decision-making intertwines with the dictats of a loosely regulated global market economy, the AME may experience an increase in the incidence of bread riots. What makes this scenario a plausible one is the fact that the national non-oil economies are faced with a global system they cannot afford to boycott. Hence their dilemma: how to reconcile the rewards they seek from the global system (integration/capital/technology transfer/markets) with the penalties that come with it (some loss of sovereignty). Foreign capital can mean certainty; it can also mean uncertainty when it is repatriated (e.g. Indonesia's riots of May 1998 and the fall of the Suharto regime weeks later). Likewise, IMF and World Bank loans in impoverished Arab states may bring some relief; but they may entail imposition of austerity programs, among other attached strings. In this regard, and given the vitality of the neo-liberal agenda, austerity programs and the cutting of subsidies are commonplace IMF and World Bank prescriptions for the states, including those in the AME, which seek integration in the global system. Generally, social expenditures as a percentage of the GDP have decreased markedly since the early 1990s in the AME. Universal food subsidies are fast becoming something of the past; the notable exception is Yemen. Food subsidies, the chief rationale of which according to Qaiser Khan of the World Bank is to buy peace among urban consumers, as a percentage of the GDP in 1995 were 1 per cent in Algeria; 1.3 per cent in Egypt; 2.9 per cent in Jordan; 1.7 per cent in Morocco and in Tunisia; and 10.4 per cent in Yemen.[144] Most of these states have experienced multiple bread riots and are likely to do so in the future.

The politicization and radicalization of these riots embolden and broaden the rioters' demands for change, shifting their focus from the economic to the political. This is more so when religious morality is invoked and deployed to argue against the immorality of the inequity and economic mismanagement of secular establishments. Increasingly, there is a mixing of religion with issues of social protection. Nowhere has this been more apparent than in Jordan and Lebanon. Islamist leaders, some of whom double up as preachers in mosques around Jordan, voice criticism of the increasing tendency by government to reduce food subsidies. Mansur, a leading member of the Islamic Action Front, equates this line of action with a starvation policy.[145] Food riots were almost endemic to Jordan with the 1997 protests forcing a cabinet reshuffle. In 2007 Egypt's textile labour force staged many strikes that confirm the symbiosis between welfare and quietism, on the one hand, and inequity and anomie, on the other. Minimum measures for protecting workers and agreeing bonus awards had to be agreed under the pressure of rioters. The rise in food and bread prices coupled with the shortage of bread in Egypt returned to haunt the Mubarak regime in the first half of 2008. Many rioters were killed; many dissidents found it an opportune moment to strike back at the authoritarian state; and Mubarak intervened by raising wages and ordering the police and army's bakeries to supply the civilian market with bread (in order to feed and not kill the Egyptian people for a change, as it were). Morocco experienced similar riots over food prices in the first half of 2007. Bread riots can be expected to continue to affect future state–society relations as well as the growth of political institutions, including opposition, regime legitimacy, and reform processes, in the populous and impoverished AME.

The challenge to state authority in Lebanon by Subhi Tufaili, the Shi'ite cleric expelled from Hizbullah in 1991,[146] is a good example of the mixing of religion with issues of social justice. In reference to his eight-month-long public disobedience campaign to press the economically rationalist Hariri government into easing poverty in the Bekaa

Valley, Tufaili speaks of his instigation of revolt of the hungry (*thawratu al-jiyā‘*) as a 'religious duty'.[147] In January 1998, Tufaili along with a group of zealous supporters barricaded themselves in a Bekaa school in a move calculated to highlight the plight of this region and its people whose neglect by the state makes it one of abject poverty and poor resources. No less than 50 people were either killed or injured before the Lebanese army 'freed' the school. More peaceful and success-ful, however was the 4 July 1997 demonstration by Tufaili's revolt of the hungry, a street march and a successful disobedience protest joined by several thousand citizens. Although hunger and marginalization were the departure point of the protests led by Tufaili, the ultimate aim was about how to affect change in the system and hold it responsible and responsive to the people:

From his headquarters in Baalbek, [Tufaili] proclaimed a revolt of the hun-gry... [B]ecause [he] was able to assemble between seven and ten thousand demonstrators on the square in front of the seraglio, the radical Shi'ite cleric... has once again become one of the most influential politicians in Lebanon. 'we start in Bekaa', he shouted to the crowd, 'and soon our movement will spread to every region. The next step will be a march on Beirut. We will call on government employees not to report for work. We shall march on Beirut, and their entire house of cards will collapse'. This was the first climax of a campaign of civil disobedience. At the beginning of May, [Tufaili] had called on the people to stop paying their taxes, and water and electricity bills... With this idea, he scored a bull's eye, since the prevailing popular belief is that only the little man is relentlessly forced to obey and pay, while the big businessmen in Beirut enjoy tax breaks and special relationships with the ministry of finance.[148]

The Tufaili phenomenon cannot be dismissed as an inconspicuous footnote in the history of the AME. The concern about issues of social justice and welfare is a genuinely serious business among Islamists everywhere in the Arab region. But it is equally a serious busi-ness among non-Islamists. Again, the postmortem done by various Lebanese parliamentarians indicates that social and regional inequal-ity and lack of social protection for the needy spell a grave danger for mutual state–society relations as well as for lasting social peace. Statements by prominent deputies such as the former House Speaker, Husayn al-Husayni, Marwan Faris, and Sami al-Khatib that hunger and unemployment cry for urgent state just socio-economic programs not coercion. Al-Husayni blames the state for not taking responsibility for its ill-thought policies that led to the neglect of the Bekaa Valley; Faris sums up the revolt of the hungry led by Tufaili as resulting from 'historical deprivation;' whereas al-Khatib describes the state's unintelligent resort to violence to put an end to the uprising as a 'natural outcome to an unnatural treatment'.[149]

A few conclusive observations can be made. The assumption that the better a country's economic performance the better its chances for democracy presents problems in the AME. The bias of this theory against poorer states is obvious. Arab electoralism in the late 1980s seems to have benefited from austerity, not bounty. Contrary to the arguments of Western theorists such as Lipset, it is the poorer not the richer Arab states that first took the steps toward electoralism in the 1980s. Only in the late 1990s has electoralism swept the Arab Gulf. Democracy can be said to be a technique for bridging political and economic impasses; it is not simply a product of socio-economic development or of unique cultural attributes. The logical flaw evident in much Western writing on the topic is that deductions made from the experience of mature democracies are of doubtful relevance for states that are only beginning the process of democratization. The problem is not that the ideal of democracy as celebrated in the West is irrelevant to the AME. Rather, analyses of non-Western political transitions do not take account of the special circumstances and severe challenges facing late-developing states.

The relationship between anti-government bread riots and electoralism, and election fetishism, is one of strong correlation, even if their democratizing effects in Sudan (1985) Algeria (1988), and Jordan (1989) suggest a causal association. Here, Rustow's warning not to confuse correlation with causation is heeded. Empirical evidence suggests a link between mass agitation and political reforms in many polities. Evidence from the American Civil rights movement, as ably shown by Piven and Cloward, is instructive.[150] From the Arab context, fieldwork data collected by the author from Sudanese Islamists who under the leadership of Hasan al-Turabi were organized under the banner of the National Islamic Front between 1985 and 1989, and Jordanian Islamists from the Islamic Action Front supports this finding. Interviewees from both movements unequivocally acknowledge a definite role of bread riots in subsequent democratic openings.[151]

There should be no mistake, however, concerning the real motives and motivations of the liberalizing regimes: Political reforms following mass riots are often carried out with the intention of manipulating the public and defusing serious crises of legitimacy and challenges to the rulers' hold on power. The superficiality of Arab political reforms attest to this: government accountability and respect for the social and economic rights of individuals are not demands that the ruling elites are anxious to grant. The breakdowns of liberalization in Sudan (1989) and Algeria (1992) and other setbacks (Tunisia, Egypt,

Morocco, and Yemen) highlight the fragility and uncertainty of Arab electoralism.

While Nieburg's thesis on the democratizing function of domestic political violence is pertinent mainly to consolidated democracies, it has some relevance to emerging democracies, on several grounds. The threat of violence and its 'occasional occurrence' are 'essential elements in peaceful and social change'.[152] Among the democratizing functions of violence is to 'instill dynamism into the structure and growth of the law, the settlement of disputes, the process of accommodating interests, and ... [to] induce general respect for the verdict of the polls'.[153] In countries where elections have until recently not been a regular practice, bread riots served to express disdain for unjust and authoritarian rule as well as to mediate the public interests and concerns to the rulers. From this perspective, bread riots represent a kind of a verdict on incompetent management of political and economic affairs that induce some 'respect' in the form of concessionary responses (rescinding decisions to cut off bread subsidies—for example, Tunisia in 1984; electoral politics) accommodating the public interest, especially after the failure of coercive tactics. Similarly, the electoral gains can be said to have strengthened legality and the rule of law, foundations for peaceful social change.

Consequently, the finding by Dixon and Moon that domestic political conflict is always negative must be rejected.[154] Obvious openings in the authoritarian structure of the *police* state in Arab polities have resulted from domestic conflict. Furthermore, Bienen and Gersovitz's chief assumption that domestic political violence has always only short-term effects should also be questioned.[155] Domestic conflict and protest can have long-term effects and beneficial outcomes, in the form of political reform. Despite the superficiality of Arab political reforms and regressive and retractive setbacks (Egypt, Tunisia, Sudan, Algeria), there is a reformist momentum that hinders return to single party/man rule in many key 'electoralizing' countries. Trepidations are inevitable in any democratization experience: the extension of the franchise to blacks (United States), Aborigines (particularly Australian), and women (many European examples) is a relatively new phenomenon, considering that one or two hundred years passed since the onset of democratic transition. The threat of domestic political violence or its eruption (1977) has kept electoralism alive in Egypt. Electoralism and party politics have been sustained there for 30 years. Even the abortion of the democratic experiment in Algeria has not terminated the democratic momentum. The ongoing quasi civil war[156] was waged in the name of 'democracy', with both the military-backed regime and the armed Islamists labeling themselves 'democratic' and their opponents 'anti-democratic'. There is some oppositional presence with many inter-locutors taking part in the few government-sponsored talks to negoti-ate a way out of the present maelstrom. Although the 1995 presidential elections and the parliamentary elections of June 1997 re-launched the return to electoralism, they are yet to fulfill the promises of social peace and democracy.[157] Electoralism in the midst the state of ordered chaos in the 1990s is evidence that the reform momentum, albeit slow and stalled, is alive.

The role of anomie, social upheaval, and political protest is largely presented as marginal to democratization. Substantial research has stressed the importance of civil society and an enlightened bourgeoisie as chief instruments of democratization, but without the development of a methodological and theoretical background to enable more focused analysis of the phenomenon of *khubz*-istes, understanding of Arab democratization will remain incomplete. Ever since the revolts of the radically minded 'seceders' (*al-khawārij*) in the seventh century AD, a tradition of protest, whether in the pursuit of liberation from foreign rule or of justice, has been present in Arabo-Islamic history.[158] Nine-teenth century Lebanon is a microcosmic example of an Arab semi-autonomous geopolitical unit where popular uprisings ('*āmmiyyahs*) in 1820, 1821, and 1857 by peasants not only struck at the very foundations of the feudal (*iqta'*) system, but also led to the re-writing of the rules of the principality's (*imārah*) political game.[159] According to Baaklini, the covenant that was conceived in the aftermath of the sec-ond '*āmmiyyah* revolutionized, and in a sense democratized, Lebanese politics through the institution of such notions as popular sovereignty and popular consensus. That element of protest has resurfaced in recent history, most evidently in the bread riots of the 1970s and 1980s in many Arab countries. Whether in Morocco or Egypt, these uprisings are part of a historical pattern:

In January 1952, rioters attacked symbols of Western influence in Cairo, discredited the Wafdist government, and paved the way for Nasser's military coup. Every decade has witnessed a major *jacquerie*. A student rebellion stunned Nasser in 1968 and simmered for the following six years. Violent strikes have periodically paralyzed the country's major industrial complexes, including al-Mahalla al-Kubra (1975), Kafr al-Dawwar (1976 and 1984), and Hulwan (1989). When Egyptians mention the memory of 1977 they are not referring to an event, but invoking a symbol of a powerful and ancient tradition of revolt.[160]

These popular uprisings have established that political deference is a function of the state's capacity for redistributive justice and equity that renders political authority *ipso facto* good and worthy of deference.

These have been the chief articles of the unwritten pact between state and society. Defectiveness on the part of the state, whereby what society has been accustomed to as inviolable rights—literacy, subsidized health care, and strategic staple foods—become subject to recall, cancels that pact. Bread riots not only radicalize the street but also serve as reminders of illegitimate political authority and pernicious governance. Burhan Ghalyun links Arab democratic transition not only to Arab regimes' realization of the futility of oppression and the necessity of bridging the gap between themselves and their peoples but also to the masses' revitalized confidence and increased capacity for sacrifice in order to secure their rights, among other things.[161]

Similarly, the significance of the independent media especially in terms of nurturing an aware and vocal public in the AME is worth considering. This is useful for a fuller picture the linkage between forces below the state and consolidation of Arab struggles for democracy. In the last chapter I consider the connection between democratic struggle and other bottom-up dynamics, al-Jazeerah satellite TV, online polling, and blogs.

Notes

1. Hamied Ansari, *Egypt: The Stalled Society* (New York: State University of New York Press, 1986), 185, 187.
2. See Bahgat Korany, 'Arab Democratization: A Poor Cousin?', in *Political Science and Politics*, XXVII (September 1994), 511. For other definitions of democratization criteria see, for instance, Georg Sørensen, *Democracy and Democratization* (Boulder: Westview Press, 1993), 13.
3. Edward P. Thompson, 'The Moral Economy of the English Crowd in the Eighteenth Century', *Past and Present*, 50 (February 1971), 76–136.
4. Ibid. 76–7.
5. Ibid. 76.
6. Ibid.
7. Ibid. 78–9.
8. Ibid. 78.
9. Ibid. 79.
10. Ibid. 78.
11. Burke, 'Understanding Arab Protest Movements', *Arab Studies Quarterly*, 8 (Fall 1987), 336.
12. Ibid. 342–3.
13. Ibid. 343.
14. Ibid. 342–3.
15. Ibid. 342.
16. Author's interview with Hasan al-Turabi, 12 May 1994, Khartoum.

17. Author's interviews with Ishaq Ahmad al-Farhan, 5 February 1992, Amman; and Ibrahim Khrisat, 6 February 1992, Amman.
18. Author's interview with 'Abd-Allatif 'Arabiyyat, 18 June 1994, Amman.
19. Author's interviews with al-Farhan and with al-Turabi.
20. Author's interview with Abu Bakr Jamil, 19 June 1994, Amman.
21. Interviewees from the NIF and the IAF strongly endorse this view.
22. A point stressed by most interviewees.
23. See, *al-barnamaju al-intikhabi li-murashshihi hizb jabhatu al-'amal al-islami 1993–1997* [The Electoral Program for the Islamic Action Front's Candidates, 1993–1997] (Amman, Jordan: The Islamic Action Front, n/d), 35–6.
24. Ibid. 35.
25. Author's interview with al-Farhan.
26. Author's interview with al-Turabi.
27. See the statement by member of parliament, Ibrahim Zayd al-Kilani, in al-nuwwab al-islamiyyun haddadu bi al-istiqalah' [The Islamist Deputies Threatened Resignation] *al-Sabil*, 6 August 1996, 13.
28. Ibid. 13.
29. See *al-barnamaju al-intikhabi li-murashshihi hizb jabhatu al-'amal al-islami 1993–1997*, 35.
30. Author's interview with al-Farhan.
31. See *al-barnamaju al-intikhabi li-murashshihi hizb jabhatu al-'amal al-islami 1993–1997*, 36.
32. Author's interview with 'Arabiyyat.
33. See *al-barnamaju al-intikhabi li-murashshihi hizb jabhatu al-'amal al-islami 1993–1997*, 36.
34. For a non-Islamist viewpoint, see Sa'id Dhiyab, 'Al-hiwar wa al-bahth 'an asbabi al-azmah' [Dialogue and the Search for the Causes of the Crisis] *al-Dustur*, 29 August 1996. Sa'id Dhiyab is one of the leaders of the Jordanian Democratic Popular Union Party known as HASHD.
35. Nabil al-Ghayshan, 'nuwwab jabhatu al-'amal al-Islami yutalibuna bi-'adami raf'i as'ara al-khubz . . .', *al-Aswaq*, 7 July 1996.
36. See, for instance, 'al-islamiyyun yatlibuna liqa 'a jalalata al-malak', *al-Hadath*, 15 July, 1996.
37. Author's interview with Hamzah Mansur, 4 February 1998, Amman.
38. See 'al-nuwwabu al-islamiyyun haddadu bi al-istiqalah' [The Islamist Deputies Threatened Resignation] *al-Sabil*, 6 August 1996.
39. According to one leader from HASHD, close to 50% of the total population live below the line of poverty. See Dhiyab, 'Al-hiwar wa al-bahth 'an asbabi al-azmah' [Dialogue and the Search for the Causes of the Crisis] *al-Dustur*, 29 August 1996.
40. See al-Ghayshan, 'nuwwab jabhat al-'amalu al-Islami yutalibuna . . .'
41. See 'al-islamiyyun yatlibuna liqa'a jalalata al-malak'.
42. Al-Ghayshan, 'nuwwab jabhatu al-'amalu al-Islami yutalibuna . . .'
43. See 'al-nuwwabu al-islamiyyun haddadu bi al-istiqalah' [The Islamist Deputies Threatened Resignation] *al-Sabil*, 6 August 1996, 1; 13.

44. See his statement in Ibid. 13.
45. Author's interview with 'Arabiyyat.
46. Author's interview with Su'ad al-Fatih, 10 May 1994, Khartoum.
47. Author's interview with Hamzah Mansur, 14 June 1994, Amman.
48. See his statement in, Al-Ghayshan, 'nuwwab jabhatu al-'amalu al-Islami yutalibuna . . .'
49. See 'al-nuwwabu al-islamiyyun haddadu bi al-istiqalah', 13.
50. Author's interview with Tariq al-Tall, 20 June 1994, Amman.
51. According to author's interviews with al-Turabi; and with al-Farhan.
52. Author's interview with Yusuf al-'Azm, 5 June 1994, Amman.
53. Author's interview with Ibrahim Muhammad al-Sanusi, 28 May 1994, Khartoum.
54. Author's interview with Muhammad Abu Faris, 13 June 1994, Amman.
55. Author's interview with 'Arabiyyat.
56. Author's interview with al-Turabi.
57. Author's interview with al-Fatih.
58. Author's interview with al-Turabi.
59. Author's interview with Hafiz al-Shaykh al-Zaki, 18 May 1994, Khartoum.
60. Burke, 'Understanding Arab Protest Movements', 334.
61. Ibid.
62. Ibid.
63. Ibid. 335.
64. Ibid.
65. Ibid. 343.
66. Author's interview with Professor Shalabi, 15 March 1993, Cairo.
67. Rashid al-Ghannushi, 29 January 1998, London.
68. See Steven Heydemann, 'Taxation without Representation: Authoritarianism and Economic Liberalization in Syria', in Ellis Goldberg, Resat Kasaba and Joel S. Migdal (eds.), *Rules and Rights in the Middle East: Democracy, Law and Society* (Seattle: University of Washington Press, 1993), 74.
69. Heydemann, 'Taxation without Representation', 76.
70. See Malik Bin Nabi's essays written in the 1950s and 1960s in Wijhatu al-Alim al-Islami [The Muslim World's Direction], trans. Abd al-Sabur Shahin (Damascus: Dar al-Fikr, 1981), 5; 133.
71. See how John P. Entelis applies the term when describing Algeria's political culture, describing *bulitik* as 'maneuvering and scheming to acquire more power' by Algerian politicians. See his *Comparative Politics of North Africa: Algeria, Morocco and Tunisia* (New York: Syracuse University Press, 1980), 102.
72. See David Seddon, 'Riot and Rebellion in North Africa: Political Responses to Economic Crisis in Tunisia, Morocco and Sudan', in Berch Berberoglu (ed.), *Power and Stability in the Middle East* (London: Zed Books, 1989), 114–35.
73. Ibid. 126.

74. Ibid. 127.
75. Ibid.
76. Ibid. 128–9.
77. P. Dougherty and S. Edge, 'Amman Attempts to Strike a Balance', *Middle East Economic Digest,* 33/49, 15 December 1989, 4.
78. Richard U. Moench, 'The May 1984 Elections in Egypt and the Question of Egypt's Stability', in Linda L. Layne (ed.), *Elections in the Middle East: Implications of Recent Trends* (Boulder: Westview Press, 1987), 60.
79. See, for instance, Jon Marks, 'Algeria: The Debt Dilemma', *Middle East Economic Digest,* 36, 6 March 1992, 8.
80. See J. King, 'Algeria: The New Political Map', *Middle East International,* 379, 6 July 1990, 18. For details on the oil impact on Arab economies see Samih K. Farsoun, 'Oil, State, and Social Structure', *Arab Studies Quarterly,* 10 (Spring 1988), 155–75.
81. D. Pryce-Jones, 'Self-determination Arab Style', *Commentary,* 87 (January 1989), 40.
82. John Mortimer, 'We'll Help Because We Have To', *The Middle East,* 191 (September 1990), 36.
83. P. Goslin, 'Algeria Stumbles on the Road to Reform', *The Middle East,* 179 (September 1989), 23.
84. Mark N. Cooper, *The Transformation of Egypt* (London and Canberra: Croom Helm, 1982), 238.
85. Ahmad N. Azim, 'Egypt: The Origins and Development of a Neo-colonial State', in Berberoglu (ed.), *Power and Stability in the Middle East,* 12.
86. Khalid Duran, 'The Second Battle of Algiers', *Orbis,* 33 (Summer 1989), 403.
87. For a similar argument see, for instance, Cooper, *The Transformation of Egypt,* 240.
88. On this question see the monograph by Karima Korayem, *Distributing Disposable Income and the Impact of Eliminating Food Subsidies in Egypt* (Cairo: The American University in Cairo/Cairo Papers in Social Science, 1982).
89. See Duran, 'The Second Battle of Algiers', 406.
90. Cooper, The Transformation of Egypt, 239–40.
91. Ibid. 240.
92. Ibid.
93. Hugh Roberts, 'The Algerian State and the Challenge of Democracy', *Government and Opposition* 27 (Autumn 1992), 435.
94. Ibid. The transliteration is added by the author.
95. Duran, 'The Second Battle of Algiers', 406.
96. Author's interview with Jonathan Kuttab, 18 August 1988, Sydney, Australia.
97. Cooper, The Transformation of Egypt, 239.
98. Seddon, 'Riot and Rebellion in North Africa', pp. 119–24.
99. According to Satloff, 12 people were killed in the Jordanian riots. See his article 'Jordan Looks Inward', p. 58. For the Algerian figure see

P. Goslin, 'Algeria Stumbles on the Road to Reform', *The Middle East*, no. 179 (September 1989), 23.

100. Dougherty and Edge, 'Amman Attempts to Strike a Balance', 4.
101. J. Hooper, 'Fundamentalists Sweep Algerian Elections', *Guardian Weekly*, 24 June 1990, 11.
102. Gene Sharpe, 'The Intifadah and the Non-Violent Struggle', *Journal of Palestinian Studies*, XIX (Autumn 1989), p. 5.
103. Author's interview with Hamzah Mansur, 4 February 1998, Amman.
104. See his statement in 'al-nuwwabu al-islamiyyun haddadu bi al-istiqalah', *al-Sabil*, 6 August 1996, 13.
105. See, 'Kitabatun 'ala judurani ma'duba tutalibu bi-rahili al-kabariti' [Graffiti on Maduba Walls Demand Kabariti's Departure] *al-Hadath*, 2 September 1996.
106. See, 'al-islamiyyun yatlibuna liqa'a jalalata al-malak'.
107. See 'al-nuwwabu 'l-islamiyyun haddadu bi al-istiqalah', 13.
108. See, 'al-Kabariti: al-ifraju 'an 521 mu'taqalan min asli 572' [al-Kabariti: The Release of 521 Detainees from a Total of 572] *al-Ra'y*, 5 September 1996, 1; 15; Nayif al-Ma'ani, 'al-ifraju 'an 10 mu'taqalan min mantaqati al-tufaylah' [The Release of 10 Detainees from al-tufaylah Region] *al-Aswaq*, 7 September 1996; see also the press conference by al-Ma'shar, the Information Minister in, 'al-Ma'shar: itlaqu saraha kaffati al-mu'taqalin khilala yawmayni' [al-Ma'shar: The Release of all Detainees in Two Days] *al-Dustur*, 2 September 1996; Tariq al-Mumini, 'al-Kabariti: ihalatu al-mutawarritin bi al-ahdathi al-akhirah ila al-qada' wa al-al-ifraju 'an baqi al-ashkhas khilala 24 sa'ah' [al-Kabariti: Referral of those Guilty [of Wrongdoing] in the Recent Incidents to the Judiciary and the Release of the Rest in 24 Hours] *al-Ra'y*, 2 September 1996, 1, 21.
109. See his statement in, 'al-aswaq tutabiu' al-hiwar...' [Al-Aswaq follows the Dialogue...] *al-Aswaq*, 3 September 1996, 6.
110. For more details on Ahmad al-Kasasibah's speech see, 'liwa 'Ayy yujaddidu al-bay'ah li qa'idi al-watan' ['Ayy Renews its Oath of Allegiance to the Leader of the Homeland] *al-Dustur*, 28 August 1996, 6.
111. See Henry S. Bienen and Mark Gersovitz, 'Consumer Subsidy Cuts, Violence and Political Stability', *Comparative Politics* 19 (October 1986), 25–44.
112. On the imposition of taxes, see Giacomo Luciani, 'Economic Foundations of Democracy and Authoritarianism: The Arab World in Comparative Perspective', *Arab Studies Quarterly* 10 (Fall 1988), 465.
113. For the rescinding of prices in Tunisia and Morocco see Seddon, 'Riot and Rebellion in North Africa', 114.
114. For the reinstating of food subsidies following the 1977 riots in Egypt see Yahya M. Sadowski, *Political Vegetables? Businessmen and Bureaucrats in the Development of Egyptian Agriculture* (Washington, D.C.: The Brookings Institution, 1991), p. 156. See also, Paul Rivlin, *The Dynamics of Economic Policy Making in Egypt* (New York: Praeger, 1985), 178.
115. Seddon, 'Riot and Rebellion in North Africa', 121.

116. Ibid. 121.
117. Ibid. 122.
118. Barrington Moore Jr., *Social Origins of Dictatorship and Democracy: Lord and Peasant in the Making of the Modern World* (Boston: Beacon Press, 1966).
119. Rustow, 'Transitions to Democracy', *Comparative Politics*, 2 (April 1970), 337–63.
120. Seymour Martin Lipset, 'Some Social Requisites of Democracy: Economic Development and Political Legitimacy', *The American Political Science Review*, 53 (March 1957), 75.
121. While Lipset's correlation meets with wide acceptance, it does not mean there is not controversy or opposition. Cutright, who followed on Lipset's footsteps, carried out empirical research to substantiate that high socio-economic development corresponds with higher levels of democratic development. His findings have, for instance, been disputed by Deane E. Neubauer, 'Some Conditions of Democracy', *The American Political Science Review*, LXI (December 1967), 1002–09.
122. Robert A. Dahl, *Polyarchy: Participation and Opposition* (New Haven: Yale University Press, 1971), 68.
123. Ibid. 68–74.
124. Ibid. 59.
125. Charles Issawi, 'Economic and Social Foundations of Democracy in the Middle East', in *International Affairs*, 32 (1956), 27–42.
126. As ranked by Coleman on the basis of 11 indices of economic development in 1960. See table in Gabriel A. Almond and James S Coleman (eds.), *The Politics of the Developing Areas* (Princeton: Princeton University Press, 1960), 543.
127. Michael C. Hudson, 'The possibilities for Pluralism', *American–Arab Affairs*, 36 (Spring 1991), 4. Most of this edition is dedicated to the subject of democratization in the Middle East.
128. Those that accrue huge earnings from external oil rent. The deviation applies to all the Gulf oildoms, Iraq and Libya. Huntington points out examples of these deviations—Saudi Arabia, Kuwait, UAE, Oman, Libya, and Iraq. See his work, *The Third Wave*, 59–72.
129. For definition of rentier state see, Hazem Beblawi, 'The Rentier State in the Arab World', in Giacomo Luciani (ed.), *The Arab State* (London: Routledge, 1990), 87–8.
130. This view is, for instance, articulated, *inter alia*, by Luciani, 'Allocation vs. Production States', in Luciani (ed.), *The Arab State*, 84; Samih K. Farsoun, 'Oil, State and Social Structure in the Middle East', *Arab Studies Quarterly* 10 (Spring 1988), 166.
131. Farsoun, 'Oil, State and Social Structure in the Middle East', 166. See also useful statistical data provided by H. Batatu showing a tenfold growth of Syria's state bureaucracy between 1960 and 1979 and a nearly eightfold increase in Iraq's between 1958 and 1978. See his 'Political Power and

Social Structure in Syria and Iraq', in Samih K. Farsoun (ed.), *Arab Society* (London: Croom Helm, 1985), 38, 43.

132. See the case study on Egypt by Robert Springborg in 'Egypt', in Tim Niblock and Emma Murphy (eds.), *Economic and Political Liberalization in the Middle East* (London and New York: British Academic Press, 1993), 160.

133. A good reference on the question of interdependence is by Saad Eddin Ibrahim, *The New Arab Social Order* (Boulder: Westview Press, 1982).

134. Farsoun, 'Oil, State and Social Structure in the Middle East', 166.

135. Ibid.

136. Ibid. 167.

137. Ibid.

138. See Almond and Powell, *Comparative Politics: System, Process and Policy*, 286–8.

139. Farsoun, 'Oil, State and Social Structure in the Middle East', 167.

140. Huntington, *The Third Wave*, 65.

141. Ibid.

142. For some Arab scholars democratization is a necessary process for integrating Arabs in a future Federal State. Refer to Haseeb et al., *The Future of the Arab Nation*, 395–9.

143. Huntington lists this as one of three factors contributing to third wave democratizations, in *The Third Wave*, 59.

144. These figures were given by Qaiser Khan, from the World Bank, in a seminar entitled 'Issues in Social Protection in Middle East and North Africa', 27 August 1998, ANU, Australia.

145. Author's interview with Hamzah Mansur, 14 June 1994, Amman.

146. For further details see 'Hizbullah: Tufaili lam ya'ud wahidan min masiratina al-mutawasilah' [Hizbullah: Tufaili is no longer a member of our continuous procession], *al-Hayat*, 25 January, 1998, 2.

147. See 'Abd al-Rahim Shalhah, 'fashalu al-ittisalat...yukarrisu al-talaq' [Failure of Mediation...Marks the Divorce (Between Hizbullah and Tufaili)], in a*l-Safir*, 26 January, 1998.

148. See 'Hunger Rebellion in Baalbek: Growing Opposition to Lebanese Prime Minister', in Neue Zuercher Zeitung (Switzerland), 22 July 1997.

149. See 'Imad Marmal, 'al-thawrah khamadat...wa lakin matalibu al-jiya' baqiyah' [The Uprising Died out, but the Demands of the Hungry are Lasting] in *al-Safir*, 2 February, 1998.

150. F. F. Piven and R. A. Cloward, *Regulating the Poor: The Functions of Public Welfare* (New York: Pantheon Books, 1971).

151. The interviewees from Jordan are Ishaq Ahmad al-Farhan, 5 February 1992, Amman; Ibrahim Khrisat, 6 February 1992, Amman; Hamzah Mansur, 14 June 1994, Amman; Hammam Said, 4 June 1994, Amman; Yusuf al-Azm, 5 June 1994, Amman; Ruba al-Farkh, 11 June 1994, Amman; Bassam La 'mush, 12 June 1994, Amman; Muhammad Abu Faris, 13 June 1994, Amman; Arwa al-Kilani, 13 June 1994, Amman; Nawal al-Fa'uri, 13 June 1994, Amman; Muhammad 'Uwidah, 13 June

1994, Amman; Fadwa Abu Ghayda', 14 June 1994, Amman; Asma' al-Farhan, 14 June 1994, Amman; Muhammad Abd al-Rahman Khalifah, 14 June 1994, Amman (then grand master of the Muslim Brethren in Jordan); Hayat al-Misimi, 15 June 1994, Amman; 'Abd-Allatif 'Arabiyyat, 18 June 1994, Amman; Abu Bakr Jamil, 19 June 1994, Amman; Tariq al-Tall, 20 June 1994, Amman. The interviewees from Sudan are Sumayyah Ja'far 'Uthman, 27 April 1994, Khartoum; Walid Fayit, 27 April 1994, Khartoum; Muhammad Khayr Fath al-Rahman, 27 April 1994, Khartoum; Zakiyyah Awad Sati, 3 May, 1994, Khartoum; Usal al-Mahdi, 3 May 1994, Khartoum; Sumayyah Abu Kashawwah, 5 May 1994, Khartoum; Lubabah al-Fadl, 7 May 1994, Khartourm; Su'ad al-Fatih, 10 May 1994, Khartoum. Hasan al-Turabi, 12 May 1994, Khartoum; Hasan Makki, 16 May 1994, Khartoum; Hafiz al-Shaykh al-Zaki, 18 May 1994, Khartoum; Ghazi Salah al-Din, 19 May 1994, Khartoum; Al-Tijani Abd al-Qadir Hamid, 28 May 1994, Khartoum; Ibrahim Muhammad al-Sanusi, 28 May 1994, Khartoum.

152. H. L. Nieburg, 'The Threat of Violence and Social change', *American Political Science Review*, 56 (1962), 865.

153. Ibid. 865.

154. W. J. Dixon and B. E. Moon, 'Domestic Political Conflict and Basic Outcomes: An Empirical Assessment', *Comparative Political Studies*, 22 (1989), 178–98.

155. H.S. Bienen and M. Gersovitz, 'Consumer Subsidy Cuts, Violence, and Political Stability', *Comparative Politics*, 19 (1986), 25–44.

156. Lucile Provost, *La Seconde guerre d'algérie. Le Quiproquo franco-algérien* [The Second Algerian War] (Paris: Flammarion, 1996).

157. See Salima Ghezali, 'Fausse éclaircie en Algérie' [False Dawn in Algeria] *Le Monde Diplomatique*, no. 503 (February 1996), 1, 12.

158. See Khalid Kishtainy, 'Violent and Non-Violent Struggle in Arab History', in Ralph E, Crow, Philip Grant, and Saad E. Ibrahim (eds.), *Arab Non-Violent Political Struggle* (Boulder and London: Lynne Rienner, 1990), 9–24.

159. Abdo I. Baklini, *Legislative and Political Development: Lebanon, 1842–1972* (Durham: Duke University Press, 1976), 42–3.

160. Sadowski, Political Vegetables?, 157.

161. Burhan Ghalyun, 'al-dimuqratiyyatu al-'Arabiyyah: judhuru al-azmah wa afaqu al-numuw' [Arab Democracy: Roots of the Crisis and Prospects of Development] in Burhan Ghalyun et al. (eds.), *hawla al-khiyar al-dimuqrati: dirasat naqdiyyah* [On the Democratic Option: A Critique] (Beirut: markaz dirasat al-wihdah al-Arabiyyah, 1994), 110–11.

6

Al-Jazeerah and the Internet as Sites
of Democratic Struggle

The information revolution, and particularly the daily dose of
uncensored television coming out of local TV stations like al-
Jazeerah and international coverage by CNN and others, is shaping public opinion, which, in turn, is pushing Arab governments
to respond. We don't know, and the leaders themselves don't know,
how that pressure will impact on Arab policy in the future.

Dale Eickelman[1]

While Arab polities remain largely undemocratic, structural shifts
in the means of public communication and opinion formation have
contributed to the emergence of a transnational Arab public sphere
that increasingly shapes politics through the region. New media,
including satellite television stations such as *al-Jazeerah*, Arabist
and Islamist newspapers distributed free of charge on the Internet,
and rapid distribution of news via email, listservs, and instant
messaging, have given citizens in states such as Jordan, Egypt,
Lebanon, and throughout North Africa and the Gulf the means to
undermine state censorship and control. This public sphere does
not substitute for democracy; it has few institutional channels by
which to translate its preferences into outcomes, and it has met
with substantial state counter-pressures. However, it also has dra-
matically reshaped the dynamics of Arab politics and conceptions
of Arab political identity.

Mark Lynch[2]

By illustrating the role of al-Jazeerah and the Internet in strengthening 'Arab opinion' and lending support to democratic struggles in the
AME, my intention in this chapter is to underscore their importance
in widening the site of bottom-up struggle against authoritarianism.
Election fetishism, I have argued, has not diminished the capacity

of the state to reinvent itself, by reproducing the same rulers and the same power relations. More research is needed by students of democratization in the AME to understand more deeply what happens below the state. Protest politics takes many forms that are not confined to bread riots. Satellite Television and the Internet today provide new sites for democratic struggles. The added value of Blogs and online opinion polling is twofold. They bolster the rise of Arab public opinion. In tandem with other societal bottom-up strategies they help frame the moment of democratic struggles from below. The rise of both, I suggest, is starting to play an important role in helping society respond to the stalled top-down or managed democratization. I shall preface the analysis with an examination of the new contests of state authority and control over citizens made possible by the 'goods' of globalization—such as the Internet and blogs (*mudawwināt*). To this end, I look at how the new information and communication technologies (ICT) seem to be empowering vocalization of dissidence, noting implications of this for state–society relations.

Cyberspace: Wither the Authoritarian Arab State?

Can the species of autocratic state in the AME weather the forces of globalization and information technologies? The AME is increasingly being swept by the new communications technologies and other integrative forces. One of the very few revelations about the late Iraqi dictator, Saddam Hussein, made possible by the 1991 Gulf War was his CNN viewing habit. Against the backdrop of these forces which can prove to be corrosive to the police state, the question about its inviolability in a globalizing world is addressed below. Two insights come to the fore. First, new communications technologies such as cellular telephones and the Internet have intensified the old contest over control of ideas, values, and information. Cyber technology opens up space for societal forces, something authoritarian states are resisting. Note how Tunisia's hosting of the UN-sponsored World Summit on the Information Society in November 2005 sat paradoxically with its continuous use of Internet filtering against political dissidents.[3] Second, this cyberspace, and the emerging cyber-dissidence flowing from it, is important for the erosion of the authoritarian state. Its utility is twofold. New democratic struggles come to the fore; and new solidarities emerge across borders. Cyberspace not only gives oppositional forces self-confidence but also makes the technologies of protest increasingly difficult to police or proscribe. The 'official transcript', to use a phrase coined by Eickelman, no longer commands monopoly over the populace in the AME. Similarly, Marc Lynch argues that a 'public transcript' is emerging in the AME. This transcript, which is helped by the rise of al-Jazeerah, is constructed by the news coverage of the suffering Iraqis in the 1990s and beyond. This transcript feeds into the 'private transcript' of the conventional opinion-makers, giving rise to what he calls 'the new Arab public'.[4] A degree of levelling of the playing field, at least in the realm of discourse, is unfolding thanks to globalization and its goods. State–society contests are thus intensified, as I argue below.

The buzz word globalization[5] has not spared the AME. Globalization is paired with religion,[6] and culture.[7] Questions of globalization and change,[8] of globalization and the durability or relevance of the nation-state,[9] and of globalization and the meaning of citizenship[10] have all moved to the centre of the current academic multidisciplinary research agenda. So are issues of globalization and identity,[11] of globalization and domination,[12] and of globalization and Orientalism.[13] The corrosive effects of globalization on the nation-state need not be recited here. Suffice it to say that globalization represents challenges to the boundaries of institutional and territorial/local understanding and practice of politics, identity, and culture. Global forces operate above the state—the stateless TNCs and jet-setting traders and businessmen. But among the new actors are also grass-roots publics made up of activists of all kind as well as NGOs. They have been empowered by new information and communication technologies. These new actors will not change regimes; but they have the potential to eat into the body politic of the nation-state. Everywhere nation-states, communities, and individuals are increasingly forced to tune into the new age of information technology and adapt to the global village.

The AME is no exception.[14] Satellite TV and the Internet are among the few 'goods' of globalization becoming widespread in the AME, with reception dishes being a common sight on the roofs of Doha, Rabat, Riyadh, Amman, and Manama. Different countries are plugged into the new age of cyber technology in varying degrees. Footage of Saudi Prince Sultan bin Salman aboard the space shuttle on 17 June 1985 was played and replayed in Arab news bulletins many times over. It signalled a new era for the Arab world's encounter with high-tech. As the AME becomes relatively attuned to the new age of information technologies, old contests are rekindled. One of the more tense contests in the AME is taking place in the sphere of information and culture. The contest within the AME is between states but more importantly between states and societies because the historical monopoly[15] of information by regimes is being broken due to the empowerment of non-state users of the new technologies. This empowerment is being resisted by many Arab states. States are willing to go with the current of technological innovation only in so far as it serves their reproduction—value assignment and consolidation of their resource and power bases.

Undeniably, most states face a very acute dilemma. On the one hand, they realize that holding back the tide of information technologies can be a liability in the long run. It could place them on the periphery in many vital domains pivotal for development. On the other, these new technologies open up a new world of information to their users that carry risks for state authority. Control-freak authoritarian regimes do crackdown on the use of new technologies. Note how most Arab states have had strained relations with the State of Qatar over critical programmes by al-Jazeerah. These programmes either host Islamists or secular dissidents or broadcast documentaries that expose torture, nepotism, corruption, and autocratic regime practices. Hence President Hosni Mubarak of Egypt nicknamed al-Jazeerah a 'box of matches'. But there is also a risk of exaggerating the subversive potential of these new technologies especially when they are not as widespread as they are in other regions. Satellite broadcasting can turn out to be an 'opiate' of the masses. There is an entertainment value that must be assumed to be important for apolitical millions of Arab users. The Saudi-funded 'Rotana' music channel, with its scantily clad divas of the video-clip revolution, is a far cry from anything of which the puritanical Wahhabi doctrine would approve. Yet it has a wide viewing public, most of which would have little interest in Al-Jazeerah's serious and critical new brand of journalism. The risk to the durability of the authoritarian state is most likely to be a cumulative one and over a long-term span of time as both the number of users and the level of political awareness augment. However, it is a limited circle of hardcore and committed activists whose use of the new technologies, especially the Internet, will continue to attempt to further erode the authority and legitimacy of the authoritarian state. Indeed, as Anderson argues the Internet is being 'Arabized' and this can be expected to have implications for state–society relations.[16]

Whatever the potentialities of the new technologies, their current is unstoppable. Going against it can be costly not only for achieving a threshold level of democratic rule but also a threshold degree of development in information technology. The state alone cannot lead technological advancement just as it has proved, with ample evidence, that it could not lead democratic development. Society has to be brought in. Stemming the tide of societal empowerment through strict regulation of the new technologies can exacerbate problems of development, politically, socially, economically, technologically, and informationally. The authoritarian state's mendacity about information and information technologies is puzzling. Its holders are critical of a unipolar information order whereby a one-way flow of Western values or ideologies from the North compromises their own. Yet rulers of the authoritarian state hardly practise what they preach. They continue to be hegemonic and homogenizing in the sphere of information, culture, and discourse. Many states in the AME still have an information ministry, which is gradually becoming extinct. State-owned media are still the predominant norm in most of the AME. They smother the unofficial media, even though many of these states are increasingly licensing private radio and television networks (e.g. Egypt, Lebanon, Oman, Syria, and Tunisia). But Arab regimes seem to have adapted themselves to the age of information with many of them having satellite channels[17] and official home pages. Similarly, numerous government departments in most Arab countries have their own websites, a fledgling move towards 'e-government'. This is as true of the Palestinian National Authority, a state in formation, as it is of the more consolidated states in the AME.[18]

The contest is tense, pitting parties with shared and no shared cultural worlds and with common and uncommon nationalities. It exemplifies how several countries in the Mid-East region have reacted to the borderless society facilitated by satellite technology. In doing so, they have expressed concern about the effect of certain television images on their national cultures, about the political purposes that might be attributed to certain programmes, and about the military and security potential of surveillance satellites. They have moved both to restrict direct access to programmes beamed from abroad, and to relay domestically select foreign ones of their own choice. These complementary objectives have revealed an inherent deficiency in national information ministries. They were ineffectual in propagating their own cultural values abroad in counterbalance to the values of the 'other' (Euro-American).[19]

Non-state actors are as adept at acquiring, using, and deploying the Internet to gain cyberspace and contest state monopoly of public space. Transnational Islamism, aided by the Internet and other high-tech communications media, is an undeniable part and parcel of globalization. The exchange between the global and the local is manifest, for example, in the Islamist discourse on a whole range of issues from the AIDS virus to the question of democracy. Such a discourse illustrates a degree of interconnectedness flowing from the long reach of cyber technology and the travel of ideas. The forces and agents of transnational Islamism, in the AME as well as in Europe and North America, are communication technologies friendly. Through them they are becoming transnational, that is, a globally oriented movement. From this perspective, at least, the phenomenon of transnational Islam, no less than other globally oriented grassroots movements and actors, is, with necessary nuances, a by-product of globalization. The forces of transnational Islamism have been successful in accommodating themselves to technological innovations and to the flow of ideas they propagate at a global scale. With equal resourcefulness as the use by Khomeini's revolution of the Xerox machine and the cassette in the 1970s, the forces of transnational Islam are consuming and utilizing the Internet and Satellite TV in the twenty-first century. The London-based 'AL-Hiwar' TV, which groups a constellation of Islamist voices such as the exiled Tunisian Nahdah Party and Palestinian Hamas, proves how transnational Islam is shaping as well as being shaped by globalization.

Internet Activism and the Rise of Blogs in the AME

Like al-Jazeerah in the mid-1990s, the explosion of blogs in the turn of the millennium is the newest threat to state authority, control, secrecy, and confidence. The hunger for political self-expression and participation is being satiated by new forms of grass-roots and non-conventional activism throughout the AME. As many Arab states police the conventional political territory and practise exclusion within it, Arab youth and dissidents are being pushed to cyberspace to seek meaning, expression and citizenship in 'virtual reality'. The website of Tunisia's protest blog 'Fock Yezzi' (enough is enough) states: 'Since we are physically unable to demonstrate peacefully within Tunisian public space, we will use the Internet to organize permanent demonstration in order to express our total disapproval with the Tunisian dictatorial regime.'[20] The website's activism led to the first conviction and imprisonment in the entire AME of a blogger. Another, Egyptian Karim Nabil Sulayman, was jailed for four years in February 2007. He was convicted of insulting Islam and slurring President Mubarak. Cyberspace activism has placed authoritarianism on the defensive in the AME. Egypt's bloggers have been inventive. Many published daily stories covering the 2005 parliamentary elections, giving their publics a non-mainstream take on the elections. This included obstruction by police to voting in areas where Muslim Brotherhood candidates were favourites.[21] Never before has the exposure of torture by the Egyptian regime, which has ruled under the Emergency Law since

1981, been so widely publicized. The wide use of the Internet by bloggers has in the turn of the millennium created problems of self-confidence and image to the Egyptian authorities equal in importance to the annual reports of Amnesty International and Human Rights Watch. Torture in police and other detention centres has been the focus of many bloggers. The revelation is not that torture happens. That fact is widely known. What the blogs have revealed is the wide use of sexual humiliation and abuse by the police and security forces, which is not specific to Egypt. Video evidence, medical reports, victims' testimonies, and interviews are all techniques used by bloggers to corroborate their stories. Two accounts arrested attention in 2007. Bloggers revealed in them the extent of torture and sexual abuse in Egypt. The victims were Mohammed Abdelqadir and Imad Al-Kabir; the former was severely tortured, the latter sexually abused. Unlike thousands of Arab male prisoners, including Islamists, who might have been humiliated through sexual abuse, Al-Kabir told his story via a blog, leading to a court case against two members of the security forces from the Bulaq Dakrur Police Station.[22] Even if the trial leads to no conviction, the security forces may be deterred from use of torture for fear of exposure through Egypt's mushrooming blogs. The systematic campaign against torture was taken up by Arab Satellite TV stations. In 2007 Egyptian Huwayda Taha, a producer with al-Jazeerah, was given a six-month jail term for doing a documentary that followed up the bloggers' graphic revelations about torture in Egypt's police stations.

All sorts of Islamic groups can be found in the Internet. In fact, the emergence of the Internet has forced dissidents throughout the AME to adjust their political strategies. The case of jailed Muslim Brotherhood blogger and journalist Abdel-Moneim Mahmoud has publicized the skill with which the Brotherhood has moved to use the Internet first, by creating a website for the Muslim Bortherhood Youth at the University of Cairo in 1999. Speaking to Tunisian blogger Sami Gharbia, Mahmoud shows how the youth within the Muslim Brotherhood was adept at using blogs, which multiplied as the movement's elders gave their blessing to its use to spread their message. Mahmoud was the catalyst for the creation of many blogs by the Brotherhood's youth. Mahmoud's launch of his blog 'I am a Brother' (*Ana Ikhwān*), encouraged others to follow suit. He was the catalyst for the Brotherhood's youth to create blogs such as 'Son of a Brother' (*Ibn Akh*), 'Brotherhood Youth' (*Chabab Al Ikhwān*), 'Muslim Brother' (*Ikhwānī*), 'Muslim Brother' (*Ikhwānjī*), and a female member created 'Daughter from the Brotherhood' (*Bint min El Ikhwān*). Mahmoud points to how blogs provide an alternative to conventional media, and with a developmental role:

The Egyptian authorities are blocking access to the Muslim Brotherhood website. It is very common and we are regularly changing the IP address and the URL to keep the web site running. However, it is important to mention that the Egyptian authorities are not targeting bloggers *per se*. They are more likely to be against activists who have been recently been using blogs as political tools... Still, the next period represents a turning point in the media. Traditional media will fail when faced with these sources of new information technologies. In my opinion, they will not be able to keep up. Television will find it hard to cover stories. Let's take the example of the incident of the rape of the bus driver by police. No newspaper or TV channel could cover that... The blog is a free technology, which means that it is out there for anyone to use. It does not mean it is labelled as Muslim Brotherhood only. Anyone can use as they wish, whether you are a Brother, secularist, a leftists.... This means it is designed to be used at any time, at any moment, and in any way, as long as it is being used for development and improvement.[23]

The Internet is equally helping create solidarities that were inconceivable in the past because of distances and borders. It is no exaggeration to say that this medium is partly making the ideal of the Islamic community more of a reality than ever before, especially since the abolition of the Caliphate in the 1920s in Turkey. In effect, the Internet is helping dismantle the borders drawn by the Europeans and solidified with the emergence of independent Muslim nation-states. This medium is binding Muslim groups across continents, for 'holy' and 'unholy' reasons. One such group calls itself the World Islamic Front, comprising the '*Jihād* and *al-Jamā'ah al-Islāmiyyah*' (Islamic Group) of Egypt, 'Jamiat ul-Ulema-e-Pakistan', the Jihad movement from Bangladesh, and the Saudi Shaykh Osama bin laden. It has used the Internet to issue a *fatwā* declaring 'holy war' against Americans in the Arabian Peninsula in the late 1990s.[24] Another group, the Islamic Association for Palestine continues to rally many individuals and groups (e.g. its attention to the Palestinian Society for the Protection of Human Rights and the Environment) to the defence of the Palestinian cause through the Internet. Its home page is rich of news, press releases, and information documenting human rights abuses by both the Israelis and the Palestinian Authority.

Besides Egypt's Muslim Brotherhood, the Lebanese Hizbullah, the Nahdah Party of Tunisia, and the Algerian FIS have sites on the Internet and/or e-mail services.[25] So do individuals and seminal thinkers of an Islamist persuasion such as Hasan al-Turabi.[26] Gulf states are not spared. From their safe base in London, opponents of the Saudi regime, Muhammad al-Mas'ari and his Committee for the Defence of Legitimate Rights, and Sa'ad al-Faqih, leader of the Movement of Islamic Reform, use the Internet to air their criticisms and the aims of their political opposition. At home the most well-known blog, owned by Muhammad Milyani, was blocked by the Saudi Internet Services Unit in 2007. Also from London, the Bahrain Freedom Movement has until the partial liberalization of the regime in 2003 practised opposition via its World Wide Web homepage.[27] The same goes for the London-based Syrian Muslim Brotherhood whose newsletter continues to be put up on the web on a weekly basis. It is no surprise then that Arab regimes keep on lobbying European governments and the United States to expel their opponents. Although removed from the homeland political theatres, these groups can wreak havoc against the regimes they oppose via information technology, establishing wide contacts with other Arab opposition movements, Arabs living in the Diaspora, and Westerners. The Internet has thus empowered groups and individuals who operate outside the consensus of most Arab ruling elites to exclude political Islam from public affairs, censor its literature, cut off all communication channels it has with the people, and limit its leaders' activities. The Internet is increasingly making this difficult, especially that many Islamic movements have got links in the Diaspora. These links are used effectively to tap into the various resources information technology offers them. The Internet is one such resource that many have acquired and deployed to fight back the systems that seek to silence them. From London, Paris, or Washington Islamist movements, already do carve for themselves a significant cyberspace that keeps them alive and well beyond the capacity of their country regimes to interfere with their cyber activities and political survival.

The same is true of secularist forces struggling for better environment or active citizenship, dynamic civil society, and good government in the AME. The Cairo-based Group for Democratic Development (GDD) is one good example with its own website. Its focus is pan-Arab, being the founding member of the Arab Network for Democratic Development.[28] Whereas the GDD's focus is on gradual democratic development within the existing system, other groups tend to be bolder about the struggle for human rights and good government in open challenge to the state's authoritarian structures. One such active group whose dynamism has made it very prominent in Egypt and in the rest of the AME is the Centre for Human Rights and Legal Aid (CHRLA).[29] Its solidaristic style, solid belief in the universality of rights and politics of coalition with other groups and forces struggles for the same ideals makes it uniquely formidable in helping erode authoritarian rule. CHRLA joins a host of Arab human rights organizations whose combined activism in 'cyberia' and outside it is a great source of discomfort, embarrassment, and unease to the authoritarian state in the AME.

Cyberspace is being currently occupied by Arab environmentalists. Perhaps one of the most conspicuous globalizing effects in the AME is the recent travel of the ideas of environmentalism. The fight to save the environment is central to the struggles of many NGOs which are already involved in struggles for human rights, women's rights and democracy. These fairly recent NGOs cover the entire AME.[30] In Egypt, there has been a Greens' political party—al-Khodor—concerned with the cause of the environment since 1990. A like-minded group has since 2003 been licensed in Tunisia as a political party. The oppositional scene is fast changing; it begins with the Internet and sometimes ends up carving out a margin of existence in political society such as the Greens of Egypt and Tunisia. The array of opposition groups and struggles and solidarities being formed cannot be ignored indefinitely by the authoritarian state. The state's monopoly of wisdom in the age of cyberspace is no longer assured. But this does not mean the end of state resistance against the rise of rival voices who partly owe their increasing empowerment, visibility, and influence to the Internet. The authoritarian state has historically had a problem with proactive literacy and awareness. The same is true of computer or information technology proactive literacy, especially when they spell danger for state control and durability.

The implications of this proactive literacy are manifold. None perhaps is more devastating for the authoritarian state than the exposure of its illiberal practices. Negative publicity travels rapidly and widely in the global village. More damage has been done to Egypt from bloggers exposing torture and sexual abuse in detention centres and police station than decades of oppression of the country's opposition. Even the well-known *Lonely Planet* travel guides draw readers' attention to human rights violations; and some Arab countries which depend on the tourist dollar feature in these reminders. The Internet enables movements struggling for human rights and democracy to widen their audiences outside the homeland boundaries. The cyberspace they get to occupy throughout the Western world where computers are commonplace is tremendous. Their contacts with Westerners and Western NGOs and even officials become more immediate, frequent, and unmediated. Note the number of international campaigns to free Arab bloggers and other dissidents. The Internet is a medium that facilitates self-representation. Through their press releases and information, for instance, these movements can communicate with the world directly, giving their own side of the story of their stand-off with their regimes. This not only helps demystify unanswered questions (about the kind of government they would like to see in the AME, the nature of relations they want with the 'West', their political strategies) thousands of people have about political Islam, but it also forces many Islamic movements to liberate themselves of both insulation and isolation. As they increasingly cease shrouding their activities in secrecy, these movements gradually gain the confidence of others as well as in self-confidence to deal with the 'other'.

The gains for non-religious movements and NGOs from the AME are no less important. Thanks to the Internet the grass-roots movement, 'Kifayah' has gained global support for its activities outside Egypt. Its peaceful and sustained campaigns against hereditary rule and oppression are widely publicized online, drawing the attention from both the international media and officials in the EU and North America.[31] Similarly, Arab environmentalists have widened their networks with Western NGOs like Greenpeace. The Greens in Lebanon are a case in point. Similarly, Arab human rights organizations have international links which provide moral and material support. These international links make it increasingly difficult for Arab regimes to interfere with their activities and activists. For instance, GDD is a member of CIVICUS—World Alliance for Citizen Participation. It receives technical and financial support from the National Endowment for Democracy, the National Democratic Institute for International Affairs, both US-based, and the European Human Rights Foundation. GDD is not unique in this regard. The Internet has facilitated many of these solidarities and communities as well as globalized local struggles for human rights and democracy. What is being created is a sense of 'international citizenship' and camaraderie transcending territorial, religious or ethnic boundaries.

The authoritarian state survives but is enfeebled and lacking in self-confidence. The very essence of the authoritarian state—centralization, control, surveillance, censorship—goes against the grist of information technology and the age of information and of democracy. Essentially, they are about de-centering not concentrating, openness not secrecy, and free access to and freedom of information not its control. In the long run, the corrosive effects to the authoritarian state bode well for the prospects of democratic struggles in the AME. Autocracy and democracy will continue to be a restless pair. The authoritarian state has proved its resilience over time and ability to rebound and reinvent itself. That ability is not likely to diminish in the age of the Internet. What will certainly diminish is the capacity of centres of power to control the sphere of values and culture in the global village or stop the impact of communications technology on society. Already some Gulf States and individual princes are forced to adapt to information technology even more so than less conservative states and rulers. Princes like Saudi al-Walid bin Talal are investing in Apple and in satellite nets.[32] But there is a *cruel paradox*. The new media barons who are opening the floodgates of new communications technology to millions of Arabs come from the most conservative ruling families.[33] It is these barons who are, on one hand, unwittingly undermining hegemonic state authority over values through their ownership of satellite TV channels with provocative programmes. On the other, they are 'royal' and 'loyal' media tycoons, either by lineage or patronage. Thus they are authority-minded setting 'red lines' for regulating non-conformity and non-compliance. Even the most liberal satellite TV channel al-Jazeerah, owned by one of the most conservative royal families (Qatar) in the AME, is not 'red lines' free. But its talk-show programmes on religion and politics are uniquely open and critical. No TV channel in Tunis, Cairo, or Casablanca has the audacity to stage similar shows without impunity. Al-Jazeerah has an additional distinction. Its online opinion polls are drawing hundreds of thousands of respondents who are eager to have a voice in Arab affairs. In the section below I attempt to examine how online participation by this newly emerging public is a boost to bottom-up democratic struggles, consolidating further the formation of a pan-Arab public opinion in the AME.

Al-Jazeerah Online Opinion Polls and Democratic Struggles

I identify al-Jazeerah's online opinion polls, which arrive at a time when the AME seems to be awash in elections, as a new site of anti-authoritarian struggle by marginalized publics. These online polls deserve to be considered for consolidating democratic struggles (e.g. led through electoral participation, petitions, protests, and blogs by Islamist and secular centrifugal forces). I single these polls out for discussion for two interrelated reasons. First, opinion polling is a fairly new phenomenon that is strengthening Arab 'public opinion'. This phenomenon is without precedence in postcolonial Arab history. Arab public opinion has largely been conspicuous by its silence and absence. This is due to the region's authoritarian states' control of free expression in the Arab world. There has since the mid-1990s been increasing Arab interest in opinion polling. Jordan University's Strategic Studies Centre has been very proactive in this regard, having conducted polls and surveys about public attitudes towards democracy, for instance. Zogby International has conducted public opinion surveys that elicited some public debate.[34] Most Arab media and newspapers with large circulation today conduct their own surveys. However, these are largely consumer-focused surveys.

Second, as a new point of reference, this emerging Arab public opinion increasingly helps expand the terrain and the opportunities for democratic vocalism and activism, helping empower the Arab 'subaltern' to speak and the marginals to participate. This trend, however, cannot be equated with a Habermasian-like public sphere. Nonetheless, al-Jazeerah's modest 'democratizing effect' (and far from being a 'CNN effect'), especially through its talk shows is corroborated by recent research.[35] The talk-shows are today supplemented and bolstered by al-Jazeerah's online surveys. The level of debate facilitated by the new medium offers a support system for dialogue, expression, acquisition of wide-ranging ideas, and discussion of most taboo topics. It is a forum that has given dissidents and regime partisans alike a medium to articulate their positions and defend them publicly. This trend can cumulatively deepen the idea that Arabs can talk and that they are entitled to talk openly to voice difference, agreement, or disagreement. So sceptics should not expect miracles from these media. In the 12 years since its founding, al-Jazeerah has already given a voice to all those representing political and religious currents persecuted by all Arab regimes. In so doing, it has also introduced their narratives to Arab audiences.

It is the dialogical content of these media rather than the positions represented therein that must be appreciated and recognized as instrumental in lending support to democratic struggles in a region that has until recently been distinguished by a media order in service of failed or authoritarian states. Hence Faysal al-Qasim, al-Jazeerah's presenter of the most polemical and most widely viewed Arab programme, understands the role of his talk show ('In the Opposite Direction') to be that of generating dialogue and debate in a way that disperses discourse and refigures Arab politics:

Dialogue is something missing among the Arabs. It is missing in schools, as much as it is missing everywhere else in life of the Arabs. At home the father is a dictator. At work, the employer is a dictator, and in the life of the Arab countries, the political leader is a dictator. Through programmes such as mine, we hope to implement new rules, those that educate the Arab human being to listen, not only to his own opinion, but to that of the other side as well. The debate-based media must enter in force and strongly in the political life of the Arabs, whether the Arab regimes like it or not.[36]

The operative term in what appears to be a committed form of journalism in al-Qasim's above statement is 'educate the Arab human being'. This didactic mission as expressed by probably al-Jazeerah's most famous polemicist gives credence to the process of consolidating democratic struggle set in motion by the Qatari Satellite station.

Information and awareness are vital for any fruitful process of democratization in the long term. Al-Qasim's credits his programme and al-Jazeerah with offering a 'ray of hope' by providing Arab viewers with the opportunity to debate taboo subjects, social and political. Several online polls resulted directly from his programme. It is not surprising that he is of the opinion that 'it is high time that [Arabs] "de-iconise" many of the thoughts and sacred myths [and political dogma] that have dominated the Arab World for decades'.[37]

Al-Jazeerah's webcasts, are not creating democracy; nor are its talkshows. They are simply providing a 'virtual' space, adding to other processes of widening participation in the Arab world. From this perspective, al-Jazeerah's online polling is a medium that releases millions of Arabs from the political restraints on free self-expression placed on them by their own central governments. Specifically, online voting exercises can be regarded as a form of unofficial mini referenda—or online quasi tele-enfranchisement, which release webcast voters from the geographical territoriality and non-democratic authority they have been accustomed to within their own homelands. This has resulted in some paradoxes and tensions. Arab satellite TV enfranchises but paradoxically de-nationalizes Arab 'citizens'. The Arab press has since the 1960s, 1970s, and 1980s largely served to consolidate the nationalist state. To an extent, Arab satellite TV has since the 1990s contributed to the undoing of the imagining of nationalist community or nation-formation. However, one consistency persists: satellite TV reinforces prejudices—pan-Arab and pan-Islamic sentiments, a point I shall return to towards the end of this chapter. These are not necessarily anti-democratic even if they tend to be anti-American or anti-Western.

'Arab Street' or 'Arab Public Opinion'?

It is no exaggeration to say that 'public opinion' has not had any presence to speak of in the Arabic political vocabulary. If public opinion refers to the 'spoken' and 'channelled' thinking of relevant 'publics' and 'pressure groups' with the potential to influence government policy, then it can be asserted that it is totally absent in the AME except through elections.[38] It is within elite circles of 'special publics' that opinion narrowly and privately feeds into Arab statecraft. Arab leaders rely on impressionistic means such as intelligence to discover about public feeling. There are no records indicating interest in public opinion by nineteenth-century reformers like Egypt's Muhammad Ali and Tunisia's Khayr al-Din who were inclined to copy Europe's parliaments and introduce limited participation. There were no records of Arab 'straw polls' in the nineteenth century, such as in the United States. Today there are no analogues to the West's professional pollsters like Gallup or Roper or an Arab counterpart to the American Institute of Public Opinion. No parallel notion of public opinion was conceived in tandem with the idea of full adult suffrage when it started to emerge early in the twentieth century in the Arab World. Generally, public opinion (as having consequence for mass, open, and deliberative politics) remains absent in the Arab World. Thus the absence or marginalization of an Arab public opinion has historically translated into the prominence of an undefined 'Arab street'. If applied to a Western setting the term would sound strange: 'the American street' or the 'British street'. The term has Orientalist overtones. A 'street' does not denote the varying degrees of 'ruliness', 'political competence', or 'intelligence' the term 'public opinion' connotes.

Western and Arab media alike have used the term 'Arab street' in a sensational fashion. The headlines speak for themselves: 'Has Saddam lost the Arab Street?'; 'The Battle on Arab Street'; 'Where is the Arab "Street"?'; 'Subverting the Arab Street'; 'Allies PR War Targets Arab Street'; 'Examining the Arab Street'; 'The Arab Street Explodes'; and 'Anger on the Arab Street'.[39] Combining the ideas of 'Saddam', 'battle', 'subversion', 'PR war', 'explosion' and 'anger' communicate a Hobbesian-like 'state of nature' not short of 'brutishness' or 'nastiness', highlighting conflict and unruliness. Academic scholarship is equally guilty of uncritical use of this pejorative nomenclature. In 'Subverting "the Arab Street"' Massad uses the term between inverted commas. Nonetheless, he offers no justification for its use. In the title 'Where is the Arab "street"?' Daniel Pipes gives his CNN interviewer, Lou Dobbs, no cautious instruction as to the problematic nature of such a term. Fortunately, Ari Melber uses it critically, noting that the term is 'inaccurate' and 'disrespectful' given its negative connotations, namely, 'a mob mentality'. Melber adds that the term is 'obstructive to US efforts to engage the Middle East'. Thus he cautions against the understanding that there is a 'monolithic Arab street stewing with a singular hatred of the United States'.[40] He is equally insightful, noting how Arab autocrats' political rhetoric use the 'Arab street' as though it is a volcano, a 'beast', a 'weapon' or a 'time-bomb' awaiting detonation by foreign-power meddling into the Middle East.

Defenders say the term emphasizes the gap between Arab dictators and their citizens. But it is precisely those rulers who advance the impression that the 'street' may erupt at any moment (even as they control information and limit expression). This is the most dangerous part of perpetuating the 'street' fiction. It feeds the scare tactics of dictators in the Middle East. Last year Egyptian President Hosni Mubarak incorrectly predicted that if the United States invaded Iraq, 'not a single ruler will be able to curb the popular sentiments' and 'chaos may prevail in the region'. Amr Moussa, the Secretary-General of the Arab League, warned the war would lead to hellish violence in the Arab street.[41]

Melber is right. Autocratic rulers almost invariably turned politics into the exclusive bastion of the few as though to express disdain for any notion of 'democracy' that gives power to the 'mob'. This is akin to the Hellenic derogatory understanding of democracy as power of the 'plebeian masses'. There is, however, another take on the subject of 'Arab street': passive, weak, and without agency. In this vein, Arab journalist Wahid Abdel-Meguid criticizes another usage in relation to the 'Arab street', mainly one of powerlessness. 'The "Arab street" deserves pity', he writes. 'Some people are treating it like a joke, while others are lamenting its imminent death.'[42] But what is interesting in Abdel-Meguid's analysis is how US foreign policymakers, among others no doubt, seem to be convinced either of a dangerous or irrelevant 'Arab street':

The Western media aren't the only ones singing about the demise of the 'Arab street' or dismissing it as irrelevant. Condoleezza Rice, the [former] American National Security Advisor, took the same line in a recent interview with the *Financial Times*. She judged that the Arab peoples are too weak to ask for democracy, meaning the task of liberating Arab and Islamic countries from tyranny must fall to Washington.[43]

In response to Rice, nothing matches the eloquence of the failure to impose democracy in Iraq. David Pollock goes furthest in highlighting the flaws of treating the 'Arab street' as monolithic or static. He points to a diversity of Arab 'publics' and 'streets'.[44] Moreover, the so-called Arab streets do not always see either eye to eye with one another or with their governments. Similarly, they are not always at odds with their regimes. He records instances of peak influence of Arab public opinions, which contradicts with the view expressed above of powerless Arab peoples. Specifically, post Iraqi invasion of Kuwait, Arab regimes in Jordan, Tunisia, and Yemen, among others, had no choice but to respond to the attitudes of their publics against the anti-Iraq US-led coalition for liberating Kuwait. The urgency of the crisis was such that never before since independence have Arab regimes embraced their publics and responded to their attitudes as they did during the build-up of anti-Iraq forces in 1991. Pollock notes Arab regimes' accounting for public opinion in a rare historical instance by 'calibrat[ing] their policies partly according to what the traffic—on the "street"—would bear'. He poignantly stresses the point further: 'Even entrenched Arab leaders appeared unable to mould their publics' attitudes at will, or to turn off the flow of independent information and opinion. Rather, public opinion appeared able to substantially modify—or substantially reinforce—the initial policy inclinations of major Arab governments on either side of this very high-stakes issue.'[45] Nonetheless, this response remains rare. Arab public opinion is still amorphous as a force, side-lined as a complex of interests and preferences, and underresearched as a subject.

But the blame for this state of affairs does not rest with Orientalists and 'Western' journalists or scholars. Arabs alone bear responsibility for the sad state of public opinion. The concept 'public opinion' is a neologism. The Arabic term *al-ra'y al-'āmm* is a direct translation of the English term 'public opinion'. There is no other Arab term that conveys an equivalent meaning. To an extent the dearth of literature in Arabic on public opinion reflects its impoverished history, theo-retically and practically. One of the very few titles on the subject tackles public opinion from an external not domestic perspective, a point to be returned to below.[46] Arab scholarship has until recently been silent on opinion polling. It has so far drawn little or no academic curiosity and there are no references in Arabic on it. The rare effort in 1978 by a respected Arab think-tank, the Beirut-based Arab Unity Studies Centre, to collect direct evidence about attitudes on Arab unity from a sizable cross-section of the Arab citizenry remains till this day incomplete. Eleven of the 21 Arab states declined to give permission for such polling to go ahead within their territories.[47] There has until very recently been a poor record of systematic surveying of public opinion in the Arab world. Public opinion has not been tested on its feelings towards public debt, or hereditary rule in republican systems. Peace with Israel has been the subject of specific polls but only recently.

Democracies seek scientific soundings about voters' attitudes towards a myriad of issues of concern to politicians contesting power or decision-makers in charge of distributing political resources or allocat-ing economic goods. Arab autocracies do not. The contrast is so stark with Israel whose 'science of public opinion has been turned into a fine art'.[48] There still seems be a sense of unease by many Arab regimes about what their publics think, value, or oppose. A rare example of polling appears in a pioneering work, which systematically surveys public opinion in 10 Arab countries. It confirms the idea of unease.[49] Michael Suleiman offers an explanation of Arab regimes' aversion to public opinion. He puts it down to the regimes' sensitivity to find-ings that may reveal disdainful attitudes and contemptuous feelings towards political authority. Officialdom deploys censorship to avoid 'potentially embarrassing or harmful consequences of research'.[50] Suleiman also notes how censorship driven by fear of imagined threats to state security renders polling impossible.

Consideration of public opinion in the Arab world has for the greater part of post-independence history had an external focus: the non-Arab 'publics' around the world. It is thus conceived of as a potential to be tapped into and grabbed. The aim is to sensitize world opinion, through diverse publics, to the Palestinian cause in a way that swings it in favour of the Arab side. In this vein, a study by Rasim Muhammad al-Jammal assigns the pan-Arab media a key role in shaping international public opinion as one strategy for winning its sympathy and for mobilizing it to support the Palestinian cause.[51]

The satellite TV revolution gives great help today in reaching wider non-Arab audiences and communicating to them pan-Arab or nationalistic perspectives (e.g. al-Jazeerah in English). It continues to carry out this role today with around-the-clock coverage of Israeli occupation and since 2003 of the Anglo-American invasion of Iraq, for instance. This is one reason why the Bush Administration has continuously expressed displeasure with al-Jazeerah and set up in 2004 its own Arab satellite TV 'Al-Hurrah' to counter Al-Jazeerah's propaganda. Public opinion has existed only in so far as it is an external resource to be won and mobilized for the benefit of Arab causes. Domestically, by contrast, public opinion is largely occluded. It is treated as a given. Specifically, under the varying degrees of authoritarian rule it is treated like a clean slate onto which are grafted state-centric values, attitudes, and preferences. The publics do not opine. The state opinion-makers opine on their behalf. Such a mode of political socialization aims at reconstituting subjectivity and identity and the attitudes or values underpinning them. The newly imagined or invented post-colonial nationalist identity contradicts potentially rival norms of identification and loyalties derived from religion or tribal solidarity. Domestic public opinion is not then viewed as a complex of preferences and choices that different publics offer to a given cause without either the autonomy of individuals or the integrity of polls' democratic process being compromised. Rather, public opinion as an agency is demoted.

Webcast Opinion Polls and Consolidating Democratic Struggles

I now proceed to corroborate the case of al-Jazeerah's role in aiding democratic struggles and the specific role of online opinion polls in this process. With regard to the online opinion polls sampled below it is worth pointing to their tentative and formative nature. They do not seem to be systematic and therefore have serious biases. These online polls tend to drive the formation of public opinion rather than passively reflect it. In the developed world media polls can better reflect opinion. Of course, it is a well-known factor that polls do alter opinion in the 'West', but properly conducted polls can offer a useful account of the state of opinion. The online opinion polls conducted by al-Jazeerah must be appreciated for being a trend-setting practice that simply helps vocalism. Their real added value therefore is qualitative not quantitative. The 'scientific' content and value of al-Jazeerah's webcast opinion polls may on close scrutiny call for questioning. But that does not in any way compromise their 'democratic' *symbolism*. In terms of value, science loses and politics gains. Quantitatively, in the sense of the webcast polls being a scientific device for sounding out public opinion, they are defective for failing important polling rules. Briefly, the webcast polls sampled below, like all polling done by al-Jazeerah, flouts the fundamental test of the simple random sample. Being online, al-Jazeerah's polls are based on self-selection. The respondents to the polls in Table 6.1 do not represent a random sample of a parent population. The simple random sample is valued for producing generalizable results applicable to a cross-section of a given population randomly selected according to variables such as age, gender, area, profession, or income. Random selection is vital for fairness; that is, equality of chance in terms of voting and representation. Renka and Blake agree that 'random' does not mean unsystematic or non-scientific. Quite to the contrary, equality of a calculable chance of sampling all respondents in a targeted population is necessary for scientific results that can be used for the purpose of systematic extrapolation.

There is no information whatsoever about the respondents, which flouts another important polling rule. But what can be surmised is that thousands of the 'voters' in al-Jazeerah's webcast polls most probably belong to the body of Arab opinion-makers. Opinion-makers refer to that social stratum whose members are educated, computer-literate, informed, politicized, and relatively well-to-do (since they own personal computers, have access to a family computer or have the money to buy Internet time). In this case, thousands of them can also be assumed to be regular or at least frequent viewers of al-Jazeerah's talk-shows and count among the network's 'website-addicts'. Al-Jazeerah online polls provide figures which are devoid of any clues as to why a majority of respondents vote overwhelmingly for the acquisition of an Arab nuclear weapon (80.3%, total voters: 61,000, 13 January

Table 6.1 Al-Jazeerah webcast opinion polls—democracy and Arab rule

No.	Question	Total respondents	Date
1	Do you think there is genuine freedom of expression in the Arab world?	20,197	27 June 2001
2	Do you think human rights violations in Syria are real or false?	8,652	02 September 2001
3	What are the causes that contribute most to the weakness of democracy in the Arab homeland?	1,356	09 September 2001
4	Will Arab states accept to practise genuine democracy voluntarily?	31,381	14 January 2003
5	Do you think that democracy in Iraq [would] harm the Sunni Arabs?	37,126	20 January 2003
6	Do you expect the creation of a democratic government in Iraq?	29,442	06 May 2003
7	Is the state's insistence on the single vote law in Jordan an obstacle to democracy?	3,692	15 June 2003
8	Does the separation of the post of Prime Minister and the role of heir to the throne consolidate the democratic experience in Kuwait?	2,638	04 July 2003
9	Will the new Iraqi Constitution meet with the people's acceptance in case of Washington's interference in its draft?	27,946	13 August 2003
10	Do municipality elections in Saudi Arabia represent a beginning towards democratic transition?	38,451	15 August 2003
11	Do you trust in the fairness of the presidential elections in Mauritania?	11,300	05 November 2003
12	Do you consider the Accord between Taha and al-Mirghani a step to end power struggle in the Sudan?	22,600	05 November 2003
13	Nine years after its creation, do you believe in the usefulness of the continuity of the [National] Palestinian Authority?	46,306	08 November 2003
14	Do you support the Peace Accord between the Sudanese Government and the Sudan People's Liberation Army?	4,648	03 February 2004
15	To what [factors] do you put down Arab regimes' silence on the torture of Iraqi prisoners?	94,827	09 March 2004
16	Will reform succeed in [Arab] Gulf States?	4,086	12 March 2004
17	Is there a conspiracy to destabilize Syria?	10,000	20 March 2004
18	Do you support Khartoum's accusing Turabi of an attempted coup in the Sudan?	38,771	31 March 04
19	Will the Algerian Army stick to neutrality vis-à-vis presidential candidates?	7,925	06 April 2004
20	Do you support America's efforts to diffuse democracy in the Arab world?	60,633	09 December 2004

2004), in the utility of suicide bombings in Iraq (72.1%, total voters: 42,126, 14 September 2004), or in the legitimacy of foreign hostage-taking by the Iraqi resistance (79.9%, total voters: 91,775, 15 April 2004). Al-Jazeerah's online voting records high voter turnouts in some polls that seem to press sensitive buttons (Iraq, Palestine, Islam, US involvement in Arab affairs). National politics does not elicit as high a response as Iraq or Palestine from al-Jazeerah's online voters. More than hundred thousand voted when requested to consider whether Israel's slaying of Hamas leader, Abd al-Aziz Rantissi, would weaken Hamas, with a majority voting it would not (84.6%, total voters: 100,504, 18 April 2004). That number of voters continues to be the fourth highest to-date. The 94,827 voters on the question of torture of Iraqi prisoners and Arab regimes' silence (question 15 in Table 6.1) or the 60,633 respondents voting (question 20 in Table 6.1) on America's democracy promotion efforts in the Arab world may not be so significant if taken as a sample for the entire Arab population which approximates 300 million.

The premier Arab broadcaster may be said to be more concerned with the conclusions and the sweeping statements derived from the results more than the depth of analysis, nuance in response, or rigour of polling. Like other mass media, al-Jazeerah's online polls are not action-oriented. But their results are not always simply transient news. They must be understood as coinciding with al-Jazeerah's pan-Arab agenda and its mission to be vociferous about taboo issues worthy of debate, thus promoting interaction with and among its wide Arab audience.[52]

The questions use wording that is not neutral. But what is missing in many polls is what Renka calls the 'no option option'. Al-Jazeerah polls are in their bulk fashioned around yes–no responses. A no-option option such as a 'do not know' response leads to more nuanced voting. Renka notes that a recurring fact is that many respondents do not always formulate a position for or against a particular poll question.[53] Questions with multiple choice responses are sometimes used as in the examples 3 and 15 shown in Table 6.1 and explained below Table 6.2. But these are the exception not the rule in al-Jazeerah's polls.

Qualitatively, there are some very modest gains, which must not be exaggerated since multiple voting cannot be excluded. Nonetheless, voter participation liberates the respondents from the apathy too often displayed by Arab citizens in despair at the futility of local politics, which is marked by lack of opportunities for either substantive political contestation or meaningful participation. Voting freely and without state hindrance and, above all else, absence of fear from state reprisals,

Table 6.2 Voting results on questions in Table 6.1

Question No.	Yes/for	No/against	Unsure
1	3.8	94.9	1.3
2	12.6	86	1.3
3[a]	57.5	21.8	9.5
4	11	86.4	2.7
5	54.5	39.5	6
6	19.2	76.7	4.1
7	74.7	17.3	7.9
8	59.2	35.5	5.3
9	16.9	83.1	—
10	25.2	74.8	—
11	53.3	46.7	—
12	55.6	44.4	—
13	33.2	66.8	—
14	67.2	32.8	—
15[b]	66	29.6	4.3
16	17.7	82.3	—
17	59.8	40.2	—
18	28.1	71.9	—
19	38.1	61.9	—
20	23.2	76.8	—

Non–Yes or No Answers: [a]Question 3: 57.5 per cent put the cause down to oppression; 21.8 per cent to negativity of Arab peoples and their conformism to despotism; and 10.5 per cent to poverty and ignorance. [b]Question 15: 66 per cent took fear of the United States to be the main factor; 29.6 per cent put the silence down to Arab regimes' own embarrassment of practising torture in their own prisons; and 4.3 thought there were other factors.

which would otherwise be the case in conventional political activism in the AME, may all account for the high propensity of opinion-makers to cast their votes online.

No gain perhaps is greater than the questions voted on. They are taboo questions that closely scrutinize Arab politics, both as a subsystem (questions 1, 3, 4, 15, and 20 in Table 6.1) and as national units (questions on single states in Table 6.1). To an extent, al-Jazeerah online polls provide voters with a unique opportunity to have their say on the pan-Arab subsystem and the various Arab states, systems that have functioned for decades with little or no accountability and without the benefit of input from the non-ruling Arab publics. The questions voted on have largely been absent from public discourse much less subject to direct scrutiny institutionally. Arab regimes waged wars and lost them, 'putschists' took over many a state and 'possessed' or 'colonized' them, and the fortune of many an Arab state vacillated between trial and error, failure or collapse without the inputs of the silenced Arab masses. Al-Jazeerah's online opinion polls have therefore become a channel for venting pent-up anger about political marginalization, thus raising the level of societal vocalism. Those who could speak and never were offered the chance to do so are today striking back at the Arab state and misrule in general. The polls sampled in Table 6.1 ask respondents to consider questions on democracy and political rule, items that have not until recently been flagged for public debate. What political territoriality has forbidden in terms of participation and vocalism on misrule, virtual reality, and online interactivity have made possible. Suddenly the marginals can speak and can opine. Questions on specifically national politics (e.g. questions on Iraq, Algeria, or the Sudan in Table 6.1) have both an edifying and mobilizing function. They enmesh the respondents in discourses that have relevance to their own political environment. Pondering the question of elections in Algeria forces consideration of similar issues in most Arab countries where elections are held and where there are always doubts about the neutrality of state institutions and apparatuses. The issue of the army's neutrality in the Algerian elections may be common to the Sudan or Yemen. The very question of neutrality has an analogue in media impartiality given the fact that ruling parties are known to benefit from their monopolistic use of this resource during elections. The request to consider the question of Arab regimes' silence on human rights abuses in Iraq (question 15 in Table 6.1) is a leading question. It focuses the respondents' thinking on their own countries' human rights violations. At least 30 per cent of the 94,827 voters put the silence down to Arab regimes' embarrassment at the practice of torture against their own citizens.

The interactivity stimulated by these taboo questions helps break silence. Arab elections come and go with no polls preceding them. Largely, presidential elections from Mauritania to Yemen take place with no scientific soundings of the populace on the candidates. Similarly, no such soundings exist to probe politics in general or specific policies, ranging from hereditary rule to defence expenditure. This is one reason why election fetishism in the AME is suspect. It reduces and sums the democratic game into a single exercise of vote-casting periodically. Between periodic elections the populace are relegated to a form of 'political clay', with no say or role to speak of in public affairs.

Voting in all the polls (Table 6.2) displays a diverse range of taboo questions the official media in the AME has yet to summon the courage to conduct soundings on. Neither it nor the public at large are coached in acquiring the skills needed to help engender democratic citizenship.

The history of post-independence is noted for a glaring absence of the kind of political socialization that entrenches acceptance of difference and of contest over political resources, meanings, and values as being part and parcel of democratic politics. For democratic politics is an ever unfolding construction. In it indeterminacy and permanence of crisis are not negative. Rather, they help reify politics as an art in the hands of competing interests constantly challenged by turning uncertainty into possibility, even if only ephemerally. By contrast, the construction of political identity in the AME is coloured by the Arab states' preference for uniformity in the name of national unity and of political deference over difference. Online voting, regardless of who participates in it and of its questionable scientific standard, provides limited opportunities to enmesh formerly excluded publics into vocalizing their views in a relatively risk-free forum. This adds, even if in a modest fashion, a 'space' of vocalism that, if and when universalized to other media outlets, serves to support existing forms of democratic struggle. This struggle will not unseat regimes. But when adopted more widely it has the potential to help the forming and communicating of political opinion. This is vital for any durable process of reform.

There should be no illusion as to the influence on policy or representation of citizens' views to be generated by the online polls. Most likely, the state of public opinion generated by al-Jazeerah's polls will more often than not be ignored by the rulers even if they are inclined to use them to learn about public sentiments. If Arab rulers allow themselves to be guided by some of the opinion surveyed by al-Jazeerah they will set their regimes on a collision course with Western governments and international norms. For they will have to ignore global norms of disarmament and develop an Arab nuclear capability; help the resistance in Iraq; and boycott the US-sponsored government in Baghdad, etc. The cliché 'stand up and be counted' applies here when the question arises about the responsiveness to this newly emerging public opinion inhabiting 'virtual reality'. The responsiveness must not be measured in the state's reactive capacity. The real learning curve resides in the invigoration of democratic struggles. Globally, the refashioning of vocalism and activism away from the straightjacket of political territoriality to virtual reality is about opening a non-policed space for free interactivity and ongoing democratization. There is some evidence of this trend in the AME, a gain flowing from the rise of the phenomenon of satellite TV in the AME. The online opinion polls give a flavour of the potentialities for Arab societies to partner in the hitherto state-driven reform processes. These societies may never be in a position to support reform if their members do not possess the democratic skills to participate, opine, differ, tolerate, and vote. Al-Jazeerah's online opinion polls provide a glimpse of the kind of interactivity that can in the long run help vocalism (opinion polls) and the acquisition of democratic knowledge (my forthcoming work on 'Salon democracy' in the Arab world).

A Critical Reflection

The online opinion polls pioneered by al-Jazeerah are making public engagement more possible. In a context of state-directed information, difference, and especially political difference, is either underrepresented or completely denied even a margin of existence. Al-Jazeerah's polls challenge that order, by offering opportunities for bolstering expression by publics long marginalized from political participation in various Arab states. Webcasts that reach millions of households give the largely silenced Arab publics and their dissidents, even if in a minimal way, a voice and a degree of representation. From this perspective, they are helping create a quasi *vox populi* in virtual reality, further strengthening both democratic struggles and the nascent Arab public opinion. However, this nascent public opinion remains largely amorphous. While some doubt can be cast about the reliability of online polling, a limited utility can be drawn from it. It discloses some information about Arab public sentiments. These sentiments seem to be at loggerheads with policies favoured in the AME by the United States and other Western governments as well as Arab regimes aligned with them.

So who are these 'publics' and what are their positions on some of the questions voted on? Part of the answer lies in the soundings obtained through al-Jazeerah's online opinion polls. These publics show Egypt's Muslim Brotherhood's real political weight to be far greater than its share of the seats the banned Islamist organization gained in the 2005 multi-party elections for Parliament (Poll conducted 17–20 November 2005 [out of 27,929 voters 76.1% were for]). They returned a resounding yes to 'vindictive action' by Hizbullah against Israel's bombing of Qana during the 34-day war of 2006 (Poll conducted 30 July 2006–02 August 2006 [86.9% were in favour from a total of 124,688—against 13.1% who favoured a ceasefire with Israel]). As to whether they considered Hizbullah's confrontation with Israel to be 'legitimate resistance' they overwhelmingly responded in the positive, in the highest voter participation in record (Poll conducted 15–18 July 2006 [of 197,641 voters 180,365 or 91.3% were in favour—17,276 or 8.7% thought Hizbullah's war with Israel was a miscalculated adventure]). The results were a direct snub to Egypt, Jordan, and Saudi Arabia who blamed the war on Hizbullah and accused it of adventurism. Again, in relation to Hizbullah a majority of online voters sided with the option of keeping the 'Islamic resistance' in Southern Lebanon. Alternative peace-keeping options voted on included the Lebanese Army, Multi-national Forces, and a combination of Lebanese-Multinational Forces. They scored respectively 18.2, 1.3, and 6.7 per cent. Hizbullah won the vote by 73.9 per cent of a total voting population of 94,558 (Poll conducted 08–11 August 2006). Hamas received similar support in al-Jazeera's online polling, suggesting the Palestinian cause to still command wide loyalty within Arab public opinion. Opinion sampled in late 2006 in al-Jazeerah opposed recognition of Israel by Hamas. The polling sample might have been low (2,256 voters); but the no-vote was 93 per cent (Poll conducted 12–16 November 2006). The killing of Palestinians in Beit Hanoun in November 2006 drew online-voter responses in favour of 'increased resistance' (Poll conducted 09–12 November 2006 [18,971 voted with 94.4% answering yes for more resistance and the rest favouring diplomatic approaches]). As in Palestine and Lebanon, al-Jazeerah's polls pointed to a staunchly anti-US and anti-Western policy preferences in Iraq. For instance, in a poll involving 31,915 respondents, 78.8 per cent opposed sentencing to death the former Iraqi dictator, Saddam Hussein (Poll conducted 06–09 November 2006). Similarly, US democracy promotion seemed to meet with rejection. Some 76.8 per cent opposed US democracy promotion in the Arab region (Poll conducted 09–12 February 2006 [the total number of respondents was 60,633]). NATO, and by implication French and British policy in the Arab World, had only minority support. In a question regarding the UN deployment in Southern Lebanon 96,305 respondents, compared with 13,884 in favour, voted against (Poll conducted 24–27 July 2006). Online voters approved highly of Iran's pursuit of nuclear capability (Poll conducted 17–20 June 2004 [81.3% in favour]).

Thus, there appears to be overwhelming support for Hizbullah and Hamas. The respondents seem to favour resistance over diplomacy. In the same vein, they seem to oppose the United States and NATO. They are against imposition of Western democracy. They have no problem with Iran's nuclear policy. Al-Jazeerah's opinion polls have 'constructed' this amorphous public. This online-voting public may be faceless but not voiceless. It may not be able to 'stand up and be counted'. However, its respondents (whether they are members of both 'moderate' and 'extremist' Islamist organizations and other dissidents) point to a disturbing trend: a form of collision of Western policy preferences and the desiderata of an incipient body of pan-Arab public opinion-formulators. Whether this collision merits concern by

Arab and Western policymakers is another matter as many would be ready to dismiss the reliability of the online polls. The polls, as suggested above, are not 'scientific'. Given the fierce contests ongoing within the AME and between its various societies and several Western powers the responses marked by hostility and opposition against the questions voted on are not implausible. Here lies the irony of al-Jazeerah's polls. Their results disclose a bias against the policies of consolidated democracies. The polls may be consolidating bottom-up democratic struggles by presenting wider sections of the computer-literate and educated pan-Arab public with opportunities for vocalizing dissidence. However, the fledgling pan-Arab public opinion does not seem to be allied with Western democracies' policy choices, including, democracy promotion. The strengthening of public opinion and consolidation of democratic struggles do not ironically translate into automatic compatibility with democratic governments in North America and Europe. This irony is only matched by the paradox of United States and EU democracy promotion in the Arab world: Washington stands for democracy except when those democratically elected happen to be Islamists such as Hamas. Al-Jazeerah may be providing political channels towards greater public engagement that has the potential to support democratization. However, support of democratization does not lead to change of attitudes towards Western powers. Nonetheless, the de-territorialized space for vocalizing dissidence and difference opened up by al-Jazeerah's polls (as well as talk-shows) is a boon for the future of sustained and incremental democratization in the AME. This captures the paradox of al-Jazeerah in which coincides both anti-Western hostility and democratic potentiality.

Conclusion

Blogs and online opinion polls add to the momentum brought about and maintained by the satellite revolution in the AME. Thus new sites of democratic struggles are formed, widening the arena of state–society contests. These new sites boost the existing conventional modes of democratic struggles, opening up an arch of possibilities for corroding, be it in a piecemeal fashion, autocracy in the AME. Some of these sites (namely, elections) of democratic struggle are initiated by the Arab state. But they were never intended for mounting challenges against entrenched centres of power (whether these belong to Arafat's Fatah, Morocco's so-called *makhzen*, a reference to the state, or the ruling Sunni 'clan-state' in Bahrain). Elections do not unseat the autocracies of the AME. But they do introduce formerly silenced and excluded political actors (e.g. Hamas, Muslim Brotherhood parties, Shi'ites in Bahrain, Lebanon, and now Iraq, trade unions in Morocco, and less so secular dissidents in several Arab states). Other sites of democratic struggle such as petitions (e.g. by learned scholars and women in Saudi Arabia), protests (e.g. 'Kifayah' in Egypt, and hunger strikes Tunisia), vociferous talk-shows, and online polls (e.g. al-Jazeerah's among others) have become moral support systems that dissidence in general draws confidence from. The satellite television revolution and the Internet have meant dissidence is de-territorialized. Protests by 'Kifayah' make instantaneous news in Arab satellite television networks. The same networks scrutinize elections in every corner of the AME. The content of petitions in Saudi Arabia travels fast. Abuses by the security apparatus in the AME are expeditiously picked up and diffused by bloggers. Al-Jazeerah's online polls widen the terrain of democratic struggles, giving opinion-formulators and other voters the opportunity to opine on taboo subjects. Hence technology, which breaks and reduces temporal and spatial barriers, combines with moral protest, conventional (elections) and non-conventional (online polls) to refigure the nature of the democratic struggles in the AME from parochial and territorial into transnational and de-territorialized. These online polls strengthen the ongoing construction of an Arab public opinion (e.g. by Zogby International, and The Pew Research Centre for the People and the Press). They rise to defy Orientalisms that have for so long, and still do, typecast is as 'Arab street'. It may then be said that a dawn of an era of Arab public opinion is in the offing. The next generation of Arab citizenries could be voting in opinion polls about 'inherited' rule, nepotism, corruption, human rights violations, and economic management. These are taboo subjects. Democracy is inconceivable without public opinion. Public opinion matters to the democratic process as do elections, rule of law, pluralism, equal opportunity, among others institutions. From this perspective, al-Jazeerah's online polls have implications for 'democracy learning', an area is still underresearched in the context of the AME. Future focus by transitologists on this unexplored territory can potentially unlock answers and provide considerable specificity about the political attitudes and behaviour patterns needed for engendering Arab citizenship and the factors that either promote or demote their emergence. The scholarly capacity to invigorate the debate about the viability of good government in the Arab world remains contingent upon refashioning the debate in order to account for how democracy is learnt. What is certain is that democracy learning shall take the route defended by Whitehead. That is, 'a complex, long-term, dynamic, and open-ended process'.

Perhaps it is still premature to say that the time of autocracies in the AME is up, especially that Internet access remains limited in some countries. But this is changing very fast as computers become more widespread and costs of Internet access decrease. The authoritarian state will use whatever power it possesses to fend off the onslaught against its authority and control, especially by political activists. This it may do through electronic defences, select bans on satellite broadcasting and via locks on access to web sites with subversive ideas by political opponents. In the age of electronics, there is no limit to the defences (e.g. Internet filtering in Saudi Arabia, Tunisia, Egypt, Libya, and Syria) that the authoritarian state may deploy to hold back the tide of cyber-dissidence, blogging, and 'chat rooms'. Regardless, time in the twenty-first century will in the AME be on the side of political renewal, not authoritarianism's election fetishism. The writing may be on the net.

Notes

1. Dale F. Eickelman, 'Bin Laden, the Arab "Street", and the Middle East's Democracy Deficit', *Current History* (January 2002), 36–9.
2. Mark Lynch, 'Beyond the Arab Street: Iraq and the Arab Public Sphere', *Politics & Society*, 31/1 (March 2003), 55.
3. According to findings by the OpenNet Initiative, a collaborative work by the universities of Toronto, Harvard and Cambridge. For more details, see Clark Boyd, 'Hungry for Net Freedom in Tunisia', BBC News, 21 November 2005, in http://newsvote.bbc.co.uk/mpapps/pagetools/print/news.bbc.co.uk/1/hi/techn, 15 November 2007.
4. Marc Lynch, *Voices of the New Arab Public: Iraq, Al-Jazeerah and Middle East Politics* (New York: Columbia University Press, 2006).
5. Roland Robertson, 'Mapping the Global Condition: Globalization as the Central Concept', in M. Featherstone (ed.), *Global Culture: Nationalism, Globalization and Modernity* (London: Sage, 1990), pp. 15–30; Marjorie Ferguson, 'The Mythology about Globalization', *European Journal of Communication*, 7 (1992), 69–93.
6. Peter Beyer, *Religion and Globalization* (London: Sage, 1994); R. Robertson and W. R. Garrett (eds.), *Religion and Global Order* (New York: Paragon Press, 1991); Roland Robertson, *Globalization: Social Theory and Global Culture* (London: Sage, 1992).
7. Frederick Buell, *National Culture and the New Global System* (Baltimore and London: Johns Hopkins University Press, 1994); Richard Madsen, 'Global Monoculture, Multiculture and Polyculture', *Social Research*, 60 (1993), 493–511; Will Kymlicka, *The Rights of Minority Cultures* (Oxford: Oxford University Press, 1995); David Rieff, 'A Global Culture?', *World Policy Journal*, 10 (1993), 73–81; Bryan S. Turner, 'Postmodern Culture.

Modern Citizens', in B. van Steenbergen (ed.), *The Condition of Citizenship* (London: Sage, 1994), 153–68.

8. Paul Ekins, *A New World Order: Grassroots Movements for Global Change* (London: Routledge, 1992).

9. Paul Hirst and Grahame Thompson, 'Globalization and the Future of the Nation-State', *Economy and Society*, 24 (1995), 408–42.

10. Richard Falk, 'The Making of Global Citizenship', in B. van Steenbergen (ed.), *The Condition of Citizenship* (London: Sage, 1994), 127–40; Will Kymlicka, *Multicultural Citizenship: A Liberal Theory of Minority Rights* (Oxford: Clarendon Press, 1995); James Rosenau, 'Citizenship in a Changing World Order', in James Rosenau and E. Czempiel (eds.), *Governance without Government* (Cambridge: Cambridge University Press, 1992), 272–94.

11. Zdravko Mlinar (ed.), *Globalization and Territorial Identity* (Aldershot: Avebury, 1992); Stuart Hall, 'The Local and the Global: Globalization and Ethnicity', in A.D. King (ed.), *Culture, Globalization and the World System* (Houndmills: Macmillan Press, 1991), 19–39.

12. Anthony Smith, *The Geopolitics of Information: How Western Culture Dominates the World* (London: Faber and Faber, 1980).

13. Bryan S. Turner, *Orientalism, Postmodernism and Globalism* (London: Routledge, 1994).

14. See the articles in Ray E. Weisenborn (ed.), *Media in the Midst of War: The Gulf War from Cairo to the Global Village* (Cairo: The Adham Centre Press, 1992).

15. For more details on this point, see Douglas Boyd, *Broadcasting in the Arab World* (Philadelphia: Temple University Press, 1982).

16. Jon W. Anderson, *Arabizing the Internet* (Abu Dhabi: Centre for Strategic Studies and Research, 1998).

17. Hussein Amin, 'Egypt and the Arab World in the Satellite Age', in John Sinclair, Elizabeth Jacka and Stuart Cunningham (eds.), *New Patterns in Global Television: Peripheral Vision* (Oxford: Oxford University Press, 1996), 101–25.

18. Examples of home page addresses are Egypt state information service http://www.sis.gov.eg/; Syria's: http://www.personal.umich.edu/~kazamaza/soph.html; Jordan's: http://petra.nic.gov.jo/jordan.html; Fateh's: http://www.fateh.org/; see also, web site by Tunisia's new Ministry of Environment on this address: http://www-iasc.enst-bretagne. fr/~hicheri/envir.html. For more official sites, see http://www.arab.net/.

19. To counterbalance the information available on the global network, Saudi Arabia set up a satellite channel solely concerned with Islamic affairs—the TV Channel 'Iqra'. See 'Information Minister on New Islamic TV Channel', FBIS-NES-94–216, 6 November 1994.

20. See http://www.yezzi.org, 12 December 2006.

21. See the transcript of al-Jazeerah special programmme on the phenomenon of bloggers in Egypt. Many bloggers were hosted on this programmme, giving insights about their motivations and activism. It can

be found on http://www.aljazeera.net/NR/exeres/E6A0A606-DDE9-49DB-820A-9E0562D9DAF8.htm, 1 May 2007.

22. See details in Amnesty International, 'Egypt: Systematic Abuses in the Name of Security' (11 April 2007).

23. The interview by Sami Gharbia can be found on http://www.globalvoicesonline.org/2007/05/03/abdel-monem-mahmoud-the-egyptian-totalitarian-regime-is-the-problem/, 16 April 2007.

24. See 'Jihad Against Jews and Crusaders', online at http://www.fas.org/irp/world/para/docs/980223-fatwa.html], 15 October 1999.

25. Egypt's Muslim Brotherhood's web-page address is http://www.ummah.org.uk/ikhwan; that of al-Nahdah Party is http://www.ezzeitouna.org/annahdha/english/princip/govprinc.HTM; the FIS's: http://fisalgeria.org/ or http://www.hackintosh.com/~bgeste/algeria_fis.html.

26. See http://www.turabi.com/body_index.html.

27. Rathmell, 'Netwar in the Gulf', 31.

28. The Group for Democratic Development's home page address is http://www.gdd.org.eg/.

29. Its home page is: http://www.chrla.org/. See also, http://www.chrla.org/releases.htm.

30. Two good examples come from Lebanon: http://www.almashriq.hiof.no/base/environment.lebanon.html, and from Palestine: http://www.palestine.org/palestine-environment.html.

31. Author's interview with Kifayah's spokesperson, George Ishaq, 15 September 2006, Cairo, Egypt.

32. See 'Saudi Investor Buys Five per cent Stake in Apple', in http://www.news.com/News/Item/0,4,9338,00.htm. See also 'Saudi Prince to Invest in Teledesic' in http://www.news.com/News/Item/0,4,17638,00.htm, 12 December 1997.

33. See Lara Marlow, 'The New Saudi Press Barons', *Time*, 22 June 1992.

34. Mark Tessler, 'Building Capacity for Public Opinion and Social Research in the Arab World', Workshop by the Institute for Social Research and the Centre for Political Studies, University of Michigan, 27 June–15 July 2005.

35. Mark Lynch, *Voices of the New Arab Public: Iraq, Al-Jazeera, and Middle East Politics Today* (New York: Columbia University Press, 2006).

36. Louay Y. Bahry, 'The New Arab Media Phenomenon: Qatar's al-Jazeera', *Middle East Policy*, VIII/2 (June 2001), 92–3.

37. Mohamed El-Nawawy and Adel Iskandar, *Al-Jazeera: The Story of the Network that is Rattling Governments and Redefining Modern Journalism* (Cambridge, MA: Westview Press, 2003), 98–104.

38. T. Harrisson, 'What is Public Opinion', *Political Quarterly*, 11 (1949), 368–83.

39. Gary C. Gambill, 'Has Saddam Lost the Arab Street', *Middle East Intelligence Bulletin* 5 (January 2003) in http://www.meib.org/articles/0301_ir1.htm, 14 December 2003; Derwin Pereira, 'The Battle on Arab Street', in: http://straitstimes.asia1.com.sg/iraqwar/story/0,4395,179520, 00.html, 14 December 2003; 'Where is the Arab "Street"?' in

http://www.danielpipes.org/pf.php?id=1093, 14 December 03; Joseph Massad, 'Subverting "the Arab Street"', in *Al-Ahram Weekly Online*, 15–21 May 2003, in http://weekly.ahram.org.eg/print/2003/638/op172.htm, 14 December 2003; Howard LaFranchi, 'Allies' PR War Targets Arab Street', *Christian Science Monitor*, 24 September 2002, in http://www.csmonitor.com/2002/0924/p01s01-uspo.htm, 14 December 2003; John Lovejoy, 'Examining the Arab Street', *Chicago Maroon*, 22 April 2003, in http://maroon.uchicago.edu/viewpoints/articles/2003/04/22/examining_the_arab, 14 December 2003; Michelle Goldberg, 'The Arab Street Explodes', in http://www.salon.com/news/feature/2003/03/22/arab_street/index_np.htm, 14 December 2003; and Amy Radwan, 'Anger on the Arab Street', *Time*, 25 August 2003, in http://www.time.com/time/europe/me/printout/), 9869,227255,00.htm, 14 December 2003.

40. Ari Melber, 'Debunking the Myth of the Arab Street', *Baltimore Sun*, 31 August 2003, in http://www.topdog04.com/000364.html, 14 December 2003.

41. Ibid.

42. Wahid Abdel-Meguid, 'The Abused Arab Street', *Al-Hayat*, 6 November 2002, in http://www.worldpress.org/article_modle.cfm?article_id=922&dont=yes, 14 December 2003.

43. Ibid.

44. David Pollock, '"The Arab Street"? Public Opinion in the Arab World', *The Washington Institute Policy Papers*, No. 32 (Washington DC.: The Washington Institute for Near East Policy, 1992), 37–41.

45. Ibid. 39.

46. Mukhtar al-Tuhami, *Al-Ra'y al-'Amm wal-Harb al-Nafsiyyah* [Public Opinion and Psychological Warfare] (Cairo: Dar al-Ma'arif, 1974).

47. The 10 countries that gave their consent for the polling to go ahead were Egypt, Jordan, Kuwait, Lebanon, Morocco, North Yemen, Palestine (diaspora), Qatar, Sudan, and Tunisia. See, W. Suleiman, 'Foreword', in Elia Zureik and Fuad Moughrabi (eds.), *Public Opinion and the Palestine Question* (London & Sydney: Croom Helm, 1987), xii.

48. Fuad Moughrabi and Elia Zureik, 'Public Opinion and the Palestine Question: An Introduction', in Elia Zureik and Fuad Moughrabi (eds.), *Public Opinion and the Palestine Question* (London & Sydney: Croom Helm, 1987), 4.

49. Tawfic E. Farah and Yasumasa Kuroda (eds.), *Political Socialization in the Arab States* (Boulder, Colorado: Lynne Rienner, 1987). Farah, Kuroda, and their co-authors systematically survey, among others, Kuwaiti students, Gulf women, and camp Palestinians. In these three cases evidence is sought via scientific questionnaires about respectively the relationship between political trust and efficacy and political behaviour, gender equality, and identity/nationalism. See the chapters by Tawfic Farah and Faisal Al-Salem, 21–2; Ahmad J. Dhaher and Maria Al-Salem, 91–104; and by Rosemary Sayigh, 185–205.

50. Michael W. Suleiman, 'Foreword', in Farah and Kuroda (eds.), *Political Socialization in the Arab States*, xi.

51. Rasim Muhammad al-Jammal, *Al-I'lam al-'Arabi al-Mushtarak* [The Joint Arab Information (System)] (Beirut: Marakz Dirasat al-Wihdah al-'Arabiyyah, 1986), 111–21.

52. These tests are based on two fine sources: Russell D. Renka, 'The Good, the Bad, and the Ugly of Public Opinion Polls', in http://cstl-cla.semo.edu/renka/Renka_papers/polls.htm, 15 December 2004; and Ken Blake, 'The Ten Commandments of Polling', in http://parklibrary.jomc.unc.edu/pollcommand.html, 22 December 2004.

53. Renka, 'The Good, the Bad, and the Ugly of Public Opinion Polls'.

Conclusions

> I woke up at 8AM. Food was scarce in my kitchen. All I could find
> was some sugar and salt but no tea. Hikes in food prices wipes off
> half of my monthly salary these days. My depressing thoughts were
> interrupted by a knock at the door. A man stood at the entrance.
> 'How can I help you?' I asked. He invited me to sell my vote for
> 50 dinars cash. I accepted but on the condition he bought my
> husband's vote too. He agreed and we shook on it. Praise be to
> Allah, we shan't starve this month. I pray that elections are held
> every month!
>
> A citizen, after the November 2007 Jordan elections[1]

The ideas about good government are invented, applied, and tested
in Europe and North America before they 'travel' in search for a new
career in the AME. The nation-state, nationalism, socialism then the
free market, and now democratization have all followed the same
travel itinerary, from the 'West' to the rest. Globalization has to an
extent rendered the nation-state almost past its prime in the EU, for
instance. Democratization, too, seems to be losing even if partly its
explanatory power at the time of its arrival in the AME. Carothers
declares it at an end point as a paradigm. The same goes for the 'reverence' attached to the 'church' that is 'third-wave' transition theory.
Whitehead, among others such as O'Donnell across the vast terrain
of transitology, strongly notes the specificity of transition. Huntington's 'third-wave' theory resonates with the same specificity of process
(consolidation), of time (1840s to 1970s), and of space (the Americas
and Europe). Its utility where the AME is concerned may not stop
at the northern rims of the Mediterranean. But the 1974 Portuguese
coup that was to herald a new wave of democratization in Southern Europe never 'washed' southwards onto the shores of contiguous
Tanger, Algiers, or Tunis. One sea for Arab and European may be; but
the 'wave' has not been one for all. The polarity of 'word' and 'world',

theory and experience, rhetoric and reality, and what 'should be' and what 'is' in the field of democratic transition varies according to time and space. As democracy continues to rekindle its moral flame across the globe, the full panoply of diverse 'modernities', histories, cultures, religions, languages, levels and models of development, and memories dictate against paradigmatic fixity or singularity. The contest continues unabated. If democracy is an essentially contested concept, so is democratization. Thus Whitehead, *inter alia*, interrogates the monism of democratization qua 'consolidation'. Like Carothers, Whitehead's interrogation 'resist' the reign of third-wave wisdom across boundaries of time and space. Specific knowledge-making about transition in specific space and specific time invites comparison but not standardization of the terms and tools of analysis. The contest affirms the view that democratization defies linearity, unfolding through contingency, incompleteness, and open-endedness. But this incompleteness is the impetus for continuing the search for clues in the 'narration' of democratization from disparate geographies, modernities, theories, and experiences. In the AME, democratization may not yet be the only 'game in town'. Democratization competes with other ongoing currents—primordialism, pan-Arabism, Islamization, unruly civism, and empire-building. Guided by this 'revisionism', I have in the foregoing analysis attempted to open to inspection the peculiarities of Arab states and societies' grappling with democratic transition. They have objectified their wrestling with democratization in election fetishism and electoralism. This electoral quintessence, a feast of voting processes without democratic finality, masks numerous faultlines. Through the 'Conclusions' below I aim to capture the tension inherent in the competing imaginings of transition to good polity in the AME. This tension results from the implicit and explicit contests over power, meaning, identity, resources, knowledge-making, and self-other validation.

Conclusion 1

The antonymy between democracy and authoritarianism and the democratic impasse in the Arab world cannot be oversimplified to a polarity between democrats and dictators. Rather, the apocryphal nature of democratic transition in the AME has its roots in a deeper tension between two worldviews. The first is formalist and systemic and reveres the centre as the only locus of loyalty, legitimacy and power. The second harbours aversion to formalized, monopolized, and centralized power. The worlds of Weber and Ibn Khaldun collide in the

AME. Weberian imagining of the state with its centralized and juridically protected and legitimized monopoly of power continues to test its Khaldunian counterpart. For Ibn Khaldun the centre can only be narrow, fluid, ephemeral, and less formal. Centralized tribal solidarity (*'aṣabiyyah*) is in a constant state of flux.[2] Its contract to rule, after it unseats a rival and decaying incumbent tribal solidarity, does not cancel out other group solidarities, that is, potential centres of power. In the seat of power the triumphant *'aṣabiyyah* is the sum of atomized solidarities, loyalties, and coercive potentialities that freely lurk to vie for power, coalesce with other solidarities to make and unmake the state. Thus the Khaldunian covenant of power does not affirm a single centre of power and leaves competition for power constantly open as a bulwark against singularity, fixity, and political decay. Lack of homogeneity spells danger for social peace, order, centralization, and even democracy under the 'Western' worldview. Homogeneity is *sui generis* a ready-made unifying force, an *esprit de corps*, that links state and society. In Ibn Khaldun's world heterogeneity and the social bonds that obtain from competing forms of tribal solidarity engender state-making and unmaking.

This notion of social solidarity persists today in the AME. It is entangled in the political process. For Salamé modern forms of group solidarity complicate the search for democracy in the AME. The continuing legitimacy of community organization and identity is not always receptive to the dogmas of Western democracy, such as individualism. Thus the struggle for democracy in the AME can be directed concomitantly at the authoritarianism of the state and of the group.[3] Zubaida contends that traditional group solidarities continue to interpenetrate with nation-states, political parties, and parliaments in the AME.[4] He argues that the constitution of political forces relates to various and shifting bases of social solidarities, which are themselves affected by changes in political and economic conjecture, including state structures and policies.[5] Today modeling polity and imagining democracy by adhering to the Weberian model of organizing politics around a centre is being challenged in the AME by the persistence of Khaldunian solidarities that threaten to unmake the state. The Yemeni centre has been waging a war of attrition against a religio-tribal revolt led by Al-Houthi's movement 'The Young Believers' (*Shabab al-Mu'umineen*), and the Shi'ite Zaidi tribes, among others, continue to weaken the centre. Similar examples in the AME are legion. Numerous centres on the margins of power refuse to pay deference to the centre occupying the state. The obsession with Weberian formalism and its centralized armour is not only deflecting attention from viable and rival centres of power but is also, and more importantly, undermining democratization in the AME. The hostility against the rise of rival centres of powers in the name of national unity is used by centralized authorities in the AME to inhibit pluralism. This is happening to the point that when the state or regime collapses there are no 'government-in-waiting' to lead anywhere in the AME. Iraq illustrates the point vividly. In Lebanon and the Occupied Territories fear of the rise of 'state-within-a-state', respectively in reference to Hizbullah and Hamas, is being used to undermine pluralism. Both stand against the United States and Israel, which is reciprocated. But they are nonetheless rival centres of power which remain vital for democratization. Democratization in the AME cannot be engineered without opposition or dissidents.

The AME faces the challenge of imagining democratization in ways that allow for rival solidarities and centres to exist and compete for state power. The alternative is simply chaos. Forms of unruly civism, including by groups like al-Qaidah, are not going to disappear by force alone. They have thrived under authoritarian structures of power that deny them expression, inclusiveness, and organization. Democratization has the potential to rein them in by allowing them a wider sphere of political activity. Khaldunian solidarities not part of the political contract to rule coexisted with the centre as autonomous but potentially rival centres without threatening social peace. Only political decay signalled power was up for grabs and group feelings were mobilized to compete for unmaking the dying order and make in its stead a state held by moral and decisive coalition of solidarities. Ethno-nationalism in the AME reveres the centre to the point of entrenching a single group solidarity (e.g. tribal and religious in the Arab monarchies, and praetorian ideological in secular states) that denies rival centres of power any form of autonomy much less existence. The presidential elections of late have all mediated self-succession. What must be borne in mind is that Arab rulers would not initiate the sort of democratic processes that would either produce challenges to their authority, or force them into early retirement or fall from grace, or invalidate them as political players. They have proven themselves to be quite resourceful and versatile, invoking when the need arises all sorts of menaces and threats to engage in 'political cleansing'.

Conclusion 2

Primordialism is back in most Arab polities, especially non-monarchical systems. From Syria to Libya, a quasi type of dynastic rule is emerging. Ibn Khaldun has for over 600 years been accurate about the role of social bonds that obtain from kinship and sanguine ties for state-making. In the 1950s and 1960s monarchies were being phased out of the AME's political landscape. At the turn of the millennium Arab republicanism faces the tests of hereditary succession in Egypt, Libya, and Yemen. In Tunisia, a repeat of the Argentine handover between spouses in the 2007 presidential elections, the First Lady, Madame Leila Bin Ali, could give the AME its first female head of state when Zinelabidine Bin Ali eventually vacates the seat of power. In Libya, Gadhafi's heir apparent, Saif al-Islam, would face little or no challenge from the populace which have no channels for public expression or political organization. In Egypt, Gamal Mubarak will face stiff opposition to succeed his father. Civil society, led by 'Kifayah' and the Muslim Brotherhood, is already campaigning against hereditary succession. He, too, could inherit power but perhaps without retaining it for a long spell of time.

Lebanon represents an exaggerated form of feudal politics where political leaders are still born into the big 'dynastic' families. Maronite General Michel Aoun and Shi'ite Hizbullah General Secretary, Hassan Nasrallah, are prototype 'Hugo Chavez' figures, breaking into politics on the back of populism and confessional solidarity. This brand of politics defeats democratic transition. It manifests itself in Arab electoralism where confessional loyalties determine voting behaviour. A billboard showing a picture of the late Rafiq Al-Hariri and his son Sa'ad, leader of the parliamentary majority bloc, during the 2005 elections in the Sunni quarters of Beirut reads: *'li'uyounak'*. That is, 'for the sake of your eyes'. It communicates an affective, not a political, message. Voters oblige. In this instance, their vote to Sa'ad al-Hariri and his allies was motivated by loyalty as well as gratitude for his father's charity and philanthropy. Indeed, Lebanon is *par excellence* the country of pluralism in the AME. But Lebanon is not a democracy. Fragmented and pilloried power has created multiple centres. But clientelism expunges all meaning from voting and elections. The choice is made for most of Lebanon's voters whose sects are rigid templates of religious, social, and political identity. Tribal solidarity largely influences voting behaviour in Jordan, Yemen, and most of the Arab Gulf. Some families are more equal than others by dint of wealth and 'possession' of the state. The 'clan-state' as a species of polity is unique to the contemporary AME. What O'Donnell ascribes to 'patrimonial if not sultanistic [regimes] rul[ing] . . . on some combination of [coercive power], tradition, and hierocratic sanction' partly survives in the AME. Electoralism has thus far served only to 'mask...tribal and hierarchical structures with a parliamentary façade'.[6]

Conclusion 3

Electoralism and election fetishism are everywhere but democracy is nowhere in the AME. They have become badges of democratic pretence worn by traditional monarchs and secular presidents. O'Donnell notes how 'electoral authoritarianism' periodically mobilizes voters but in the interval between elections neither cultivates nor relies on citizens. This applies to the AME. In the AME where electoralism is being routinized voter turnout is on the decrease. The elections in late 2007 in Morocco (34%—against 51% in 2002) and Jordan (62%) point to voter disillusionment. Citizens protest through boycott. These elections do not lead to the kind of 'breakthroughs' that empower civil society or the opposition to compete for power in fair contests. The state has historically relied on the judiciary and the media to play roles in manipulating outcomes and images. But the elections of 2005 in Egypt will go out in history as the elections when the judiciary revolted against fraud and against its own role in covering it up. The letter published that year in the press by a female judge, Noha Al-Zaini, Assistant Head of the Administrative Prosecution Authority, confirmed what many have doubted for decades. Al-Zaini's letter documented on the pages of '*Al-Masri Al-Yom*' fraud that led to a seat won by the Muslim Brotherhood candidate, Jamal Hishmat, to be allocated to the ruling party's candidate, Mustafa El-Feqi.[7] The stand-off between the independent judges and the regime continues. In Morocco, where civil society and political parties enjoy a wider margin of existence, the electoral process and infrastructure do not support transition. Early in 2007 Democracy Reporting International and the Moroccan monitoring group 'Transparency' found many flaws that undermine transition. There are no mechanisms for checking voters' signatures, vetting funds, including political parties in the final vote count of their candidates, and for prolonging election campaigns.[8] These flaws were not attended to in the September 2007 House of Representatives elections. As a result, according to the 'Moroccan Democratic Civil Forum' the lower voter turnout was due to three factors: lack of credibility in the opposition parties' electoral platforms and policies; negative perception of parliament as toothless; and inadequate technical electoral know-how, which left a large segment of the voting population without voting cards.[9] It identifies three categories of voters: The first and largest boycotts elections for reasons of disillusionment or apathy. The second is made up of 'those who negotiate their votes with the aim of...financial profit', noting the rise of unofficial economy at election time. The third and smallest category 'votes out of conviction'.[10] Like Jordan, Morocco and Kuwait are the Arab monarchies with periodic elections and a modicum of competition. However, the royal houses are arbiters of the political game and possess unfettered powers that elected parliaments cannot limit. In Morocco, there are signs that the palace could, in future, help to sponsor and create a 'loyal' political party.

In some countries (e.g. Egypt and Jordan) the only formidable forces to challenge the state exercise self-restraint. They prefer to limit the number of candidates they field to contest seats so not to rouse the wrath of the state. The Egyptian elections of 2005 were over three rounds a fight for survival for Islamist (independent) candidates. In some constituencies the election booths were barred before voters sympathetic to the Muslim Brotherhood and violence (*baltagah* in the Egyptian vernacular) by the regime cronies and security marred the polls like never before. Entering parliament has become commodified, used by some as a form of social and economic mobility. As a result voting itself has become commercialized and all of the new elections in the Arab Gulf, including Kuwait with its longstanding parliamentary tradition, vote-buying is commonplace (see opening quote). The same practice exists in elections of the impoverished Arab states (e.g. Morocco, Jordan, and Egypt).[11] Writing on what he calls 'upgrading authoritarianism in the Arab World', Heydemann notes that despite the seeming increase in contestation, regimes control electoral processes very tightly, distorting outcomes.[12] He gives examples of other draconian measures, in addition to fraud and detention of leaders, taken to curtail free contestation and participation by regime opponents: 'coercion and repression, as in the cases of Saad Eddin Ibrahim and Ayman Nour in Egypt... and Algeria, Egypt, and Syria... continue to be governed under emergency rule.'[13] He adds to this the arbitrariness of licensing or proscribing political parties and restricted media access to the opposition. Ayman Nour of 'Al-Ghad Party' (Tomorrow Party) who won 12 per cent of the popular vote in a three-candidate presidential race in 2005 was put in prison on charges of fraud after the elections, and not before. But Arab political parties are part of the problem of authoritarianism and electoralism. Internally, many are not democratically organized; they select candidates arbitrarily; they are elitist and urban-based; they are secretive; they are obsessed with power and ideology not policies; and many mirror the Arab state with leaders clinging to power to the bitter end. Al-Wafd's Nu'man Gom'ah of Egypt invaded the party's headquarters by force in April 2006. He was ousted for his 'tyrannical ways' by the party's supreme committee, of which he disapproved. In a way, this blemishes democratic struggles in the AME considering that Gom'ah was presidential material, and was one of three candidates, including Mubarak, that contested the 2005 presidential elections.

In yet other states in the AME cosmetic plebiscites (e.g. Syria) with pre-ordained results and some of the ills such as vote-buying persist. Like in Syria, elections in the AME happen on one day, in some so swiftly with hardly any time for the candidates or the voters to learn from the brief and periodic democratic experience. Kuwait's traditional gatherings and Mauritania's communal tents are the exception. Partial suffrage in the UAE and Saudi Arabia renders transition patriarchal, elitist, or both. In none of these elections society or its civil potential stands any fair chance to rival the centre, much less dislodge it from power. To date, the fact remains that no Arab incumbent president has ever been voted out of power.

Conclusion 4

Electoralism at the turn of the millennium happens in the age of American imperialism in the AME. To invoke Timothy Mitchell the AME is being subjected to a quasi process of 'enframing'.[14] It could be referred to as 'democratic enframing'. Enframing, used by Mitchell in reference to the modernizing of Egypt, deploys penetrative, discursive, and disciplinary methods for the purpose of control, infiltration, re-ordering, and of colonizing an object society.[15] 'Democratic enframing', as a companion to Pax-Americana, resembles by dint of its use of a disciplinary 'new mode of authority'—mediated by military might/invasion—has a *fixing* effect to that observed by Mitchell in Muhammad Ali's modernizing of Egypt. Fixing involves 'physical confinement of groups' and 'continuous monitoring of behaviour'.[16] Indeed, there is a quasi 'cordoning off' of the Arab region, especially after September 11, as a lawless territory rife with so-called jihadists, incorrigibly flawed by barbarity, and misruled by tyrants. This is 'confinement' of a whole region to the realm of un-civility, which necessitates 'monitoring' for the purpose of neatly cutting up the Arab World into zones of 'democracy', 'autocracy', 'jihadism', 'terrorism', etc. 'Enframing', Mitchell observes, is a method of dividing up and containing'.[17] But this *fixing* effect is more dangerous in its manifestation as an act of *freezing* time, space, history, culture, identity in the pursuit of a democracy promotion—read American pluralism. As if Arab history starts on 11 September 2001. What precedes that date is ahistory. The

'construction of hierarchies', pertinent to enframing, applies to 'democratic enframing'. For, the unruly, uncivil, autocratic, and barbarian
order is no match to the ruly, civic, democratic, and civilized order
that obtains from democracy. There is an ordering process central to
enframing. It operates by dividing 'the neutral surface . . . called space'
into an inside and outside.[18] Through this binary logic, the apparatus
acting upon an object assumes positional superiority and dominance.
Thus a whole pattern of power relations and subject–object posture
are defined. In the pursuit of democracy promotion, the United States
has set in motion a process of 'democratic enframing' that gives the
American side (and its attendant discursive and disciplinary systems)
the position of the distributor of order, the dispenser of moral value,
the arbiter of democratic truth, the architect of hierarchy, and the only
knower as displayed in the wording of the GMEI. Mitchell sums it
up: the 'techniques of enframing, of fixing an interior and an exterior,
and of positioning the observing subject, are what create an appearance of order, an order that works by appearance. The world is set up
before an observing subject as though it were the picture of something.
Its order occurs as the relationship between observer and picture . . .'[19]
What is in effect taking place is a quasi American-led drive to modern-
ize the AME and order it in its image and according to the dictats of
US interests and superpower status.

US pressure has nonetheless induced electoralism in all of the Arab
Gulf states. The US democracy promotion is part of a frenzied effort
to order the Arab world in its image and to hold it together by univer-
salizing values—political and economic liberalism. Three observations
are in order. First, the GMEI, the US 'road-map' for democratizing
the AME is tainted by the invasion of Iraq, Abu Ghraib, and hostility
to democratic outcomes in favour of Islamists (e.g. Hamas, Muslim
Brotherhood). Democratization via invasion has not gone beyond electoralism, as in the rest of the AME. This is reason why the GMEI
is discredited in Arab discourses. Galal Amin views its objectives to
coincide with the UNDP Arab Human Development Report. Amin finds
no connection between the empowerment of women and democratic
transition. He deconstructs the report as condescending to Arabs, deepening the '*kawagah* complex' (foreigner complex)—inferiority vis-à-vis
Westerners which spawns imitation.[20] In a conspiratorial fashion he
dismisses the report as no more than a pretext for the invasion of Iraq
and opening up the AME to the private sector.[21] Nader Ferjani, the
very editor of Arab Human Development Report, opposes its misuse for
democratizing the Arab world by force.[22] Secular Kifayah rejects it.[23]
So does the Muslim Brotherhood whose Grand Master Muhammad
Mahdi Akif says 'all we want is for the US to do nothing'.[24] That is,

neither support Mubarak nor oppose the Brotherhood, leaving Egypt for the Egyptians to sort out their own transition. The United States is likely to be the subject of criticism for what it does and for what it does not. Second, US bias in favour of client regimes undermines its own democracy promotion. For, authoritarian regimes interpret US hostility towards formidable Islamists and liberal opposition alike as a green light to proscribe their activities and oppress them. US silence or indifference thus leads to weakening and eliminating the only potentially viable opposition in the AME. Lastly, the allocation of capital to lubricate the machineries of protégé regimes not only serves to reproduce these regimes and their ability to provide patronage to their own clients but also determine and construct the patterns of exclusion and inclusion and empowerment and disempowerment. Hence, as in the Maghrib states 'recentralization of power has paradoxically been linked in part to greater reliance on international capital needed for local development. Relatively small groups of decision makers have become allocative agents, using the 'power of the purse' to pursue specific economic and political goals.'[25]

The AME has not produced a vision of its own and the United States, in the absence of an Arab 'road-map' for democratization, intervenes to fill that vacuum. The Tunis Declaration of the 16th Arab League Summit (24 May 2004) and the 'Alexandria Declaration' are timid reactions to the US democracy promotion, as Bush was preparing to table his GMEI to the G8 Summit. The Tunis Declaration pays lip service in vague language (Point No. 3) about the AME 'endeavour . . . to pursue reform and modernization . . . and to keep pace with the rapid world changes, by consolidating democratic practice, by enlarging participation in political and public life, by fostering the role of all components of the civil society . . .'[26] The 'Alexandria Statement' is slightly more precise in endorsing democratization since its authors are representatives of Arab civil society organizations (whose participation was vetted and approved by the Egyptian regime).[27] It defines political reform as being 'all direct and indirect measures for which government, civil society and the private sector are responsible'.[28] It commits to 'genuine democracy' that accounts for specificity. But the 'essence [of such a] democracy remains the same . . . [with] freedom [being of] paramount value, ensur[ing] actual sovereignty of the people and government by the people through political pluralism, leading to transfer of power'.[29] The contagious effect from US pressure that led to election fetishism in Arab Gulf states previously without any elections is evident here. US democratic 'road-mapping' galvanized state and society to respond with 'plans' of their own. What is missing from the Tunis and Alexandria statements is practical steps to engineer democratic 'learning' through exchange of local knowledge and Arab–Arab diffusion of best-practice experiences (e.g. Kuwaiti parliamentary capacity, Egypt professional syndicates organization, and Morocco's transitional justice). Imagining a democratic polity must benefit from existing knowledge practices in the West. But it must not do so in a foundationalist fashion that simply mimics Euro-American dogmas of polity and civil society.

Conclusion 5

Electoralism may be understood as the management of democratic transition in the AME top-down and from without. There are forces from below that are striking back at the centre. Bread rioters, bloggers, and online voters all exemplify the societies in the AME are not passive. They may not be politically organized; but they are politicized. Democratic struggles for the purpose of political organization are underway. Egypt's 'Kifayah' (Enough) has emerged as a formidable protest movement that stages mass rallies against single issues (e.g. hereditary succession, prisoners of conscience, torture, corruption, imprisonment of journalists). It has proved infectious within and without Egypt. In Egypt a variety of 'sister movements' have been formed. These include the 'March 9 Movement for University Autonomy', 'Workers for Change', 'Youth for Change', 'Writers and Artists for Change', 'Journalists for Change', 'Lawyers for Change', and 'Engineers without Surveillance'.[30] Shaaban views this swell in mobilization for democratic struggle to be spawned by society's desire to reclaim political roles it lost five decades ago as well as to protest its economic marginalization.[31] 'Sister' movements have emerged in Tunisia, 'Yezzi Fokk' ('let go, or 'enough is enough'), and in Lebanon, 'Khalas' ('enough'). George Ishaq, spokesperson for 'Kifayah', when it was first formed, states that the aim of the movement is to 'break the barrier of fear'. He adds: 'Arab authoritarianism deploys brutality to cower people and this fear is found in the political and economic spheres. Politically, Arabs are over-policed and surveilled. Economically, the fear of having no income maintains clientelistic ties and depoliticizes the masses'.[32] But fear is real and electoralism has not been consistent with observation of human rights. Police acts of brutality go unchecked, much less punished. The well-known Egyptian journalist Fahmi Huwaydi, documents the case of the murder of a 12-year-old youth in a police station:

I suggest that we designate the 12th of August of each year as a day [to contemplate] torture in Egypt. It would be a day for human rights organizations to shame the torturers' heinous crimes. They have violated the human dignity of thousands of people over a quarter of a century... Why particularly the 12th of August? On that day 12-year-old Mohamed Mamdouh's soul left this world. His dead body bore visible marks of torture in al-Mansourah's police station... all for an alleged act of petty theft... This story illustrates the state of human rights in Egypt. It reveals the extent of disregard for human worthiness and the treatment of the citizen like an insect that deserves not to live. It also demonstrates the unlawfulness and cruelty of the majority of Egypt's police force.[33]

This element of fear explicates the persistence of coercion and the durability of Arab authoritarianism. The post-colonial order has been marked by a quasi re-occupation of the state. The successive new guards at the helm of the independent state have invariably stamped their rule with singularity, coercion, patronage, and exclusion. With nationalist and radical zeal they set out, and succeeded, to obliterate the vestiges and agents of conservative conviction—bourgeoisie, monarchy, and political society. When the name of the game was modernization they targeted the symbols of tradition—religion and tribalism. They oppressed the 'right' when the left was in political vogue. When they switched politics and *infitāḥ* became the fashionable wave the same political masters turned against the left. Their history as military guards can be summarized by hegemony over left and right, and over religion and tribe. When Islamism is resurgent they invoke its putative antitheses, democracy and secular politics. When society demands democratization they resist; in Sayyid Qutb or Bin Laden and the like, they have a ready-made convenience. So it happens that the long trail of exclusion is littered with 'body politics' from the left and the right, belonging to feminists, secularists, human rights activists, Islamists, and today bloggers. Such are the denials ordained by the consecutive political masters in the AME. These denials could not have formed guarantees for militating against autocracy, let alone for engineering substantive and durable democratic transitions. The occupiers of the state have of late appropriated the language of human rights, civil society, democratization, and moderate Islam. But the strange absence of the institutions, values, and practices vital for the conceptual geography of good government bespeak a reality of stalled transition in the AME. In such a transition election fetishism is largely a charade.

The war against terror has aggravated the spectre of fear and the draconian laws introduced throughout the AME threaten the citizenry in the absence of independent judiciaries. In Egypt and Tunisia, two states where state violence can be unleashed without hesitation, societies are fighting back. The two most vociferous and organized independent judges associations are fighting for survival. Both have split in the middle the old state-sponsored national judges associations, affiliated under the brands of corporatism found in Cairo and Tunis. The irony is that electoralism is not placating the fledgling civil society. To the contrary, every opportunity is grabbed by society to resist hegemony and fear of the autocratic state.

This fear is now the subject of a new genre of literary studies that use satire and allegory. A short story by Khalid Ashour entitled 'the Death of Mr President' treats a clerk's tropism toward paranoia of being surveilled by the state.[34] After a colleague happily breaks the news of the president's death as broadcast in international media, the clerk finds himself gripped by fear for merely thinking that the president could die. His silent monologue is a repetition of the same question: 'how could it be possible for the president to die?' The paranoia engulfs him further. Suspicion takes over him. Perhaps the colleague in the office opposite his is trying to spy on his inner thoughts. His colleague asks: 'finally, the president died?' He struggles to purge the thought of the president's death out of his mind. He censors himself from following such a train of thought for fear of the security services. The services know, watch, hear, and even sense everything. At the end he discovers he is not alone in his fear. His colleagues, including political foes, are all stricken by the same fear. They are all afflicted with the inner demolition that crushes all confidence needed for the travails of free citizenship. Later that day, he finds himself in the Azhar mosque square in a sea of people shouting 'long live the president . . . the president lives'. He lapses into another monologue:

This is not the first time that I join such [state-orchestrated] demonstrations. In every re-election of our president, God protects him from all harm, we were transported by [government] buses to the same Azhar square to express ourselves freely! We vowed our support for the president alone. True I did not use to be part of the organizing electoral committees. Nor did my friends or I vote for the president. But it was equally true that those who missed the Azhar square [pro-president] rallies lost a percentage of their monthly pay, which I personally could not afford to forego. What was strange, however, was that every time the president, may Allah prolong his tenure in office, scored a landslide victory of more than 99 per cent.

Thus has self-succession been engineered in many an Arab republic. The 99 per cent election victories are only one feature of the election fetishism sweeping the AME today. O'Donnell writes that the 'genie' of democracy refuses to be 'put back into the bottle'.[35] That 'genie', the Arabic word for *jinn* (spirit with supernatural power), which has entered European languages, has left the bottle and the AME in the ninth century when the Umayyads and their philosophers discovered, studied, translated, and helped transmit Greek democracy. Nearly 1,100 years later the United States sacks Baghdad to putatively introduce democracy to the AME and the AME to democracy. The genie of democracy is back but not in a bottle. It is 'embedded' within a Trojan horse-like military apparatus, and within speech and ink that call for further deciphering and narrating. The 'story' of either the search for or return to Arabia of the 'genie' that is democracy does not end here. Like all stories of democratization across time and space, it shall remain open-ended.

Notes

1. From Al-Jazeerah Net News, commentary by a Jordanian reader to the day's leading news story, 'Accusations of Vote-Buying: Highlight of Jordanian Elections' [Arabic] http://www.aljazeera.net/NR/exeres/F9096AEA-DC13-47B8-8CF5-3B086501, 21 November 2007. Fore more on vote-buying in Jordan's elections, see Oula Farawati, 'Disproportionate Democracy', *Al-Ahram Weekly*, 22–28 November 2007.
2. Franz Rosenthal, *The Muqaddimah: an Introduction to History* (London: Routledge & Kegan Paul, 1967), pp. lxxviii–lxxxi.
3. Ghassan Salamé, 'Introduction: Where are the Democrats?' in Ghassan Salamé (ed.) *Democracy without Democrats? The Renewal of Politics in the Muslim* World (London: I. B. Tauris, 1994), 9–11.
4. Sami Zubaida, *Islam, the People and the State: Essays on Political Ideas and Movements in the Middle East* (London: Routledge, 1989), 84.
5. Ibid. 90.
6. Shukri B. Abed, 'Democracy and the Arab World', in Edy Kaufman, Shukri B. Abed, and Robert L. Rothstein (eds.), *Democracy, Peace, and the Israeli-Palestinian Conflict* (Boulder: Lynne Rienner, 1993), 201.
7. See, for instance, Fatemah Farag, 'Egyptian Press, Desperate and Afraid', Al-Ahram Weekly, Issue No. 771, 1–7 December 2005.
8. Mohamed Hajiwy, 'Transparency Proposes Reform of Morocco's Electoral System' [Arabic] *Bayan al-Yawm*, 25 January 2007.
9. Moroccan Democratic Civil Forum, 'Report by MDCF & CERSS on the Elections of September 7, 2007', Centre D'Études et de Recherches en Sciences, October 2007, 1–10.
10. Ibid. 6–7.
11. For an example, see Thanassis Cambanis, 'Jordan, Fearing Islamists, Tightens Grip on Elections', *The New York Times*, 11 November 2007.
12. Steven Heydemann, 'Upgrading Authoritarianism in the Arab World', Analysis Paper No. 13 (October 2007), The Saban Centre for Middle East Policy, the Brookings Institution, 11.
13. Ibid.

14. Timothy Mitchell, *Colonizing Egypt* (Berkeley: California University Press, 1999).
15. Ibid. 35.
16. Ibid. 40.
17. Ibid. 44.
18. Ibid. 44; 55.
19. Ibid. 60.
20. Galal Amin, *The Illusions of Progress in the Arab World: A Critique of Western Misconceptions* (Cairo: American University of Cairo Press, 2006), 9.
21. Ibid. 47.
22. Nader Fergany, 'The UNDP's Arab Human Development Reports and their Readings', in Birgitte Rahbek (ed.), *Democratization in the Middle East: Dilemmas and Perspectives* (Aarhus: Aarhus University Press, 2005), 19–30.
23. Author's interview with George Ishaq, 'Kifayah' Spokesperson, 1 December 2005, Cairo, Egypt.
24. Author's interview with Muhammad Mahdi Akif, Grand Master, Muslim Brotherhood, 7 April 2006, Cairo, Egypt.
25. Abdelbaki Hermassi, 'Socio-economic Change and Political Implications: the Maghreb', in Salamé (ed.), *Democracy Without Democrats?*, 238.
26. See League of Arab States, 'Tunis Declaration', http://arableague-us.org/tunis_declaration.html, 20 January 2006.
27. The key Pan-Arab bodies that attended were Arab Academy for Science and Technology, Arab Business Council, Arab Women's Organization, Economic Research Forum, and the Arab Organization for Human rights.
28. Arab Civil Society Organizations, 'Alexandria Statement: Arab Reform Issues—Vision and Implementation', 12–14 March 2007, Bibliotheca Alexandria, Alexandria, Egypt.
29. Ibid.
30. Ahmad Bahaéddin Shaaban, 'The New Protest Movement in Egypt: Has the Country Lost Patience', in *Arab Reform Brief*, 17 November 2007, Arab Reform Initiative, Cairo, 1–8.
31. Ibid. 5.
32. Author's interview with George Ishaq, 'Kifayah' Spokesperson, 1 December 2005, Cairo, Egypt.
33. Fahmi Huwaydi, 'The Day of Torture in Egypt', Al-Dostor, 22 August 2007, 28.
34. Khalid Ashour, 'Mawt Al-Sayyid Al-Ra'is' [Death of Mr President], *Al-Quds al-Arabi*, 18–19 August 2007, 10.
35. Guillermo O' Donnell, 'The Perpetual Crises of Democracy', *Journal of Democracy*, 18/1 (January 2007), 10.

Select Bibliography

Addi, L., *L'Algérie et la Démocratie: Pouvoir et Crise du Politique dans l'Algérie Contemporaine* (Paris: La Découverte, 1995).

Al-Khaliq, A. A. A. A., *The Arab Gulf States: Old Approaches and New Realities* (Abu Dhabi: Emirates Centre for Strategic Studies and Research, 2000).

Almond, G. A., and Coleman, J. S. (eds.), *The Politics of the Developing Areas* (Princeton: Princeton University Press, 1960).

Amin, G., *The Illusions of Progress in the Arab World: A Critique of Western Misconceptions* (Cairo: American University of Cairo Press, 2006).

Ayubi, N. N., *The State and Public Policies in Egypt Since Sadat* (Reading: Ithaca Press, 1991).

Baklini, A. I., *Legislative and Political Development: Lebanon, 1842–1972* (Durham: Duke University Press, 1976).

Baloyra, E. A., *Comparing New Democracies: Transition and Consolidation in Mediterranean Europe and the Southern Cone* (Boulder: Westview Press, 1987).

Binder, L., et al., *Crises and Sequences in Political Development* (Princeton: Princeton University Press, 1971).

Bremer III, L. P., and McConnell, M., *My Year in Iraq: The Struggle to Build a Future of Hope* (New York: Simon & Schuster, 2006).

Carapico, S., *Civil Society in Yemen: The Political Economy of Activism* (Cambridge: Cambridge University Press, 1998).

Carothers, T., *Critical Mission: Essays on Democracy Promotion* (Washington, D.C.: Carnegie Endowment for International Peace, 2004).

Carter, J., *Palestine: Peace not Apartheid* (New York: Simon & Schuster, 2006).

Cohen, A., *Political Parties in the West Bank under the Jordanian Regime, 1949–1967* (Ithaca and London: Cornell University Press, 1982).

Collings, D. (ed.), *Peace for Lebanon? From War to Reconstruction* (Boulder and London: Lynne Rienner, 1994).

Cooper, M. N., *The Transformation of Egypt* (London and Canberra: Croom Helm, 1982).

Crow, R. E., Grant, P., and Ibrahim, S. E. (eds.), *Arab Non-Violent Political Struggle* (Boulder and London: Lynne Rienner, 1990).

Dahl, R. A., *Polyarchy: Participation and Opposition* (New Haven: Yale University Press, 1971).

Danchev, A., and Macmillan, J. (eds.), *The Iraq War and Democratic Politics* (London & New York: Routledge, 2005).

De Tocqueville, A., *La Démocratie En Amérique*, vols. 3 (Paris: C.L., 1888).

Deeb, M., *Party Politics in Egypt: The Wafd and its Rivals 1919–1939* (London: Ithaca Press, 1979).

Deegan, H., *The Middle East and Problems of Democracy* (Buckingham: Open University Press, 1993).

Diamond, L. (ed.), *Political Culture and Democracy in Developing Countries* (Boulder and London: Lynne Rienner, 1993).

Diamond, L., Plattner, M. F., and Brumberg, D. (eds.), *Islam and Democracy in the Middle East* (Baltimore & London: Johns Hopkins, University Press 2003).

Diamond, L., Linz, J. J., and Lipset, S. M. (eds.), *Democracy in Developing Countries* (Boulder: Westview Press, 1988–1990).

El-Nawawy, M., and Iskandar, A., *Al-Jazeera: The Story of the Network that is Rattling Governments and Redefining Modern Journalism* (Cambridge, MA: Westview Press, 2003).

Entelis, J. P., and Naylor, P. C. (eds.), *State and Society in Algeria* (Boulder: Westview Press, 1992).

Farah, T. E., and Kuroda, Y. (eds.), *Political Socialization in the Arab States* (Boulder, Colorado: Lynne Rienner, 1987).

Farsoun, S. K. (ed.), *Arab Society* (London: Croom Helm, 1985).

Gause, F. G., *Political Opposition in the Gulf Monarchies* (San Domenico di Fiesole: European University Institute, 2000).

Gibb, H. A. R., and Bowen, H., *Islamic Society and the West: A Study of the Impact of Western Civilization on Muslim Culture in the Near East*, Vol. 1 (London: Oxford University Press, 1950).

Goldberg, E., Kasaba, R., and Migdal, J. S. (eds.), *Rules and Rights in the Middle East: Democracy, Law and Society* (Seattle: University of Washington Press, 1993).

Hall, J. A. (ed.), *Civil Society: Theory, History, Comparison* (Cambridge: Polity Press, 1995).

Halper, S., and Clarke, J., *America Alone* (Cambridge: Cambridge University Press, 2004).

Haseeb, K. E., et al., *The Future of the Arab Nation* (Beirut: Markaz Dirasat Al-Wihdah Al-Arabiyah, 1991).

Hatem, M. F., *The Nineteenth Century Discursive Roots of the Continuing Debate on the Social Contract in Today's Egypt* (San Domenico di Fiesole, Florence: European University Institute, Robert Schuman Centre for Advanced Studies, 2002).

Higley, J., and Gunther, R. (eds.), *Elites and Democratic Consolidation in Latin America* (Cambridge: Cambridge University Press, 1992).

Hinnebusch, R. A., *Egyptian Politics under Sadat: The Post-Populist Development of an Authoritarian-Modernizing State* (Cambridge: Cambridge University Press, 1985).

Hobsbawm, E., *Globalization, Democracy and Terrorism* (London: Little, Brown, 2007).

Hopwood, D., *Egypt: Politics and Society 1945–90* (London: HarperCollins Academic, 1991).

Hourani, A., *Arabic Thought in the Liberal Age: 1798–1939* (London: Oxford University Press, 1962).

Huntington, S. P., *The Third Wave: Democratization in the Late Twentieth Century* (Norman and London: University of Oklahoma Press, 1991).

Ibn Khaldun, A. A., trans. F. Rosenthal, *The Muqaddimah [Prolegomenon]: An Introduction to History* (Princeton: Princeton University Press, 1967).

Ibrahim, S. E., *The New Arab Social Order* (Boulder: Westview Press, 1982).

Jonas, S., and Stein, N. (eds.), *Democracy in Latin America* (New York: Bergin and Garvey Publishers, 1990).

Kedourie, E., *Democracy and Arab Political Culture* (Washington, DC: The Washington Institute for Near East Policy, 1992).

Landau, J. M., Özbudun, E., and Tachau, F. (eds.), *Electoral Politics in the Middle East: Issues, Voters and Elites* (London: Croom Helm, 1980).

Lapidus, I. M., *A History of Islamic Society* (Cambridge: Cambridge University Press, 1991).

Layne, L. L. (ed.), *Elections in the Middle East: Implications of Recent Trends* (Boulder: Westview Press, 1987).

Linz, J. J., and Stepan, A., *Problems of Democratic Transition and Consolidation: Southern Europe, South America, and Post-Communist Europe* (Baltimore: Johns Hopkins University Press, 1996).

—— and Stepan, A. (eds.), *The Breakdown of Democratic Regimes: Latin America* (Baltimore and London: The Johns Hopkins University Press, 1978).

Lynch, M., *Voices of the New Arab Public: Iraq, Al-Jazeera, and Middle East Politics Today* (New York: Columbia University Press, 2006).

Makiya, K. (Al-Khalil, S.), *The Republic of Fear* (Los Angeles and London: University of California Press, 1998).

Malloy, J. M., and Seligson, M. A. (eds.), *The Politics of Regime Transition in Latin America* (Pittsburgh: University of Pittsburgh Press, 1987).

Mansour, F., *The Arab World: Nation, State and Democracy* (London: Zed Books, 1992).

Mcdermott, A., *Egypt from Nasser to Mubarak: A Flawed Revolution* (London: Croom Helm, 1988).

Migdal, J. S., *Strong States and Weak Societies: State-Society Relations and State Capabilities in the Third World* (Princeton: Princeton University Press, 1988).

Mitchell, T., *Colonizing Egypt* (Berkeley: California University Press, 1991).

Monshipouri, M., *Democratization, Liberalization and Human Rights in the Third World* (Boulder and London: Lynne Rienner, 1995).

Moore, C. H., and Springborg, R., *Globalization and the Politics of Development in the Middle East* (Cambridge: Cambridge University Press, 2001).

Moore, B., Jr., *Social Origins of Dictatorship and Democracy: Lord and Peasant in the Making of the Modern World* (Boston: Beacon Press, 1966).

Niblock, T., and Murphy, E. (eds.), *Economic and Political Liberalization in the Middle East* (London and New York: British Academic Press, 1993).

Norton, A. R. (ed.), *Civil Society in the Middle East*, vols. 1 and 2 (Leiden: E.J. Brill, 1995 and 1996).

O'Donnell, G., *Dissonances: Democratic Critiques of Democracy* (Notre Dame: University of Notre Dame Press, 2007).

O'Donnell, G., Schmitter, P., and Whitehead, L., *Transitions from Authoritarian Rule: Comparative Perspectives* (Baltimore: Johns Hopkins University Press, 1986).

O'Donnell, G., Schmitter, P. C., and Whitehead, L. (eds.), *Transitions from Authoritarian Rule: Prospects for Democracy* (Baltimore: Johns Hopkins University Press, 1986).

Packer, G. (ed.), *The Fight is for Democracy: Winning the War of Ideas in America and the World* (New York: Perennial & HarperCollins, 2003).

Parry, G., and Moran, M. (eds.), *Democracy and Democratization* (London: Routledge, 1994).

Peterson, J. E., *The Arab Gulf States: Steps Toward Political Participation* (New York: Praeger, 1988).

Phillips, A., *Gendered Democracy* (Cambridge: Polity Press, 1990).

Phillips, D. L., *Losing Iraq* (London: Basic Books, 2006).

Piscatori, J. P., *Islam in a World of Nation-States* (Cambridge: Cambridge University Press, 1986).

Rau, Z. (ed.), *The Reemergence of Civil Society in Eastern Europe and the Soviet Union* (Boulder: Westview Press, 1991).

Rahbek, B. (ed.), *Democratization in the Middle East: Dilemmas and Perspectives* (Aarhus: Aarhus University Press, 2005).

Rosenthal, J. H. (ed.), *Ethics and International Affairs: A Reader* (Washington, D.C.: Georgetown University Press, 1995).

Rustow, D., *A World of Nations: Problems of Political Modernization* (Washington, DC: The Brookings Institution, 1967).

Said, E. W., *Orientalism* (London: Penguin Books, 1991).

Salamé, G. (ed.), *Democracy Without Democrats? The Renewal of Politics in the Muslim World* (London: I. B. Tauris, 1994).

Salibi, K., *A House of Many Notions* (London: I.B. Taurus, 1988).

Seligman, A. B., *The Idea of Civil society* (New York: The Free Press, 1992).

Sharabi, H. (ed.), *The Next Arab Decade* (Boulder: Westview Press, 1988).

Sørensen, G., *Democracy and Democratization* (Boulder: Westview Press, 1993).

Springborg, R., *Mubarak's Egypt: Fragmentation of the Political Order* (Boulder and London: Westview Press, 1989).

Stepan, A., *Rethinking Military Politics: Brazil and the Southern Cone* (Princeton: Princeton University Press, 1988).

Tachau, F. (ed.), *Political Elites and Political development in the Middle East* (New York: John Wiley, 1975).

Tessler, M., and Garnham, D. (eds.), *Democracy, War and Peace in the Middle East* (Bloomington and Indianapolis: Indiana University Press, 1995).

Tessler, M., Nachtwey, J., and Banda, A. (eds.), *Area Studies and Social Science: Strategies for Understanding Middle East Politics* (Bloomington and Indianapolis: Indiana University Press, 1999).

Tétreault, M. A., *Stories of Democracy: Politics and Society in Contemporary Kuwait* (New York: Columbia University Press, 2000).

Turner, B. S., *Orientalism, Postmodernism and Globalism* (London and New York: Routledge, 1994).

United Nations, United Nations Development Report, *Human Development Report 2000* (New York & Oxford: Oxford University Press, 2000).

Waterbury, J., *The Commander of the Faithful: The Moroccan Political Elite—A Study in Segmented Politics* (London: Weidenfeld and Nicolson, 1970).

Weisenborn, R. E. (ed.), *Media in the Midst of War: The Gulf War from Cairo to the Global Village* (Cairo: The Adham Centre Press, 1992).

Whitehead, L., *Democratization: Theory and Experience* (Oxford: Oxford University Press, 2002).

—— (ed.), *The International Dimensions of Democratization: Europe and the Americas* (Oxford: Oxford University Press, 1996).

Wittfogel, K. A., *Oriental Despotism: A Comparative Study of Total Power* (New Haven: Yale University Press, 1957).

Woodward, P., *Sudan 1898–1989: The Unstable State* (Boulder: Lynne Rienner, 1990).

Zartman, I. W. (ed.), *Collapsed States: The Disintegration and Restoration of Legitimate Authority* (Boulder and London: Lynne Rienner, 1995).

—— et al., *Political Elites in Arab North Africa: Morocco, Algeria, Tunisia, Libya and Egypt* (New York and London: Longman, 1982).

Zubaida, S., *Islam, the People and the State: Essays on Political Ideas and Movements in the Middle East* (London: Routledge, 1989).

Articles

Addi, L., 'Algeria's Democracy Between the Islamists and the Elite', *Middle East Report*, 22/175 (March/April 1992).

Albright, M., *In Support of Arab Democracy: Why and How*, International Task Force Report No. 54 (New York: Council on Foreign Relations, 2005).

Al-Sayyid, M. K., 'Slow Thaw in the Arab World', *World Policy Journal*, 8/4 (Fall 1991).

Amnesty International, *Egypt: Abuses in the Name of Security* (11 April 2007).

Anderson, L., 'Arab Democracy: Dismal Prospects', *World Policy Journal*, XVIII/3 (Fall 2001).

—— 'Political Pacts, Liberalism, and Democracy: The Tunisian National Pact of 1988', *Government and Opposition*, 26/2 (Spring 1991).

Bahry, L. Y., 'The New Arab Media Phenomenon: Qatar's Al-Jazeera', *Middle East Policy*, 8/2 (June 2001).

Ben Ali, Z. E. A., '*La déclaration de Ben Ali à la radio*' [Ben Ali's Radio Proclamation] *Jeune Afrique* (18 November 1987).

Ben Yahmed, B., '*Chadli était la Malchance de l'Algérie*' [Chadli was Algeria's Bad Luck], *Jeune Afrique* (16–23 January 1992).

Bianchi, R., 'Islam and Democracy in Egypt', *Current History*, 88/535 (February 1989).

Bill, J. A., 'Comparative Middle East Politics: Still in Search of Theory', *PS: Political Science and Politics*, 27/3 (September 1994).

Binder, L., '"Islamic Liberalism"', *PS: Political Science and Politics*, 27/3 (September 1994).

Bourgi, A., *'Ce Regime n'etait plus qu'une Coquille Vide'* [This Regime was no more than an empty Shell], *Jeune Afrique* (16–23 January 1992).

Brown, N. K., Dunne, M., and Hamzawy, A., *Egypt's Controversial Constitutional Amendments* (Washington, D.C.: Carnegie Endowment for International Peace, 23 March 2007).

Brumberg, D., 'The Trap of Liberalized Autocracy', *Journal of Democracy*, 13/4 (October 2002).

Burke III, E., 'Understanding Arab Protest Movements', *Arab Studies Quarterly*, 8/4 (Fall 1986).

Burns, W. J., 'Political and Economic Goals of a New Generation in the Middle East', Testimony before the Senate foreign Relations Committee, Washington D.C. (19 March 2003).

—— 'Priorities in the Middle East and North Africa', Testimony before the Senate foreign Relations Committee, Washington, DC (26 March 2003).

Bush, G. W., 'Remarks by the President at the 20th Anniversary of the National Endowment for Democracy', United States Chamber of Commerce (6 November 2003).

—— 'The New Way Forward in Iraq', President's Address to the Nation (10 January 2007).

Cambanis, T., 'Jordan, Fearing Islamists, Tightens Grip on Elections', *The New York Times* (11 November 2007).

Cantori, L. J., 'The Old Orthodoxy and the New Orthodoxy in the Study of Middle Eastern Politics', PS: *Political Science and Politics*, 27/3 (September 1994).

Carapico, S., 'Elections and Mass Politics in Yemen', *Middle East Report*, 23/185 (November/December 1993).

Carothers, T., 'The End of the Transition Paradigm', *Journal of Democracy*, 13/1 (2002).

Cofman Wittes, T., 'The New US Proposal for a Greater Middle East Initiative', *Saban Centre for Middle East Policy*, Memo No. 2 (10 May 2004).

Cohen, Y., 'Democracy from Above: The Political Origins of Military Dictatorship in Brazil', *World Politics*, 40/1 (October 1987).

Dawisha, A., 'The Colonel Does it His Way', *The Middle East*, 168 (October 1988).

Deeb, M. J., 'New Thinking in Libya', *Current History*, 89 (April 1990).

Detalle, R., 'The Yemeni Elections Up Close', *Middle East Report*, 23/185 (November/December 1993).

Diamond, L., 'Elections without Democracy: Thinking about Hybrid Regimes', *Journal of Democracy*, 13/2 (April 2002).

Dixon, W. J., and Moon, B. E., 'Domestic Political Conflict and Basic Outcomes: An Empirical Assessment', *Comparative Political Studies*, 22/2 (1989).

Duran, K., 'The Second Battle of Algiers', *Orbis*, 33 (Summer 1989).

Eickelman, D. F., 'Bin Laden, the Arab "Street", and the Middle East's Democracy Deficit', *Current History*, 101 (January 2002).

Eissa, I., 'Egypt: Point/Counterpoint to the Constitutional Amendments—Part II', *Arab Reform Bulletin*, 5/3 (April 2007).

Entelis, J. P., 'Algeria Under Chadli: Liberalization without Democratization Or, Perestroika, Yes; Glasnost, No!' *Middle East Insight*, 6/3 (Fall 1988).

Esposito, J. L., and Piscatori, J. P., 'Democratization and Islam', *Middle East Journal*, 45/3 (Summer 1991).

Farsoun, S. K., 'Oil, State, and Social Structure', *Arab Studies Quarterly*, 10/2 (Spring 1988).

Feldman, N., 'Agreeing to Disagree in Iraq', *The New York Times* (30 August 2005).

Gellner, E., 'Civil Society in Historical Context', *International Social Science Journal*, 43/129 (August 1991).

Gershman, C., 'The National Endowment for Democracy in 1990: Hearing before the Subcommittee on International Operation of the Committee on Foreign Affairs', US House of Representatives (28 September, 1989).

Hagopian, F., '"Democracy by Undemocratic Means"? Elites, Political Pacts, and Regime Transition in Brazil', *Comparative Political Studies*, 23/2 (July 1990).

Hashim, A. G., 'Mauritania: Beyond the Presidential Election', *Arab Reform Bulletin*, 5/3 (April 2007).

Herb, M., 'Emirs and Parliaments in the Gulf', *Journal of Democracy*, 13/4 (October 2002).

Heydemann, S., 'Is the Middle East Different?' *Journal of Democracy*, 7/2 (April 1996).

—— 'Upgrading Authoritarianism in the Arab World', Analysis Paper, No. 13 (October 2007), The Saban Centre for Middle East Policy. Washington, DC: the Brookings Institution.

Hoffman, M., 'Restructuring, Reconstruction, Reinscription, Rearticulation: Four Voices in Critical Internal Theory', *Millennium*, 20/2 (1991).

Hudson, M. C., 'After the Gulf War: Prospects for Democratization in the Middle East', *Middle East Journal*, 45/3 (Summer 1991).

—— 'Democratization and the Problem of Legitimacy in Middle East Politics', *Middle East Studies Association Bulletin*, 22/2 (December 1988).

—— 'Democracy and Social Mobilization in Lebanese Politics', *Comparative Politics*, 1/2 (January 1969).

—— 'The Possibilities for Pluralism', *American-Arab Affairs*, 36 (Spring 1991).

Huntington, S. P., 'After Twenty Years: The Future of the Third Wave', *Journal of Democracy*, 8/4 (October 1997).

Ibrahim, S. E., 'On Democracy in Saudi Arabia', *Civil Society*, 3 (March 1992).

Ibrahim, S. E., 'The Betrayal of Democracy by Egypt's Intellectuals', *Civil Society*, 2 (February 1992).

Ibrahim, Y. M., 'Algerians, Angry with the Past, Divided over their Future', *New York Times* (19 January 1992).

—— 'Interim leaders in Algeria Stop Elections for Seats in Parliament', *New York Times* (13 January 1992).

Inkeles, A., 'Transitions To Democracy', *Society*, 28/4 (May/June 1991).

International Crisis Group, 'Iraq: Don't Rush the Constitution' (*Crisis Group*) *Middle East Report*, No. 42 (8 June 2005).

Issawi, C., 'Economic and Social Foundations of Democracy in the Middle East', *International Affairs*, 32/1 (1956).

Karl, T. L., 'Dilemmas of Democratization in Latin America', *Comparative Politics* 23/1 (October 1990).

Kerr, M., 'Arab Radical Notions of Democracy', *Middle Eastern Affairs*, 3 (St. Anthony's Papers, 1963).

Kienle, E., 'Destabilization through Partnership? Euro-Mediterranean Relations after the Barcelona Declaration', *Mediterranean Politics*, 3/2 (1998).

—— 'More than a Response to Islamism: The Political De-liberalization of Egypt in the 1990s', *Middle East Journal*, 52/2 (Spring 1998).

King, J., 'Algeria: The New Political Map', *Middle East International*, 379 (6 July 1990).

Korany, B., 'Arab Democratization: A Poor Cousin', *PS: Political Science and Politics*, 27/3 (September 1994).

Kritz, N., 'Constitution-Making Process: Lessons for Iraq', Briefings and Congressional Testimony, United States Institute of Peace (25 June 2003).

Latif, O. A., 'Syria: Elections without Politics', *Arab Reform Bulletin*, 5/3 (April 2007).

Lawson, F. H., '*Liberalisation économique en Syrie et en Iraq*' [Economic liberalization in Syria and Iraq], *Maghreb-Machrek*, 128 (April–June 1990).

Lesch, A. M., 'Democracy in Doses: Mubarak Launches his Second Term as President', *Arab Studies Quarterly*, 11/4 (Fall 1989).

Leveau, R., '*La Tunisie du Président ben Ali: equilibre interne et environnemt Arabe*' [President Ben Ali's Tunisia: Internal Equilibrium and Arab Context], *Maghreb-Machrek*, 124 (April–June 1989).

Levitsky, S., and Way, L. A., 'The Rise of Competitive Authoritarianism', *Journal of Democracy*, 13/2 (April 2002).

Lewis, B., 'Turkey is the Only Muslim Democracy', *Middle East Quarterly*, 1/1 (March 1994).

Lijphart, A., 'Typologies of Democratic Systems', *Comparative Political Studies*, 1/1 (April 1968).

—— 'Consociational Democracy', *World Politics*, 21/2 (January 1969).

Lipset, S. M., 'Some Social Requisites of Democracy: Economic Development and Political Legitimacy', *The American Political Science Review*, 53/1 (March 1957).

Luciani, G., 'Economic Foundations of Democracy and Authoritarianism: The Arab World in Comparative Perspective', *Arab Studies Quarterly*, 10/4 (Fall 1988).

Luizard, P. J., *'L'improbable démocratie en Iraq: le piège de l'etat-nation'*, [The Improbability of democracy in Iraq: The Nation-State Trap] *Egypt/Monde Arabe*, 4/4e (1990).

Lynch, M., 'Beyond the Arab Street: Iraq and the Arab Public Sphere', *Politics and Society*, 31/1 (March 2003).

Maghraoui, A., 'Problems of Transition to Democracy: Algeria's Short-lived Experiment with Electoral Politics', *Middle East Insight*, 8 (Winter 1992).

Makram-Ebeid, M., 'Political Opposition in Egypt: Democratic Myth or Reality?', *Middle East Journal*, 43/3 (Summer 1989).

Marks, J., 'Morocco: Reform Shakes up a Sleepy System', *Middle East Economic Digest*, 37/8 (26 February 1993).

Mdhaffer, Z., 'General Report', *International Symposium on the Democratic Transitions in the World Today* (Tunis: [n/p], 1990).

Melia, T. O., and Katulis, B. M., *Iraqis Discuss their Future: Post-War Perspectives from the Iraqi Street* (Washington, DC & Baghdad: National Democratic Institute for International Affairs, 28 July 2003).

Merriam, J. G., 'Egypt Under Mubarak', *Current History*, 82 (January 1983).

Moore, C. H., *'La Tunisie après Vingt Ans de Crise de Succession'* [Tunisia after Twenty Years of Succession Crisis], *Maghreb-Machrek*, 120 (April–June 1988).

Neubauer, D. E., 'Some Conditions of Democracy', *American Political Science Review*, 61/4 (December 1967).

O'Donnell, G., 'Illusions about Consolidation', *Journal of Democracy*, 7/2 (April 1996).

—— 'The Perpetual Crises of Democracy', *Journal of Democracy*, 18/1 (January 2007).

Osman, T., 'Hosni Mubarak: What the Pharaoh is like', *Open Democracy* (16 January 2006).

Ottaway, M., 'Promoting Democracy in the Middle East: The Problem of U.S. Credibility', Carnegie Endowment for International Peace, *Working Paper*, no. 35 (March 2003).

—— and Carothers, T., 'The Greater Middle East Initiative: Off to a False Start', Carnegie Endowment for International Peace, *Policy Brief*, no. 29 (March 2004).

Parens, J., 'Whose Liberalism? Which Islam?', *PS: Political Science and Politics*, 27/3 (September 1994).

Perthes, V., 'America's Greater Middle East and Europe: Key Issues for Dialogue', *Middle East Policy*, 11/3 (2004).

Quandt, W. B., 'Algeria's Uneasy Peace', *Journal of Democracy*, 13/4 (October 2002).

Rice, C., 'Transforming the Middle East', *The Washington Post* (17 August 2003).

—— 'U.S. Will Build Democracy in Iraq', *The Financial Times* (23 September 2002).

Roberts, H., 'The Algerian State and the Challenge of Democracy', *Government and Opposition*, 28/1 (Winter 1993).

Rustow, D. A., 'Transitions to Democracy: Toward a Dynamic Model', *Comparative Politics*, 2/3 (April 1970).

Sadiki, L., 'Progress and Retrogression of Arab Democratization', *Journal of Arabic, Islamic and Middle Eastern Studies*, 1/1 (1993).

—— 'The Search for Citizenship in Bin Ali's Tunisia: Democracy versus Unity', *Political Studies*, 50/3 (August 2002).

Sadowski, Y., 'The New Orientalism and the Democracy Debate', *Middle East Report*, 183 (July–August 1993).

Safa, O., 'Lebanon Springs Forward', *Journal of Democracy*, 17/1 (January 2006).

Salih, K. O., 'Kuwait's Parliamentary Elections: 1963–1985: An Appraisal', *Journal of South Asian and Middle Eastern Studies*, 16 (Winter 1992).

Seale, P., 'What Hope for Arab Democracy?', *Open Democracy* (21 April 2005).

Sehimi, M., '*Les élections législatives au Maroc*' [Legislative elections in Morocco], *Maghreb/Machrek*, 107 (1985).

Shaaban, A. B., 'The New Protest Movement in Egypt: Has the Country Lost Patience', *Arab Reform Brief* (17 November 2007), Arab Reform Initiative, Cairo).

Sharpe, G., 'The Intifadah and the Non-Violent Struggle', *Journal of Palestinian Studies*, 19/1: 73 (Autumn 1989).

Thompson, E. P., 'The Moral Economy of the English Crowd in the Eighteenth Century', *Past and Present*, 50 (February 1971).

Vandewalle, D., 'Qadhafi's "Perestroika": Economic and Political Liberalization in Libya', *Middle East Journal*, 45/2 (Spring 1991).

Ware, L. B., 'Ben Ali's Constitutional Coup in Tunisia', *Middle East Journal*, 42/4 (Autumn 1988).

Wedman, B. C., 'Let's be Capitalists', *The Middle East*, 214 (August 1992).

Wendt, A., 'Anarchy is what States Make of it: The Social Construction of Power Politics', *International Organization*, 46 (Spring 1992).

—— 'Collective Identity Formation and the International State', *American Political Science Review*, 88 (1994).

—— 'Constructing International Politics', *International Security*, 20 (Summer 1995).

Wickham, C. R., 'Beyond Democratization: Political Change in the Arab World', *Political Science and Politics*, 27/3 (September 1994).

—— 'The Problem with Coercive Democratization: The Islamist Response to the US Democracy Reform Initiative', *Muslim World Journal of Human Rights*, 1/1 (2004).

Youngs, R., 'Europe's Uncertain Pursuit of Middle East Reform', Carnegie Endowment for International Peace', *Working Paper*, No. 45 (June 2004).

Arabic

Abdullah, T. F., *Aliyyat Al-Taghyeer Al-Dimuqrati fi Al-Watan Al-'Arabi* [The Mechanisms of Democratic Transformation in the Arab Homeland] (Beirut: Markaz Dirasat Al-Wihdah Al-Arabiyyah, 2004).

Al-Ahram Centre for Political and Strategic Studies, *Al-Taqrir Al-'Arabi Al-Istratiji 1989* [The Arab Strategic Report 1989] (Cairo: Markaz Al-Dirasat Al-Siyasiyyah wa Al-Istratijiyyah bi Al-Ahram, 1990).

Al-Alawi, S. B., *Al- Mujtama'u Al-Madani fi Al-Watani Al-'Arabi wa Dawruhu fi Tahqiqi Al-dimuqratiyyah* [Civil society in the Arab Homeland: Its Role in Achieving Democracy] (Beirut: Markaz Dirasat Al-Wihdah Al-Arabiyyah, 1992).

Al-Ghayshan, N., 'Nuwwab Jabhat Al-'Amalu Al-Islami Yutalibuna bi-'Adami Raf'i As'ar Al-Khubz...', *Al-Aswaq* (7 July, 1996).

Al-Haj, S., *'Tawazunat Siyasiyyah Jadidah Tafruduha Nata'ij Al-Intikhabat Al-Yamaniyyah'* [New Power Configurations Imposed by the Yemeni Elections], *Al-Hawadith* (7 May, 1993).

Al-Hakim, I. A., *'Al-Dimuqratiyyah Al-yamaniyyah bayna Al-Najah wa Al-fashal'* [Yemeni Democracy Between Success and Failure], *Qadaya Duwaliyyah*, 4 (March/April 1993).

Al-Hurani, H., 'Intikhabat 1993 Al-Urduniyyah: Qira'ah fi Khalfiyyatiha, Zurufiha wa Nata'ijuha' [Jordan's 1993 Elections: A Reading of its Background, its Circumstances and its Results], *Qira'at Siyasiyyah* 4 (Spring 1994).

Al-Jammal, R. M., *Al-I'lam Al-'Arabi Al-Mushtarak* [The Joint Arab Information [System]] (Beirut: Marakz Dirasat Al-Wihdah Al-Arabiyyah, 1986).

Al-Kawari, A. K. (ed.), *Madakhil Al-Intiqal ila Al-Dimuqratiyyah fi Al-Buldan Al-'Arabiyyah* [Pathways to Democratic Transition in the Arab Countries] (Beirut: Markaz Dirasat Al-Wihdah Al-Arabiyyah, 2003).

—— (ed.), *Al-Dimuqratiyyah wa Al-Ahzab fi Al-Buldan Al-'Arabiyyah: Al-Mawaqif wa Al-Makhawif Al-Mutabadalah* [Democracy and Political Parties in Arab Countries: Reciprocal Positions and Fears] (Beirut: Marakz Dirasat Al-Wihdah Al-Arabiyyah).

Al-Kilani, I. Z., 'Al-Nuwwab Al-Islamiyyun Haddadu bi Al-Istiqalah' [The Islamist Deputies Threatened Resignation], *Al-Sabil* (6 August, 1996).

Al-Ma'Ani, N., 'Al-ifraju 'an Al-Mu'taqalin min Mantaqati Al-Tufaylah' [The Release of 10 Detainees from Al-Tufaylah Region], *Al-Aswaq* (7 September, 1996).

Al-Mumini, T., 'Al-Kabariti: Ihalatu Al-Mutawarritin bi Al-Ahdath Al-Akhirah ila Al-Qada' wa Al-Al-Ifraju 'an Baqi Al-Ashkhas Khilal 24 Sa'ah' [Al-Kabariti: Referral of those Guilty [of Wrongdoing] in the Recent Incidents to the Judiciary and the Release of the Rest in 24 Hours], *Al-Ra'y* (2 September, 1996).

Al-Solh, R., and Al-Kawari, A. K., 'Mashru li Ta'ziz Al-Masa'i Al-Dimuqratiyyah fi Al-Buldan Al-'Arabiyyah' [The Project of Consolidating Democracy Orientations in the Arab Homeland], *Al-Mustaqbal Al-'Arabi*, 15/161 (July 1992).

Al-Tuhami, M., *Al-Ra'y Al-'Amm wa Al-Harb Al-Nafsiyyah* [Public Opinion and Psychological Warfare] (Cairo: Dar Al-Ma'arif, 1974).

Arab Human Rights Organisation, *'Al-Ta'dilat ala Qanuni Al-Ahzabi Al-Siyasiyyah, Khutwah fi Al-Ittijah Al-Mu'akis'* [Political Parties Law Amendments: A Step in the Wrong Direction], *AHRO Background Briefing*, nos. 60–61 (February–March 1993).

Belqaziz, A. A.-I. (ed.), *Al-Mu'aradah wa Al-Sultah fi Al-Watan Al-'Arabi: Azmatu Al-Mu'aradah Al-Siyasiyyah Al-'Arabiyyah* [Opposition and Government in the Arab Homeland: The Crisis of Arab Political Opposition] (Beirut: Marakz Dirasat Al-Wihdah Al-Arabiyyah, 1987).

Bin Nabi, M., and Shahin, A. A. -S. (trans.), *Wijhat Al-'Alim Al-Islami* [The Muslim World's Direction] (Damascus: Dar Al-Fikr, 1981).

Dhiyab, S., 'Al-Hiwar wa Al-Bahth 'an Asbabi Al-Azmah' [Dialogue and the Search for the Causes of the Crisis], *Al-Dustur* (29 August, 1996).

Ghalyun, B., et al. (eds.), *Hawla Al-Khiyar Al-Dimuqrati: Dirasat Naqdiyyah* [On the Democratic Option: A Critique] (Beirut: Markaz dirasat Al-wihda Al-Arabiyya, 1994).

Hafiz, S. A.-D., *Sadmatu Al-Dimuqratiyyah* [The Shock of Democracy] (Cairo: Sina" Li-Nashr, 1993).

Hilal, A. A.-D., et al., *Al-Dimuqratiyyah wa Huququ Al-Insan fi Al-Watani Al-'Arabi* [Democracy and Human Rights in the Arab Homeland] (Beirut: Markaz Dirasat Al-Wihdah Al-Arabiyyah, 1986).

Huwaydi, F., *Al-Islamu wa Al-Dimuqratiyyah* [Islam and Democracy] (Cairo: Markaz Al-Ahram, 1993).

Ibn Baz, A. A.-A., *Hukm Al-Islam* [The Ruling of Islam] (Medina: The Islamic University Publications, 1980).

Ibrahim, H. T., and Abdallah, A. A.-J. A. (eds.), *Al-Tahawwulat Al-Dimuqratiyyah fi Al-Iraq: Al-Quyud wa Al-Furas* [Democratic Transition in Iraq: Constraints and Opportunities] (Dubai: Markaz Al-Khaleej Lil Abhath, 2005).

Ibrahim, S. E. (ed.), *Azmatu Al-Dimuqratiyyah fi Al-Alam Al-'Arabi* [The Crisis of Democracy in the Arab World] (Beirut: Markaz Dirasat Al-Wihdah Al-Arabiyyah, 1984/1987).

Marmal, I., 'Al-Thawrah Khamadat . . . wa Lakin Matalibu Al-Jiya' baqiyah' [The Uprising Died out, but the Demands of the Hungry Linger], *Al-Safir* (2 February, 1998).

Mis'ad, N. (ed.), *Al-Ada' Al-Barlamani Lil-Mar'ah Al-'Arabiyyah: Dirasat Halat Misr was Suriya wa Tunis* [Parliamentary Performance of the Arab Woman: Case Studies of Egypt, Syria and Tunisia] (Beirut: Markaz Dirasat Al-Wihdah Al-Arabiyyah, 2005).

Rashid, A. H., *Al-Tahawwul Al-Dimuqrati fi Al-'Iraq: Al-Mawarith Al-Tarikhiyyah, Al-Ususs Al-Thaqafiyyah, wa Al-Muhaddadat Al-Kharijiyyah* [Democratic Transition in Iraq: The Historical Heritage, the Cultural Foundations, and the External Constraints] (Beirut: Markaz Dirasat Al-Wihdah Al-Arabiyyah, 2006).

Shalhah, A. A.-R., 'Fashalu Al-Ittisalat... Yukarrisu Al-Talaq' [Failure of Mediation... Marks the Divorce [Between Hizbullah and Tufaili]], Al-*Safir* (26 January, 1998).

Talabah, M., Manzumatu Al-Ta'limi Al-'Arabi wa Tahiddiyat 'Asru Al-Ma'lumat [The Arab Education System and the Challenges of the Age of Information], *Al-Iqtisad wa Al-A'mal*, 197 (May 1996).

The Islamic Action Front, *Al-Barnamaju Al-Intikhabi li-Murashshihi Hizb Jabhatu Al-'Amal Al-Islami 1993–1997* [The Electoral Program for the Islamic Action Front's Candidates, 1993–1997] (Amman, Jordan: The Islamic Action Front, n/d).

Index